ALL-IN-ONE
Student Workbook
Version A

Prentice Hall

Course 3 MATHEMATICS Common Core

Charles
Illingworth
McNemar
Mills
Ramirez
Reeves

Taken from:

Prentice Hall Mathematics, Course 3, All-in-One Workbook, Version A

PEARSON

Front Cover: Boden/Ledingham/Masterfile
Back Cover: Gary Randall/Getty Images.

Taken from:
Prentice Hall Mathematics Course 3: ALL-IN-ONE Student Workbook Version A, Global Edition

Published by Prentice Hall
Upper Saddle River, New Jersey 07458

Pearson Learning Solutions, 501 Boylston Street, Suite 900, Boston, MA 02116
A Pearson Education Company
www.pearsoned.com

Printed in the United States of America

1 2 3 4 5 6 7 8 9 10 V011 17 16 15 14 13 12

000200010271665671

SD

ISBN 10: 1-256-73723-2
ISBN 13: 978-1-256-73723-0

Daily Notetaking Guide

Practice, Guided Problem Solving, Vocabulary

Chapter 1: Real Numbers and the Coordinate Plane

Chapter 2: Solving Linear Equations

Chapter 3: Introduction to Functions

Chapter 4: Graphing Functions

Chapter 5: System of Linear Equations

Chapter 6: Exponents

Chapter 7: An Introduction to Geometry

Chapter 8: Transformations

Chapter 9: Geometry and Measurement

Chapter 10: Data Analysis

A Note to the Student:

This section of your workbook contains notetaking pages for each lesson in your student edition. They are structured to help you take effective notes in class. They will also serve as a study guide as you prepare for tests and quizzes.

Name ______ Class ______ Date ______

Lesson 1-1

Rational Numbers

Lesson Objective	**Common Core Standard**
To write equivalent fractions and decimals	The Number System: 8.NS.1

Vocabulary

A rational number is ______

______

A terminating decimal is ______

______

A repeating decimal is ______

______

Example

1 Writing a Terminating Decimal Find the batting average of a hitter with 27 hits in 120 times at bat.

$\frac{27}{120}$ or ☐ ÷ ☐ = $120\overline{)27.000}$ with quotient 0.225 ← **This is a ☐ decimal.**

− ☐

300

− ☐

600

− ☐

0 ← **There is no remainder.**

So the player's batting average is ☐.

Quick Check

1. Find the batting average of a hitter with 22 hits in 80 times at bat.

Name ______________________ Class ______________ Date ______________

Examples

2 Writing a Repeating Decimal Write $\frac{28}{77}$ as a decimal.

$\frac{28}{77}$ or ☐ ÷ ☐ $= 77\overline{)28.0000}$ with quotient ☐ ← **This is a ☐ decimal.**

$$\begin{array}{r} 77\overline{)28.0000} \\ -\ 231 \\ 490 \\ -\ \square \\ 280 \\ -\ 231 \\ \square \\ -\ \square \\ 28 \end{array}$$

← **There will always be a remainder of ☐ or ☐.**

So $\frac{28}{77} =$ ☐.

3 Writing an Equivalent Fraction Write 1.24 as a mixed number in simplest form.

$1.24 = \frac{1.24}{1}$ ← **Write as a fraction with the denominator 1.**

$= \frac{\square}{100}$ ← **Since there are ☐ digits to the right of the decimal point, multiply the numerator and the denominator by ☐.**

$= \frac{124 \div \square}{100 \div \square}$ ← **Divide the numerator and the denominator by the ☐.**

$= \frac{31}{25} = \square\frac{\square}{\square}$ ← **Simplify. Write as a mixed number.**

Quick Check

2. Write $\frac{55}{60}$ as a decimal.

3. Write 1.42 as a mixed number in simplest form.

Name ______________________ Class ______________ Date ______________

Lesson 1-2

Irrational Numbers and Square Roots

Lesson Objective	Common Core Standards
To find and estimate square roots and to classify numbers as rational or irrational	The Number System: 8.NS.1, 8.NS.2 Expressions and Equations: 8.EE.2

Vocabulary

A perfect square is ______________________

The square root of a number is ______________________

____

Irrational numbers are ______________________

____

The real numbers are ______________________

Examples

1 Finding Square Roots of Perfect Squares Find the two square roots of each number.

a. 81

$\square \cdot \square = 81$ and $\square \cdot \square = 81$

The two square roots of 81 are $\square$ and $\square$.

b. $\frac{1}{36}$

$\square \cdot \square = \frac{1}{36}$ and $\square \cdot \square = \frac{1}{36}$

The two square roots of $\frac{1}{36}$ are $\square$ and $\square$.

2 Estimating a Square Root Estimate the value of $-\sqrt{70}$ to the nearest integer and to the nearest tenth.

$-\sqrt{81}$ $\square$ $-\sqrt{64}$

-9 -8

Since 70 is closer to 64 than it is to 81, $-\sqrt{70} \approx \square$.

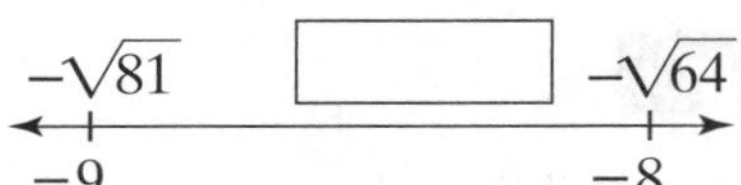

Since 70 is closer to 70.56 than to 68.89, $-\sqrt{70} \approx \square$.

Quick Check

1. Find the square roots of each number.

a. 36 $\square$

b. 1 $\square$

c. $\frac{1}{16}$ $\square$

2. Estimate the value of $\sqrt{38}$ to the nearest integer and to the nearest tenth. $\square$

Name ______________________ Class ______________ Date ______________

Examples

3 Comparing Square Roots Which is greater, $\sqrt{28}$ or 5.1?

First, estimate the value of the square root to the nearest tenth. $\sqrt{28} \approx$ [ ]

Since [ ] [ ] 5.1, $\sqrt{28}$ [ ] 5.1.

4 Surface Area of a Sphere The formula S.A. $= 13r^2$ gives the approximate surface area S.A. in square units of a sphere with radius r. Find the radius of a sphere with surface area 650 square units.

S.A. $= 13r^2$ ← **Use the formula for the surface area of a sphere.**

[ ] $= 13r^2$ ← **Substitute** [ ] **for S.A.**

$\frac{650}{13} = r^2$ ← **Divide each side by** [ ] **to isolate r.**

[ ] $\approx r^2$ ← **Simplify.**

$\sqrt{50} \approx \sqrt{r^2}$ ← **Find the positive square root of each side. Use a calculator.**

[ ] $\approx r$ ← **Round to the nearest tenth.**

The radius of a sphere with surface area 650 square units is about [ ] units.

5 Classifying Real Numbers Is each number *rational or irrational*? Explain.

a. $-9333.\overline{3}$ [ ]; the decimal repeats.

b. $4\frac{7}{9}$ [ ]; the number can be written as the ratio [ ].

c. $\sqrt{90}$ [ ]; 90 is not a [ ] square.

d. 6.363663666 . . . [ ]; the decimal does not terminate or repeat.

Quick Check

3. Which is greater $\sqrt{20}$ or 4.7?

[ ]

4. Use the formula S.A. $= 13r^2$ to find the radius of a sphere with a surface area of 520 square units. Round to the nearest tenth of a unit.

[ ]

5. Is $0.\overline{6}$ *rational* or *irrational*? Explain.

[ ]

Name ______________________ Class ______________ Date ______________

Lesson 1-3

Cube Roots

Lesson Objective	**Common Core Standard**
To find cube roots and to solve cube root equations	Expressions and Equations: 8.EE.2

Vocabulary

A perfect cube is a ____.

A cube root is a ____.

____

Example

1 Finding Cube Roots of Perfect Cubes Find the cube roots of each number.

a. 27

$\square \cdot \square \cdot \square = 27$

So, the cube root of 27 is $\square$.

b. -343

$\square \cdot \square \cdot \square = -343$

So, the cube root of -343 is $\square$.

c. $\frac{1}{512}$

$\square \cdot \square \cdot \square = \frac{1}{512}$

So, the cube root of $\frac{1}{512}$ is $\square$.

Quick Check

1. Find the cube root of each number.

a. 216

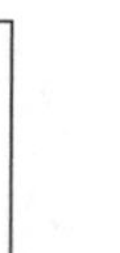

b. -1

c. $\frac{1}{27}$

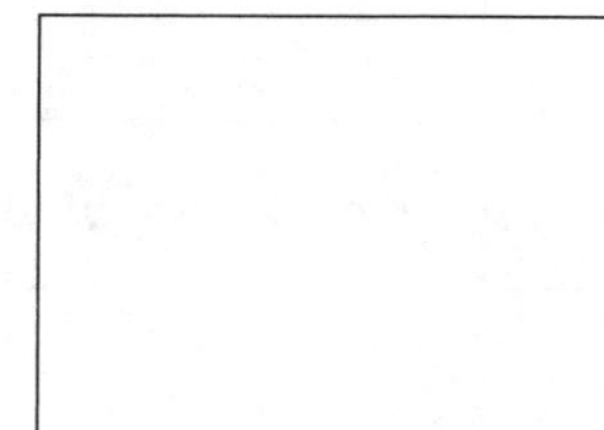

Name ______________ Class ______________ Date ______________

Example

2 Finding the Side Length of a Cube A cube-shaped storage container has a volume of 1,728 cubic inches. What is the side length of the container?

$V = s^3$ ← Volume formula

$\square = s^3$ ← Substitute $\square$ for V.

$\square = \sqrt[3]{s^3}$ ← Find the cube root of each side.

$\square = s$

The side length of the storage container is $\square$.

Quick Check

2. A different cube-shaped packing box has a volume of 125 cubic feet. What is the side length of the box? $\square$

Example

3 Solving a Cube Root Equation Solve $x^3 = \frac{343}{729}$.

$x^3 = \frac{343}{729}$

$\sqrt[3]{x^3} = \sqrt[3]{\frac{343}{729}}$ ← Find the cube root of each side.

$x = \frac{\sqrt[3]{343}}{\sqrt[3]{729}}$ ← Find the cube root of the $\square$. ← Find the cube root of the $\square$.

$x = \square$ ← Simplify. *Think:* 343 = $\square$ and 729 = $\square$.

Quick Check

3. Solve $x^3 = \frac{27}{216}$.

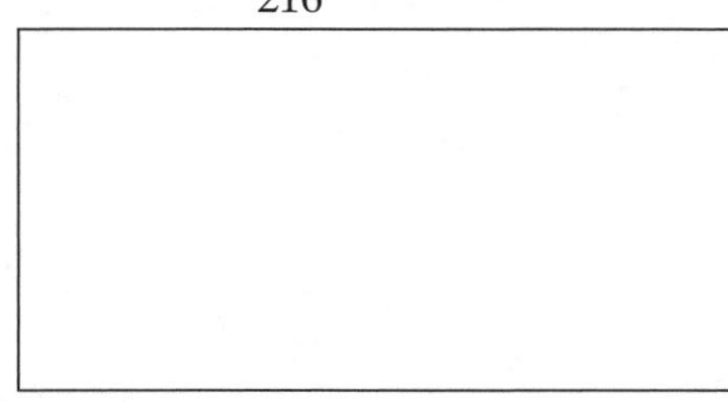

Name ______________________ Class ______________ Date ______________

Lesson 1-4

The Pythagorean Theorem

Lesson Objective	Common Core Standard
To use the Pythagorean Theorem to find the length of the hypotenuse of a right triangle	Geometry: 8.G.7

Vocabulary and Key Concepts

The Pythagorean Theorem

In any right triangle, the sum of the squares of the lengths of the ______ is equal to the square of the length of the ______.

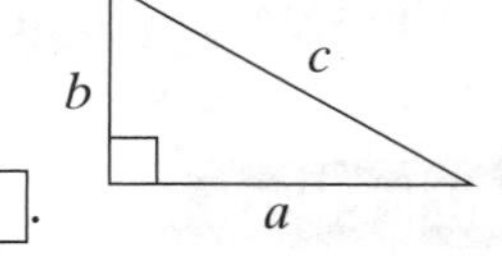

$a^2 + b^2 = \square$

The legs of a right triangle are ____

The hypotenuse of a right triangle is ____

Examples

1 Finding the Hypotenuse Find the length of the hypotenuse of a right triangle with legs of 6 ft and 8 ft.

$\square$ ← **Use the Pythagorean Theorem.**

$\square^2 + \square^2 = c^2$ ← **Substitute $\square$ for *a* and $\square$ for *b***

$\square + \square = c^2$ ← **Simplify.**

$\square = c^2$ ← **Add.**

$\sqrt{\square} = \sqrt{\square}$ ← **Find the positive square root of each side.**

$\square = c$ ← **Simplify.**

The length of the hypotenuse is $\square$ ft.

2 Multiple Choice The bottom of a ladder is 10 ft from the side of a building. The top of the ladder is 24 ft from the ground. How long is the ladder.

A. 22 ft **B.** 26 ft **C.** 30 ft **D.** 34 ft

$\boxed{}$ ← **Use the Pythagorean Theorem.**

$\square^2 + \square^2 = \square^2$ ← **Substitute**

$\square + \square = c^2$ ← **Simplify.**

$\square = c^2$ ← **Add.**

$\sqrt{\square} = \sqrt{\square}$ ← **Find the positive square root of each side.**

$\square = c$ ← **Simplify.**

The ladder is ☐ ft long. The correct answer is choice ☐.

Quick Check

1. Find the length of the hypotenuse of a right triangle with legs of 12 cm and 16 cm.

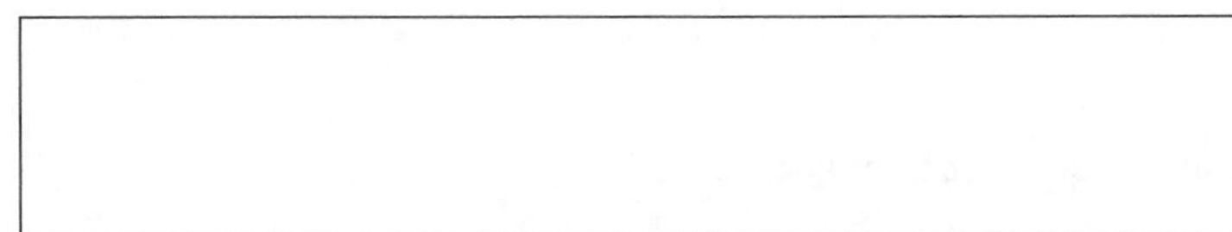

2. A bridge has 22-ft horizontal members and 25-ft vertical members. Find the length of each diagonal member to the nearest foot.

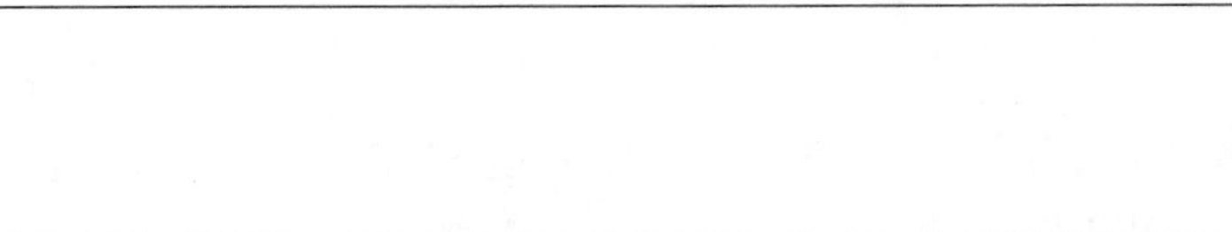

Name ____________________ Class ____________ Date ____________

Lesson 1-5

Using the Pythagorean Theorem

Lesson Objective	Common Core Standard
To use the Pythagorean Theorem to find the missing measurements of triangles	Geometry: 8.G.7

Example

1 Finding a Leg of a Right Triangle Find the missing leg length of the triangle below.

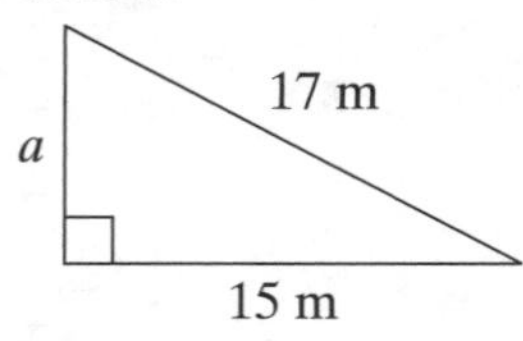

[ ] ← **Use the Pythagorean Theorem.**

$\square^2 + \square^2 = \square^2$ ← **Substitute [ ] for *b* and [ ] for *c*.**

$a^2 + \square = \square$ ← **Simplify.**

$a^2 = \square$ ← **Subtract.**

$\sqrt{\square} = \sqrt{\square}$ ← **Find the positive square root of each side.**

$a = \square$ ← **Simplify.**

The length of the other leg is [ ] m.

Quick Check

1. The hypotenuse of a right triangle is 20.2 ft long. One leg is 12.6 ft long. Find the length of the other leg to the nearest tenth.

[ ]

Name ______________________ Class ______________ Date ______________

Example

2 Multiple Choice You are riding on a carousel. You choose a horse near the outer edge of the carousel. Your friend is standing on the ground. Before the carousel starts moving, your friend is 9 m from you and 11 m from the center of the carousel. To the nearest tenth of a meter, how far are you from the center of the carousel?

A. 5.2 m **B.** 6.3 m **C.** 7.5 m **D.** 8.8 m

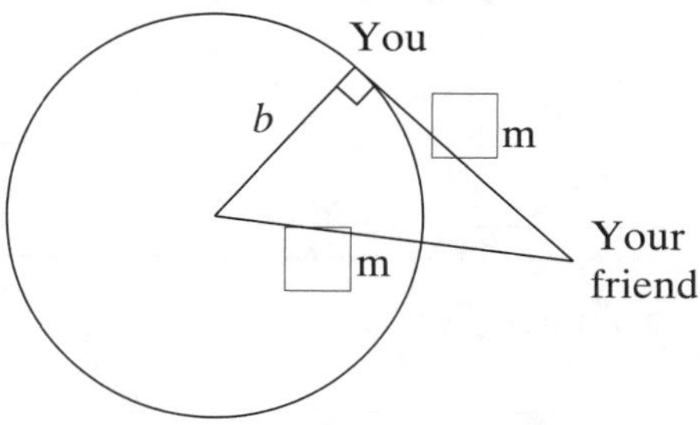

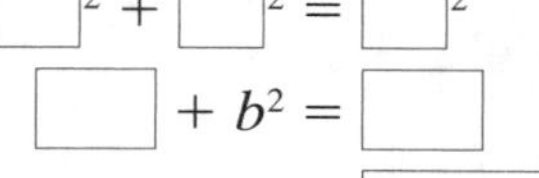 ← **Use the Pythagorean Theorem.**

$\square^2 + \square^2 = \square^2$ ← **Substitute** ☐ **for *a* and** ☐ **for *c*.**

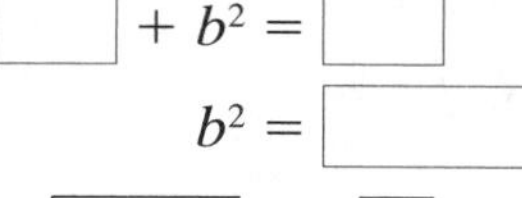

$\square + b^2 = \square$ ← **Simplify.**

$b^2 = \square$ ← **Subtract.**

$\sqrt{\square} = \sqrt{\square}$ ← **Find the positive square root of each side.**

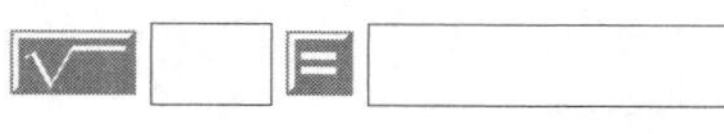

√ ☐ = ☐ ← **Use a calculator.**

$b \approx \square$ ← **Simplify.**

You are about ☐ m from the center of the carousel. The correct answer is choice ☐.

Quick Check

2. Construction The bottom of an 18-ft ladder is 5 ft from the side of a house. Find the distance from the top of the ladder to the ground. Round to the nearest tenth of a foot.

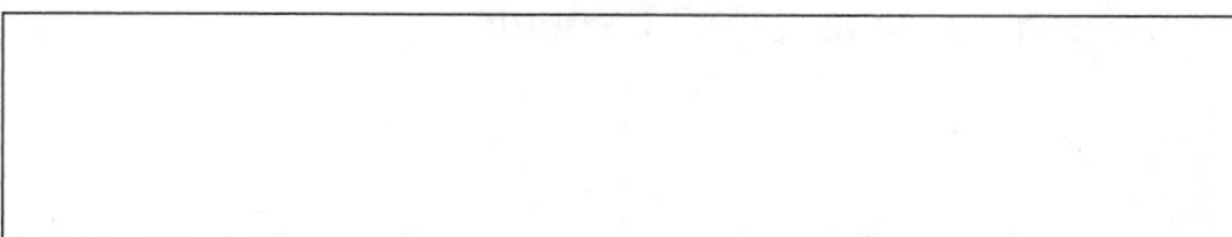

Name ________________ Class ________ Date ________

Lesson 1-6

Converse of the Pythagorean Theorem

Lesson Objective	**Common Core Standard**
To solve problems using the Triangle Inequality Theorem and the Converse of the Pythagorean Theorem	Geometry: 8.G.6

Vocabulary and Key Concepts

Triangle Inequality Theorem

The sum of ________________

is greater than ________________

According to the Converse of the Pythagorean Theorem, a triangle is a right triangle if

____

Example

1 Using the Triangle Inequality Theorem Is it possible to construct a triangle with the given side lengths? Explain.

a. 8 yd, 12 yd, 5 yd

☐ + ☐ ☐ 5

☐ + ☐ ☐ 8

☐ + ☐ ☐ 12

Yes. The sum of any two lengths is ☐ the third length.

b. 25 mm, 14 mm, 8 mm

☐ + ☐ ☐ 8

☐ + ☐ ☐ 14

☐ + ☐ ☐ 25

No. The sum of ☐ and ☐ is *not* greater than ☐.

Quick Check

1. Is it possible to construct a triangle with the given side lengths? Explain.

a. 6 mi, 10 mi, 20 mi ☐

b. 1.5 m, 2.5 m, 3.5 m ☐

Name ______________________ Class ______________ Date ______________

Example

❷ Identifying a Right Triangle Determine whether the triangle is a right triangle. Explain.

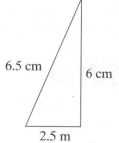

$a^2 + b \stackrel{?}{=} c^2$ ← **Use the Pythagorean Theorem.**

$\square^2 + \square^2 \stackrel{?}{=} \square^2$ ← **Substitute $\square$ for *a*, $\square$ for *b*, and $\square$ for *c*.**

$\square + \square \stackrel{?}{=} 42.25$ ← **Simplify. Use a calculator.**

$\square = \square$

The equation is true, so the triangle is a $\square$ triangle.

6.5 cm
6 cm
2.5 m

Quick Check

2. Determine whether the given lengths can be side lengths of a right triangle. Explain.

a. 10 in., 24 in., 26 in. $\square$

b. 8 cm, 9 cm, 12 cm $\square$

Example

❸ A carpenter has built two adjoining walls of a room and wants to make sure the walls meet at a 90° angle in the corner. One wall is 16 feet long and the other wall is 12 feet long. He measures the diagonal between the walls to be 20 feet. Do the walls meet at a right angle?

$a^2 + b \stackrel{?}{=} c^2$ ← **Use the Pythagorean Theorem.**

$\square^2 + \square^2 \stackrel{?}{=} \square^2$ ← **Substitute $\square$ for *a*, $\square$ for *b*, and $\square$ for *c*.**

$\square + \square \stackrel{?}{=} \square$ ← **Simplify.**

$\square = \square$

The equation is true, so the given lengths form a right triangle. The walls meet at a 90° angle in the corner.

Quick Check

3. A triangular field has boundary lines that are 40 yd, 75 yd, and 85 yd long. Determine whether the boundary lines form a right triangle. Explain.

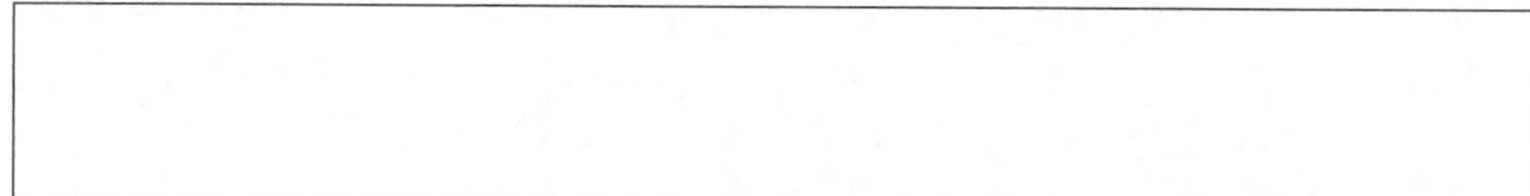

Name ______________________ Class ______________ Date ______________

Lesson 1-7

Distance in the Coodinate Plane

Lesson Objective	Common Core Standards
To graph points and to use the Pythagorean Theorem to find distances in the coordinate plane	Geometry: 8.G.7, 8.G.8

Vocabulary

A coordinate plane is ______________________

The x-axis is ______________________

The y-axis is ______________________

Quadrants are ______________________

The origin is ______________________

An [ ] gives the coordinates of the location of a point.

The [ ] tells the number of horizontal units a point is from the origin.

The [ ] tells the number of vertical units a point is from the origin.

Example

1 Finding Distance on a Coordinate Plane Find the distance between points $A(-2, 4)$ and $B(4, -4)$.

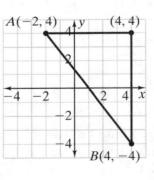

horizontal leg: [ ] − [ ] = 6 units

vertical leg: [ ] − [ ] = 8 units

[ ] ← **Pythagorean Theorem**

$[\ ]^2 + [\ ]^2 = c^2$ ← **Substitute.**

$[\ ] + [\ ] = c^2$ ← **Simplify.**

$[\ ] = c^2$ ← **Add.**

$[\ ] = \sqrt{c^2}$ ← **Find the positive square root of each side.**

$[\ ] = c$

The distance between $A(-2, 4)$ and $B(4, -4)$ is [ ] units.

Name ______________________ Class ______________ Date ______________

❷ **Multiple Choice** The park is 4 kilometers west of the bus station. The grocery store is 7 kilometers south of the bus station. To the nearest kilometer, how far is the grocery store from the park?

A. 5 km

B. 6 km

C. 7 km

D. 8 km

Park

y Bus Station

x

Grocery Store

$\square$ ← **Use the Pythagorean Theorem.**

$\square^2 + \square^2 = \square^2$ ← **Substitute**

$\square + \square = \square$ ← **Simplify.**

$\square = c^2$ ← **Add.**

$\sqrt{\square} = \sqrt{\square}$ ← **Find the positive square root of each side.**

[√] $\square$ [=] $\square$ ← **Use a calculator.**

$c \approx \square$ ← **Simplify.**

The correct answer is choice $\square$.

Quick Check

1. Find the distance between points (2, 1) and (7, 9). If necessary, round to the nearest tenth.

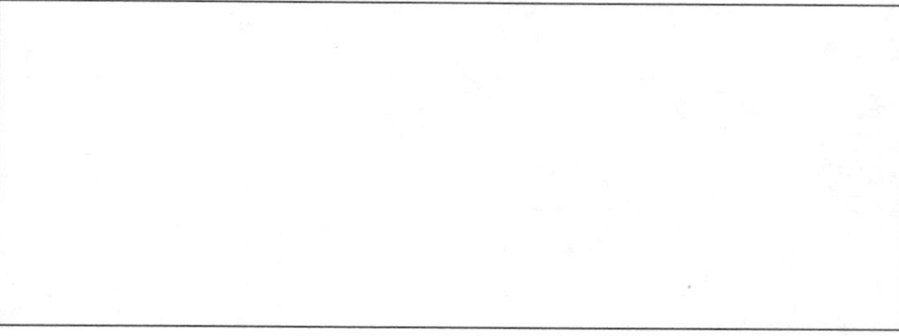

2. Your school is 3 miles south of your house. The park is 5 miles east of your school. To the nearest mile, how far is your house from the park?

Name ____________________ Class ____________ Date ____________

Lesson 2-1

Solving Two-Step Equations

Lesson Objective	**Common Core State Standards**
To solve two-step equations and to use two-step equations to solve problems	Expressions and Equations: 8.EE.7, 8.EE.7.b

Example

1 Solving Using Subtraction and Division Solve $4p + 7 = -13$.

$4p + 7 = -13$

$4p + 7 - \square = -13 - \square$ ← **Subtract $\square$ from each side.**

$4p = \square$ ← **Simplify.**

$\frac{4p}{\square} = \frac{\square}{\square}$ ← **Divide each side by $\square$.**

$p = \square$ ← **Simplify.**

Check $4p + 7 = -13$

$4(\square) + 7 \stackrel{?}{=} -13$ ← **Substitute $\square$ for *p*.**

$\square = -13$ ✓ ← **The solution checks.**

Quick Check

1. Solve $4g + 11.6 = -23.2$. Check the solution.

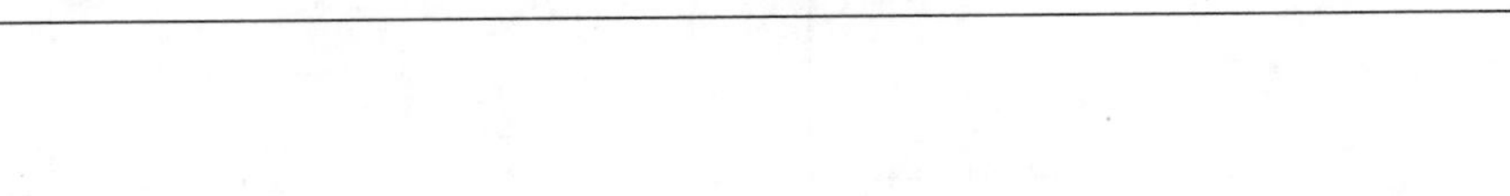

Name ______________________ Class ______________ Date ______________

Example

❷ Sharing Costs Six people at dinner shared equally a total bill of \$180. This total included a tip of \$30. Which equation can be used to find the amount of each person's share for dinner without the tip?

A. $6s = 180$ **B.** $6s - 30 = 180$

C. $6s + 30 = 180$ **D.** $6(s + 30) = 180$

Words | each person's share for dinner | ___ | 6 | ___ | tip | is | \$180 |

Let s = each person's share for dinner.

Equation ___ ___ ___ ___ ___ = ___

The equation is ______.

The correct answer is choice ___.

You can solve the equation to find each person's share.

$6s + 30 - \square = 180 - \square$ ← **Subtract ___ from each side.**

$6s = \square$ ← **Simplify.**

$\frac{6s}{\square} = \frac{\square}{\square}$ ← **Divide each side by ___.**

$s = \square$ ← **Simplify.**

Each person's share for dinner without the tip is \$ ___.

Quick Check

2. Telephone Bill To make a long-distance call, it costs \$.50 per call and \$.85 per minute. You make a long-distance call that costs \$3.90. Write and solve an equation to find the length of the call.

Name ______________________ Class ______________ Date ______________

Lesson 2-2

Simplifying Algebraic Expressions

Lesson Objective	Common Core State Standards
To combine like terms and simplify algebraic expressions	Expressions and Equations: 8.EE.7.b

Vocabulary

A term is ______________________

____

Like terms have ______________________

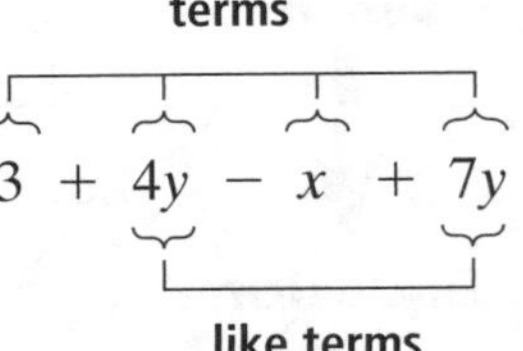

Examples

1 Combining Like Terms Combine like terms in the expression $q - 9q$.

$q - 9q = 1q - 9q$ ← **Rewrite q as $1q$.**

$= (1 \square 9)q$ ← $\square$ **Property**

$= \square$ ← **Combine like terms by subtracting.**

2 Application: Shopping Karen buys 12 bottles of water and 8 cans of fruit juice for a camping trip. Monica buys 6 bottles of water and 16 cans of fruit juice. Define and use variables to represent the total cost.

Words Karen: 12 bottles of water plus 8 cans of juice

Let b = the cost of a bottle of water.

Let c = the cost of a can of fruit juice.

Expression $\square b \quad \square \quad 8\square$

Words Monica: 6 bottles of water plus 16 cans of juice

Expression $\square b \quad \square \quad 16\square$

Combined Expression $\square b \square 8 \square + \square b \square 16 \square$

$\square b \square 8 \square + \square b \square 16 \square$

$= \square b + 6b + 8\square + \square c$ ← **Commutative Property of Addition**

$= (\square + 6)b + (8 + \square)c$ ← **Distributive Property**

$= \square b + \square c$ ← **Simplify.**

Name ______________________ Class ______________ Date ______________

3 Distributing and Simplifying Simplify $4(b - 3) + 2.3b$.

$4(b - 3) + 2.3b = 4b - \square + 2.3b$ ← $\square$ **Property**

$= 4b + 2.3b - \square$ ← $\square$ **Property of Addition**

$= (\square + \square)b - 12$ ← $\square$ **Property**

$= \square - \square$ ← **Simplify.**

Quick Check

1. Combine like terms in the expression $2t + t - 17t$.

2. In one trip to a hardware store, you buy 16 boards, 2 boxes of nails, and a hammer. On a second trip, you buy 10 more boards and a box of nails. Define and use variables to represent the total cost.

   Let $\square$ = ______________

   Let $\square$ = ______________

   Let $\square$ = ______________

3. Simplify the expression $11 - 2(3.4b + 1)$.

Name ______________________ Class ______________ Date ______________

Lesson 2-3

Solving Multi-Step Equations

Lesson Objective	**Common Core State Standards**
To write and solve multi-step equations	Expressions and Equations: 8.EE.7, 8.EE.7.b

Example

1 Simplifying Before Solving an Equation Solve $2c + 2 + 3c = 12$.

$2c + 2 + 3c = 12$

$2c + 3c + 2 = 12$ ← ☐ **Property of Addition**

$\square + 2 = 12$ ← **Combine like terms.**

$\square + 2 - \square = 12 - \square$ ← **Subtract ☐ from each side.**

$5c = \square$ ← **Simplify.**

$\frac{5c}{\square} = \frac{\square}{\square}$ ← **Divide each side by ☐.**

$c = \square$ ← **Simplify.**

Check $2c + 2 + 3c = 12$

$2(\square) + 2 + 3(\square) \stackrel{?}{=} 12$ ← **Substitute ☐ for c.**

$\square = 12$ ✓ ← **The solution checks.**

Quick Check

1. Solve $-15 = 5b + 12 - 2b + 6$. Check the solution.

Name ______________________ Class ______________ Date ______________

Example

❷ **Using the Distributive Property** Eight cheerleaders set a goal of selling 424 boxes of cards to raise money. After two weeks, each cheerleader has sold 28 boxes. How many more boxes must each cheerleader sell?

A. 15 boxes **B.** 25 boxes **C.** 50 boxes **D.** 53 boxes

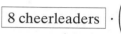

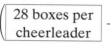

Words 8 cheerleaders · (28 boxes per cheerleader + additional boxes per cheerleader) = 424 boxes

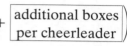

Let x = the number of additional boxes per cheerleader.

Equation ☐ · (☐ + ☐) = ☐

$8(28 + x) = 424$

☐ $+ 8x = 424$ ← ☐ **Property**

☐ − ☐ $+ 8x = 424 -$ ☐ ← **Subtract** ☐ **from each side.**

$8x = 200$ ← **Simplify.**

$\frac{8x}{☐} = \frac{200}{☐}$ ← **Divide each side by** ☐.

$x =$ ☐ ← **Simplify.**

Each cheerleader must sell ☐ more boxes. The correct answer is choice ☐.

Quick Check

2. **Class Trips** Your class goes to an amusement park. Admission is $10 for each student and $15 for each chaperone. The total cost is $380. There are 12 girls in your class and 6 chaperones on the trip. How many boys are in your class?

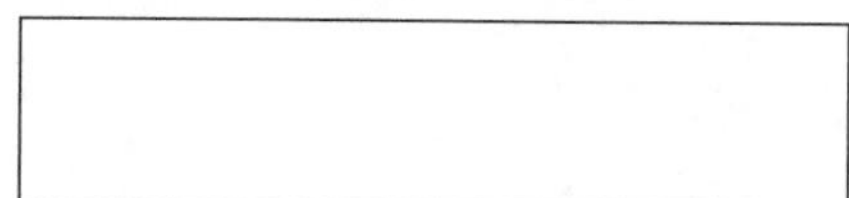

Name ________________ Class ________ Date ________

Lesson 2-4

Solving Equations With Variables on Both Sides

Lesson Objective	Common Core State Standards
To write and solve equations with variables on both sides	Expressions and Equations: 8.EE.7, 8.EE.7.b

Example

1 Variables on Both Sides Solve $9 + 2p = -3 - 4p$.

$9 + 2p = -3 - 4p$

$9 + 2p + \square = -3 - 4p + \square$ ← **Add** $\square$ **to each side.**

$9 + \square = -3$ ← **Combine like terms.**

$9 - \square + 6p = -3 - \square$ ← **Subtract** $\square$ **from each side.**

$6p = \square$ ← **Simplify.**

$\frac{6p}{\square} = \frac{\square}{\square}$ ← **Divide each side by** $\square$.

$p = \square$ ← **Simplify.**

Check $9 + 2p = -3 - 4p$

$9 + 2(\square) \stackrel{?}{=} -3 - 4(\square)$ ← **Substitute** $\square$ **for** ***p*****.**

$\square = 5$ ✓ ← **The solution checks.**

Quick Check

1. Solve $7b - 2 = b + 10$. Check the solution.

Name ______________________ Class ______________ Date ______________

Example

2 Using the Distributive Property The chess club decides to sell shirts and hats for fundraising. The total cost of a shirt and a hat is $21. Paula purchased 4 hats for the same price as 3 shirts. What is the cost of one shirt?

Words [cost of 4 hats] is the same as [cost of 3 shirts]

Let x = cost of one shirt.

Equation $4 \cdot (21 - x) \quad = \quad 3x$

$4(21 - x) = 3x$

$\square - 4x = 3x$ ← $\square$ **Property**

$\square - 4x + \square = 3x + \square$ ← **Add** $\square$ **to each side.**

$\square = 7x$ ← **Simplify.**

$\frac{84}{7} = \frac{7x}{7}$ ← **Divide each side by** $\square$.

$\square = x$ ← **Simplify.**

The cost of one shirt is $\$\square$.

Quick Check

2. One cell phone plan costs $29.94 per month plus $.10 for each text message sent. Another plan costs $32.99 per month plus $.05 for each text message sent. For what number of text messages will the monthly bill for both plans be the same?

Name ______________________ Class ______________ Date ______________

Lesson 2-5

Types of Solutions of Linear Equations

Lesson Objective	Common Core State Standards
To identify whether a linear equation in one variable has one, infinitely many, or no solutions	Expressions and Equations: 8.EE.7, 8.EE.7.a, 8.EE.7.b

Key Concepts

Algebraic Form	Number of Solutions	Description
$a = b$	None	There are ☐ values of the variable for which the equation is true.
$x = a$	One	The equation is ☐ for exactly one value of the variable.
$a = a$	Infinitely many	The equation is true for ☐ values of the variable.

Examples

1 Identifying Types of Solutions Tell whether each equation has one solution, infinitely many solutions, or no solution. Justify your answer.

a. $6w + 3 = 4w - 1$

$6w - \square + 3 = 4w - \square - 1$ ← **Subtract ☐ from each side.**

$\square + 3 = -1$ ← **Simplify.**

$2w + 3 - \square = -1 - \square$ ← **Subtract ☐ from each side.**

$2w = -4$ ← **Simplify.**

$\frac{2w}{\square} = \frac{-4}{\square}$ ← **Divide each side by ☐.**

$w = \square$ ← **Simplify.**

The result is an equation of the form ☐ = ☐. So, the equation has ☐ solution(s).

b. $6w + 3 = 6(w + 0.5)$

$6w + 3 = \square + \square$ ← **Use the Distributive Property.**

$6w - \square + 3 = 6w - \square + 3$ ← **Subtract ☐ from each side.**

$3 = \square$ ← **Simplify.**

The result is an equation of the form ☐ = ☐. So, the equation has ☐ solution(s).

Name ______________________ Class ______________ Date ______________

c. $6w + 3 = 6(w - 4)$

$6w + 3 = \square - \square$ ← **Use the Distributive Property.**

$6w - \square + 3 = 6w - \square - 24$ ← **Subtract** $\square$ **from each side.**

$3 = \square$ ← **Simplify.**

The result is an equation of the form $\square = \square$. So, the equation has $\square$ solution(s).

Quick Check

1. Tell whether each equation has one solution, infinitely many solutions, or no solution. Justify your answer.

a. $5x + 8 = 5(x + 3)$ **b.** $9x = 8 + 5x$ **c.** $6x + 12 = 6(x + 2)$ **d.** $7x - 11 = 11 - 7x$

Example

2 **Comparing Costs** A movie club card costs \$10. Cardholders pay the member's cost for a movie ticket. A person without a club card pays \$2 more for a ticket. A friend tells you that the cost of 5 tickets is the same for both members and nonmembers. Is this true? Justify your answer.

Words $\square + 5 \cdot \square = 5 \cdot (\square + \$2)$

Let t = cost of one member's ticket in dollars.

Equation $\square + 5t = 5(t + 2)$ ← **Substitute 10 for cost of card in dollars.**

$10 + 5t = \square + \square$ ← **Use the Distributive Property.**

$10 + 5t - \square = 5t - \square + 10$ ← **Subtract** $\square$ **from each side.**

$10 = 10$ ← **Simplify.**

The result is an equation of the form $\square = \square$. So, the equation has $\square$ solution(s), and the statement is $\square$.

Quick Check

2. Admission to the museum is \$8 for students and \$16 for adults. Yesterday, twice as many students as adults came to the museum. The total admissions paid by students and the total admissions paid by adults were equal. How many adults came to the museum yesterday? Justify your answer.

Name ____________ Class ____________ Date ____________

Lesson 3-1

Relating Graphs to Events

Lesson Objective	Common Core Standard
To interpret and sketch graphs that represent real-world situations	Functions: 8.F.5

Vocabulary

Change in data is linear if ____________

Change in data is not linear if ____________

Example

1 Interpreting a Graph The graph shows the altitude of a helicopter during a flight.

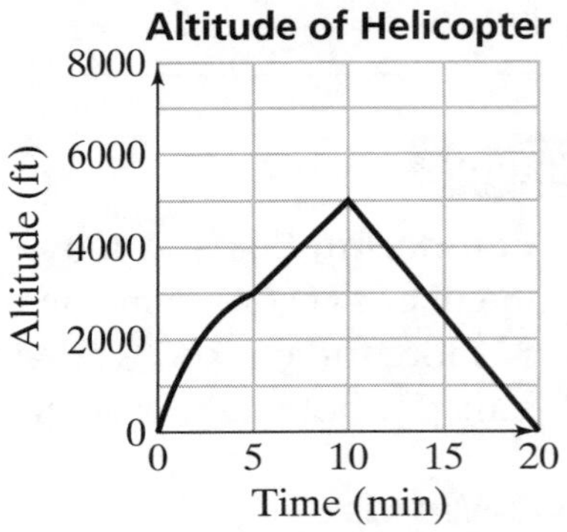

a. Is the helicopter's altitude increasing or decreasing during each of the following times?

0 to 2 min

7 to 8 min

12 to 16 min

b. Is the helicopter's altitude linear or nonlinear during each of the following times?

3 to 4 min

9 to 10 min

15 to 18 min

Altitude of Helicopter

Quick Check

1. Between which two times did the speed increase the most?

Name ______________________ Class ______________ Date ______________

Example

❷ Sketching a Graph An athlete jogs for 30 min, sprints for 5 min, and walks for 10 min. Sketch and label a graph showing his speed.

As the athlete starts jogging, the speed increases and then becomes constant for about 30 minutes. Then the speed increases again for the sprint and becomes constant for about 5 minutes. Then the speed decreases when the athlete slows to a walk for 10 minutes.

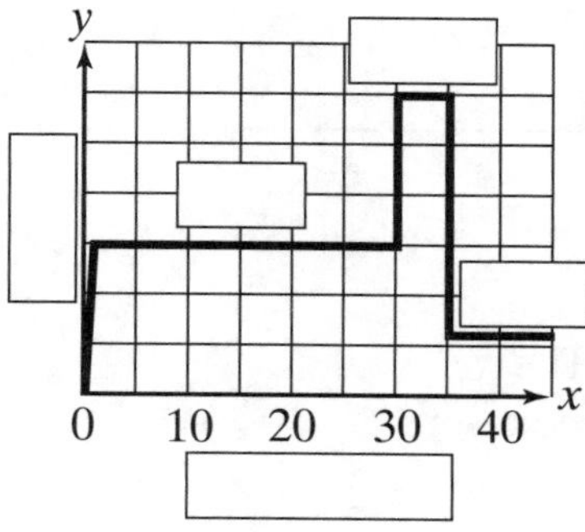

Quick Check

2. You walk to your friend's house. For the first 10 min, you walk from home to a park. For the next 5 min, you watch a ball game in the park. For the last 5 min, you run to your friend's house. Sketch and label a graph showing your distance from home during your trip.

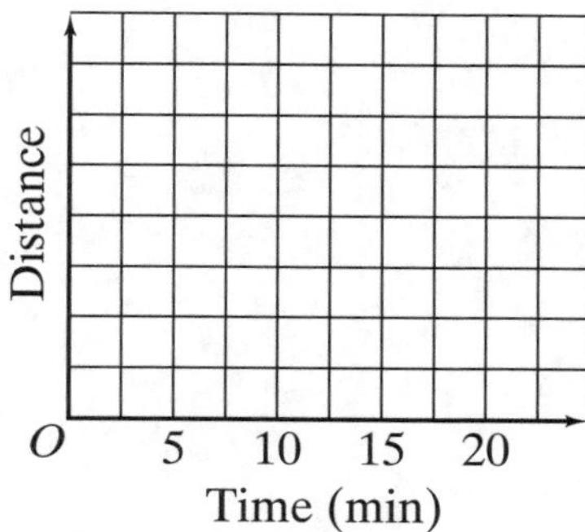

Name ______________________ Class ______________ Date ______________

Lesson 3-2

Functions

Lesson Objective	**Common Core Standard**
To evaluate functions and complete input-output tables	Functions: 8.F.1

Vocabulary

A function is ____

A function rule is ____

Examples

❶ **Evaluating Functions** Julia deposited $40 in a savings account. The function $s = 5w + 40$ gives the total savings s in dollars after w weeks that Julia has been saving. Find the output s for the input $w = 12$.

$s = 5w + 40$ ← **Write the function.**

$s = 5 \cdot \square + 40$ ← **Substitute the input value for *w*.**

$s = \square + 40$ ← **Simplify.**

$s = \square$

The output s for the input $w = \square$ is $\square$. So, after depositing $40, Julia's total savings is $\square$.

❷ **Input-Output Tables** The function $t = 2h + 15$ gives the outdoor temperature t in degrees Fahrenheit h hours before, at, and after sunrise on a cold winter day. Use the function to complete the table for $h = -4, -2, 0, 2, 4$.

Input *h*	Output *t*
−4	
−2	
0	
2	
4	

← $2(\square) + 15 = \square$

← $2(\square) + 15 = \square$

← $2(\square) + 15 = \square$

← $2(\square) + 15 = \square$

← $2(\square) + 15 = \square$

Name ______________________ Class ______________ Date ______________

❸ Input-Output Table Application Complete the table of input-output values for the function rule $t = 4c$, where c represents the number of cars and t represents the number of tires.

Input c (number of cars)	Output t (number of tires)
3	
6	
9	

← 4 · ☐ = ☐

← 4 · ☐ = ☐

← 4 · ☐ = ☐

Quick Check

1. The function $F = \frac{9}{5}C + 32$ converts temperatures in degrees Celsius, C, to degrees Fahrenheit, F. Evaluate the function for $C = 20$.

2. Use the function $m = \frac{1}{3}n + 1$ to make an input-output table for $n = -1, 0, 1,$ and 2.

Input n	Output m
−1	
0	
1	
2	

3. The deposit on a drink container is \$.10 in the state of Michigan. Use the function rule $d = 0.1c$. Make a table of input-output pairs to show the total deposits on 5, 10, and 15 containers.

Input c	Output d

Name ______________________ Class ______________ Date ______________

Lesson 3-3

Proportional Relationships

Lesson Objective	Common Core Standard
To determine if relationships are proportional	Expressions and Equations: 8.EE.5

Vocabulary

A proportional relationship is ______________________________

____

Examples

1 Proportional Relationships in Tables: Distance-Time Relationships
Determine if the relationship is proportional.

Jason's Hiking Trip	
Time t (days)	Distance d (mi)
1	12
2	24
3	36
4	48

Write the ratio of each input to its corresponding output. Then simplify.

$\frac{1}{\square}$

$\frac{2}{\square} = \square$

$\frac{\square}{\square} = \square$

$\frac{\square}{\square} = \square$

The ratios are ______________, so the relationship is ______________.

2 Proportional Relationships in Tables: Comparison Shopping Determine if the relationship is proportional.

Polo Shirts
2 for \$16
4 for \$32
5 for \$40
7 for \$49

Write the ratio of each input (number of shirts) to its corresponding output (cost). Then simplify.

$\frac{2}{\square} = \square$

$\frac{4}{\square} = \square$

$\frac{\square}{\square} = \square$

$\frac{\square}{\square} = \square$

The ratios are ______________, so the relationship is ______________.

Name ______________________ Class ______________ Date ______________

❸ Input-Output Tables and Graphs Sarah makes and sells quilted tablet covers for \$18 each. She uses the function $s = 18c$, where s represents sales in dollars and c represents number of covers sold. Complete the input-output table and graph your results. Does the function have a proportional relationship? Explain.

Tablet Cover Sales	
Number of Covers c	Sales s (in dollars)
0	0
1	18
2	36
3	54

Write the ratio of each input to its corresponding output. Simplify.

$\frac{0}{0}$ **undefined**

$\frac{1}{\square}$

$\frac{\square}{\square} = \square$

$\frac{\square}{\square} = \square$

Write a title. →

Label the vertical axis using s and a title. →

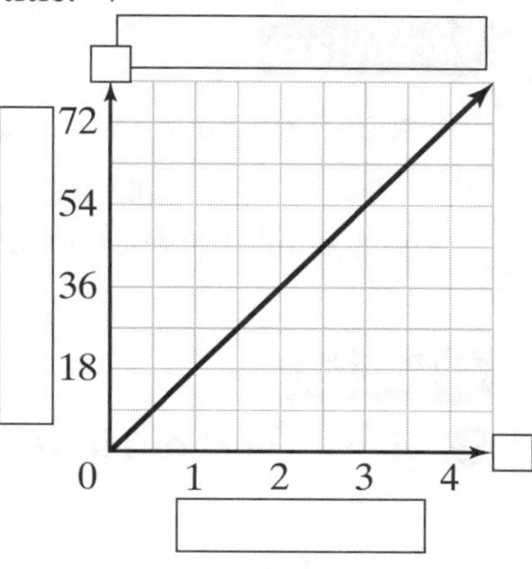

← Label the horizontal axis using c and a title.

The function ______________ a proportional relationship because

____

Quick Check

1. The ratios of all the inputs to the outputs in a table are $\frac{1}{4}$. Is the relationship proportional?

2. Pizza slices are selling as follows: 1 for \$2, 2 for \$3, or 4 for \$5. Is this relationship proportional? Explain.

3. The function $t = 4m$ gives the temperature t in degrees Celsius after m minutes of a liquid during a science experiment. Determine if the function has a proportional relationship.

Lesson 3-4

Linear Functions

Lesson Objective	Common Core Standard
To recognize linear functions and use tables and equations to graph them	Functions: 8.F.3

Vocabulary

A linear function is ____

[ ] data are data that involve a count of objects. [ ] data are data where numbers between any two data values have meaning.

Examples

1 Linear Functions in Tables Determine which function represented by a table is linear.

Find the changes in variables.

Function 1

x	−2	0	2	4
y	4	7	10	16

Function 2

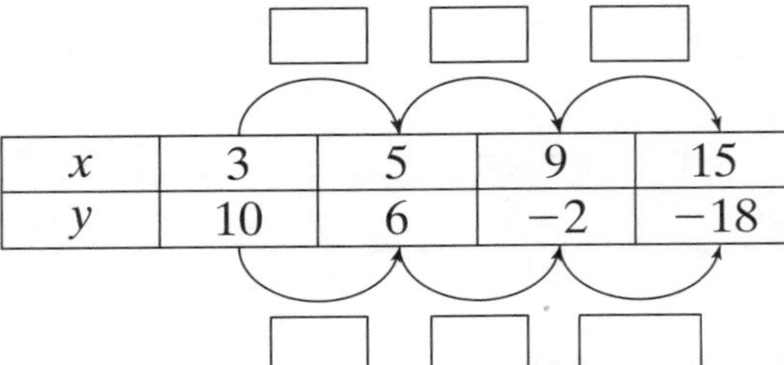

x	3	5	9	15
y	10	6	−2	−18

Ratios in changes between variables:

__________, __________, __________

The ratios are ______________, so

the function ______________ linear.

Ratios in changes between variables:

__________, __________, __________

The ratios are ______________, so

the function ______________ linear.

2 Graphing Discrete Data It costs $9.50 to download a book to an e-reader. The total cost of downloading books is a function of the price of one book. Make a table and graph the function. Determine whether the data are discrete or continuous.

You ______________ buy part of a book, so the data are ______________.

Complete the table.

Number of Books	Total Cost (dollars)
0	
1	
2	
3	

Connect data points with a dashed line.

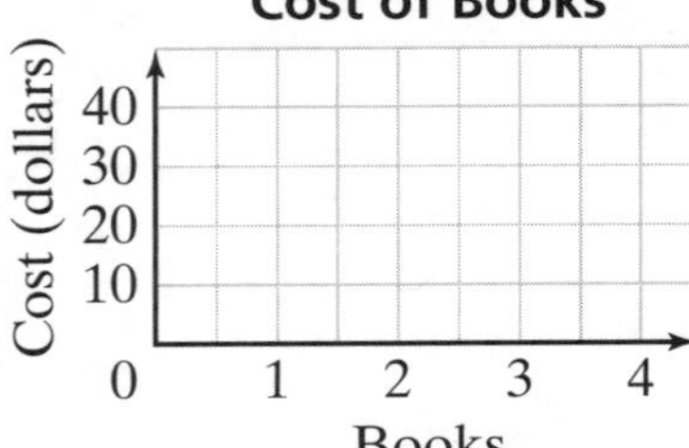

Name ____________________ Class ____________ Date ____________

❸ Graphing Continuous Data A shopper buys some grapes that cost \$2.19 per pound and a watermelon that costs \$4.00. The function $c = 2.19p + 4$ gives the total the shopper spent on produce where c represents total cost and p represents number of pounds of grapes. Use the equation to make a table and graph the function.

Determine whether the data are discrete or continuous.

You ____________ buy part of a pound of grapes, so the data are ____________.

Complete the table.

Pounds of Grapes	Total Cost (dollars)
0	
1	
2	
3	

Connect data points with a solid line.

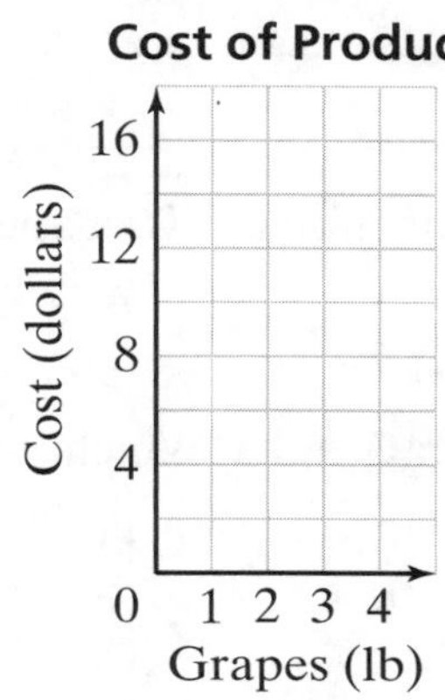

Quick Check

1. Determine if the function represented in the table is linear. Explain.

x	5	9	17	21
y	−12	−13	−15	−16

2. **Tickets** The function $c = 15t$ represents the cost (in dollars) of t adult tickets to a museum. Make a table and graph the function.

3. **Flying** The function $a = 4{,}000 - 600m$ gives the altitude a of a plane in feet after m minutes. Make a table and graph the function.

Name ______________________ Class ______________ Date ______________

Lesson 3-5

Nonlinear Functions

Lesson Objective	**Common Core State Standard**
To identify nonlinear functions	Functions: 8.F.3

Vocabulary

A nonlinear function is ______________________________

A quadratic function is ______________________________

____

The graph of a quadratic function is a U-shaped curve called a ______________.

Examples

1 Nonlinear Functions from Graphs Which functions appear to be nonlinear?

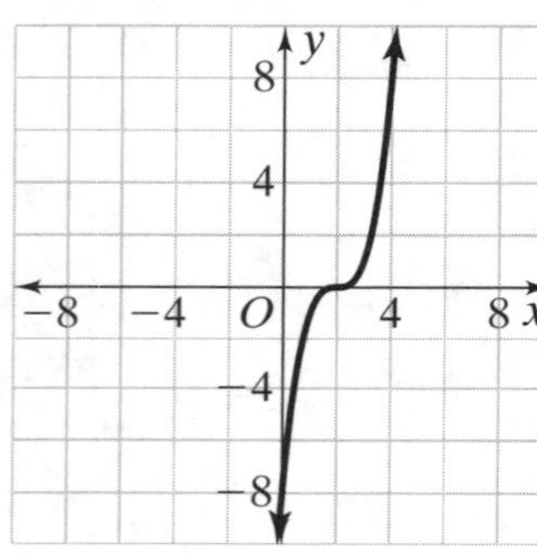

Function 1

Function 2

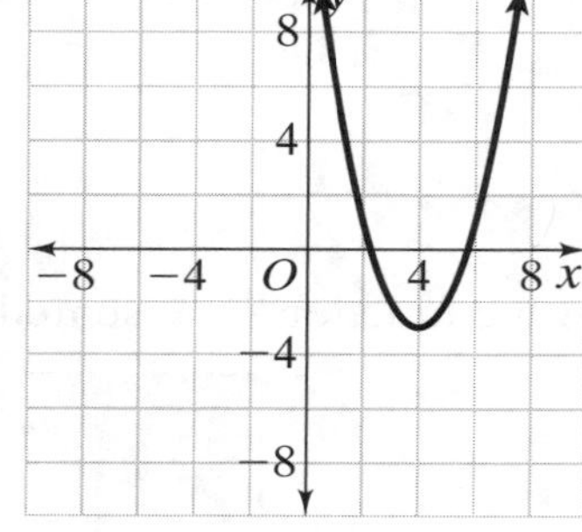

Function 3

The graph of function 1 ______________ a straight line.

The graph of function 2 ______________ a straight line.

The graph of function 3 ______________ a straight line.

So, function(s) ______________ is/are nonlinear.

2 Nonlinear Functions from Tables and Equations Determine which function is nonlinear.

a. Simplify each equation if possible.

$y = 3(x + 4) - 5$ $\qquad$ $y = 2x^3 + 5$

______________ $\qquad$ ______________

The greatest exponent in the first function is ______________.

The greatest exponent in the second function is ______________.

The ______________ function is nonlinear because its greatest exponent is 2 or greater.

Name ______________________ Class ______________ Date ______________

b. Find the ratios between the changes in variables for each table.

x	5	7	10	14
y	2	4	6	8

x	3	6	9	12
y	5	3	1	−1

______________________ ______________________

The ratios are not the same in the ______________ table, so it represents a ______________ function.

3 Nonlinear Functions from Descriptions Decide if the function described is linear or nonlinear.

Samantha throws a softball into the air. A function relates the height of the ball above the ground to time.

Decide if the height per second of the ball changes at a constant rate. Explain.

____

So, this function is ______________________.

Quick Check

1. Sketch the function that passes through the points in the table. Does the function appear to be nonlinear?

x	2	4	6	8
y	4	8	12	16

2. Which of the two given functions is nonlinear?

a. $y = 17 - 4^x$

$y = 4 + 2(x + 7)$

b.

x	3	6	9	12
y	3	5	7	10

x	6	7	8	9
y	−2	1	4	7

3. John mows lawns. He charges his customers \$15 per hour. A function relates the number of hours John works and the amount he earns. Is the function nonlinear? Explain.

Name ______________________ Class ______________ Date ______________

Lesson 4-1

Understanding Slope

Lesson Objective	**Common Core Standards**
To find the slope of a line from a graph or table	Functions: 8.F.4 Expressions and Equations: 8.EE.6

Vocabulary and Key Concepts

Slope of a Line

slope of a line = $\dfrac{\text{change in } \square\text{-coordinates}}{\text{change in } \square\text{-coordinates}}$ ← rise / ← run

Slope is ______________________

Examples

1 Finding the Slope of a Line Using coordinates, find the slope of the line between $P(-2, 3)$ and $Q(-1, -1)$.

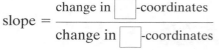

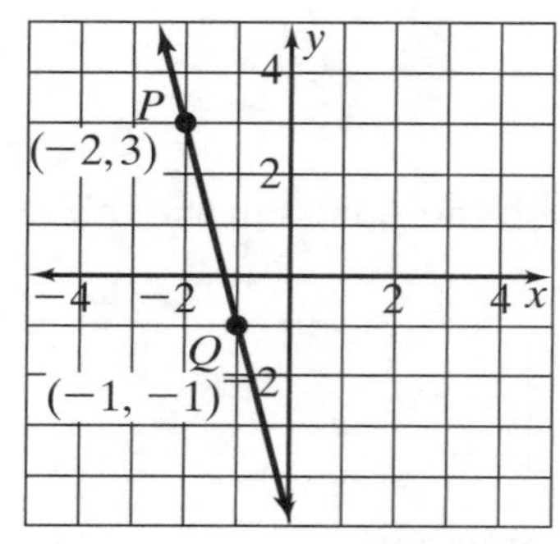

slope = $\dfrac{\text{change in } \square\text{-coordinates}}{\text{change in } \square\text{-coordinates}}$

$= \dfrac{\square - (\square)}{\square - (\square)}$ ← **Subtract coordinates of *Q* from coordinates of *P*.**

$= \dfrac{\square}{\square}$ or $\square$ ← **Simplify.**

2 Slopes of Horizontal and Vertical Lines Find the slope of each line. State whether the slope is zero or undefined.

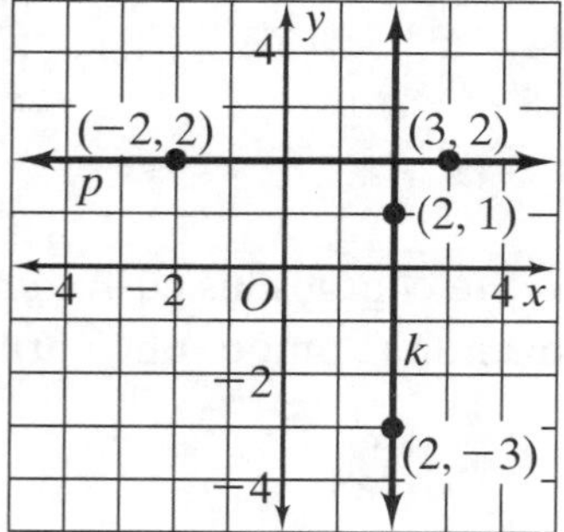

a. line k

slope = $\dfrac{1 - (\square)}{\square - 2} = \dfrac{\square}{\square}$

Division by zero is $\square$

The slope of a vertical line is $\square$.

b. line p

slope = $\dfrac{2 - \square}{\square - 3} = \dfrac{\square}{\square} = \square$

The slope of a horizontal line is $\square$.

Name ______________________ Class ______________ Date ______________

❸ Finding Slope From a Table Graph the data in the table. Connect the points with a line. Then find the rate of change.

Distance (mi)	Cost ($)
100	25
200	50
300	75
400	100

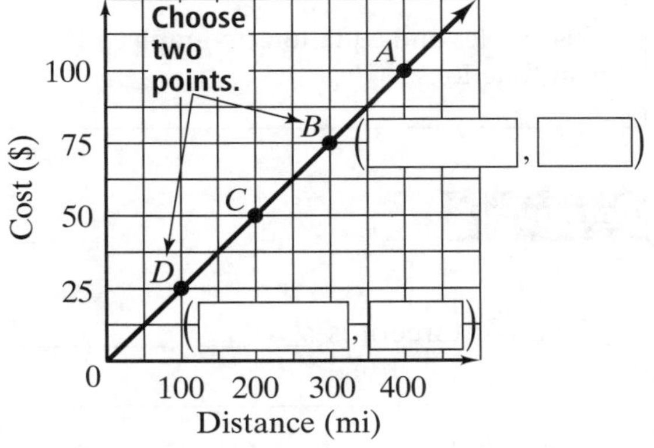

rate of change = slope = $\dfrac{\text{change in } \square}{\text{change in } \square}$

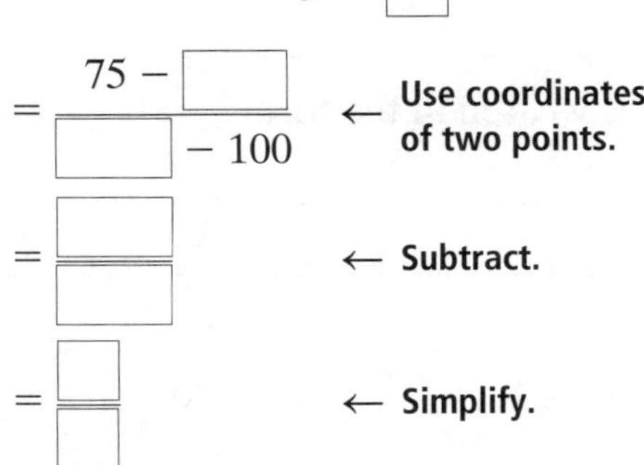

$= \dfrac{75 - \square}{\square - 100}$ ← **Use coordinates of two points.**

$= \dfrac{\square}{\square}$ ← **Subtract.**

$= \dfrac{\square}{\square}$ ← **Simplify.**

The cost increases by $ ☐ for every ☐ miles traveled.

Quick Check

1. Find the slope of each line.

a. (2, 4) (−3, 2)

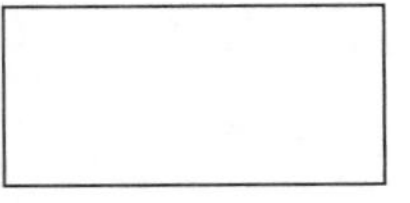

b.

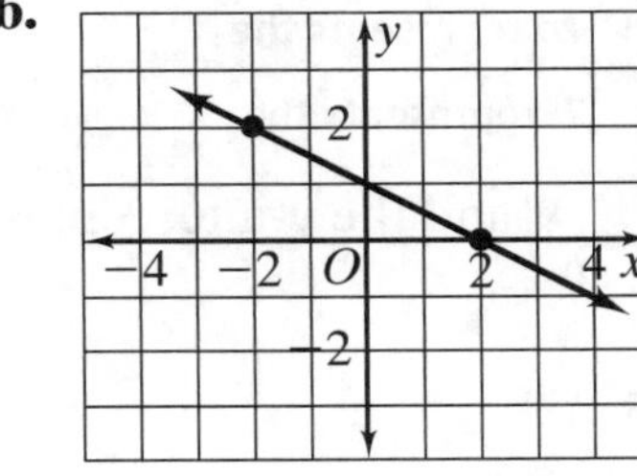

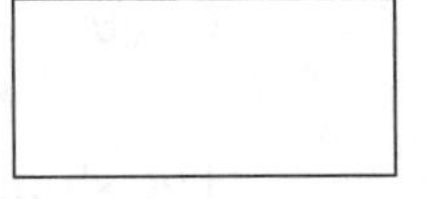

2. Find the slope of a line through the points (3, 1) and (3, −2). State whether the slope is zero or undefined.

3. Graph the data in the table and connect the points with a line. Then find the slope.

x	−1	0	1	2
y	2	0	−2	−4

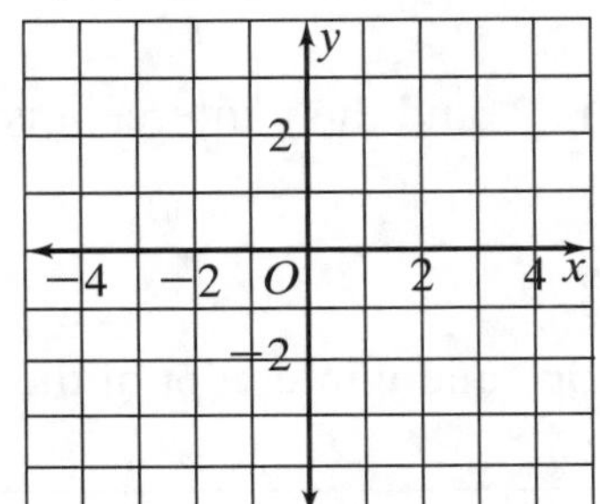

Slope = ☐

Name ______________________ Class ______________ Date ______________

Lesson 4-2

Graphing Linear Functions

Lesson Objective	Common Core Standards
To use tables and equations to graph linear functions	Expressions and Equations: 8.EE.6 Functions: 8.F.1, 8.F.3, 8.F. 4

Vocabulary

The y-intercept is ______________________

____

An equation written in slope-intercept form is written in the form ______________________

____

A linear function is ______________________

____

Example

1 Finding Slope and y-intercept Find the slope and y-intercept of the graph of each function.

a. $y = 3x \ + 7$

$y = 3x \ + 7$

$\uparrow \quad \uparrow$

$y = mx + b$ **m represents the** ☐.

b represents the ☐.

The slope is ☐ and the y-intercept is ☐.

b. $y = 3x + 7$

$y = \frac{3}{4}x - 5$

$\uparrow \quad \uparrow$

$y = mx + b$

The slope is ☐ and the y-intercept is ☐.

Quick Check

1. Find the slope and y-intercept of the graph of $y = x - 3$.

____

Name ________________ Class ________________ Date ________________

Example

❷ **Graphing Functions of the Form $y = mx$** The amount that Amber earns from her job is given by the function $y = 7x$, where y represents her earnings and x represents the number of hours she works. Graph $y = 7x$.

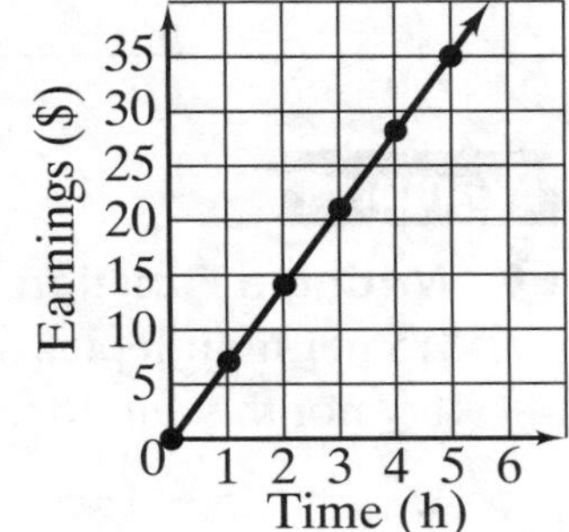

Use slope-intercept form.

The y-intercept is ☐ and the slope is ☐.

Move ☐ units ☐ from (0, 0) since the slope is positive and ☐ unit ☐. Repeat to find more points on the line.

Draw a line through the three points.

Quick Check

2. Graph the function $y = \frac{1}{5}x$.

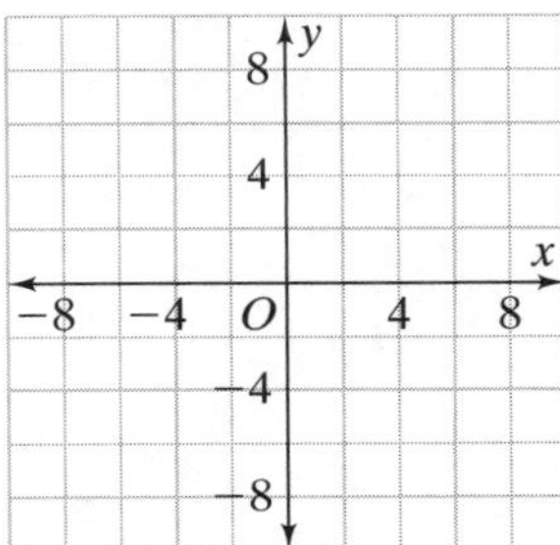

Name ______________________ Class ______________ Date ______________

Lesson 4-3

Writing Rules for Linear Functions

Lesson Objective	Common Core Standard
To write function rules from words, tables, and graphs	Functions: 8.F.4

Examples

1 Writing a Function Rule From Words A rate for Internet access is \$15 per month plus \$.25 per hour of use. Which function rule represents the monthly bill for x hours of use?

A. $y = 0.25 + 15x$ **C.** $y = 15 - 0.25x$

B. $y = 15 + 0.25x$ **D.** $y = 0.25x - 15$

☐ = \$15 plus \$.25 times ☐

Let ☐ = the number of hours. ← **input**

Let ☐ = the monthly cost. ← **output**

☐ = ☐ + ☐ · ☐

y = ☐ + ☐ x

The function rule ☐ = ☐ + ☐ represents the monthly cost for x hours of use. The correct answer is choice ☐.

2 Writing a Rule From a Table Do the values in the table below represent a linear function? If so, write a function rule.

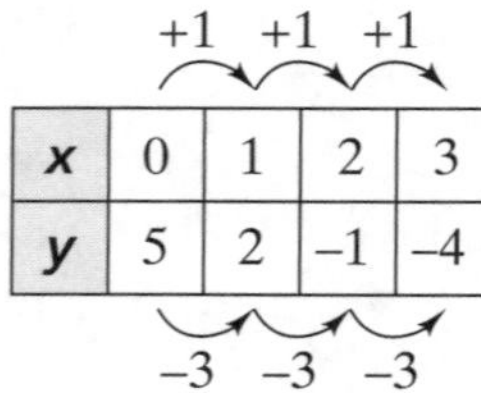

x	0	1	2	3
y	5	2	–1	–4

+1 +1 +1 ← **Find the changes in inputs.**

–3 –3 –3 ← **Find the changes in outputs.**

$\frac{\text{change in } y}{\text{change in } x} = \frac{-3}{1} = \frac{-3}{1} = \frac{-3}{1}$ ← **Compare the changes as ratios.**

Since each ratio is the same, the function ☐ linear. The slope is ☐.

The point (0, ☐) lies on the graph of the function. So the y-intercept is ☐. Use the slope-intercept form to write a function rule.

$y =$ ☐ $x +$ ☐ ← **Substitute ☐ for *m* and ☐ for *b*.**

Name ____________________ Class ____________ Date ____________

3 Writing an Equation From a Graph An insurance salesperson earns an annual base salary plus a commission for each insurance policy that she sells. The graph shows this relationship. Write a function rule. What is base salary and rate of change?

y
50,000
40,000
(5, 30000)
30,000
Salary ($)
20,000
10,000
0
x
0 1 2 3 4 5 6 7 8 9 10
Number of Policies Sold

The point ______ lies on the y-axis so the y-intercept, b, is ______.

Two points are shown, so use them to find the slope, m.

$$m = \frac{\text{change in } \square \text{-coordinates}}{\text{change in } \square \text{-coordinates}}$$

$$= \frac{\square - \square}{\square - \square}$$

$$= \frac{\square}{\square}$$

$$= \square$$

The function rule is $y =$ ______ $x +$ ______.

The base salary is ______. The rate of change is ______, which is the commission for each policy the salesperson sells.

Quick Check

1. An orchestra buys music stands for $42 each with $298 in its bank account. Write a function rule that shows how the account balance depends on the number of stands bought. What are the initial value and rate of change of the function?

____

2. The table shows the inches of snow during a snowstorm. Write a function rule. What is the initial value and rate of change?

Number of Hours, x	3	6	9	12
Inches of Snow, y	4.5	9	13.5	18

____

3. The graph shows the height of a snowman over time. Write a function rule. What is the initial height and rate of change?

____

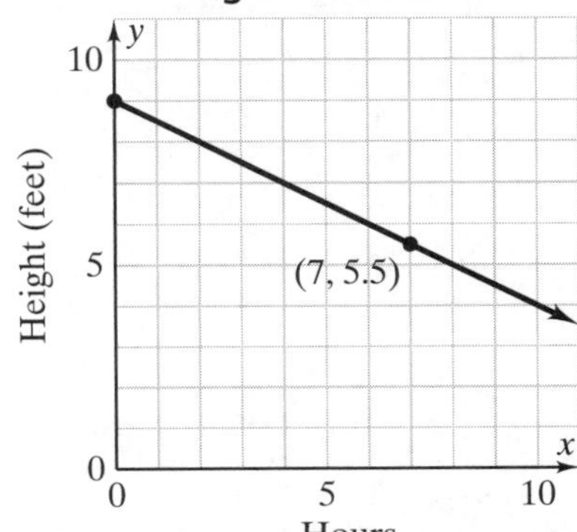

Name ______________________ Class ______________ Date ______________

Lesson 4-4

Comparing Functions

Lesson Objective	Common Core Standards
To compare properties of two functions represented in different ways	Functions: 8.F.2 Expressions and Equations: 8.EE.5

Examples

1 Comparing Linear Functions Which function has a greater rate of change?

Rates of Change

x	1	2	3	4
y	4	9	14	19

$y = 6x + 1$

Step 1 Find the slope from the table.
Use the points (1, 4) and (4, 19).

$$\text{slope} = \frac{\square - \square}{\square - \square} = \frac{\square}{\square} \text{ or } \square$$

Step 2 Find the slope from the equation using $y = mx + b$.

$y = 6x + 1$

↑

$y = mx + b$ **The slope is** $\square$.

Since $\square > \square$, the function $y = 6x + 1$ has a greater ______.

2 Comparing Initial Values of Linear Functions A company is deciding on its location for its annual employee appreciation dinner. A reception hall charges a \$300 rental fee and \$18 per person for meal service. Some rental rates for a hotel banquet room are the ordered pairs (20, 690) and (35, 1020) in the form (number of people, total cost in dollars). Which has the greater initial cost?

Reception Hall: The initial cost for the reception hall is represented by the ______ fee, which is ______.

Hotel Banquet Room: To find the initial cost of the hotel banquet room, use the ordered pairs to write an equation in slope-intercept form.

The ______ represents the initial cost.

Find the slope.

$$\text{slope} = \frac{\square - \square}{\square - \square}$$

$$= \frac{\square}{\square} \text{ or } 22$$

Find the *y*-intercept using $y = mx + b$.

$y = mx + b$

$690 = \square(20) + b$

$690 = \square + b$

$\square = b$

The initial cost for the hotel is ______.

Since ______ > ______, the ______ has a greater initial cost.

Name ______________________ Class ______________ Date ______________

❸ Comparing Nonlinear Functions Maria and Cory are both participating in a 6-mile bike-a-thon to raise money for charity. Sponsors can give a flat donation or pledge a certain amount of money for each mile they complete. Maria has $45 in flat donations and pledges totaling $12.50 per mile. Cory's donations are represented in the graph. Compare the functions.

Maria's Donations	Cory's Donations
increases	
not continuous	
Minimum ____	Minimum $30
Maximum $120	Maximum ____

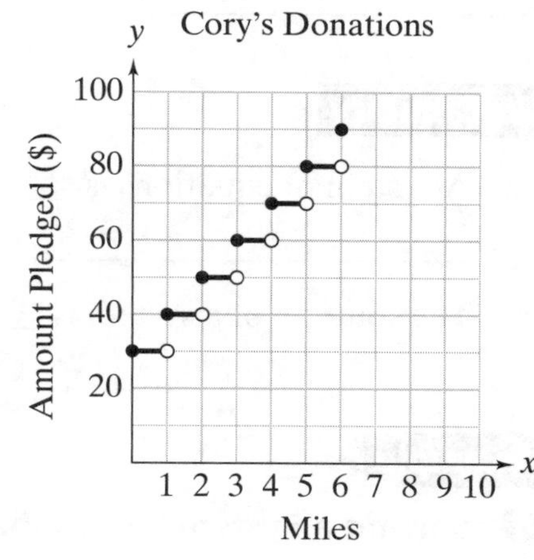

Quick Check

1. Which function has the greater rate of change?

x	1	3	4	6
y	5	13	17	25

$y = 2x + 1$

____

2. Vikram opened a savings account with $150. He deposits $150 every two weeks. Compare Vikram's account to Jack's account.

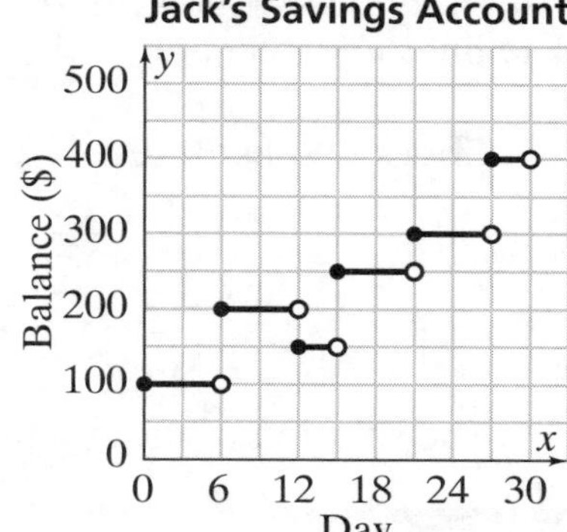

____

____

____

____

3. Steve's Scooter Rentals charges $17 per hour plus a $29 rental fee. Scooter World charges $48 for 1 hour and $108 for 4 hours. Both relationships are linear. Which company has the greatest initial cost?

Name ______________________ Class ______________ Date ____________

Lesson 5-1

Solving Systems by Graphing

Lesson Objective	**Common Core State Standards**
To solve systems of two linear equations in two variables by graphing the equations	Expressions and Equations: 8.EE.8.a, 8.EE.8.b, 8.EE.8.c

Vocabulary

A system of equations is ______________________________

____

The solution of a system is ______________________________

____

Example

1 Solving a System by Graphing Solve the system by graphing.

$$y = 3x - 5$$
$$y = -2x + 5$$

$y = 3x - 5$ ← **The slope is** ☐.

← **The y-intercept is** ☐.

$y = -2x + 5$ ← **The slope is** ☐.

← **The y-intercept is** ☐.

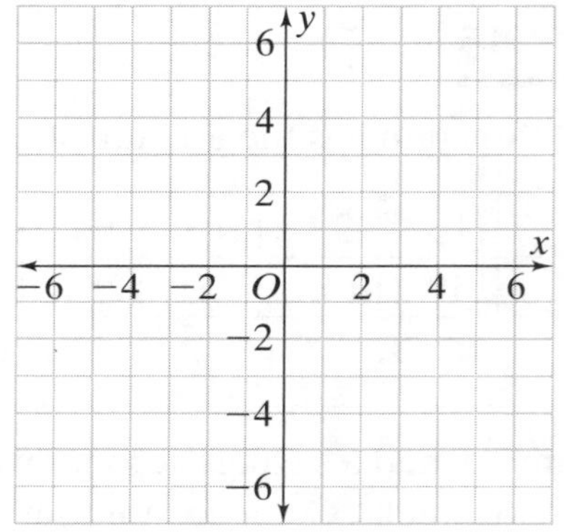

Graph both equations on the same coordinate plane.
The lines intersect at (☐, ☐).

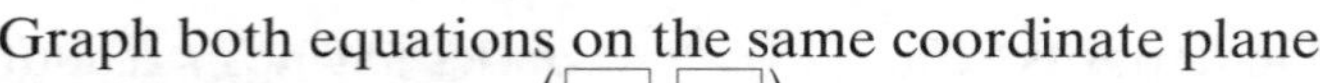

Check Substitute ☐ for x and ☐ for y in each equation.

$y = 3x - 5$	$y = -2x + 5$
☐ $\stackrel{?}{=}$ $3 \cdot$ ☐ $- 5$	☐ $\stackrel{?}{=}$ $-2 \cdot$ ☐ $+ 5$
☐ = ☐ ✓	☐ = $1 \cdot$ ☐ ✓

The solution of the system is ☐.

Quick Check

1. Solve the system of equations by graphing. Check the solution.

$$y = 2x - 4$$
$$y = -\frac{1}{2}x + 1$$

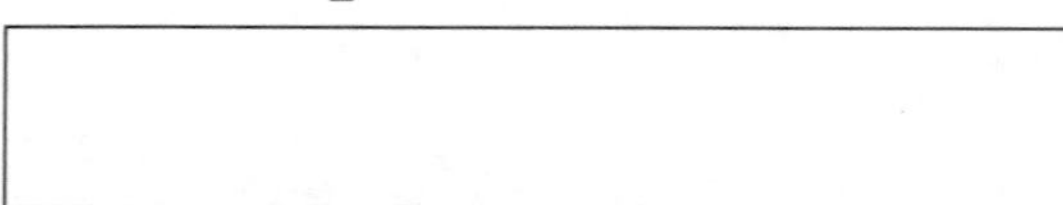

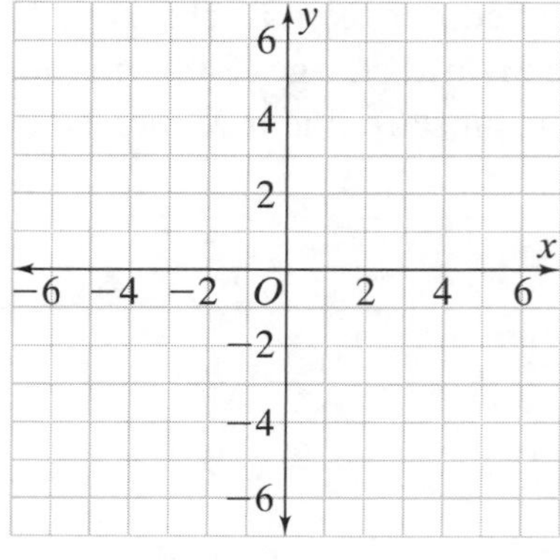

Name ________________ Class ________________ Date ________________

Example

❷ Solving a System by Graphing Solve the system by graphing.

$$-2x + y = 2$$
$$x + y = 5$$

Complete the tables.

x	$-2x + y = 2$	y	(x, y)
-2			
0			
2			

x	$x + y = 5$	y	(x, y)
-2			
0			
2			

Graph both equations on the same coordinate plane.
The lines intersect at (☐, ☐).

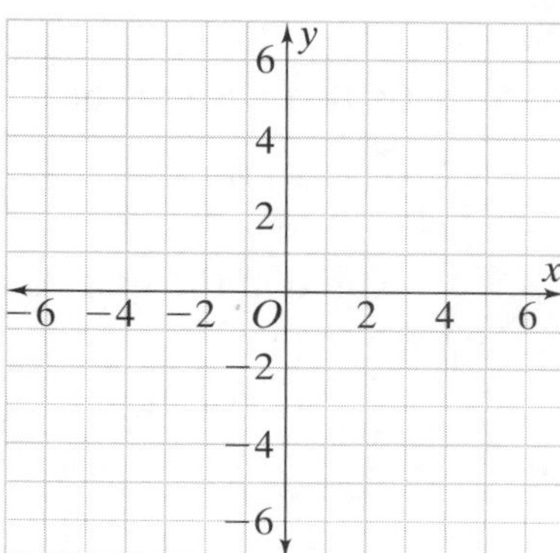

Check Substitute ☐ for x and ☐ for y in each equation.

$-2x + y = 2$ $\qquad$ $x + y = 5$

$-2 \cdot ☐ + ☐ \stackrel{?}{=} 2$ $\qquad$ $☐ + ☐ \stackrel{?}{=} 5$

☐ = ☐ ✓ $\qquad$ ☐ = ☐ ✓

The solution of the system is ☐.

Quick Check

2. Solve the system by graphing.

$$-x + y = -5$$
$$2x + y = 4$$

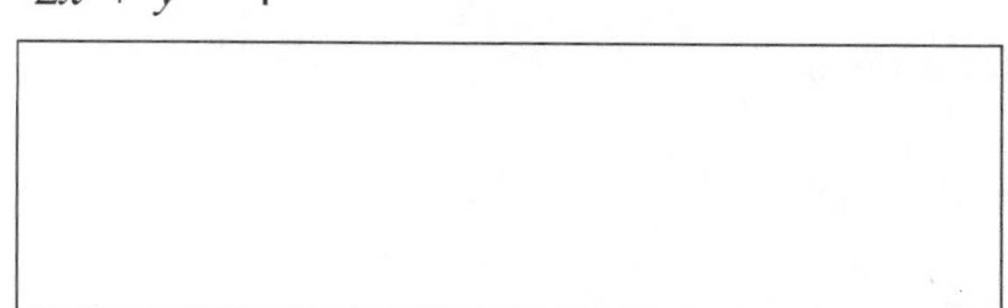

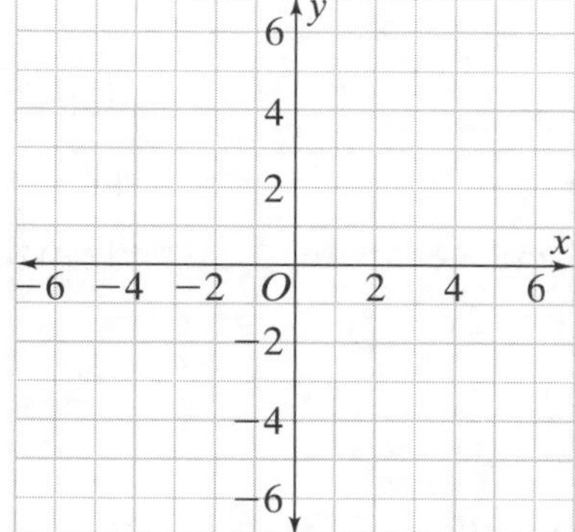

Name ______________________ Class ______________ Date ______________

Lesson 5-2

Solving Systems by Substitution

Lesson Objective	Common Core State Standards
To solve a system of equations with substitution	Expressions and Equations: 8.EE.8.b, 8.EE.8.c

Vocabulary

To solve a system of equations using the substitution method, you ______________________

____

____

Example

1 Using Substitution Solve the system by substitution.

$y = 2x + 3$
$2x - 2y = 4$

Step 1 As y is isolated in the first equation, substitute ☐ in the other equation.

$2x - 2y = 4$

$2x - 2 \cdot$ ☐ $= 4$ ← **Substitute** ☐ **for** y.

$2x -$ ☐ $-$ ☐ $= 4$ ← **Use the Distributive Property.**

☐ $= 4$ ← **Simplify.**

$-2x =$ ☐ ← **Add** ☐ **to each side.**

$x =$ ☐ ← **Divide each side by** ☐.

Step 2 Substitute ☐ for x in either equation and solve for ☐.

$y = 2x + 3$

$y = 2 \cdot$ ☐ $+ 3$ ← **Substitute** ☐ **for** x.

$y =$ ☐ ← **Simplify.**

Check Replace x with ☐ and y with ☐ in each equation.

$y = 2x + 3$	$2x - 2y = 4$
☐ $\stackrel{?}{=} 2 \cdot$ ☐ $+ 3$	$2 \cdot$ ☐ $- 2 \cdot$ ☐ $\stackrel{?}{=} 4$
☐ $=$ ☐ ✓	☐ $=$ ☐ ✓

The solution of the system is ☐.

Quick Check

1. Solve the system by substitution. Check your answer.

$y = x + 1$
$2x + y = -2$

☐

Name ____________________ Class ____________ Date ____________

Example

❷ Solving for a Variable and Using Substitution Solve the system by substitution.

$$3x + 5y = -8$$
$$5x + y = 5$$

Step 1 Solve the second equation for y.

$5x + y = 5$

$y =$ ____ ← **Subtract** ____ **from both sides.**

Step 2 Substitute ____ for y in the other equation and solve for ____.

$3x + 5y = -8$

$3x + 5 \cdot$ ____ $= -8$ ← **Substitute** ____ **for** y.

$3x -$ ____ $+$ ____ $= -8$ ← **Use the Distributive Property.**

____ $= -8$ ← **Simplify.**

$-22x =$ ____ ← **Subtract** ____ **from both sides.**

$x =$ ____ ← **Divide each side by** ____.

Step 3 Substitute ____ for x in either equation and solve for ____.

$5x + y = 5$

$5 \cdot$ ____ $+ y = 5$ ← **Substitute** ____ **for** x.

____ $+ y = 5$ ← **Simplify.**

$y =$ ____ ← **Subtract** ____ **from both sides.**

Check Replace x with ____ and y with ____ in each equation.

$3x + 5y = -8$ $\qquad$ $5x + y = 5$

$3 \cdot$ ____ $+ 5 \cdot$ ____ $\stackrel{?}{=} -8$ $\qquad$ $5 \cdot$ ____ $+$ ____ $\stackrel{?}{=} 5$

____ $=$ ____ ✓ $\qquad$ ____ $=$ ____ ✓

The solution of the system is ____.

Quick Check

2. Solve the system of equations by substitution. Check your answer.

$$-2x + y = 3$$
$$3x - 2y = 0$$

Name ______ Class ______ Date ______

Lesson 5-3

Solving Systems by Elimination

Lesson Objective	Common Core State Standards
To solve a system of linear equations by elimination	Expressions and Equations: 8.EE.8.b, 8.EE.8.c

Vocabulary

To solve a system of equations using the elimination method, you ______

______

______

Example

1 Solving a System by Adding

Solve the system by elimination.

$2x + 3y = 18$
$5x - 3y = 3$

Step 1 The coefficients of ☐ are additive inverses, so add the equations to eliminate ☐.

$2x + 3y = 18$
$+\ 5x - 3y = 3$

☐ = ☐ ← **Add the two equations.**

$x =$ ☐ ← **Solve for *x*.**

Step 2 Substitute ☐ for x in either equation and solve for ☐.

$2x + 3y = 18$

$2 \cdot$ ☐ $+ 3y = 18$ ← **Substitute** ☐ **for *x*.**

☐ $+ 3y = 18$ ← **Simplify.**

$y =$ ☐ ← **Solve for *y*.**

Check Replace x with ☐ and y with ☐ in each equation.

$2x + 3y = 18$ $\qquad$ $5x - 3y = 3$

$2 \cdot$ ☐ $+ 3 \cdot$ ☐ $\stackrel{?}{=} 18$ $\qquad$ $5 \cdot$ ☐ $- 3 \cdot$ ☐ $\stackrel{?}{=} 3$

☐ = ☐ ✓ $\qquad$ ☐ = ☐ ✓

The solution of the system is ☐.

Quick Check

1. Solve the system of equations by elimination: $3x + 4y = 16$, $-3x + 2y = 8$. Check your solution.

Name ____________________ Class ____________ Date ____________

Example

2 Solving a System by Multiplying Solve the system of equations by elimination.

$$-6x + 4y = 2$$
$$-3x - 2y = -7$$

Step 1 Multiply both sides of the one equation by a number so that the coefficients of x are additive inverses of each other ____.

$\_\_\_\_ \cdot (-3y - 2y) = \_\_\_\_ \cdot (-7)$ ← **Multiply the second equation by ____.**

$\_\_\_\_ = \_\_\_\_$ ← **Simplify.**

Step 2 Eliminate one variable by combining equal expressions.

$-6x + 4y = 2$

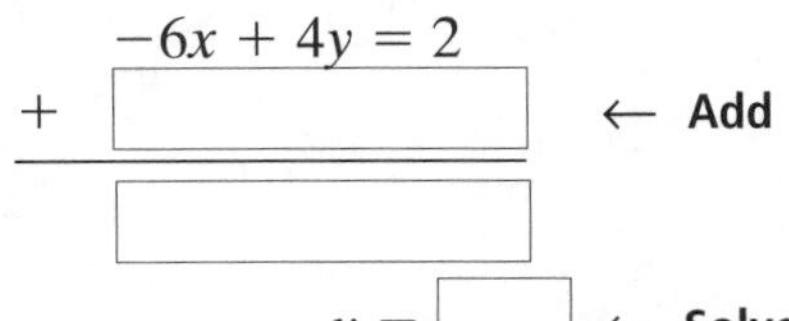

$+$ ____ ← **Add**

$y =$ ____ ← **Solve for y.**

Step 3 Substitute ____ for y in either equation and solve for ____.

$-6x + 4y = 2$

$-6x + 4 \cdot \_\_\_\_ = 2$ ← **Substitute ____ for y.**

$-6x + \_\_\_\_ = 2$ ← **Simplify.**

$x = \_\_\_\_$ ← **Solve for x.**

Check Replace x with ____ and y with ____ in each equation.

$-6x + 4y = 2$ | $-3x - 2y = -7$

$-6 \cdot \_\_\_\_ + 4 \cdot \_\_\_\_ \stackrel{?}{=} 2$ | $-3 \cdot \_\_\_\_ - 2 \cdot \_\_\_\_ \stackrel{?}{=} -7$

$\_\_\_\_ = \_\_\_\_$ ✓ | $\_\_\_\_ = \_\_\_\_$ ✓

The solution of the system is ____.

Quick Check

2. Solve the system by elimination. $8x - 3y = 4$
$-4x + 4y = 8$

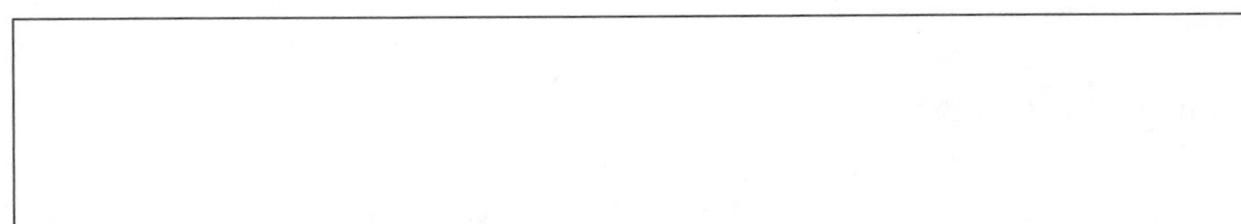

Name ______________________ Class ______________ Date ______________

Lesson 5-4

Systems in the Real World

Lesson Objective	**Common Core State Standards**
To use systems of linear equations to solve real-world problems	Expressions and Equations: 8.EE.8.b, 8.EE.8.c

Examples

1 Application: Fees The Main Street Parking Garage charges a \$30.00 monthly fee plus \$2.50 per day. The High Street Garage charges a \$40.00 monthly fee plus \$1.50 per day. Determine when it would be better to park in the Main Street garage, and when it would be better to park in the High Street garage.

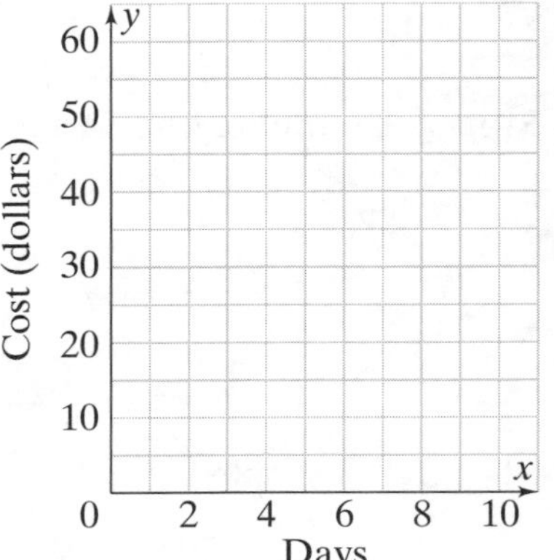

Write a system of equations to represent the situation.

Let x = __________ and y = __________.

Main Street: [ ]

High Street: [ ]

Graph both equations.

The lines appear to intersect at ([ ], [ ]).

Main Street Garage is less expensive for [ ] days.

High Street Garage is less expensive for [ ] days.

The cost is the same for [ ] days.

2 Application: Money Tina has 50 coins, all dimes and quarters. The value of the coins is \$7.10. Write a system of equations to determine how many dimes and how many quarters Tina has.

Write a system of equations to represent the situation.

Let d = __________ and d = __________.

d + [ ] = 50 ← **The number of dimes and quarters as an equation**

$0.10d$ + [ ] = 7.10 ← **The values of the dimes and the quarters as an equation**

Use the substitution method to solve the system. Check your solution.

d = [ ] q = [ ]

So, Tina has [ ] dimes and [ ] quarters.

Name ________________ Class ________ Date ________

❸ **Application: Dining** Kevin and Rose went to a deli to have lunch with their friends. The people at Kevin's table ordered 3 salads and 2 cups of soup and paid \$15.45. The people at Rose's table ordered 3 salads and 4 cups of soup and paid \$21.03. Determine the cost of each salad and each cup of soup.

Write a system of equations to represent the situation.

Let $s =$ ________________ and $c =$ ________________.

$3 \cdot \square + 2 \cdot \square = \square$ ← **The order from Kevin's table as an equation**

$\square$ ← **The order from Rose's table as an equation**

Make additive inverses. Multiply each side of either equation by $\square$.

Use the elimination method to solve the system of equations.

$s = \square$ $c = \square$

So, each salad costs $\square$ and each cup of soup costs $\square$.

Quick Check

1. Alexa is trying to decide between two hotels. Hotel A charges \$80 per night. Hotel B charges \$70 per night plus a one-time parking fee of \$20. Which hotel should she choose? Explain your reasoning.

2. Alyssa has a collection of 35 character figures. Some of the figures cost \$10 each and the others cost \$25 each. The total value of her figures is \$575. Write and solve a system of equations to find how many \$10 figures and how many \$25 figures she has.

3. Ji downloaded 15 songs and 3 movies for \$32.25. Arie downloaded 22 songs and 3 movies for \$41. What is the cost of downloading one movie?

Name ______________________ Class ______________ Date ______________

Lesson 6-1

Scientific Notation

Lesson Objective	**Common Core Standard**
To write numbers in both standard form and scientific notation	Expressions and Equations: 8.EE.3

Key Concepts

Scientific Notation

A number is in scientific notation if ______________________

____

Examples 1×10^8 1.54×10^7 9.99×10^4

Example

1 Writing in Standard Form At one point, the distance from the Earth to the moon is 1.513431×10^{10} in. Write this number in standard form.

$1.513431 \times 10^{10} = 1.5134310000.$ ← **Move the decimal point** ☐ **places to the right. Insert zeros as necessary.**

= ☐

At one point, the distance from the Earth to the moon is ☐ in.

Quick Check

1. Write 7.66×10^6 km^2, the area of Australia, in standard form.

☐

Name ______________________ Class ____________ Date ____________

Examples

❷ Writing in Scientific Notation The diameter of the planet Jupiter is about 142,800 km. Write this number in scientific notation.

142,800 = 1.42,800. ← **Move the decimal point ☐ places to the left.**

= ☐ $\times 10^{☐}$ ← **Use ☐ as the exponent of 10.**

The diameter of the planet Jupiter is about ☐ km.

❸ Scientific Notation With Negative Exponents A typical width of a human hair is about 8.0×10^{-5} m. Write this number in standard form.

8.0×10^{-5} = 0.00008.0 ← **Move the decimal point ☐ places to the ☐ to make 8 less than 1.**

A typical width of a human hair is ☐ meters wide.

❹ Numbers Less Than 1 Write the quantity 0.000089 in scientific notation.

0.000089 = 0.00008.9 ← **Move the decimal point ☐ places to the ☐.**

= ☐ $\times 10^{☐}$ ← **Use ☐ as the exponent of 10.**

Quick Check

2. Write 3,476,000 m, the moon's diameter, in scientific notation.

3. Write 2.5×10^{-4} inch, the diameter of a cell, in standard form.

4. Write 0.0000035 in scientific notation.

Name ____________ Class ____________ Date ____________

Lesson 6-2

Exponents and Multiplication

Lesson Objective	Common Core Standard
To multiply powers with the same base	Expressions and Equations: 8.EE.1

Key Concepts

Multiplying Powers With the Same Base

To multiply numbers or variables with the same base, ☐ the exponents.

Arithmetic	Algebra
$3^2 \cdot 3^7 = 3^{(2+7)} = 3^9$	$a^m \cdot a^n = a^{(m+n)}$

Examples

1 Multiplying Powers Write the expression $(-3)^2 \cdot (-3)^4$ using a single exponent.

$(-3)^2 \cdot (-3)^4 = (-3)^{(\square + \square)}$ ← **Add the exponents.**

$= (-3)^{(\square)}$ ← **Simplify the exponent.**

2 Application: Geometry Find the area of the square.

x^5 cm

A. x^{10} cm^2 **B.** x^{25} cm^2 **C.** $2x^{10}$ cm^2 **D.** $2x^{25}$ cm^2

$A = s \cdot s$ ← **Write the area formula.**

$A = x^5 \cdot x^5$ ← **Substitute ☐ for *s*.**

$A = x^{(\square + \square)}$ ← **Add the exponents.**

$A = x^{\square}$ ← **Simplify.**

The area of the square is $x^{\square}$ cm^2. The correct answer choice is A.

Name ______________________ Class ______________ Date ______________

③ Using the Commutative Property Simplify the expression $-6x^5 \cdot 3x^4$.

$-6x^5 \cdot 3x^4 = \square \cdot \square \cdot x^5 \cdot x^4$ ← **Use the Commutative Property of Multiplication.**

$= \square x^{(\square + \square)}$ ← $\square$ **the exponents of powers with the same base.**

$= -18x^{\square}$ ← **Simplify.**

Quick Check

1. Write each expression using a single exponent.

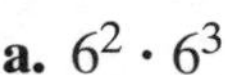

a. $6^2 \cdot 6^3$ **b.** $(-4) \cdot (-4)^7$ **c.** $3 \cdot 3^2 \cdot 3^3$

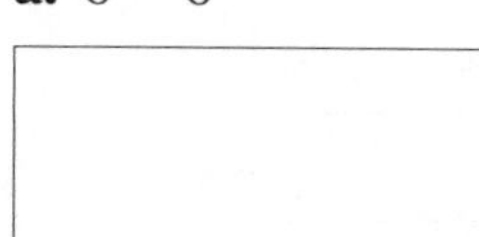
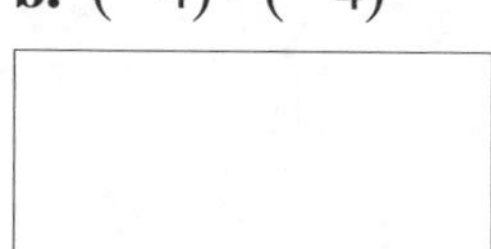
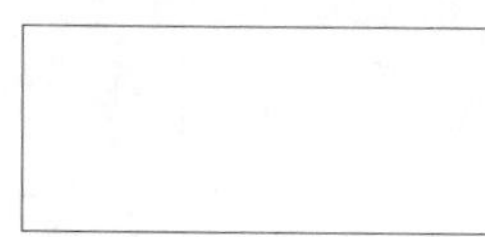

2. A square has a side length of n^3. Find the area of the square.

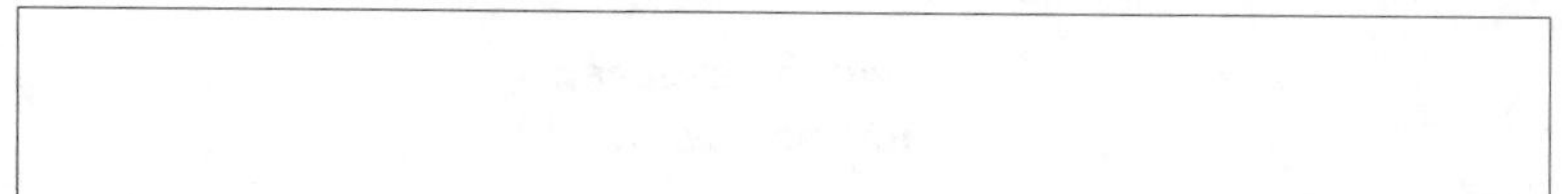

3. Simplify each expression.

a. $2a^2 \cdot 3a$ **b.** $x^{10} \cdot x^3$ **c.** $-4y^5 \cdot -3y^5$

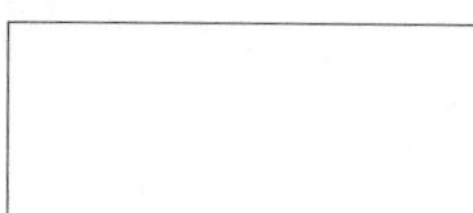

Name ____________________ Class ____________ Date ____________

Lesson 6-3

Multiplying with Scientific Notation

Lesson Objective	Common Core Standard
To multiply numbers written in scientific notation and choose appropriate units of measure	Expressions and Equations: 8.EE.4

Example

1 Multiplying With Scientific Notation Multiply $(3 \times 10^3)(7 \times 10^5)$. Write the product in scientific notation.

$(3 \times 10^3)(7 \times 10^5) = (\square \times \square) \times (10^{\square} \times 10^{\square})$ ← Use the ______ and ______ properties.

$= \square \times (10^{\square} \times 10^{\square})$ ← Multiply ___ and ___.

$= \square \times 10^{\square}$ ← Add the exponents for the powers of 10.

$= \square \times 10^{\square} \times 10^{\square}$ ← Write ___ in scientific notation.

$= \square \times 10^{\square}$ ← Add the exponents.

Quick Check

1. Multiply. Write each product in scientific notation.

a. $(2 \times 10^6)(4 \times 10^3)$

b. $(3 \times 10^5)(2 \times 10^8)$

c. $12(8 \times 10^{20})$

Name ______________________ Class ______________ Date ______________

Examples

❷ Multiple choice A light-year is about 5.9×10^{12} miles. A mile is about 1.609×10^3 meters. How many meters are in a light-year? Write your answer in scientific notation.

A. 9.5×10^{15} **B.** 9.5×10^{16} **C.** 9.5×10^{36} **D.** 9.5×10^{37}

$(5.9 \times 10^{12})(1.609 \times 10^3)$ ← **Multiply by conversion factor.**

$= (\square \times \square) \times (10^{\square} \times 10^{\square})$ ← **Use the ______ and ______ properties.**

$\approx \square \times (10^{\square} \times 10^{\square})$ ← **Multiply ______ and ______. Round to the nearest tenth.**

$= \square \times 10^{\square}$ ← **Add the exponents.**

There are about ______ meters in a light-year. The correct answer is choice ______.

❸ Choosing Units with Scientific Notation Choose the most reasonable unit to describe the quantity. Then use scientific notation to describe the quantity using the other unit.

a. The length of a school bus is 9 ______. (m, km)

$9 \square \times \frac{\square \text{ km}}{1 \text{ m}} = 9 \times \square \text{ km}$ ← **Multiply by a conversion factor.**

b. The mass of a horse is about 500 ______. (g, kg)

$500 \square \times \frac{\square \text{ g}}{1 \text{ kg}} = 500 \times 10^3 \text{ g}$ ← **Multiply by a conversion factor.**

$= 5 \times \square \text{ g}$ ← **Simplify.**

Quick Check

2. **Astronomy** The speed of light is about 3.0×10^5 kilometers/second. Use the formula $d = r \cdot t$ to find the distance light travels in an hour, which is 3.6×10^3 seconds.

3. Choose the most reasonable unit to describe the quantity. Then use scientific notation to describe the quantity using the other unit.

A pencil is 7 ______ long. (cm, m)

Name ______________________ Class ______________ Date ______________

Lesson 6-4

Exponents and Division

Lesson Objective	**Common Core Standard**
To divide powers with the same base and to simplify expressions with negative exponents	Expressions and Equations: 8.EE.1

Key Concepts

Dividing Powers With the Same Base

To divide nonzero numbers or variables with the same nonzero base, $\square$ the exponents.

Arithmetic

$$\frac{8^5}{8^3} = 8^{(5 \,\square\, 3)} = 8^{\square}$$

Algebra

$$\frac{a^m}{a^n} = a^{(m \,\square\, n)}, \text{ where } a \neq 0.$$

Zero as an Exponent

For any nonzero number a, $a^0 = \square$.

Example $9^0 = \square$

Negative Exponents

For any nonzero number a and integers n, $a^{-n} = \frac{1}{\square}$.

Example $8^{\square} = \frac{1}{8^5}$.

Examples

❶ **Dividing Powers** Write $\frac{x^{14}}{x^9}$ using a single exponent.

$\frac{x^{14}}{x^9} = x^{(14 \,\square\, 9)}$ ← $\square$ **exponents with the same base.**

$= x^{\square}$ ← **Simplify.**

❷ **Expression With a Zero Exponent** Simplify each expression.

a. $(-5)^0$

$(-5)^0 = \square$ ← **Simplify.**

b. $2y^0$, $y \neq 0$

$2y^0 = \square$ ← **Simplify.**

Name ______________________ Class ______________ Date ______________

❸ Expressions With Negative Exponents Simplify each expression.

a. 2^{-3}

$2^{-3} = \frac{\square}{2^{\square}}$ ← Use a [ ] exponent. →

$= \frac{\square}{\square}$ ← Simplify.

b. $(p)^{-8}$

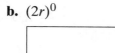

$= \frac{\square}{p^{\square}}$

Quick Check

1. Write $\frac{w^8}{w^5}$ using a single exponent.

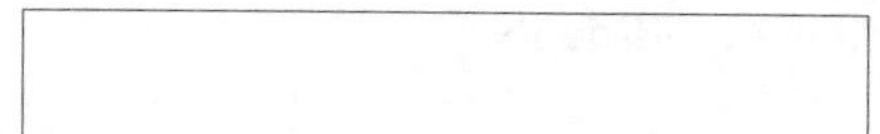

2. Simplify each expression.

a. $(-9)^0$

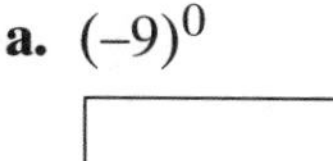

b. $(2r)^0$

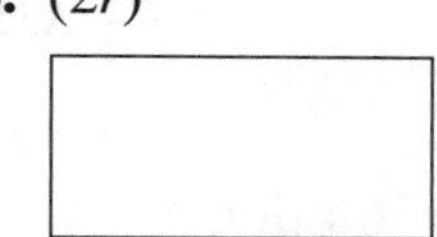

c. $2r^0$

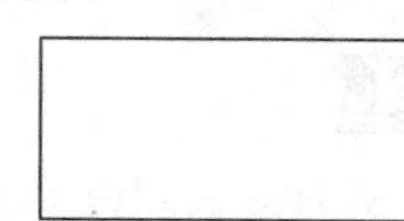

3. Simplify each expression.

a. 3^{-1}

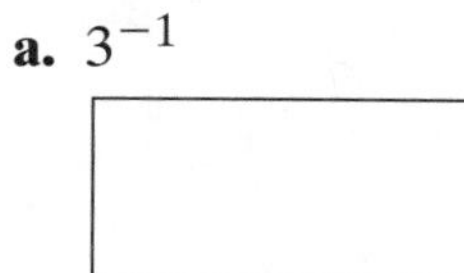

b. w^{-4}

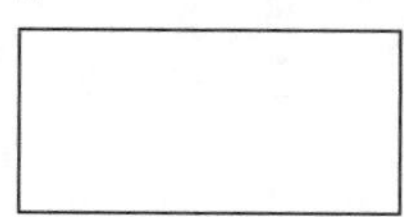

c. $(-2)^{-3}$

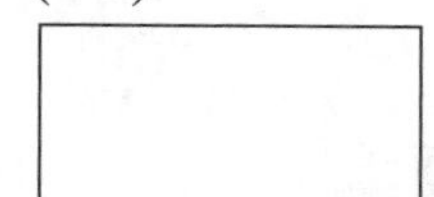

Name ______________________ Class ______________ Date ______________

Lesson 6-5

Dividing with Scientific Notation

Lesson Objective	**Common Core Standards**
To divide and compare numbers written in scientific notation	Expressions and Equations: 8.EE.3, 8.EE.4

Example

1 Dividing Numbers in Scientific Notation Simplify $(5.4 \times 10^5) \div (9.1 \times 10^2)$. Write the quotient in scientific notation.

$(5.4 \times 10^5) \div (9.1 \times 10^2) = \frac{5.4 \times 10^5}{9.1 \times 10^2}$ ← **Write a fraction.**

$= \frac{\square}{\square} \times \frac{10^5}{10^2}$ ← **Separate the coefficients and the powers of ten.**

$\approx 0.59 \times \frac{10^{\square}}{10^{\square}}$ ← **Divide the coefficients.**

$\approx 0.59 \times 10^{\square}$ ← **Subtract the exponents.**

$\approx \square \times 10^{\square} \times 10^3$ ← **Write 0.59 in scientific notation.**

$\approx 5.9 \times 10^{\square}$ ← **Add the exponents.**

Quick Check

1. Simplify. Write each quotient in scientific notation.

a. $\frac{7.9 \times 10^5}{2.3 \times 10^3}$

b. $\frac{4.8 \times 10^4}{2.95 \times 10^6}$

c. $\frac{3.7 \times 10^7}{5.2 \times 10^2}$

Examples

2 Application: Astronomy The average distance between the sun and Jupiter is about 4.8×10^8 miles. Light travels about 1.1×10^7 miles per minute. Estimate how long sunlight takes to reach Jupiter. Write your answer in standard form and round to the nearest whole number.

$\text{time} = \frac{\text{distance}}{\text{speed}}$ ← **Use the formula for time.**

$= \frac{\square}{\square} \times \frac{10^8}{10^7}$ ← **Substitute. Write as a product of quotients.**

$= \frac{4.8}{1.1} \times 10^{8 \square 7}$ ← **______ the exponents.**

$\approx 4.4 \times 10^1$ ← **Divide and simplify.**

Sunlight takes about 4.4×10^1 minutes, or ____ minutes to reach Jupiter.

Name ______________________ Class ______________ Date ______________

3 Dividing by Numbers in Standard Form Divide. Write each quotient in scientific notation.

a. $(8.2 \times 10^4) \div 5.1 = \frac{\square}{\square}$ ← **Write a fraction.**

$= \frac{\square}{\square} \times 10^4$ ← **Separate the coefficients and the powers of ten.**

$\approx \square \times 10^4$ ← **Divide the coefficients.**

b. $6 \div (8.3 \times 10^3) = \frac{\square}{\square}$ ← **Write a fraction.**

$= \frac{6}{8.3} \times 10^{\square}$ ← **Separate the coefficients and power of ten.**

$\approx \square \times 10^{-3}$ ← **Divide the coefficients and divide the powers of ten.**

$\approx \square \times 10^{-1} \times 10^{-3}$ ← **Write 0.72 in scientific notation.**

$\approx \square \times 10^{\square}$ ← **Add the exponents.**

4 Ordering Numbers Order 6.5×10^3, 6.4×10^{-3}, 5.8×10^3, and 8.9×10^2 from least to greatest.

$\square$, 8.9×10^2, $\square$, 5.8×10^3 ← **Sort the numbers using the powers of ten, least to greatest.**

6.4×10^{-3}, 8.9×10^2, $\square$, $\square$ ← **Sort the numbers with the same power of ten, using the first factor.**

Quick Check

2. The distance between the sun and Earth is about 9.3×10^7 miles. Light travels about 1.1×10^7 miles per minute. Estimate how long sunlight takes to reach Earth. Write your answer in standard form and round to the nearest tenth.

3. Divide. Write each quotient in scientific notation.

a. $\frac{6.2 \times 10^6}{4.1}$ **b.** $\frac{-3.5 \times 10^3}{5}$ **c.** $\frac{17}{1.4 \times 10^8}$

4. Order the numbers from least to greatest.
$3 \times 10^6, 3.11 \times 10^5, 3 \times 10^{-6}, 3.8 \times 10^{-5}$

Name ______________________ Class ______________ Date ____________

Lesson 7-1

Pairs of Angles

Lesson Objective

To identify types of angles and to find angle measures using the relationship between angles

Vocabulary

Adjacent angles have ______________________

____

Vertical angles are ______________________

____

Congruent angles have ______________________

Two angles are supplementary if ______________________

____

Two angles are complementary if ______________________

____

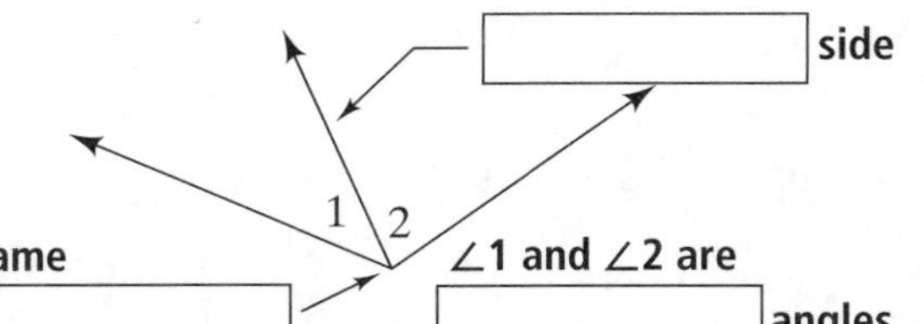

$\angle 1$ and $\angle 2$ are ______ angles.

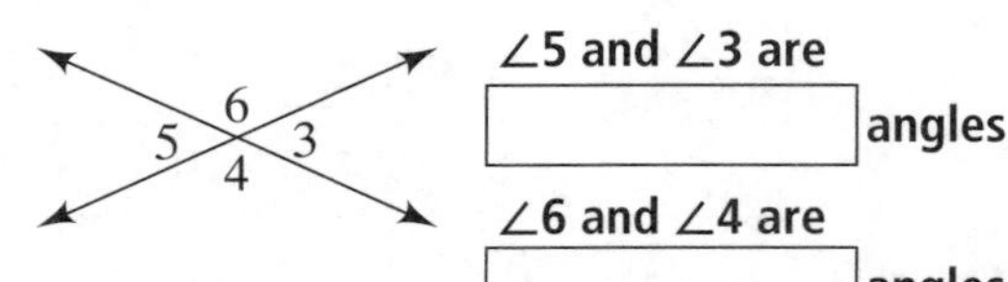

$\angle 5$ and $\angle 3$ are ______ angles.

$\angle 6$ and $\angle 4$ are ______ angles.

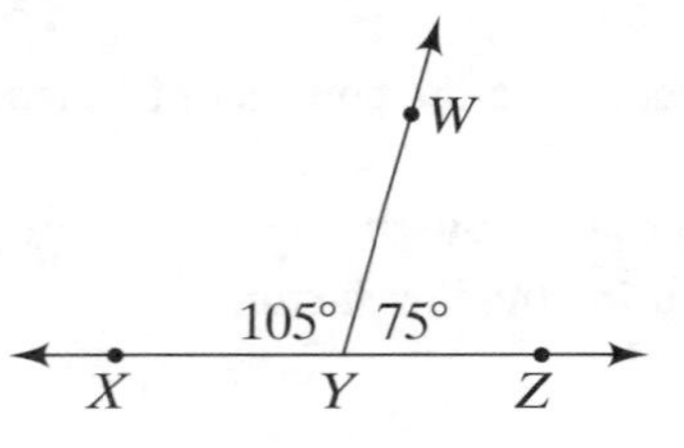

$\angle WYX$ and $\angle WYZ$ are ______ **angles.**

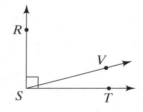

$\angle VSR$ and $\angle VST$ are ______ **angles.**

Perpendicular lines are ______________________

____

Examples

1 Identifying Adjacent and Vertical Angles Name a pair of adjacent angles and a pair of vertical angles in the figure at the right.

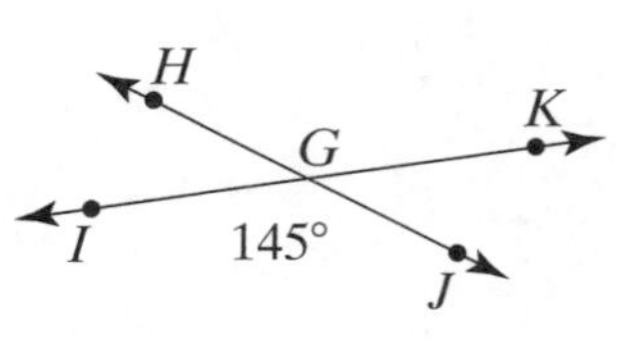

The adjacent angles are $\angle HGK$ and ______; $\angle KGJ$ and ______; $\angle JGI$ and ______; $\angle IGH$ and ______.

The vertical angles are $\angle JGI$ and ______; $\angle HGI$ and ______.

Since vertical angles are congruent, $m\angle HGK = m\angle JGI =$ ______.

Name ______________________ Class ______________ Date ______________

❷ Finding Supplementary Angles Suppose $m\angle DEF = 73°$. Find the measure of its supplement.

$x° + m\angle DEF = \boxed{}$	←	**The sum of the measures of supplementary angles is** $\boxed{}$.
$x° + 73° = 180°$	←	**Substitute** $\boxed{}$ **for** $m\angle DEF$.
$x° + 73° - \boxed{} = 180° - \boxed{}$	←	**Subtract** $\boxed{}$ **from each side.**
$x° = \boxed{}$	←	**Simplify.**

The measure of the supplement of $\angle DEF$ is $\boxed{}$.

❸ Finding Angle Measures A right angle is divided into two angles. If the measure of the larger angle is 67°, find the measure of the smaller angle.

$x° + 67° = \boxed{}$	←	**The angles are complementary.**
$x° + 67° - \boxed{} = 90° - \boxed{}$	←	**Subtract** $\boxed{}$ **from each side.**
$x° = \boxed{}$	←	**Simplify.**

The measure of the complement of an angle whose measure is 67° is $\boxed{}$.

1. $\angle DBJ$ and $\angle JBT$ are adjacent angles in the photo. $\angle DBY$ and $\angle JBT$ are vertical angles. Name another pair of vertical angles and another pair of adjacent angles.

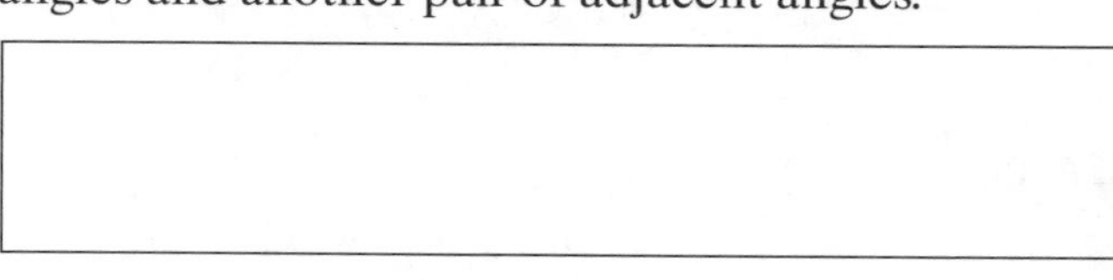

2. An angle has a measure of 47°. Find the measure of its supplement.

3. In the diagram at the right, $m\angle 5 = 36°$. Find the measures of $\angle 3$ and $\angle 4$.

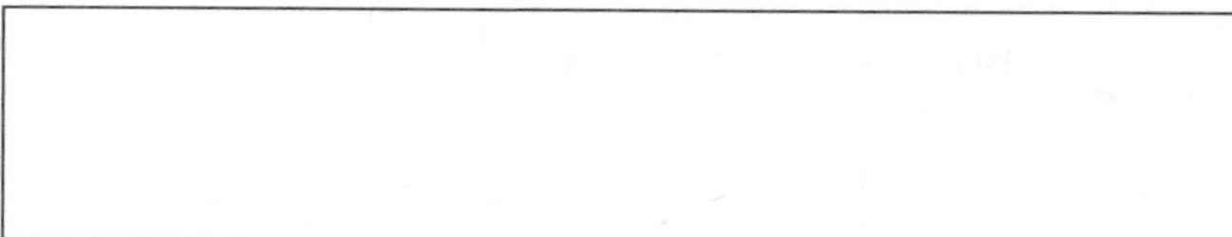

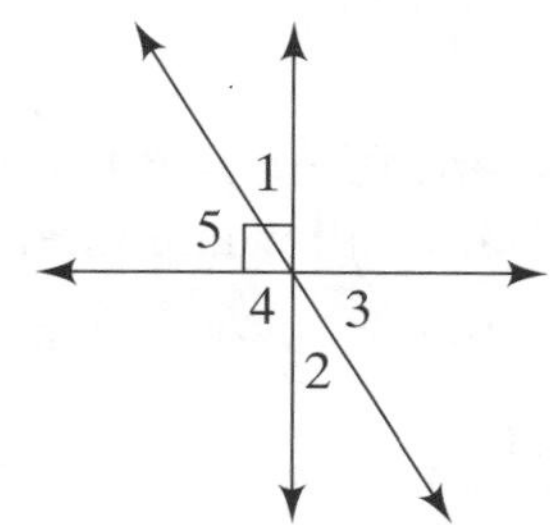

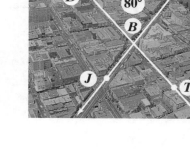

Name ________________ Class ________ Date ________

Lesson 7-2

Angles and Parallel Lines

Lesson Objective	**Common Core State Standard**
To identify parallel lines and the angles formed by parallel lines and transversals	Geometry: 8.G.5

Vocabulary and Key Concepts

Transversals and Parallel Lines

When a transversal intersects two parallel lines,

- [ ] angles are congruent, and
- [ ] angles are congruent.

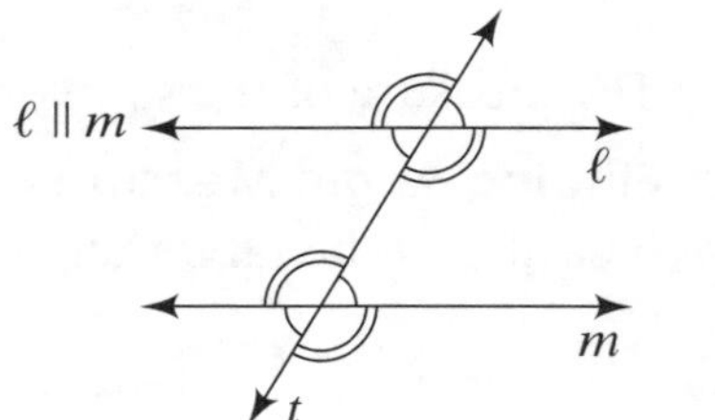

A transversal is ________________

Corresponding angles lie ________________

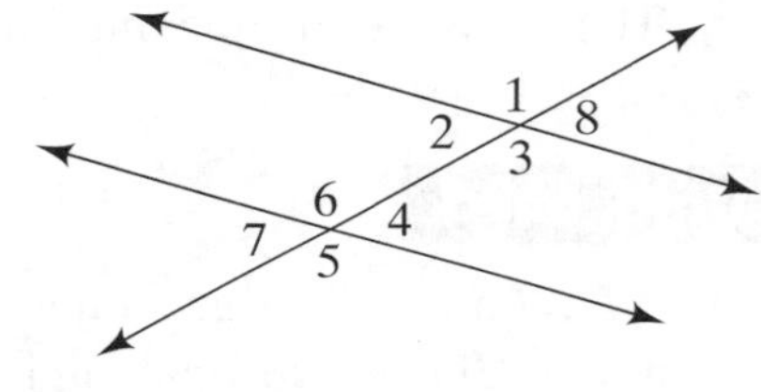

Examples: $\angle 1$ and [ ] $\angle 2$ and [ ]

$\angle 3$ and [ ] $\angle 4$ and [ ]

Alternate interior angles lie ________________

Examples: $\angle 3$ and [ ] $\angle 4$ and [ ]

Examples

Use this diagram for Examples 1 and 2.

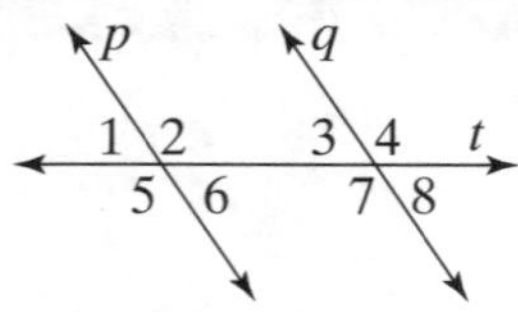

1 **Identifying Angles** Identify each pair of corresponding angles and each pair of alternate interior angles.

$\angle 1$ and [ ], $\angle 2$ and [ ], $\angle 5$ and [ ], $\angle 6$ and [ ] are pairs of [ ] angles.

$\angle 2$ and [ ], $\angle 3$ and [ ] are pairs of [ ] angles.

Name ____________________ Class ____________ Date ____________

❷ Finding Angle Measures If p is parallel to q, and $m\angle 3 = 56°$, find $m\angle 6$ and $m\angle 1$.

$m\angle 6 = m\angle 3 =$ ____ ← ____________ **angles are congruent.**

$m\angle 1 = m\angle 3 =$ ____ ← ____________ **angles are congruent.**

❸ Identifying Parallel Lines In the diagram below, $m\angle 5 = 80°$, $m\angle 6 = 80°$, and $m\angle 7 = 80°$. Explain why p and q are parallel and why s and t are parallel.

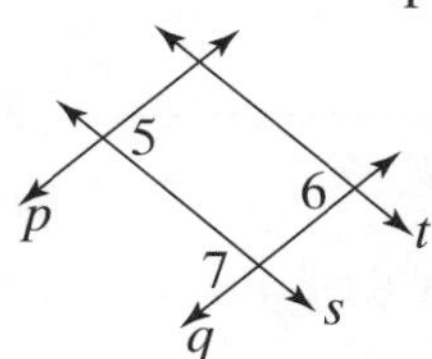

$p \parallel q$ because $\angle 5$ and $\angle 7$ are congruent ____________ angles.

$s \parallel t$ because $\angle 6$ and $\angle 7$ are congruent ____________ angles.

Quick Check

1. Use the diagram for Examples 1 and 2. Identify each pair of angles as *corresponding, alternate interior,* or *neither*.

a. $\angle 3, \angle 6$

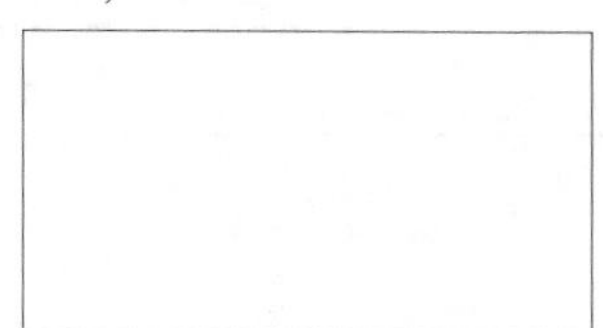

b. $\angle 2, \angle 7$

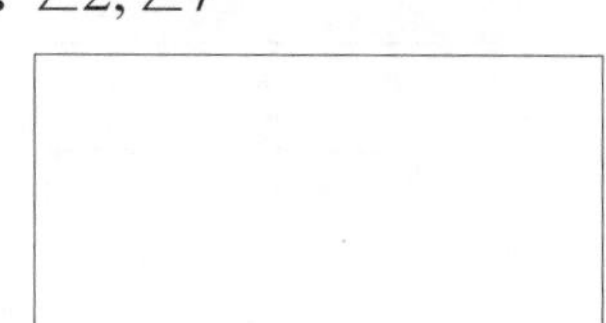

c. $\angle 1, \angle 8$

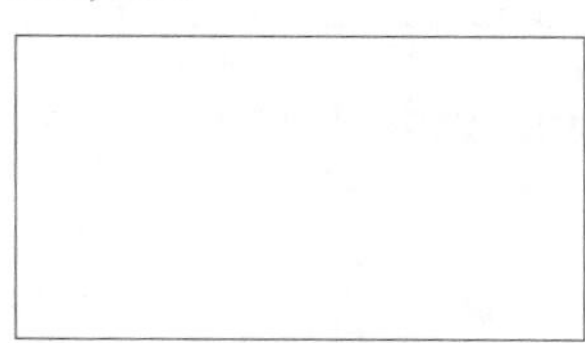

2. In the diagram for Examples 1 and 2, $m\angle 3 = 117°$. Find $m\angle 6$ and $m\angle 5$.

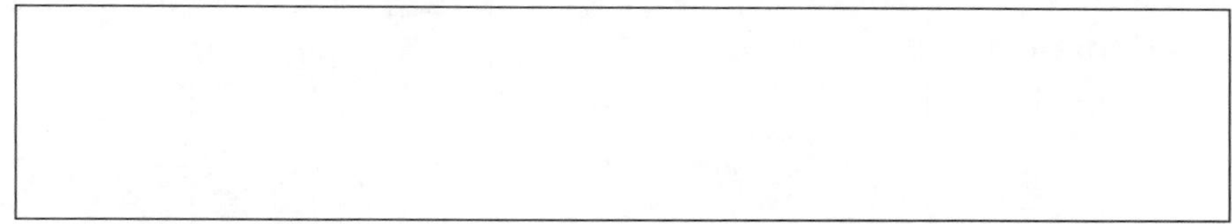

3. Transversal t is perpendicular to lines ℓ and m. Explain how you know $\ell \parallel m$.

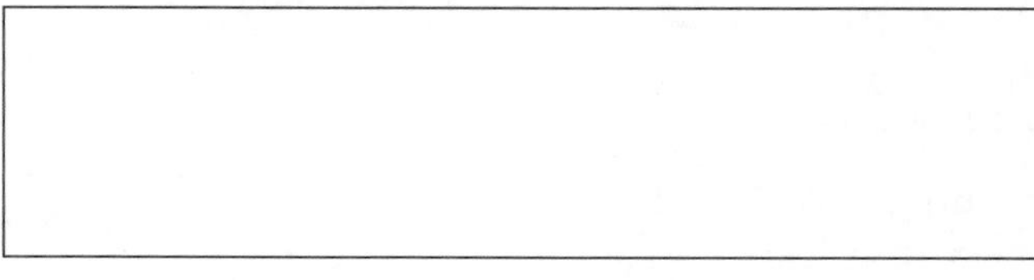

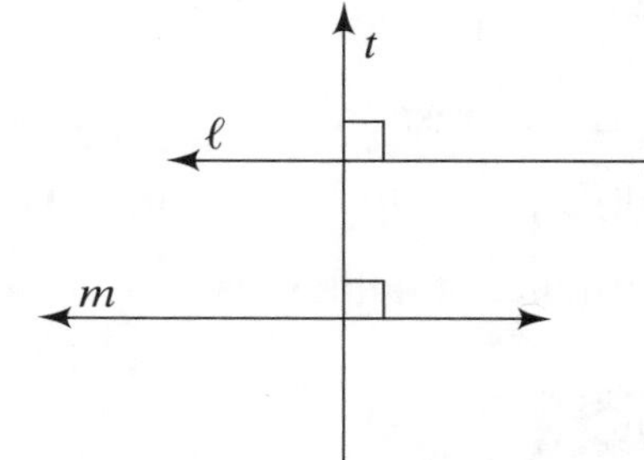

Name ______________________ Class ______________ Date ______________

Lesson 7-3

Congruent Figures

Lesson Objective	**Common Core State Standard**
To identify congruent figures and use them to solve problems	Geometry: 8.G.2

Vocabulary and Key Concepts

Showing Triangles Are Congruent

To demonstrate that two triangles are congruent, show that the following parts of one triangle are congruent to the corresponding parts of the other triangle.

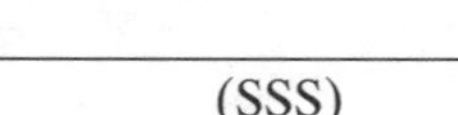

(SSS)

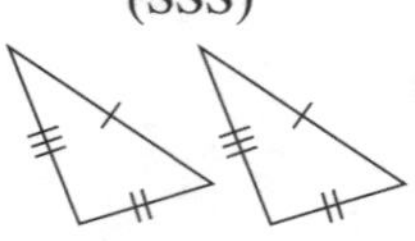

(SAS)

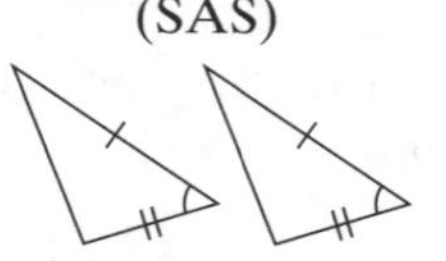

(ASA)

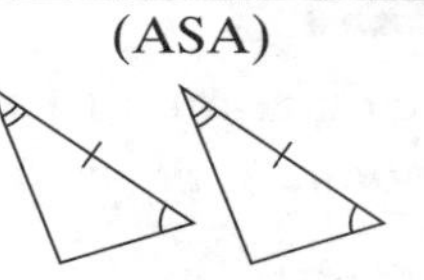

Congruent polygons are ______________________________

Example

1 Writing Congruence Statements Write a congruence statement for the congruent figures at the right.

Congruent Angles	**Congruent Sides**
$\angle A \cong$ ☐	$\overline{AB} \cong$ ☐
$\angle B \cong$ ☐	$\overline{BC} \cong$ ☐
$\angle C \cong$ ☐	$\overline{CD} \cong$ ☐
$\angle D \cong$ ☐	$\overline{DA} \cong$ ☐

Since $\angle A$ corresponds to ☐, $\angle B$ corresponds to ☐, $\angle C$ corresponds to ☐, and $\angle$D corresponds to ☐, a congruence statement is ☐ $\cong$ ☐.

Quick Check

1. Write a congruence statement for the congruent figures at the right.

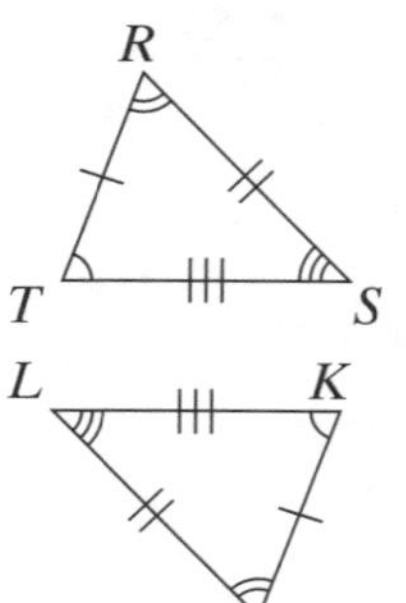

Name ______________________ Class ______________ Date ______________

Examples

❷ Congruent Triangles Show that the triangles are congruent.

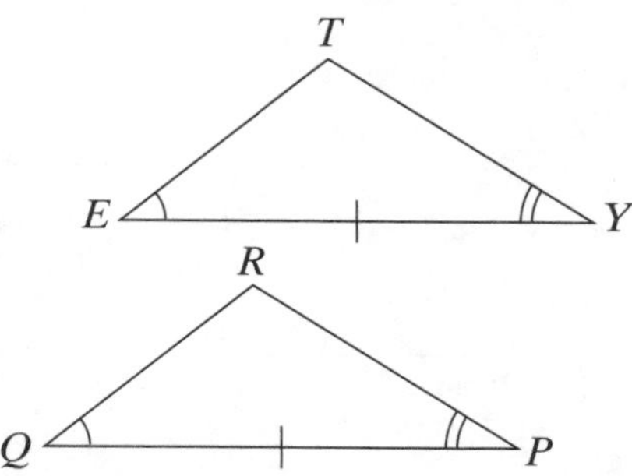

$\angle Q \cong \angle E$ [ ]

$\overline{QP} \cong \overline{EY}$ [ ]

$\angle P \cong \angle Y$ [ ]

$\triangle QPR \cong \triangle EYT$ [ ]

❸ Surveying A surveyor drew the diagram at the right to find the distance from J to I across the canyon. $\triangle GHI \cong \triangle KJI$. What is the distance $\overline{JI}$?

Corresponding parts of congruent triangles are [ ]. Since $\overline{JI}$ corresponds to $\overline{HI}$,

$\overline{JI} =$ [ ] ft.

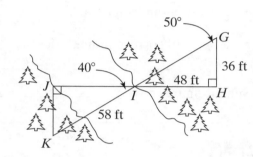

50°
G
36 ft
40°
48 ft
J
I
H
58 ft
K

Quick Check

2. Show that each pair of triangles is congruent.

a.

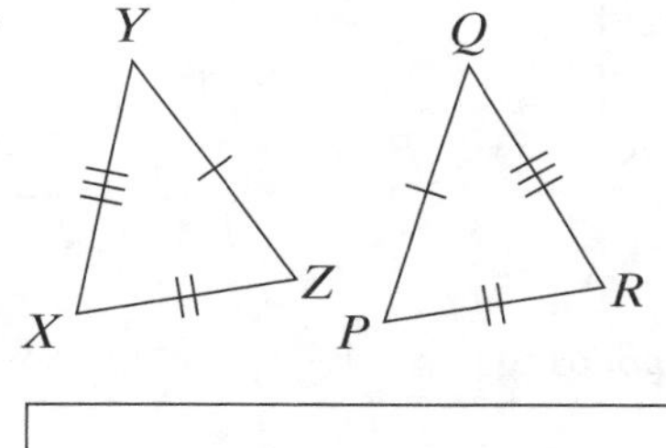

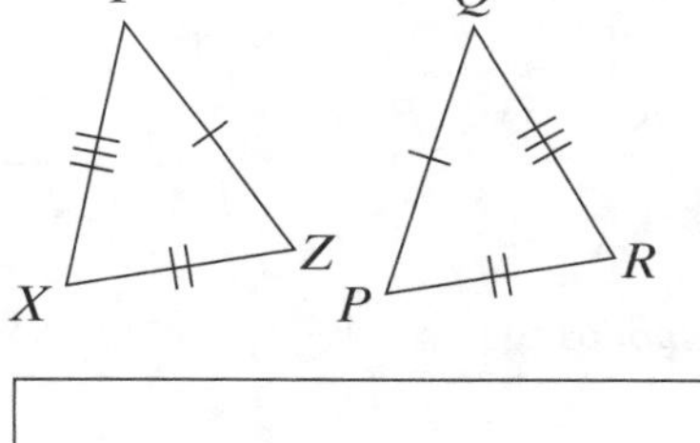

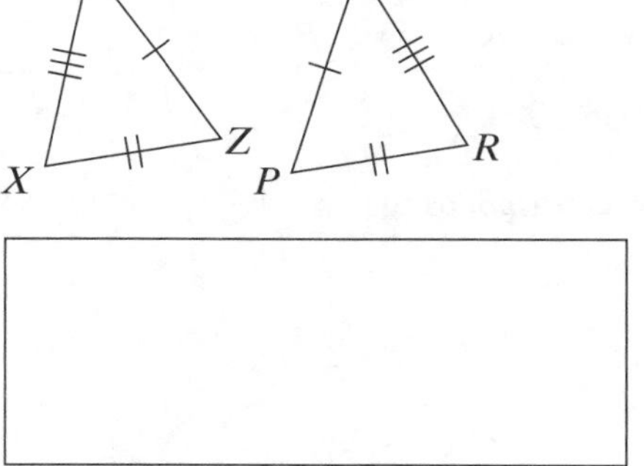

b.

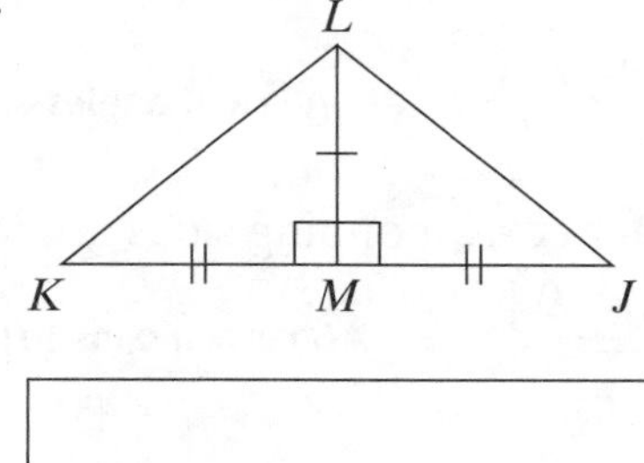

3. Use the diagram in Example 3 to find each measurement.

a. $\overline{JK}$

b. $m\angle K$

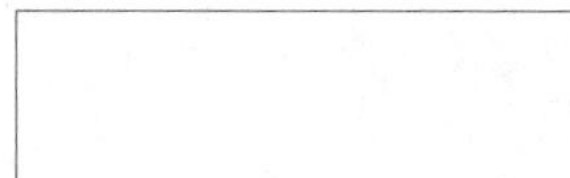

c. $m\angle GIH$

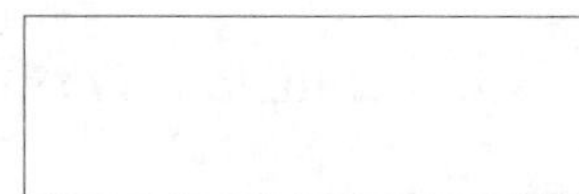

Name ________________ Class ________________ Date ________________

Lesson 7-4

Similar Figures

Lesson Objective	**Common Core State Standard**
To identify similar figures and to use proportions to find missing measurements in similar figures	Geometry: 8.G.4

Vocabulary and Key Concepts

Similar Polygons If two polygons are similar polygons, then

- corresponding angles are ☐ and
- lengths of corresponding sides are ☐.

Similar figures have ________________

____

Example

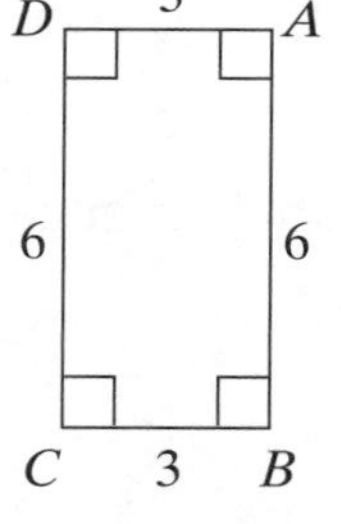

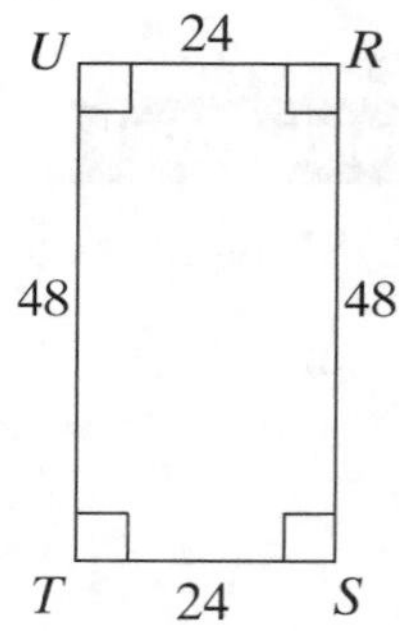

1 Identifying Similar Polygons Is rectangle $ABCD$ similar to rectangle $RSTU$? Explain.
First, check whether corresponding angles are congruent.

$\angle A \cong \angle$☐ $\angle B \cong \angle$☐ ← **All right angles are** ☐°.
$\angle C \cong \angle$☐ $\angle D \cong \angle$☐

Next, check whether corresponding sides are in proportion.

$\frac{AB}{\square} \stackrel{?}{=} \frac{DA}{\square}$ ← ***AB* corresponds to** ☐. ***DA* corresponds to** ☐.

$\frac{6}{\square} \stackrel{?}{=} \frac{3}{\square}$ ← **Substitute.**

$6 \cdot \square \stackrel{?}{=} \square \cdot 3$ ← **Write the cross products.**

$\square = \square$ ← **Simplify.**

The corresponding sides ☐ in proportion, so rectangle $ABCD$ is ☐ to rectangle $RSTU$.

Quick Check

1. Is rectangle $EFGH$ similar to rectangle $PQRS$? Explain.

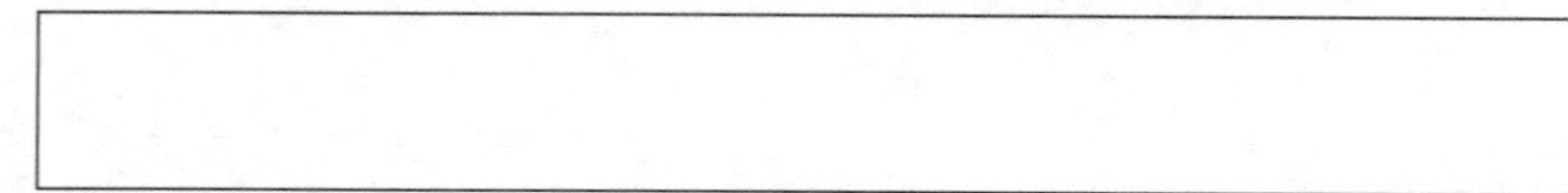

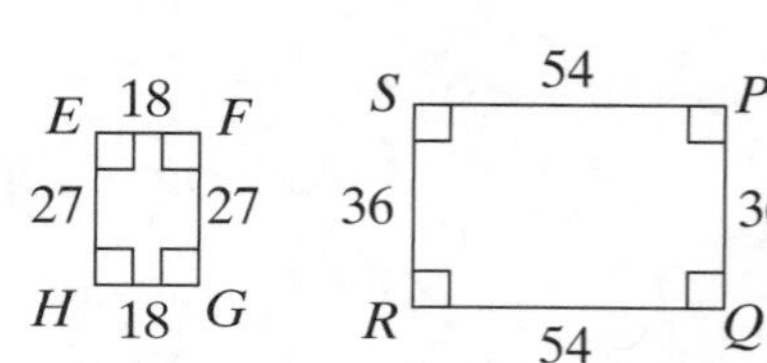

Name ______________________ Class ______________ Date ______________

Examples

❷ Application: Design Given that rectangle $EFGH$ is similar to rectangle $WXYZ$, find t.

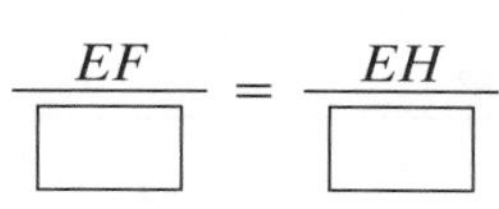

$\frac{EF}{\square} = \frac{EH}{\square}$ ← ***EF*** **corresponds to** $\square$. ***EH*** **corresponds to** $\square$.

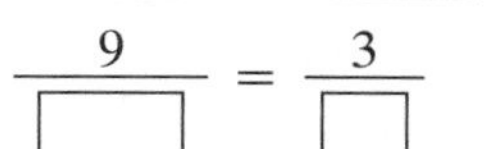

$\frac{9}{\square} = \frac{3}{\square}$ ← **Substitute.**

$9 \cdot \square = \square \cdot 3$ ← **Write the cross products.**

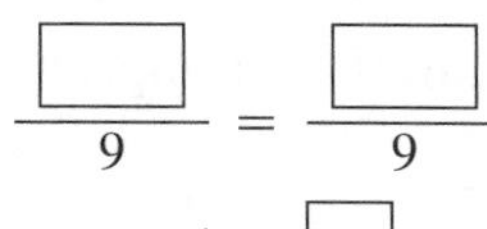

$\frac{\square}{9} = \frac{\square}{9}$ ← **Simplify. Then divide each side by 9.**

$t = \square$ ← **Simplify.**

E 9 F
3
H G

Z t W
12
Y X

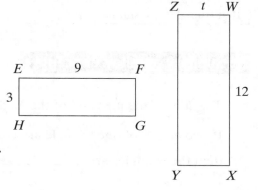

❸ Overlapping Similar Triangles $\triangle RST \sim \triangle PSU$. Find the value of d.

Step 1 Separate the triangles.

Step 2 Write a proportion using corresponding sides of the triangles.

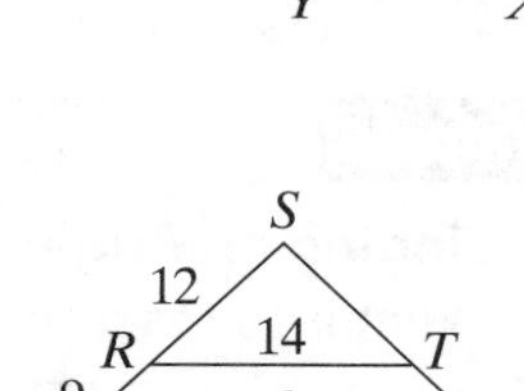

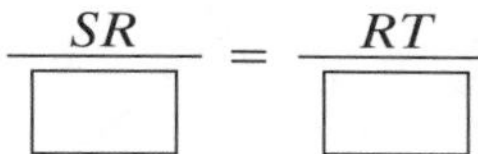

$\frac{SR}{\square} = \frac{RT}{\square}$ ← **Write a proportion.**

$\frac{12}{\square} = \frac{14}{\square}$ ← **Substitute.**

$12 \cdot \square = \square \cdot 14$ ← **Write the cross products.**

$\square = \square$ ← **Simplify.**

$\frac{\square}{12} = \frac{\square}{12}$ ← **Divide each side by 12.**

$d = \square$ ← **Simplify.**

S
12
R T
14

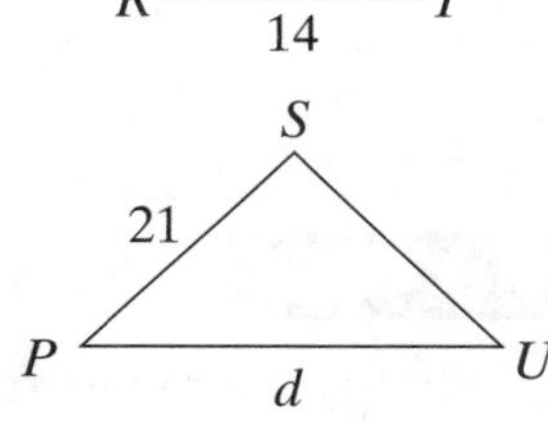

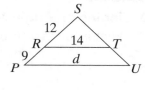

Quick Check

2. In Example 2, if the side lengths of $EFGH$ are doubled, will the resulting polygon be similar to $EFGH$? Explain.

3. If ST is 13 ft in Example 3, what is the length of $\overline{SU}$?

Name ______________________ Class ______________ Date ______________

Lesson 7-5

Proving Triangles Similar

Lesson Objective	Common Core State Standard
To determine measures of the angles of triangles and use them to help prove that triangles are similar	Geometry: 8.G.5

Vocabulary and Key Concepts

The sum of the measure of the angles of any triangle is ______________________.

If two angles of one triangle are congruent to the corresponding angles of another triangle, then the triangles are ______________________.

Example

1 Finding an Angle Measure $\triangle BAC$ forms part of a bridge truss. What is the measure of $\angle C$?

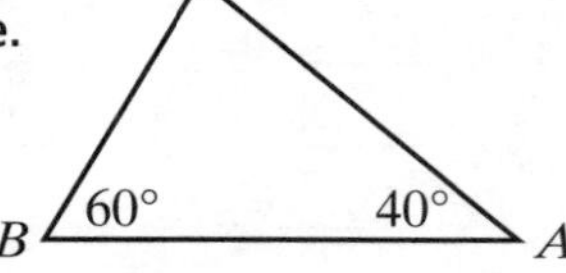

$\square + \square + m\angle C = 180°$ ← **Angle sum of a triangle.**

$\square + \square + m\angle C = 180°$ ← **Substitute.**

$m\angle C + \square = 180°$ ← **Simplify.**

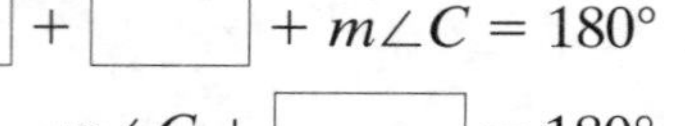

$m\angle C + 100° - \square = 180° - \square$ ← **Subtract** $\square$ **from each side.**

$m\angle C = \square$ ← **Simplify.**

Quick Check

1. What is the measure of $\angle E$ in $\triangle DEF$?

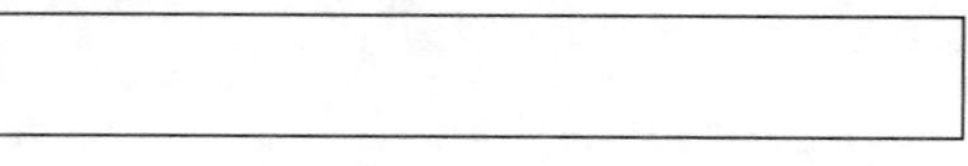

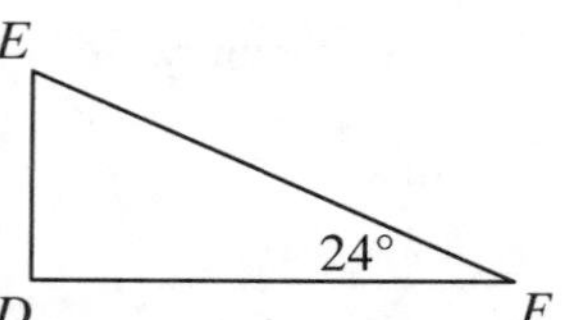

Name ____________________ Class ____________ Date ____________

Example

2 Similar Triangles Show that the pair of triangles is similar.

Step 1 Use the angle sum of a [ ] to find $m\angle R$.

$89^\circ + 43^\circ + m\angle R = $ [ ]

$132^\circ + m\angle R = $ [ ]

$132 - $ [ ] $+ m\angle R = $ [ ] $-$ [ ]

$m\angle R = $ [ ]

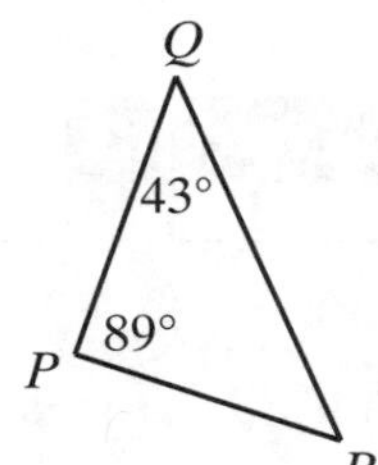

Step 2 Use AA similarity.

$\angle P \cong$ [ ] ← **Each measures** [ ].

$\angle R \cong$ [ ] ← **Each measures** [ ].

$\triangle PQR \sim \triangle LMK$ by Angle-Angle similarity.

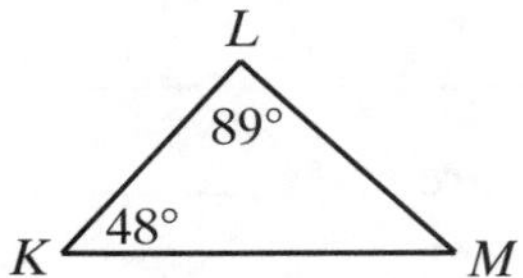

Quick Check

2. Show that each pair of triangles is similar.

a.

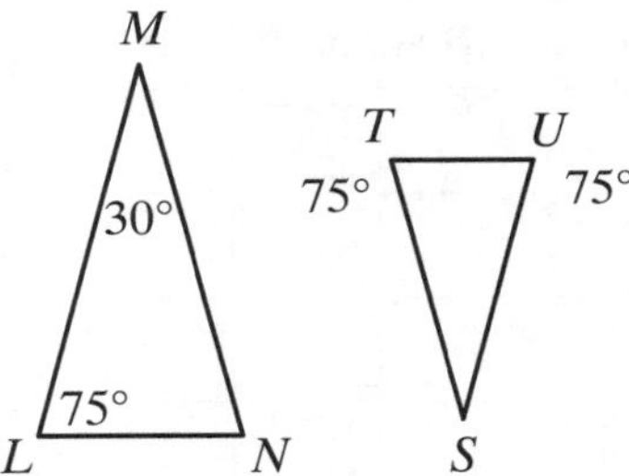

b.

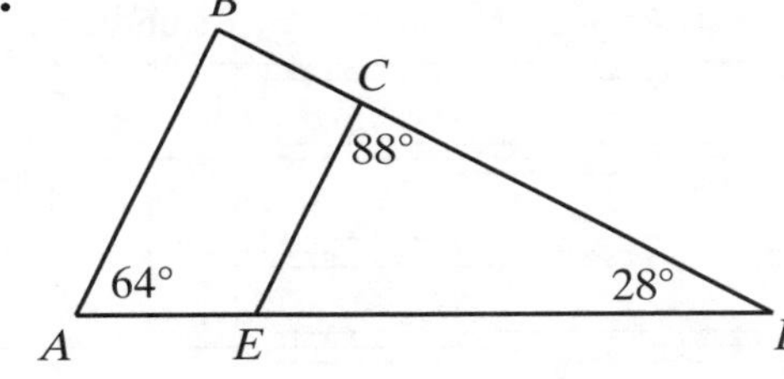

Name ______________________ Class ______________ Date ______________

Lesson 7-6

Angles and Polygons

Lesson Objective	**Common Core State Standard**
To find the angle measures of a polygon	Geometry: 8.G.5

Vocabulary and Key Concepts

Polygon Angle Sum

For a polygon with n sides, the sum of the measures of the interior angles is ______.

Exterior angles are ______________________________

Interior angles are ______________________________

Common Polygons

Polygon Name	Number of Sides	Polygon Name	Number of Sides
______	3	**Octagon**	______
______	4	**Nonagon**	______
______	5	**Decagon**	______
______	6	**Dodecagon**	______
Heptagon	______		

Example

1 Sum of the Interior Angle Measures Find the sum of the measures of the interior angles of an octagon.

An octagon has ☐ sides.

$(n - 2)180° = (\square - 2)180°$ ← **Substitute ☐ for *n*.**

$= \square°$ ← **Simplify.**

Quick Check

1. What is the sum of the measures of the interior angles of a heptagon? ☐

Name ______________________ Class ______________ Date ______________

Examples

2 Angle Measures of a Polygon Find the missing angle measure in the hexagon.

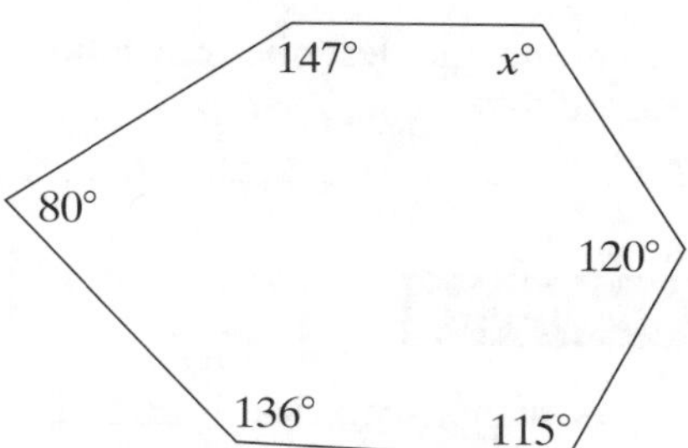

Step 1 Find the sum of the measures of the interior angles of a hexagon.

$(n - 2)180° = (\square - 2)180°$ ← **Substitute** $\square$ **for** ***n*****.**

$= \square$ ← **Simplify.**

Step 2 Write an equation.
Let x = the missing angle measure.

$\square = \square + \square + \square + \square + \square + x°$ ← **Write an equation.**

$720° = \square + x°$ ← **Add.**

$\square = x°$ ← **Subtract** $\square$ **from each side.**

The missing angle measure is $\square$.

3 Finding the Measure of an Exterior Angle $\angle 2$ is an exterior angle of $\triangle ABC$. What is $m\angle 2$?

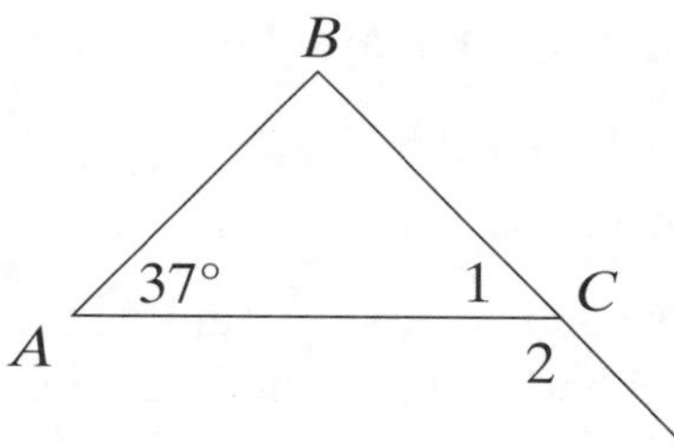

$m\angle 2 = m\angle A + m\angle B$ ← **Exterior angle of triangle**

$= \square$ ← **Substitute.**

$= \square$ ← **Simplify.**

$\angle 2$ measures 127°.

Check

By the angle sum of a triangle, $m\angle 1 = 180° - 90° - 37° = 53°$.

$\angle 1$ and $\angle 2$ are supplementary, so $m\angle 2 = 180° - 53° = 127°$. ✔

Quick Check

2. A hexagon has five angles with measures of 142°, 84°, 123°, 130°, and 90°. What is the measure of the sixth angle?

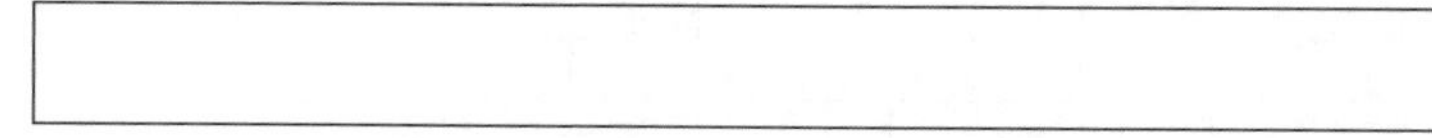

3. In $\triangle RST$, $m\angle R = 63°$ and $m\angle S = 84°$. What is the measure of the exterior angle at vertex T?

Name ______________________ Class ______________ Date ______________

Lesson 8-1

Translations

Lesson Objective	**Common Core Standards**
To graph and describe translations in the coordinate plane	Geometry: 8.G.1.a, 8.G.1.b, 8.G.1.c, 8.G.3

Vocabulary

A transformation is ____

____

A translation is ____

____

An image is ____

____

Example

1 Graphing a Translation

Multiple Choice If $\triangle ABC$ is translated 3 units to the left and 2 units up, what are the coordinates of point A'?

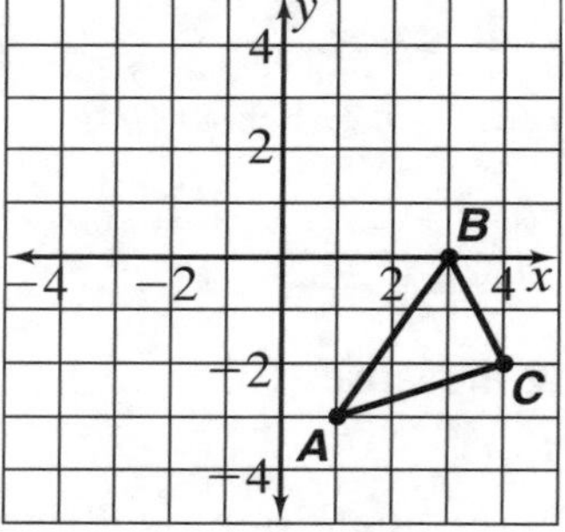

A. $A'(-2, -1)$ **C.** $A'(-2, 1)$

B. $A'(2, -1)$ **D.** $A'(2, 1)$

Slide each vertex ☐ units to the ☐ and ☐ units up. Label and connect the images of the vertices.

The correct answer is choice ☐.

Quick Check

1. $\triangle JKL$ has vertices $J\ (0, 2)$, $K\ (3, 4)$, $L\ (5, 1)$. Translate $\triangle JKL$ 4 units to the left and 5 units up. What are the coordinates of point J'?

☐

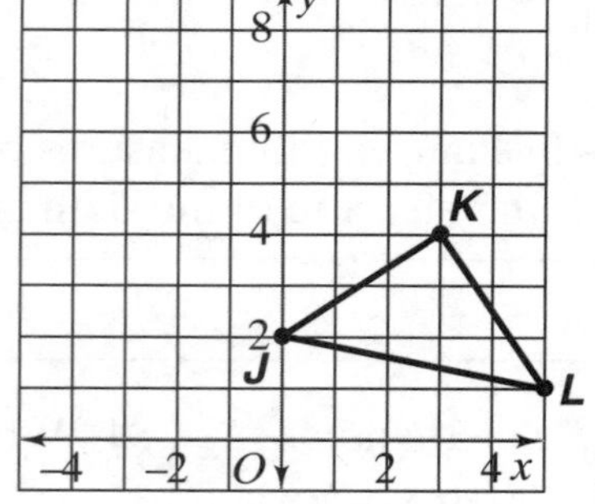

Name ______________________ Class ______________ Date ______________

Example

❷ Describing a Translation Write a rule to describe the translation of $G(-5, 3)$ to $G'(-1, -2)$.

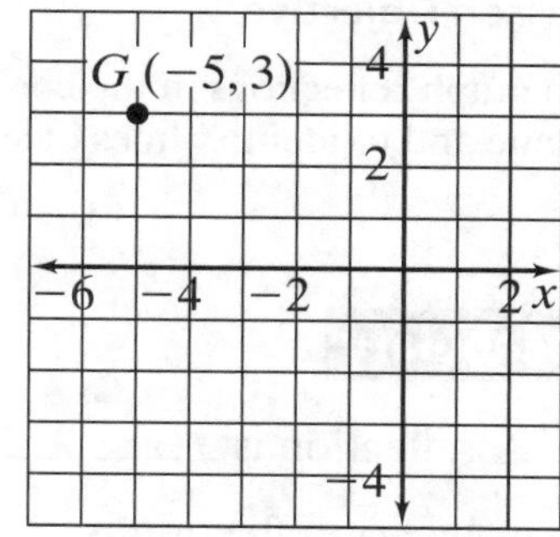

Point G moves ☐ units to the right and ☐ units down. So, the translation adds ☐ to the x-coordinate and subtracts ☐ from the y-coordinate.

The rule is ☐ → ☐.

Quick Check

2. Write a rule that describes the translation shown on the graph.

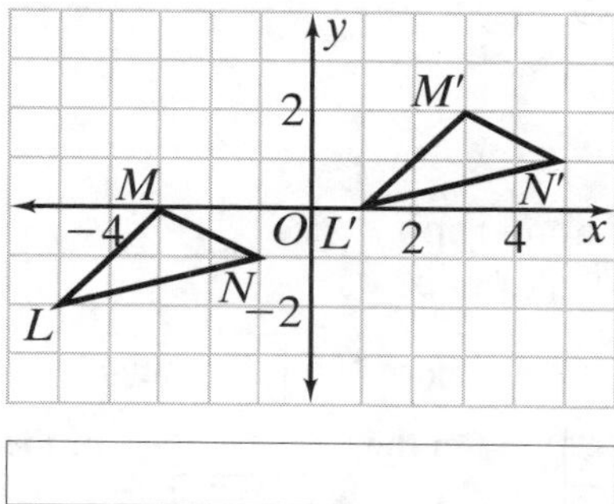

☐

Name ______________________ Class ______________ Date ______________

Lesson 8-2

Reflections and Symmetry

Lesson Objective	**Common Core Standards**
To graph reflections in the coordinate plane and to identify lines of symmetry	Geometry: 8.G.1.a, 8.G.1.b, 8.G.1.c, 8.G.3

Vocabulary

A reflection is ______________________

A line of reflection is ______________________

A line of symmetry is ______________________

A figure can be reflected over a line so that its image matches the original figure if it has ______________________

Example

1 Graphing Reflections of a Point Graph the point $H(-4, 5)$. Then graph its image after it is reflected over the y-axis. Name the coordinates of H'.

The coordinates of H' are $(\square, \square)$.

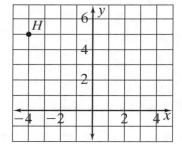

Since *H* is ☐ **unit(s) to the** ______ **of the *y*-axis, *H′* is** ☐ **unit(s) to the** ______ **of the *y*-axis.**

Quick Check

1. Graph the point $D(-2, 1)$. Then graph its image after it is reflected over the y-axis. Name the coordinates of D'.

____

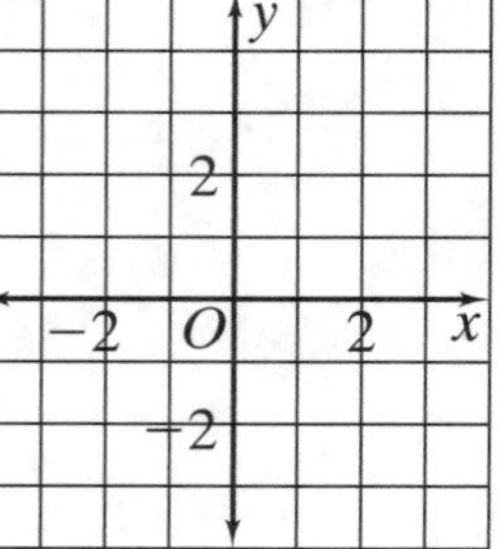

Example

2 Graphing Reflections of a Shape $\triangle BCD$ has vertices $B(-3, 1)$, $C(-2, 5)$, and $D(-5, 4)$. Graph $\triangle BCD$ and its image after a reflection over the x-axis. Name the coordinates of the vertices of $\triangle B'C'D'$.

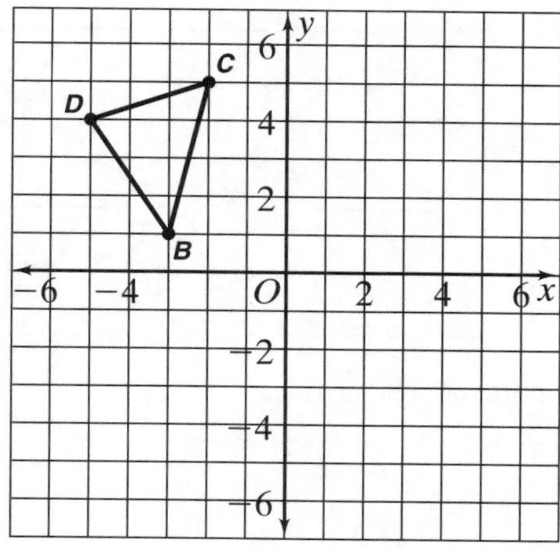

Since *B* is ☐ unit(s) ☐ the *x*-axis, *B'* is ☐ unit(s) ☐ the *x*-axis.

Reflect the other vertices.
Draw $\triangle B'C'D'$.

The coordinates of the vertices are B'(☐, ☐), C'(☐, ☐), and D'(☐, ☐).

Quick Check

2. $\triangle EFG$ has vertices $E(4, 3)$, $F(3, 1)$, and $G(1, 2)$. Graph $\triangle EFG$ and its image after a reflection over the x-axis. Name the coordinates of the vertices of $\triangle E'F'G'$.

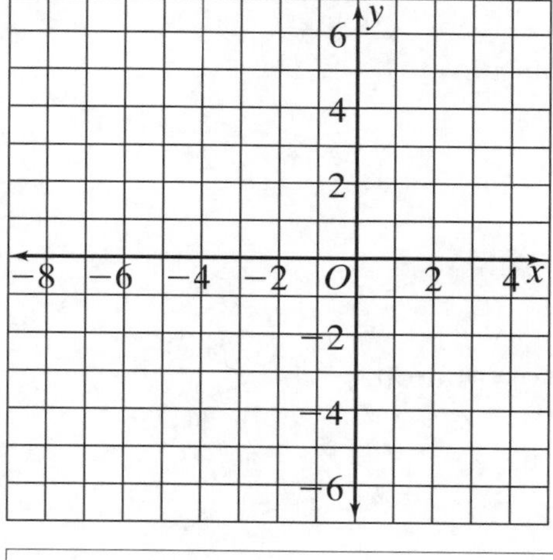

☐

Name ______________________ Class ______________ Date ______________

Lesson 8-3

Rotations

Lesson Objective	**Common Core Standards**
To graph rotations and identify rotational symmetry	Geometry: 8.G.1.a, 8.G.1.b, 8.G.1.c, 8.G.3

Vocabulary

A rotation is ______________________________

The center of rotation is ______________________________

The angle of rotation is ______________________________

A figure has [   ] if it can be rotated 180° or less and exactly match its original figure.

Example

1 **Rotational Symmetry** Does this figure have rotational symmetry? If so, give the angle of rotation.

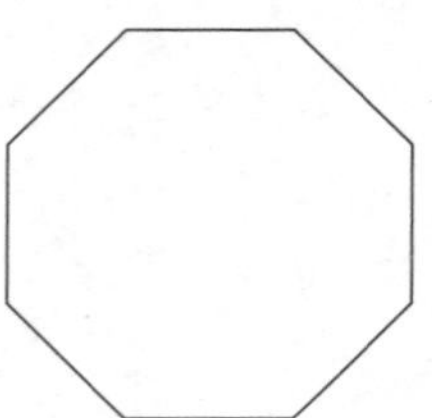

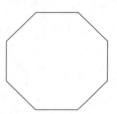

The image matches the original after [ ] of a complete rotation.

$\frac{1}{8} \cdot 360° = \square°$

The angle of rotation is $\square°$.

Quick Check

1. If the figure below has rotational symmetry, find the angle of rotation. If it does not, write *no rotational symmetry*.

Name ______________________ Class ______________ Date ______________

Example

❷ **Graphing Rotations** Draw the image of rectangle $ABCD$ after a rotation of 90° about the origin.

Step 1 Draw and trace.

- Draw rectangle $ABCD$ with vertices $(3, 2), (-3, 2), (-3, -2)$, and $(3, -2)$. Place a piece of tracing paper over your graph.
- Trace the vertices of the rectangle, the x-axis, and the y-axis.
- Place your pencil at the origin to rotate the paper.

Step 2 Rotate and mark each vertex.

- Rotate the tracing paper 90° counterclockwise. The axes should line up.
- Mark the position of each vertex by pressing your pencil through the paper.

Step 3 Complete the new figure.

- Remove the tracing paper.
- Draw the rectangle.
- Label the vertices to complete the figure.

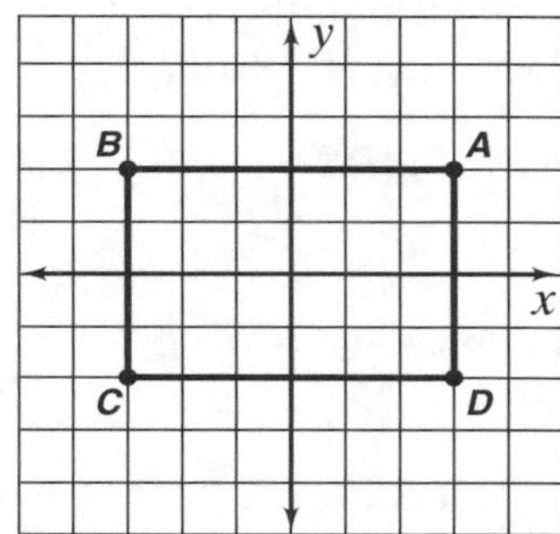

Quick Check

2. Draw the image of $\triangle ABD$ after a rotation of the given number of degrees about the origin. Name the coordinates of the vertices of the image.

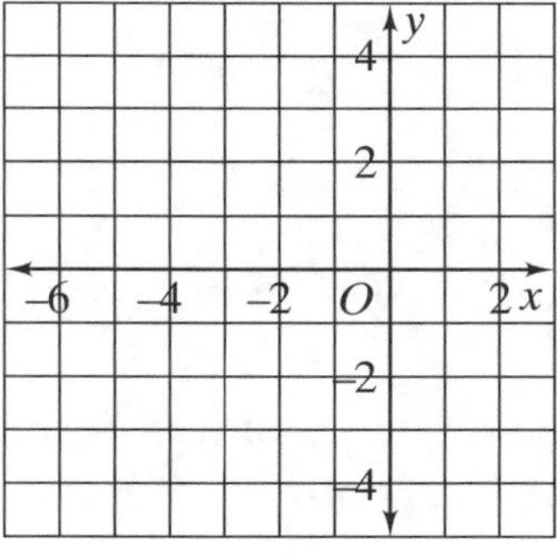

a. 180°

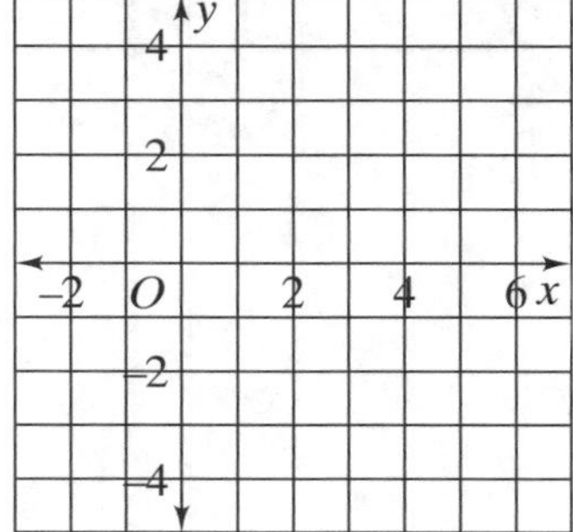

b. 270°

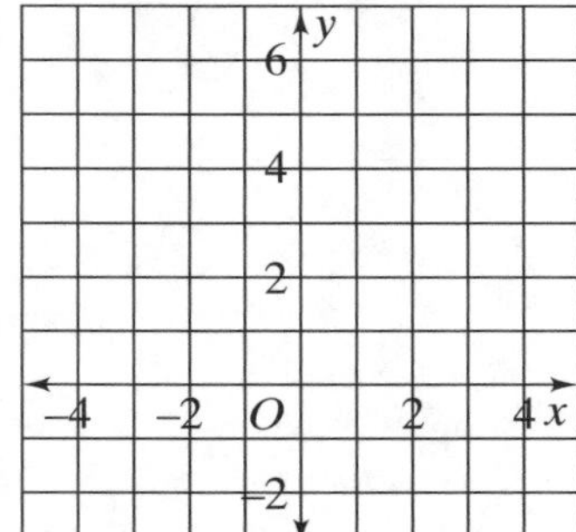

Name ______________________ Class ______________ Date ______________

Lesson 8-4

Transformations and Congruence

Lesson Objective	**Common Core Standard**
To describe a sequence of transformations that maps one figure onto another; to determine whether two figures are congruent by using a sequence of transformations	Geometry: 8.G.2

Vocabulary

You can use a sequence of transformations to ______ one figure onto another.

Example

1 Recognizing a Series of Transformations The three trapezoids are congruent. Describe the sequence of transformations that maps *PQRS* onto *P‴Q‴R‴S‴*.

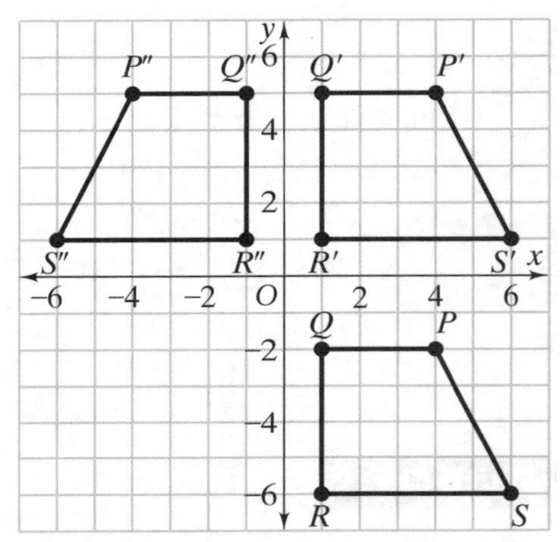

A translation ____ units ____ maps *PQRS* onto ______.

A reflection over the ____-axis maps *P′Q′R′S′* onto ______.

So, a translation ____ units ____, followed by a ______ over the ____-axis, maps *PQRS* onto ______.

Quick Check

1. Describe the sequence of transformations that maps *WXYZ* onto *W″X″Y″Z″*.

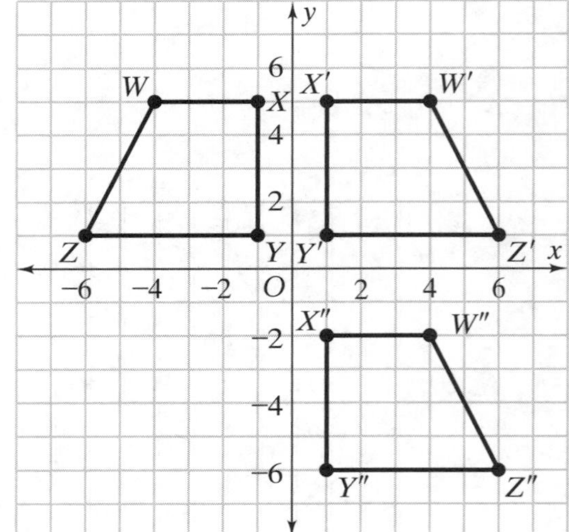

Name ______________________ Class ______________ Date ______________

Example

❷ Using Transformations to Determine Congruence

Determine whether the two triangles in the diagram are congruent. If they are congruent, write a congruence statement. If they are not congruent, explain why.

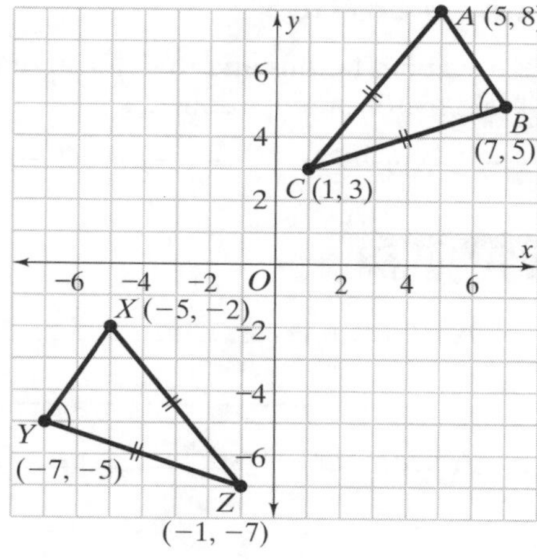

$\triangle ABC$ and $\triangle XYZ$ have ______ orientations and are on ______ sides of the y-axis.

So, first ______ $\triangle ABC$ over the ___ -axis to get $\triangle$ ______.

Then, ______ the reflected image $\triangle$ ______ ______ units ______ to map it onto $\triangle$ ______.

Finally, write your congruence statement:

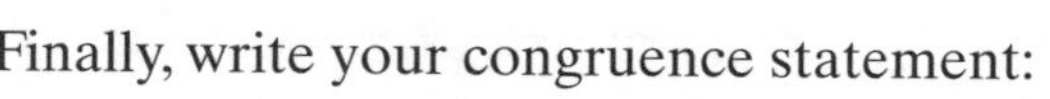

____

____

____

____

Quick Check

2. Determine whether $\triangle ABC$ is congruent to $\triangle QRS$. If the triangles are congruent, tell what sequence of transformations will map $\triangle ABC$ onto $\triangle QRS$. Then write a congruence statement. If they are not congruent, explain why.

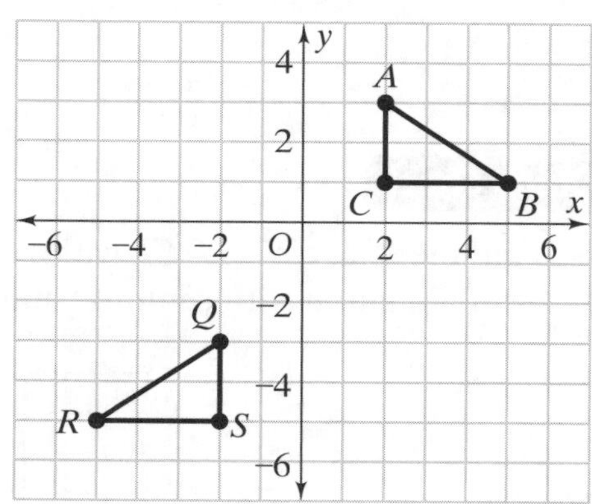

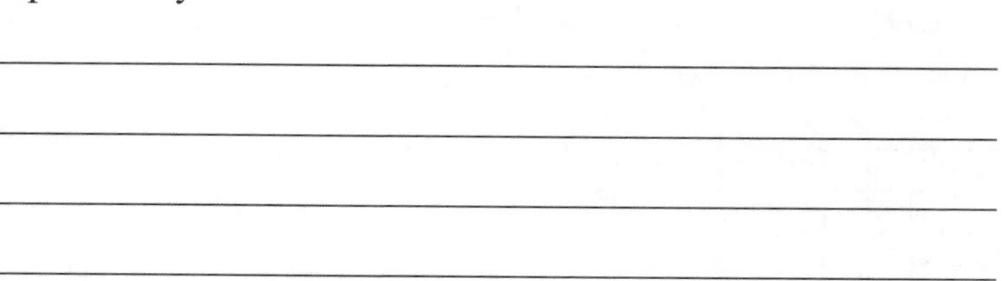

____

____

____

____

Name ______________________ Class ______________ Date ______________

Lesson 8-5

Transformations and Congruence

Lesson Objective	**Common Core Standards**
To graph dilations and to determine the scale factor of a dilation	Geometry: 8.G.3, 8.G.4

Vocabulary

A dilation is ____

____

A scale factor is ____

____

An enlargement is ____

A reduction is ____

Example

1 Finding a Dilation Find the image of $\triangle ABC$ after a dilation with center A and a scale factor of 3.

$\triangle A'B'C'$ is the image of $\triangle ABC$ after a dilation with center A and a scale factor of 3. $\triangle ABC$ ☐ $\triangle A'B'C'$.

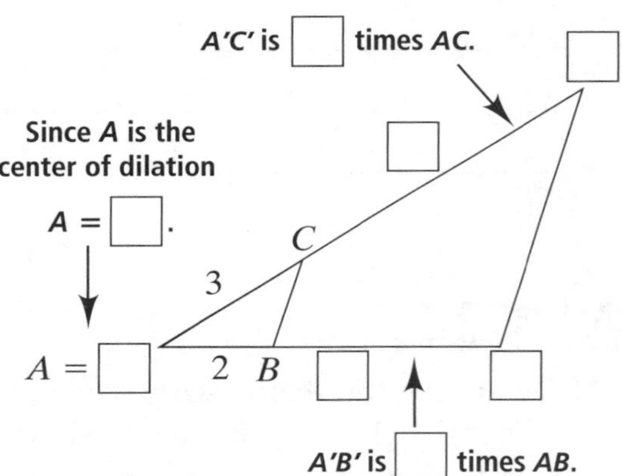

Quick Check

1. Find the image of $\triangle DEF$ with vertices $D(-2, 2)$, $E(1, -1)$, and $F(-2, -1)$ after a dilation with center D and a scale factor of 2.

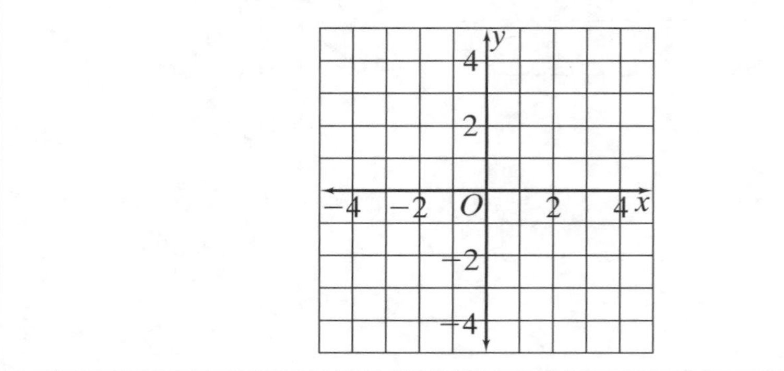

Name ______________________ Class ______________ Date ______________

❷ **Graphing Dilation Images** Find the coordinates of the vertices of the image of quadrilateral $WXYZ$ after a dilation with center $(0, 0)$ and a scale factor of $\frac{1}{2}$. Then graph the image. Quadrilateral $WXYZ$ has vertices $W(-2, -1)$, $X(0, 2)$, $Y(4, 2)$, and $Z(4, -1)$.

Step 1 Multiply the x- and y-coordinates of each point by $\frac{1}{2}$.

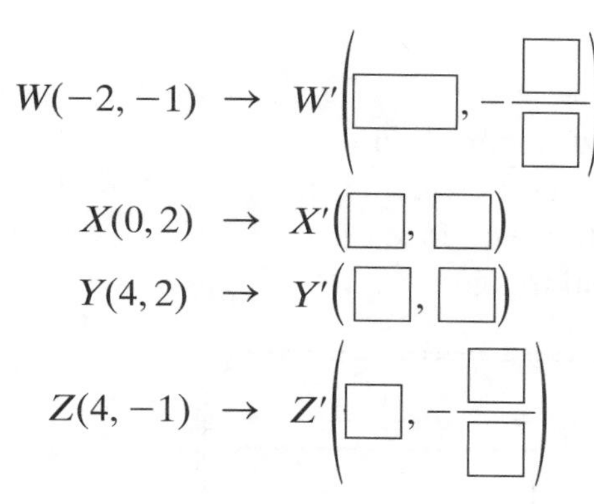

Step 2 Graph the image.

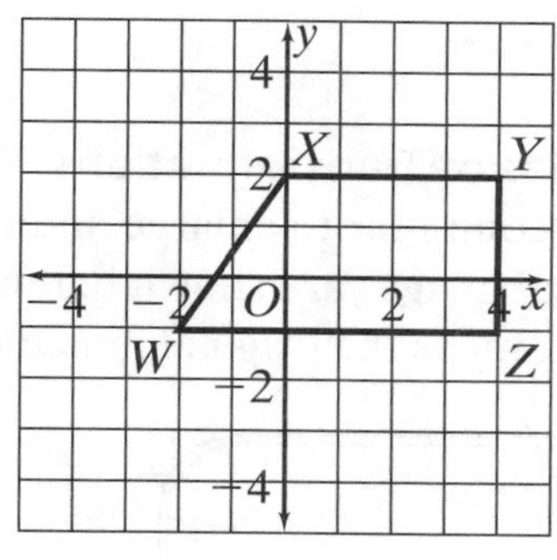

❸ **Finding a Scale Factor** $\triangle Q'P'R'$ is a dilation of $\triangle QPR$. What is the scale factor of the dilation?

image → $\frac{Q'P'}{QP}$ = $\frac{\square + \square}{\square}$ = $\square$
original →

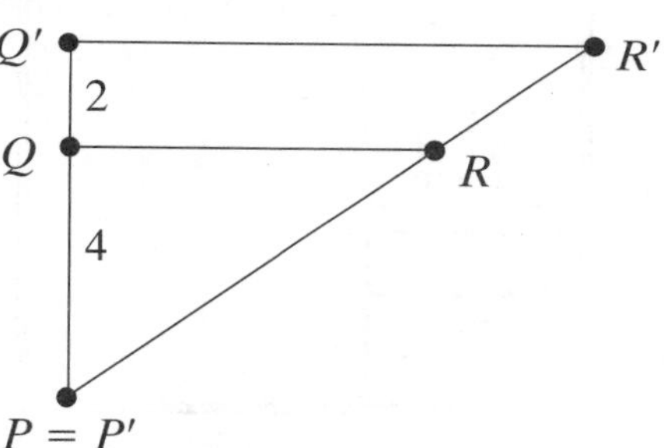

The scale factor is ______. It is ______ than 1, so the dilation is a(n) ______.

Quick Check

2. $ABCD$ has vertices $A(0, 0)$, $B(0, 3)$, $C(3, 3)$, and $D(3, 0)$. Find the coordinates of the vertices of the image of $ABCD$ after a dilation with a scale factor of $\frac{4}{3}$. Then graph the image.

3. Figure $EFGH$ shows the outline of a yard. Figure $E'F'G'H'$ is a doghouse. Figure $E'F'G'H'$ is a dilation image of figure $EFGH$. Find the scale factor. Is the dilation an enlargement or a reduction?

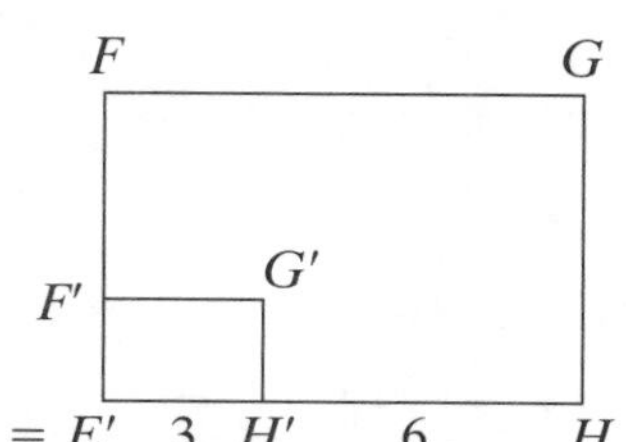

Name ________________ Class ________________ Date ________________

Lesson 8-6

Transformations and Similarity

Lesson Objective	**Common Core Standard**
To describe a sequence of transformations that maps one figure onto another; to determine whether two figures are similar by using a sequence of transformations	Geometry: 8.G.4

Example

1 Recognizing a Series of Transformations You use the zoom and swipe features on a tablet computer to enlarge and then move a geometric image. The original and final images are shown below. Describe the sequence of transformations that maps the original image onto the final image

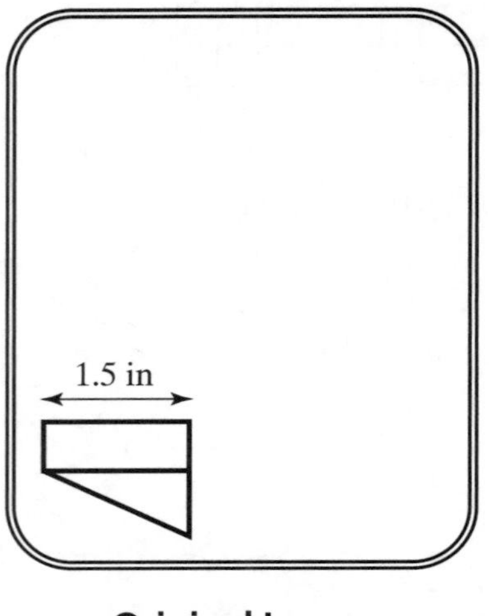

Original Image

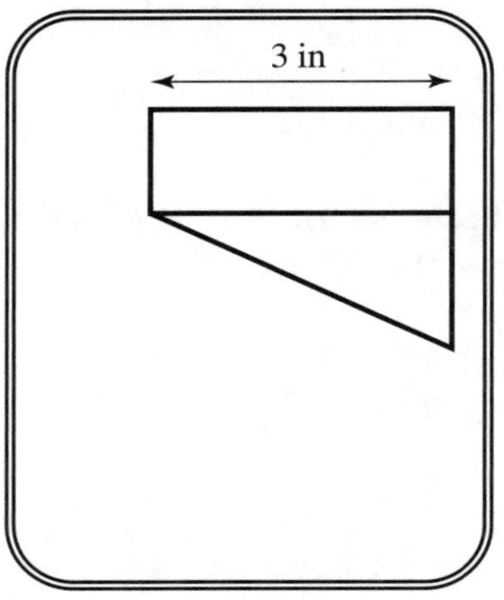

Final Image

The zoom was a ________ with a scale factor of ____.

Swiping the image mapped the original image in the direction ______ and then ______ onto the final zoomed-in image.

Name ______________________ Class ______________ Date ______________

Quick Check

1. Using a computer, a graphic designer moves a company logo from the top left of a page to the bottom center of the page and then enlarges the logo, as shown below. Describe the sequence of transformations that maps the original logo onto the final logo.

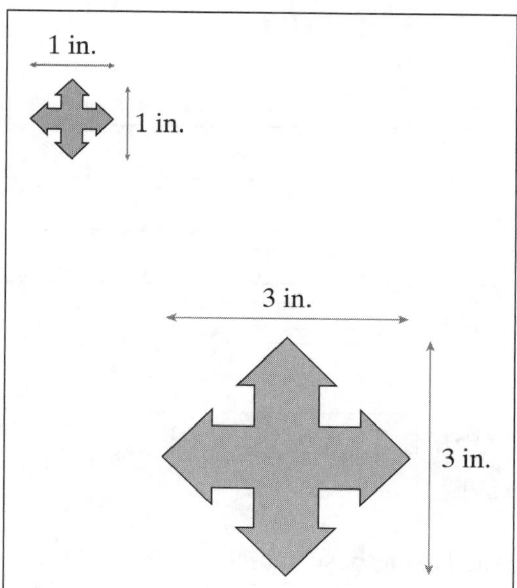

Name ______________________ Class ______________ Date ______________

Lesson 9-1

Solids

Lesson Objective	
To identify solids, parts of solids, and skew line segments	

Vocabulary

Solids are ____

____

A polyhedron is ____

____

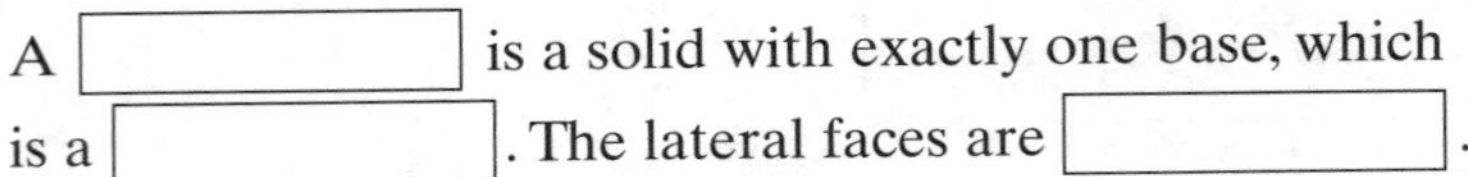

[ ] lines are lines that do not [ ] and are not [ ].

A [ ] is a solid that has two [ ] bases that are [ ] polygons.

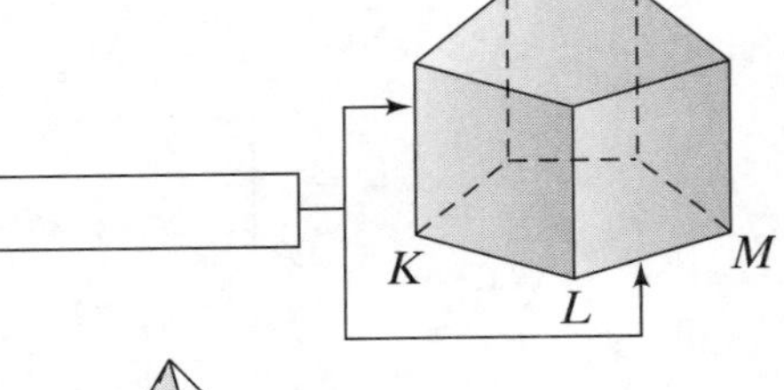

A [ ] is a solid with exactly one base, which is a [ ]. The lateral faces are [ ].

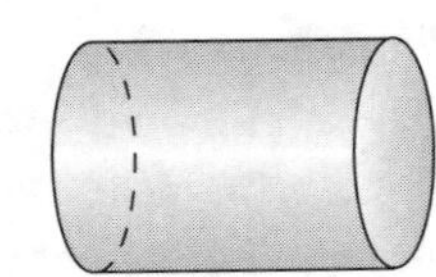

A [ ] is a solid with two bases that are parallel, congruent [ ].

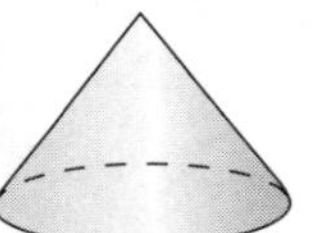

A [ ] is a solid with exactly one circular base and one [ ].

Examples

1 Naming Solids and Their Parts In the figure at right, describe the base, name the figure, and name the part labeled $\overline{CD}$.

The base is a [ ]. The figure is a [ ].

$\overline{CD}$ is a [ ].

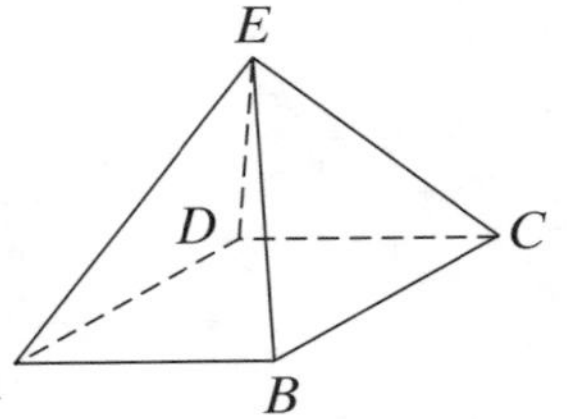

2 Recognizing Solids Which common solids make up this toy?

The box is a [ ]. The head is a [ ].

The hat is a [ ] with a [ ] on top.

Name ______________________ Class ______________ Date ______________

❸ Identifying Skew Line Segments For each figure, name a pair of skew line segments, a pair of parallel line segments, and a pair of intersecting line segments.

a.

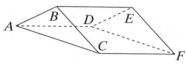

☐ and ☐ are skew. ☐ and ☐ are parallel.

☐ and ☐ intersect.

b.

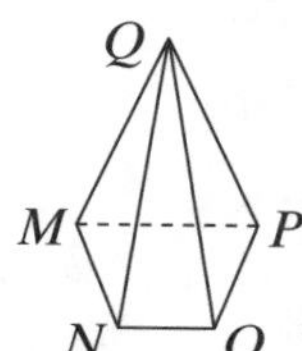

☐ and ☐ are skew. 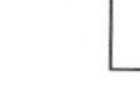 and ☐ are parallel.

☐ and ☐ intersect.

Quick Check

1. Refer to the figure at the right. Name the figure, $\overline{JK}$, and the points J and K.

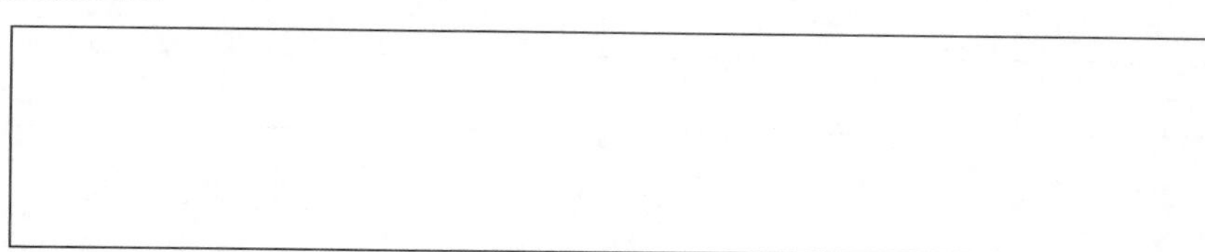

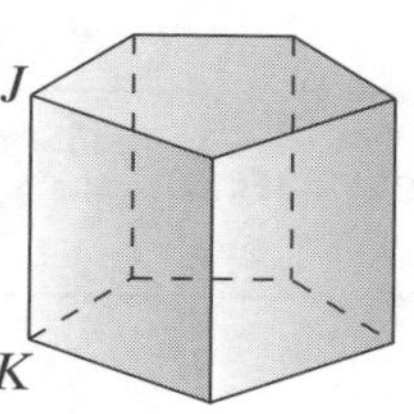

2. What common solids will a stage crew use to build the stage prop at right?

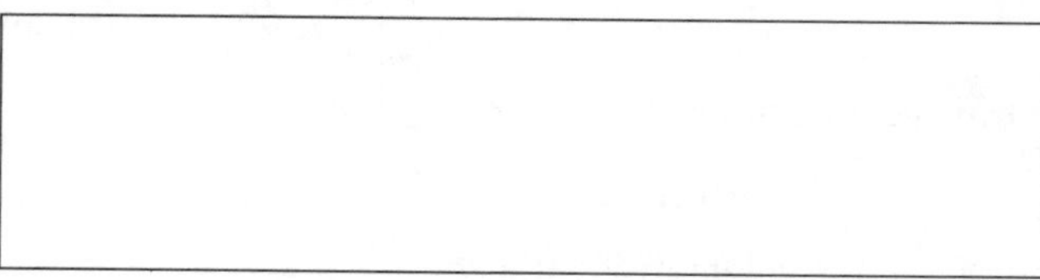

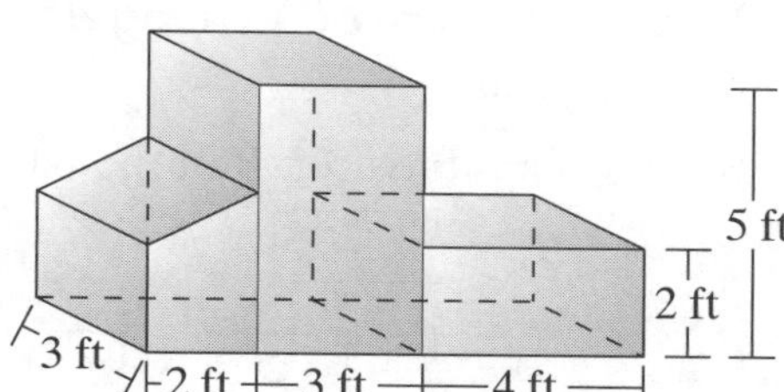

3. For the figure at the right, name a pair of intersecting line segments.

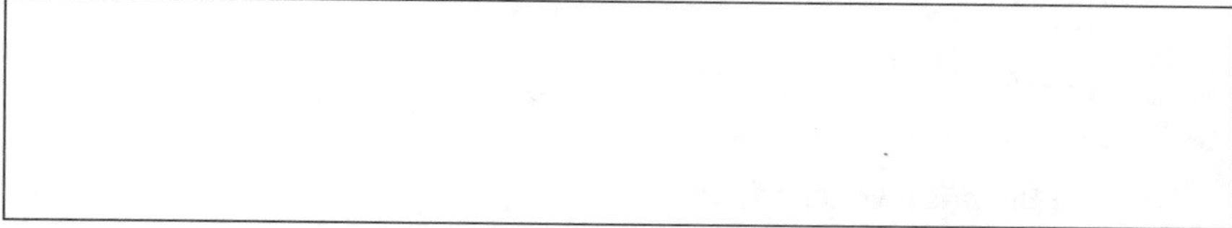

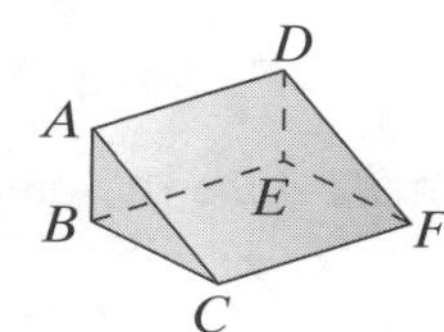

Name ______________________ Class ______________ Date ______________

Lesson 9-2

Volumes of Prisms and Cylinders

Lesson Objective	Common Core Standards
To find the volumes of prisms and cylinders	Geometry: 8.G.7, 8.G.9

Vocabulary and Key Concepts

Volume of Prisms and Cylinders

The volume V of a prism is the product of the base area B and the height h.

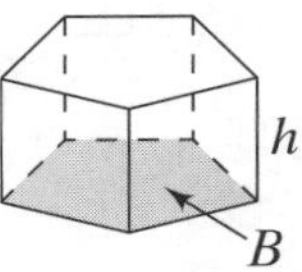

$$V = Bh$$

The volume V of a cylinder is the product of the base area B and the height h.

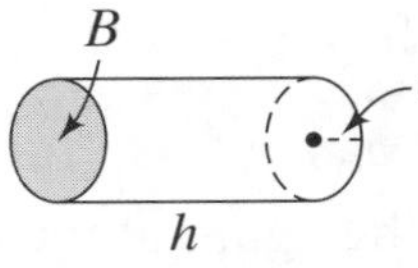

$$V = Bh$$

Integers are ____

____

Examples

1 Finding Volume of a Triangular Prism Find the volume of this prism.

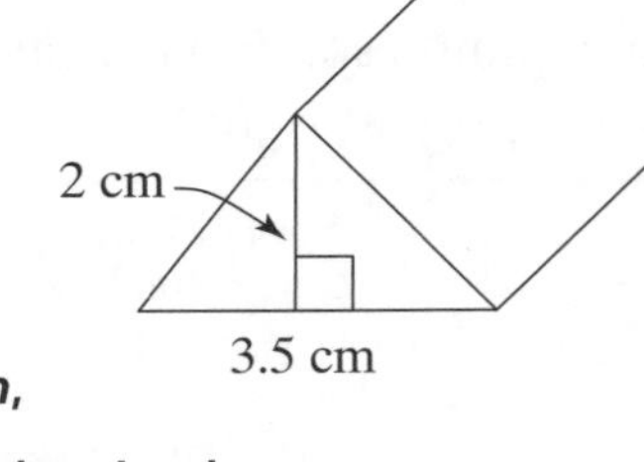

Step 1 Find the area B of the base.

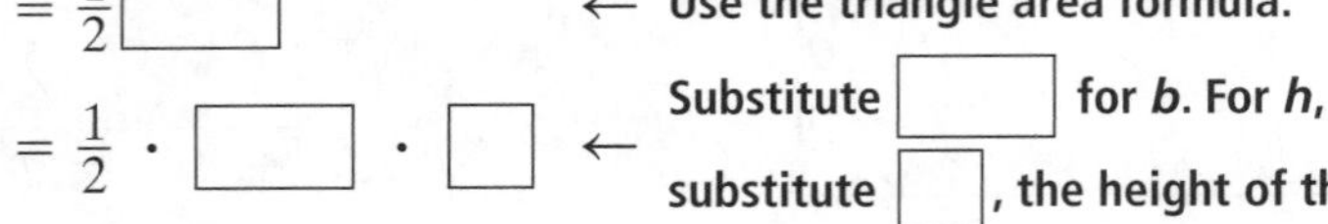

$B = \frac{1}{2}$ ____ ← **Use the triangle area formula.**

$= \frac{1}{2} \cdot$ ____ $\cdot$ ____ ← **Substitute ____ for *b*. For *h*, substitute ____, the height of the triangle.**

$=$ ____ ← **Multiply.**

The area of the base is ____ cm^2.

Step 2 Use the base area to find the volume.

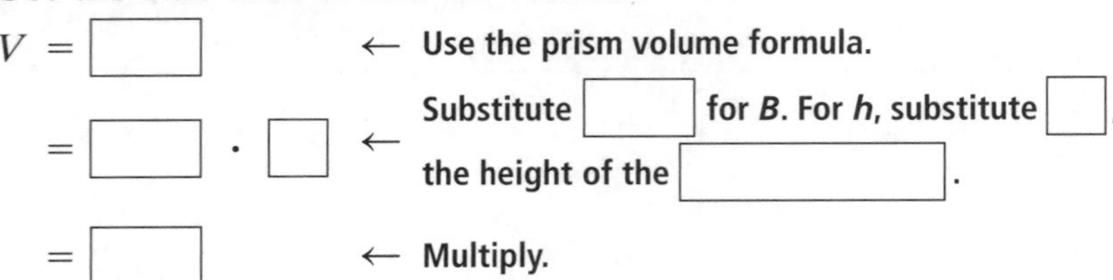

$V =$ ____ ← **Use the prism volume formula.**

$=$ ____ $\cdot$ ____ ← **Substitute ____ for *B*. For *h*, substitute ____, the height of the ____.**

$=$ ____ ← **Multiply.**

The volume of the prism is ____ cm^3.

Name ______________________ Class ______________ Date ______________

❷ Finding Volume of a Cylinder Find the volume of a cylindrical cake that is 5 in. tall with a diameter of 15 in. Give your answer to the nearest cubic inch.

Estimate Use 3 for π. The area of the base is about 3×64 in.^{2}, or ☐ in.^{2}. The volume is about 190×5 in.^{3}, or ☐ in.^{3}.

Step 1 Find the area of the base.

$B = \pi$ ☐

$= \pi($☐$)$ ← **Substitute.**

$=$ ☐ ← **Simplify.**

The base area is ☐ in.^{2}.

Step 2 Use the base area to find the volume.

$V =$ ☐

$=$ ☐ $\cdot$ ☐ **Substitute.** →

$\approx$ ☐ **Simplify.** →

The volume of the cylindrical cake is about ☐ in.^{3}.

Check for Reasonableness The answer ☐ is close to the estimate of ☐. The answer is reasonable.

Quick Check

1. Find the volume of the prism.

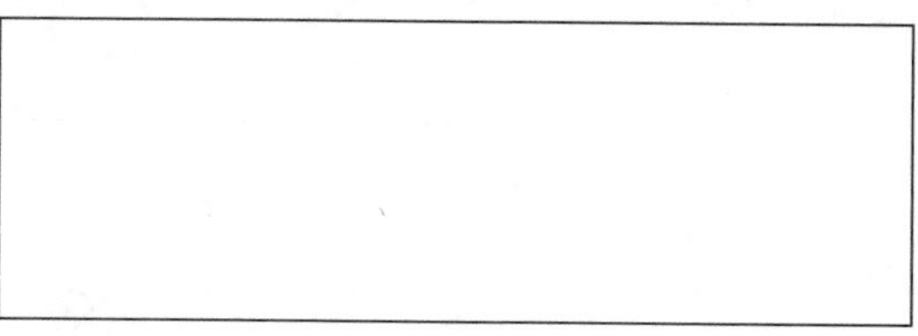

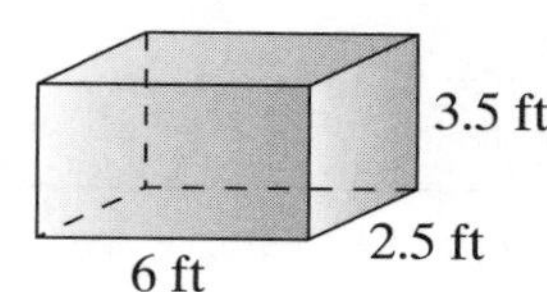

2. a. **Estimation** Estimate the volume of the cylinder at the right. Use 3 for π.

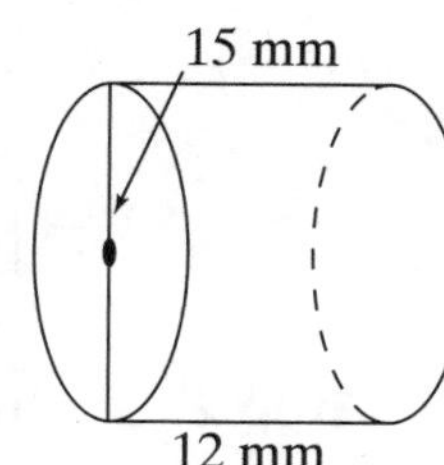

b. Find the volume of the cylinder to the nearest cubic millimeter.

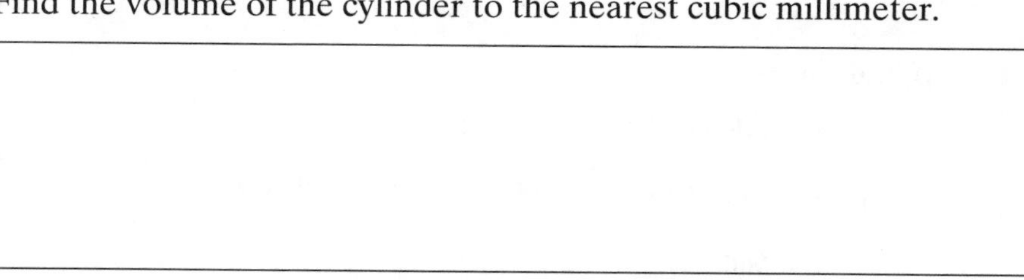

Name ____________________ Class ____________ Date ____________

Lesson 9-3

Volumes of Pyramids and Cones

Lesson Objective	**Common Core Standard**
To find the volumes of pyramids and cones	Geometry: 8.G.9

Key Concepts

Volume of a Pyramid

The volume V of a pyramid is one third the product of the base area B and the height h.

$$V = \frac{1}{3}Bh$$

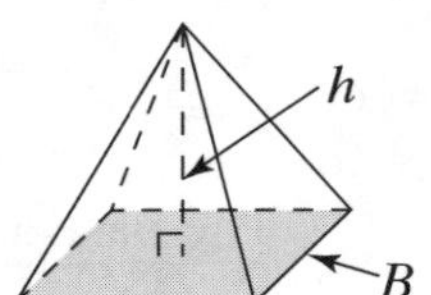

Volume of a Cone

The volume V of a cone is one third the product of the base area B and the height h.

$$V = \frac{1}{3}Bh$$

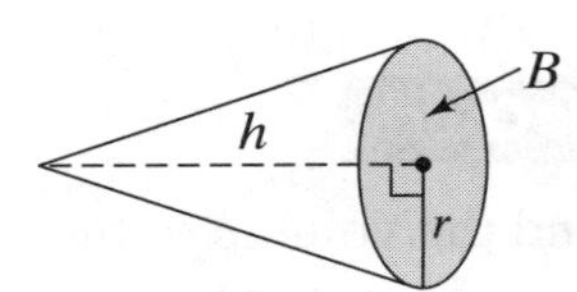

Examples

1 Finding Volume of a Square Pyramid Find the volume of this square pyramid to the nearest cubic foot.

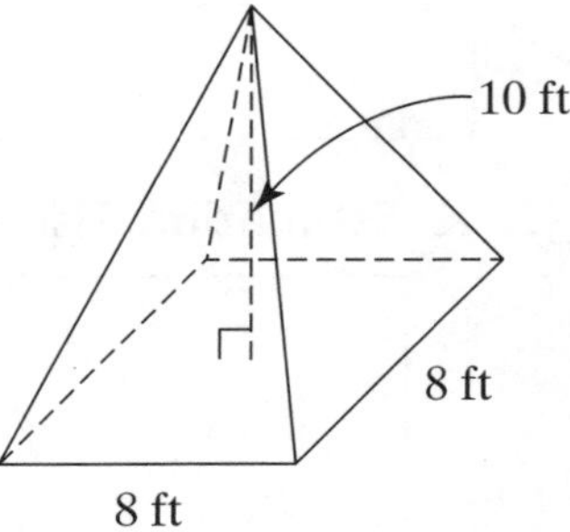

Step 1 Find the area of the base.

$B =$ ☐ ← **area of a square**

$=$ ☐ ← **Substitute** ☐ **for** ***s*****.**

$=$ ☐ ← **Simplify.**

Step 2 Use the base area to find the volume.

$V = \frac{1}{3}Bh$ ← **volume of a pyramid**

$= \frac{1}{3}$(☐)(☐) ← **Substitute** ☐ **for** ***B*** **and** ☐ **for** ***h*****.**

$\approx$ ☐ ← **Multiply.**

The volume of the pyramid is approximately ☐ ft^3.

Name ______________________ Class ______________ Date ______________

❷ **Using the Volume Formula** Find the volume of this cone to the nearest cubic centimeter.

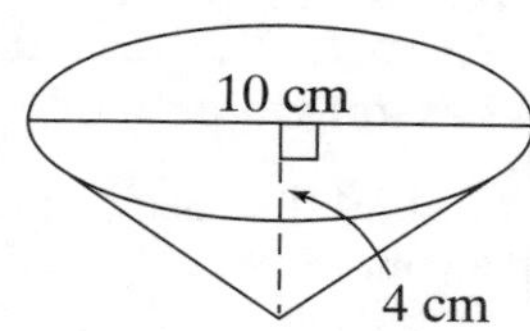

Step 1 Find the area of the base.

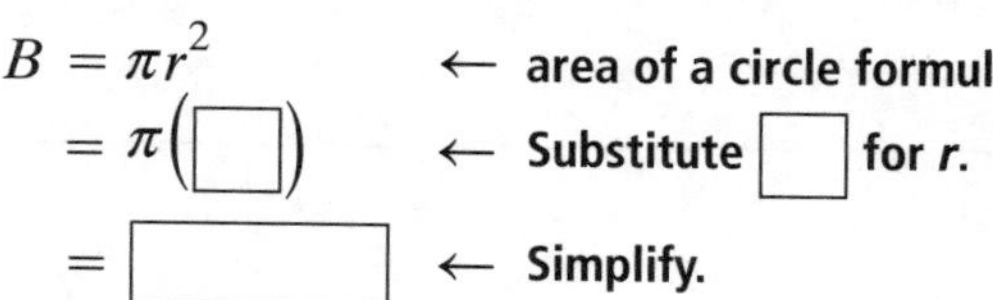

$B = \pi r^2$ ← area of a circle formula

$= \pi(\square)$ ← Substitute $\square$ for *r*.

$= \square$ ← Simplify.

Step 2 Use the base area to find the volume.

$V = \frac{1}{3}Bh$ ← cone volume formula

$= \frac{1}{3}(\square)\square$ ← Substitute $\square$ for *B* and $\square$ for *h*.

$= \square \frac{\square}{\square} \square$ ← Multiply.

≈ 105 ← Simplify.

To the nearest cubic centimeter, the volume of the cone is $\square$ cm^3.

Quick Check

1. Find the volume of the square pyramid at the right.

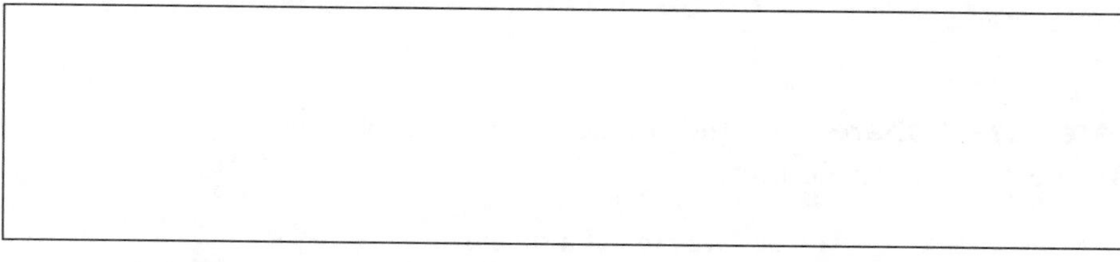

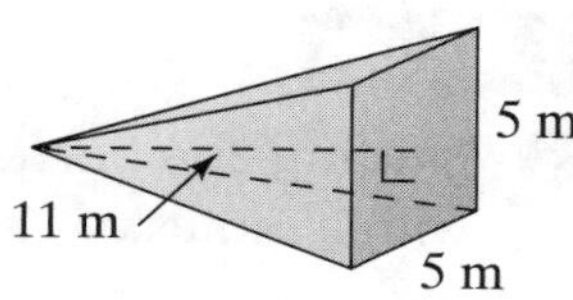

2. Find the volume of the cone at the right. Round to the nearest cubic meter.

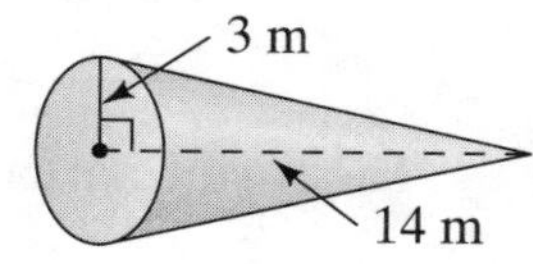

Name ________________ Class ________________ Date ________________

Lesson 9-4

Spheres

Lesson Objective	**Common Core Standard**
To find the surface area and volume of a sphere	Geometry: 8.G.9

Vocabulary and Key Concepts

Surface Area and Volume of a Sphere

The surface area of a sphere is four times the product of π and the square of the radius r.

$$\text{S.A.} = 4\pi r^2$$

The volume of a sphere is four thirds of the product of π and the radius r cubed.

$$V = \frac{4}{3}\pi r^3$$

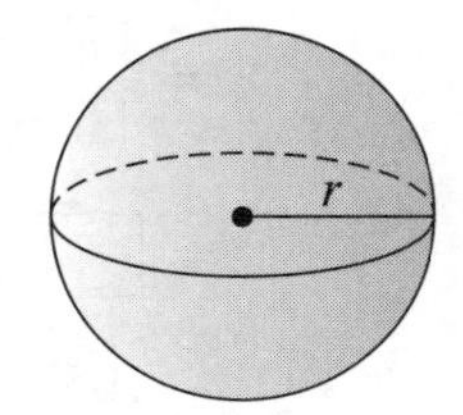

A sphere is ____

____

Example

1 Finding the Surface Area of a Sphere Find the surface area of a sphere with a radius of 12 m to the nearest whole unit.

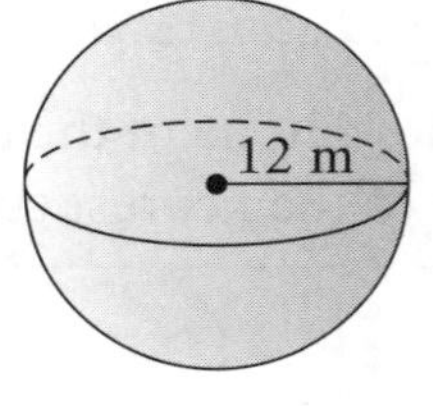

S. A. = 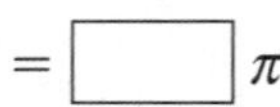 ← **surface area of a sphere**

$= 4\pi(\square)^2$ ← **Substitute** $\square$ **for** r.

$= \square\,\pi$ ← **Simplify.**

$\approx$ 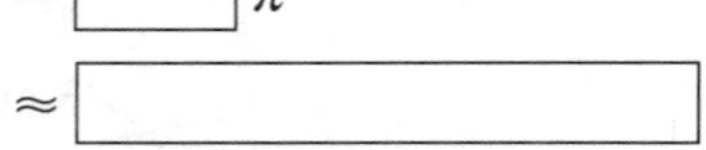 ← **Use a calculator.**

The surface area of the sphere is about $\square$.

Quick Check

1. A sphere has a radius of 7 ft. Find its surface area to the nearest square foot.

Name ______________________ Class ______________ Date ______________

Example

❷ **Finding the Volume of a Sphere** A standard men's basketball has a diameter of 9.39 inches. What is the volume of a standard men's basketball to the nearest cubic inch?

$r = \frac{\square}{\square}$ ← The radius is equal to ☐ the diameter.

$\approx \square$ in. ← Round to the nearest tenth of an inch.

$V = \square$ ← volume of a sphere

$\approx \frac{4}{3}\pi(\square)^3$ ← Substitute ☐ for *r*.

$\approx \square$ ← Use a calculator.

The volume of a standard men's basketball is about ☐.

Check for Reasonableness Use 3 for π and 5 for r. The volume is about $\frac{4}{3}(3)(5)^3$ in.^{3}, or ☐. The answer ☐ reasonable.

Quick Check

2. A globe in a brass stand has a diameter of 40 in. What is the volume of the globe to the nearest cubic inch?

Name ______________________ Class ______________ Date ______________

Lesson 9-5

Exploring Similar Solids

Lesson Objective	Common Core Standard
To use proportions to find missing measurements of similar solids, including surface area and volume	Geometry: 8.G.9

Vocabulary and Key Concepts

Surface Area and Volume of Similar Solids

If the ratio of the corresponding dimensions of similar solids is $\frac{a}{b}$, then

- the ratio of their surface areas is $\frac{a^2}{b^2}$ and
- the ratio of their volumes is $\frac{a^3}{b^3}$.

Similar solids ____

____

Example

1 Finding Dimensions of a Similar Solid At an ice cream shop, the small and large cones are similar. The small cone has a radius of 3 cm and a height of 12 cm. The large cone has a radius of 5 cm. What is the height of the large ice cream cone? Let h = the height of the large cone. Use corresponding parts to write a proportion.

$\frac{h}{\square} = \frac{\square}{\square}$ ← **dimensions of large cone** / **dimensions of small cone**

$\square \times \frac{h}{12} = \frac{5}{3} \times 12$ ← **Multiply each side by** $\square$.

$h = \frac{\square}{\square}$ ← **Simplify.**

$= \square$

The height of the large cone is $\square$.

Quick Check

1. Two cylinders are similar. The small cylinder has a diameter of 4 m and a height of h. The large cylinder has a diameter of 5 m and a height of 11 m. What is the value of h?

Name ____________ Class ____________ Date ____________

Example

2 Surface Area and Volume of Similar Solids A square pyramid has a surface area of 39 cm^2 and a volume of 12 cm^3. The pyramid is similar to a larger pyramid, but its side length is $\frac{2}{3}$ that of the larger pyramid. Find the surface area and volume of the larger pyramid.

The ratio of the side lengths is $\frac{2}{3}$, so the ratio of the surface areas is $\frac{2^2}{3^2}$, or $\frac{\square}{\square}$.

$$\frac{\text{surface area of the small pyramid}}{\text{surface area of the large pyramid}} = \frac{\square}{\square}$$ ← **Write a proportion.**

$$\frac{\square}{S} = \frac{\square}{\square}$$ ← **Substitute the surface area of the small pyramid.**

$$39 \cdot \square = S \cdot \square$$ ← **Write the cross products.**

$$S = \square$$ ← **Simplify.**

The surface area of the large pyramid is $\square$

If the ratio of the side lengths is $\frac{2}{3}$, the ratio of the volumes is $\frac{2^3}{3^3}$, or $\frac{\square}{\square}$.

$$\frac{\text{volume of the small pyramid}}{\text{volume of the large pyramid}} = \frac{\square}{\square}$$ ← **Write a proportion.**

$$\frac{\square}{V} = \frac{\square}{\square}$$ ← **Substitute the volume of the small pyramid.**

$$12 \cdot \square = V \cdot \square$$ ← **Write the cross products.**

$$V = \square$$ ← **Simplify.**

The volume of the large pyramid is $\square$

Quick Check

2. A box has a surface area of about 54 $in.^2$ and a volume of about 27 $in.^3$. The edge lengths of the box are about $\frac{1}{3}$ of the edge lengths of a larger box. Find the surface area and volume of the larger box.

$\square$

Name ________________ Class ________________ Date ________________

Lesson 10-1

Scatter Plots

Lesson Objective	**Common Core Standards**
To interpret and make scatter plots of bivariate data	Statistics and Probability: 8.SP.1, 8.SP.2

Vocabulary

A scatter plot is ________________

Bivariate data show ________________

Example

1 Reading Scatter Plots On the graph at the right, tell what the ordered pair (4, 1,500) represents.

Each point on the scatter plot represents one ordered pair:

([ ] , [ ])

So, for (4, 1,500),

4 represents [ ]

1,500 represents [ ]

Raise Received by Workers Based on Number of Years They Have Been Employed

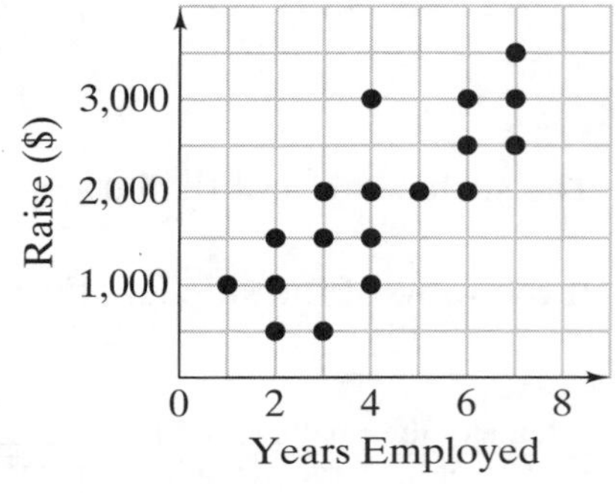

Quick Check

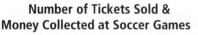

1. a. In the scatter plot to the right, what does (350, 2,275) represent?

[ ]

b. How many tickets were sold when the amount of money collected was $2,700?

[ ]

Number of Tickets Sold & Money Collected at Soccer Games

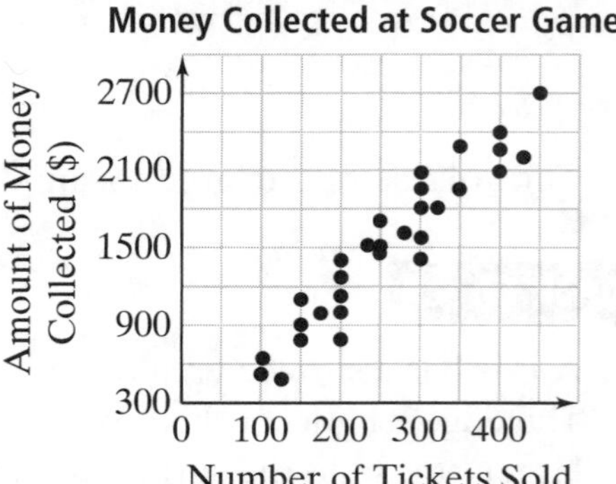

Name ______________________ Class ______________ Date ______________

Examples

❷ Making Scatter Plots Make a scatter plot for the data.

Miles Traveled and Gas used

Gas (gal)	Miles
5	150
4	112
7	217
3	87
8	216
5	155

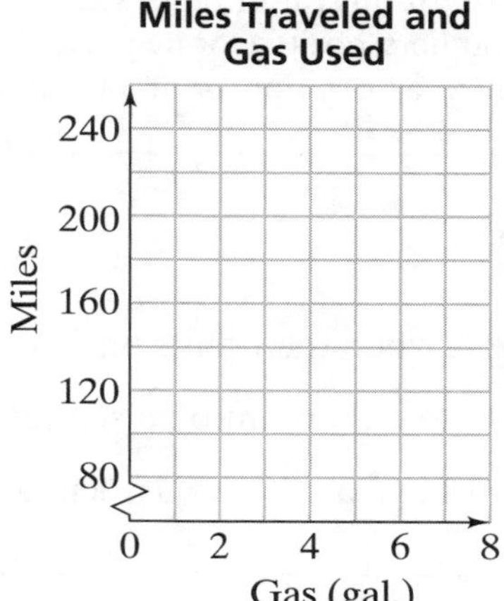

Step 1 Use the horizontal scale to show the ______________.

Use the vertical scale to represent the ______________.

Step 2 Plot each data pair (5, 150) represents a data pair.

Quick Check

2. Make a scatter plot for the data below.

Age(yr)	1	15	6	19	12	3	5	13	20	6
Sleep Time (h)	15	8.5	9.5	7	9.25	12	11	9	7	9.75

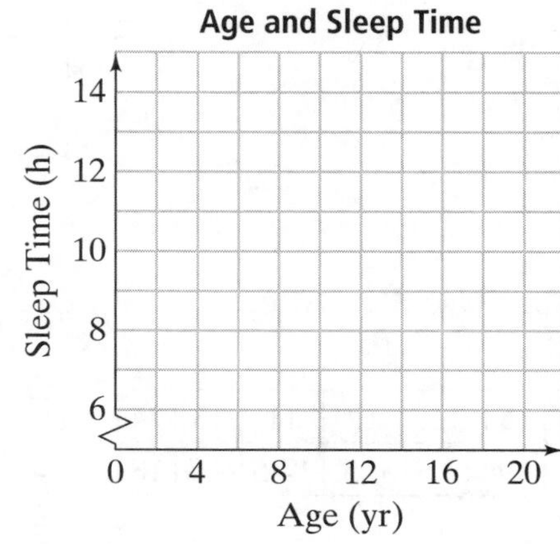

Name ______________________ Class ______________ Date ____________

Lesson 10-2

Analyzing Scatter Plots

Lesson Objective	**Common Core Standard**
To describe patterns in scatter plots, such as clustering, outliers, positive or negative association, linear association, or nonlinear association	Statistics and Probability: 8.SP.2

Vocabulary

Clustering is when the points on a scatter plot are ______________________

An outlier is a data point on a scatter plot that is ______________________

Data points have a positive association if ______________________

____

Data points have a negative association if ______________________

____

No association in data is when ______________________

Example

1 Identifying Clustering and Outliers Make a scatter plot for the data. Identify any clustering or outliers in the data.

Weekly Time Watching Television

Age (yr)	3	4	4	4	5	5	5	6	6	7
Time (hr)	2	1	2	3	1	2	3	2	3	8

Clustering occurs between the ages ☐ and ☐.

An outlier occurs at ☐.

Weekly Time Watching Television of Children of Different Ages

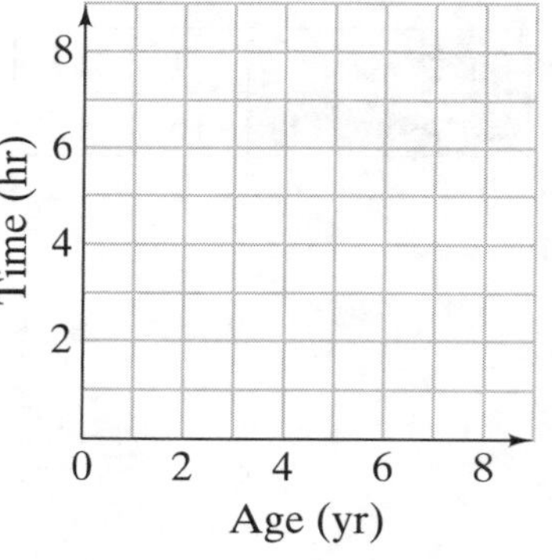

Quick Check

1. Make a scatter plot for the data in the table. Use the scatter plot to identify any clustering or outliers.

Age (yr)	13	12	13	14	13	12	12	15	11	12	11	13	14
Time (min)	10.2	12	11	10	10.6	11	11.3	9	13.5	6.5	12.5	9.5	18

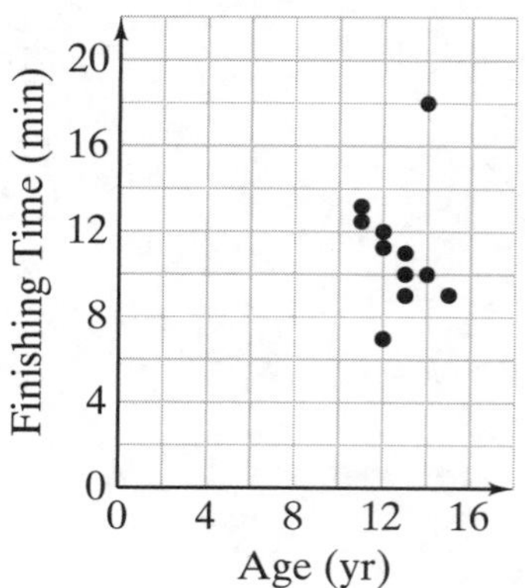

Name ____________________ Class ____________ Date ____________

Example

❷ Describing Associations in Scatterplots Make a scatterplot for each set of data. Describe the pattern of association that the scatterplot shows. Tell whether the data have a linear association or a nonlinear association.

a. (0, 100), (4, 50), (1.5, 80), (3, 60)
(2, 60), (1, 90), (2, 80)

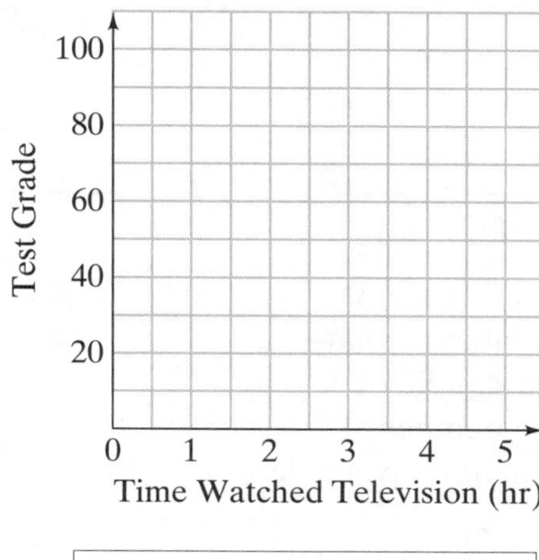

b. (5, 5), (8, 8), (1, 3), (3, 4)
(0, 2), (4, 6), (6, 7)

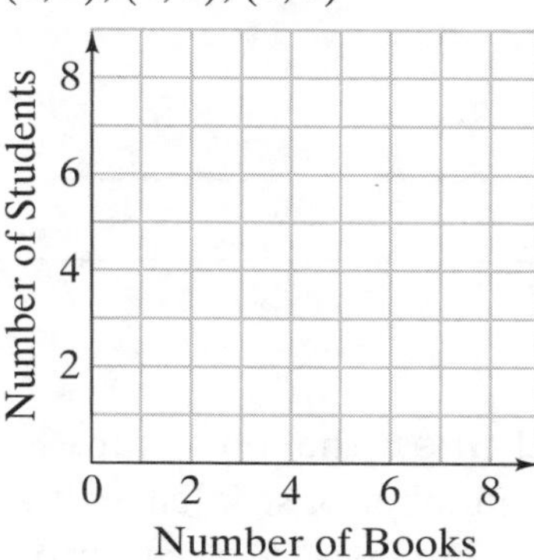

Quick Check

2. Make a scatter plot for the data. Describe the pattern of association that the scatter plot shows.

Latitude (°B)	0	32	12	15	22	20	45	37	49
Temperature (°F)	95	75	98	90	88	85	63	79	59

Maximum Daily August Temperatures in Northern Latitudes

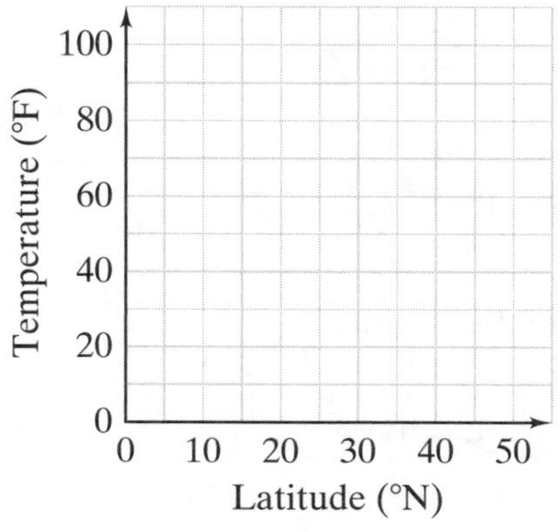

3. Make a scatter plot for the data. Tell whether the data show a linear association or a nonlinear association
(0, 3), (6, 55), (2, 9), (1, 2.5),
(3, 10), (5, 27), (4, 15), (5.5, 40)

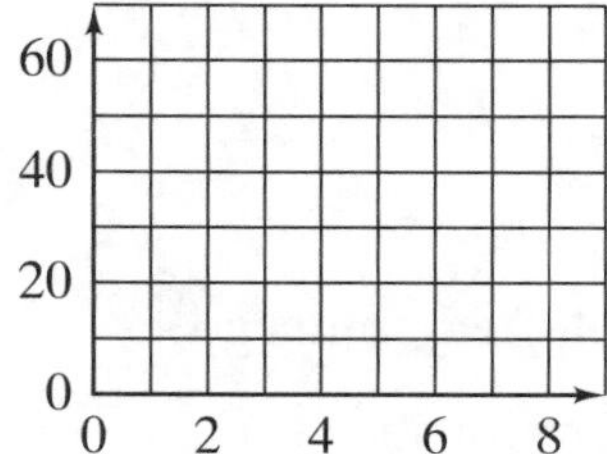

Name ______________________ Class ______________ Date ______________

Lesson 10-3

Modeling Data With Lines

Lesson Objective	Common Core Standards
To assess the fit of a trend line on a scatter plot and to use trend lines to estimate and make predictions	Statistics and Probability: 8.SP.2, 8.SP.3

Vocabulary

A trend line is ____

____

Examples

1 **Drawing Trend Lines** The table at the left shows the number of years worked and the number of sick leave days available for a sample of employees of a company. Use a scatter plot to predict the number of sick leave days an employee who has worked 30 years will have available.

Years Worked	Sick Leave (days)
1	12
8	70
12	140
17	170
21	230
23	210
26	310

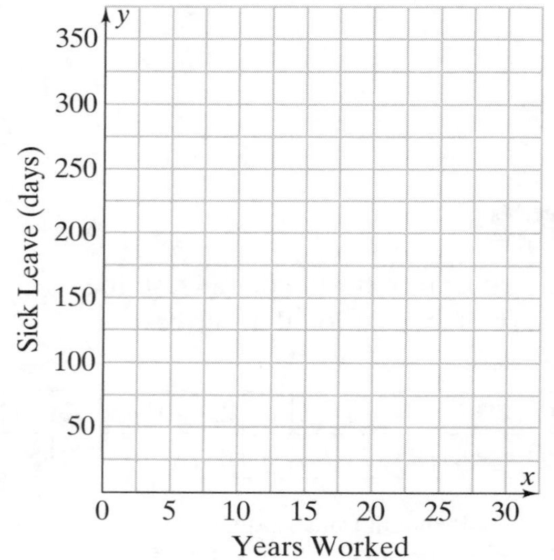

Step 1 Plot each data pair.

Step 2 The plotted points go ☐ from ☐ to ☐. This scatter plot shows a ☐, ☐ association.

Step 3 Draw a line with positive slope. Make sure there are about as many points above the line as there are below it.

Step 4 Find ☐ on the horizontal axis. Move up to the trend line. Then move left to the vertical axis.

An employee who has worked 30 years with the company should have ☐ days of sick leave available.

Name ______________________ Class ______________ Date ______________

❷ **Assessing the Fit of Trend Lines** In the scatter plots below, Jay and Aaron each drew a different trend line to approximate the relationship between monthly meeting attendance and reward points for their scout group. Which trend line appears to be a better fit? Explain.

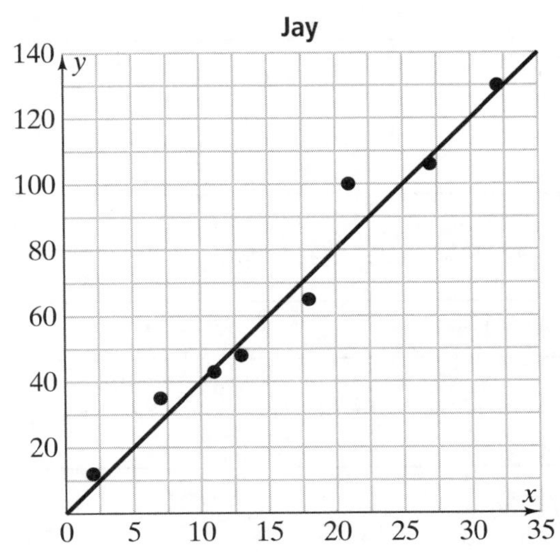

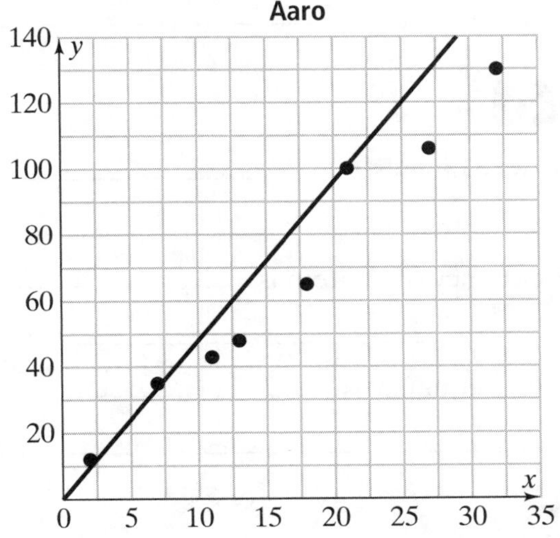

[ ] trend line has about the same number of points above it as below it. So [ ] trend line appears to be a better fit.

Quick Check

1. The table shows the age and height of a sample of girls. Use a scatter plot to predict the height of a girl who is 9 years old. ________

Age and Height of Girls

Age (yr)	2	7	11	13	14	17	15	5	18
Height (in.)	33	45	56	57	61	63	66	43	65

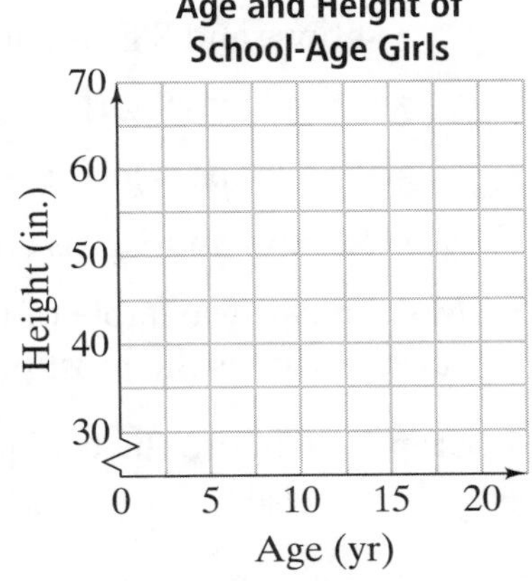

2. The scatter plot shows the results of a survey about the relationship between the number of hours spent reading and the number of hours spent watching television. Draw a trend line that fits the data better than the one shown.

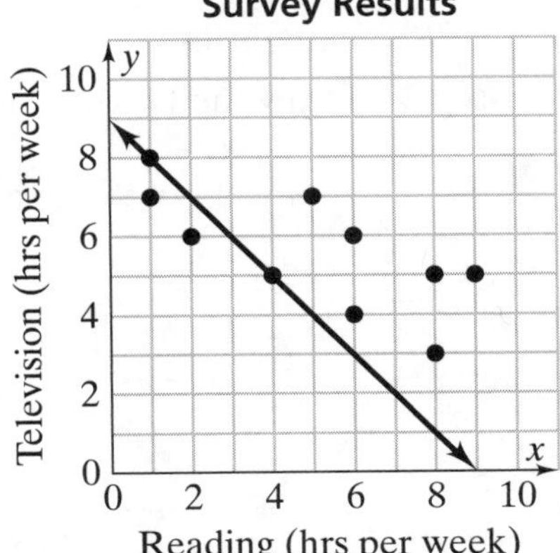

Name ______________________ Class ______________ Date ______________

Lesson 10-4

Two-Way Tables

Lesson Objective	**Common Core Standard**
To construct and interpret two-way frequency tables and two-way relative frequency tables	Statistics and Probability: 8.SP.4

Vocabulary

A two-way table is ______________________________

____

The frequency of an item is ______________________________

____

Relative frequency is ______________________________

____

Examples

1 Making a Frequency Table Fifty students were surveyed about their favorite flavors of ice cream.

- 4 boys and 8 girls chose chocolate as their favorite flavor.
- 2 boys and 9 girls chose rocky road as their favorite flavor.
- 8 boys and 4 girls chose vanilla as their favorite flavor.
- 12 boys and 3 girls chose strawberry as their favorite flavor.

Make a two-way table of frequencies for the data. According to the survey, what is the most popular flavor of ice cream?

Step 1 Choose the categories.
Use ☐ and ☐ as one set of categories. Use ☐, ☐, ☐, and ☐ as the other set of categories.

Step 2 Draw the two-way table. Fill in the table using the data above.

☐ has ☐ votes. ☐ is the most popular flavor.

Name ______________________ Class ______________ Date ______________

❷ Making a Relative Frequency Table To design a school decal, the principal surveyed students about their favorite colors and shapes. The frequency table shows the results. Is there evidence that students who like blue are more likely to like a round decal than a triangular one? Explain.

Favorite Color

Favorite Shape	Blue	Red	Green	Total
Circle	4	3	2	**9**
Square	3	5	1	**9**
Triangle	2	2	3	**7**
Total	**9**	**10**	**6**	**25**

Step 1 Make a two-way table of relative frequencies. Find the relative frequencies or each ______. Divide each frequency by its corresponding column total.

Favorite Color

Favorite Shape	Blue	Red	Green
Circle			
Square			
Triangle			
Total			

Step 2 Analyze the results. According to the table, ______, or ______%, of the students who favor blue also like circles. ______, or ______%, of the students who favor blue also like triangles.

Step 3 Draw a conclusion. For the students surveyed, there is evidence that ______ students who liked blue preferred a ______ decal than a ______ one.

Quick Check

1. Thirty students were surveyed about their favorite type of lunch. Six girls and 8 boys chose turkey sandwiches. Seven girls and 3 boys chose grilled chicken. Four girls and 2 boys chose veggie pizza. Make a two-way table of frequencies for the data. According to the survey, what is the least popular lunch choice?

	Turkey Sandwich	Grilled Chicken	Veggie Pizza	Total
Girls				
Boys				
Total				

____

____

2. Use the data from Example 2. Is there evidence that students who favor red are more likely to prefer a triangular decal than a square one? Explain your reasoning.

____

____

____

A Note to the Student:

This section of your workbook contains a series of pages that support your mathematics understandings for each chapter and lesson presented in your student edition.

- Practice pages provide additional practice for every lesson.
- Guided Problem Solving pages lead you through a step-by-step solution to an application problem in each lesson.
- Vocabulary pages contain a variety of activities to increase your reading and math understanding, ranging from graphic organizers to vocabulary review puzzles.

Name ________________ Class ________________ Date ________________

Practice 1-1

Rational Numbers

Write the decimal expansion of each fraction.

1. $\frac{12}{36}$ ________
2. $\frac{20}{25}$ ________
3. $\frac{28}{60}$ ________
4. $\frac{14}{80}$ ________
5. $\frac{77}{99}$ ________
6. $-\frac{21}{56}$ ________
7. $-\frac{15}{33}$ ________
8. $\frac{5}{40}$ ________
9. $\frac{15}{60}$ ________
10. $\frac{7}{21}$ ________
11. $\frac{24}{50}$ ________
12. $-\frac{2}{3}$ ________
13. $\frac{22}{80}$ ________
14. $-\frac{30}{48}$ ________
15. $\frac{11}{12}$ ________
16. $\frac{14}{22}$ ________
17. $\frac{35}{40}$ ________
18. $-\frac{28}{72}$ ________
19. $-\frac{42}{54}$ ________
20. $\frac{14}{30}$ ________
21. $\frac{9}{40}$ ________

Write each decimal as a mixed number or fraction in simplest form.

22. 0.006 ________
23. −4.8 ________
24. 0.97 ________
25. 0.4 ________
26. 9.05 ________
27. −0.28 ________
28. 3.082 ________
29. −1.41 ________
30. 4.23 ________
31. 8.05 ________
32. −3.02 ________
33. 7.13 ________

Solve.

34. The eighth grade held a magazine sale to raise money for their spring trip. They wanted each student to sell subscriptions. After the first day of the sale, 25 out of 125 students turned in subscription orders. Write a rational number in simplest form to express the student response on the first day.

____

35. Pete wanted to win the prize for selling the most subscriptions. Of 240 subscriptions sold, Pete sold 30. Write a rational number in simplest form to express Pete's part of the total sales.

____

Name _______________ Class _______________ Date _______________

1-1 • Guided Problem Solving

GPS Student Page 6, Exercise 33:

Population In 2003, 0.219 of the people in the United States were younger than 15 years old. Write the decimal as a fraction.

Understand

1. What are you being asked to do?

____

Plan and Carry Out

2. Write the fraction with a denominator of one.

____

3. How many digits are there to the right of the decimal point?

____

4. Multiply the numerator and denominator by 1,000.

____

5. Can the fraction be simplified? Why or why not?

____

____

Check

6. Is your answer reasonable? Write the decimal in word form.

____

____

____

Solve Another Problem

7. A group of teenagers is surveyed about their preference for music performers. Of the teenagers surveyed, 0.275 preferred individual artists. Express the decimal as a fraction.

____

Name ______________________ Class ______________ Date ______________

Practice 1-2

Irrational Numbers and Square Roots

Find the two square roots of each number.

1. 81
2. $\frac{9}{49}$
3. $\frac{1}{121}$
4. 289

Estimate the value of each expression to the nearest integer and to the nearest tenth.

5. $\sqrt{5}$
6. $-\sqrt{10}$
7. $\sqrt{3}$
8. $-\sqrt{245}$
9. $-\sqrt{21}$
10. $-\sqrt{52}$

Which number is greater?

11. $\sqrt{60}$, 7.5
12. $\sqrt{35}$, 6.1
13. $\sqrt{44}$, 4.5
14. $\sqrt{84}$, 9.3

Find each square root. Round to the nearest tenth if necessary.

15. $\sqrt{130}$
16. $\sqrt{8}$
17. $\sqrt{144}$
18. $\sqrt{160}$
19. $\sqrt{182}$
20. $\sqrt{256}$
21. $\sqrt{301}$
22. $\sqrt{350}$

Identify each number as *rational* or *irrational*.

23. $\sqrt{16}$
24. $\sqrt{11}$
25. $\sqrt{196}$
26. $\frac{4}{5}$
27. $0.\overline{712}$
28. -8
29. $\sqrt{3}$
30. 5.2
31. 0.1010010001 . . .
32. $-\sqrt{25}$
33. $\sqrt{306}$
34. 2.7064

Use $s = 20\sqrt{273 + T}$ to estimate the speed of sound s in meters per second for each Celsius temperature T. Round to the nearest integer.

35. 37°C
36. -1°C
37. 15°C
38. -18°C

Name ______________________ Class ______________ Date ______________

1-2 • Guided Problem Solving

GPS Student Page 13, Exercise 39:

Ferris Wheels The formula $d = 1.23\sqrt{h}$ represents the distance in miles d you can see from h feet above ground. On the London Eye Ferris Wheel, you are 450 ft above ground. To the nearest tenth of a mile, how far can you see?

Understand

1. What are you being asked to find?

____

____

____

Plan and Carry Out

2. What is the formula?

____

3. What is the height?

____

4. Substitute known values into the formula.

____

5. Simplify using a calculator. Round to the nearest tenth.

____

Check

6. Use estimation to check your answer.

____

____

____

____

Solve Another Problem

7. The formula $d = 1.23\sqrt{h}$ represents the distance in miles d you can see from h feet above ground. At the top of the Ferris wheel at Cedar Point, you are 140 ft above ground. To the nearest tenth of a mile, how far can you see?

____

Name ____________ Class ____________ Date ____________

Practice 1-3

Cube Roots

Find the cube root of each number.

1. 64 ________
2. 729 ________
3. -343 ________
4. $\frac{1}{8}$ ________
5. $-1{,}000$ ________
6. $\frac{27}{64}$ ________

Solve each equation by finding the value of x.

7. $x^3 = -1$ ________
8. $x^3 = 216$ ________
9. $x^3 = 1{,}728$ ________
10. $x^3 = \frac{8}{27}$ ________
11. $x^3 = \frac{64}{125}$ ________
12. $x^3 = \frac{125}{512}$ ________

Find the side length of each cube.

13. 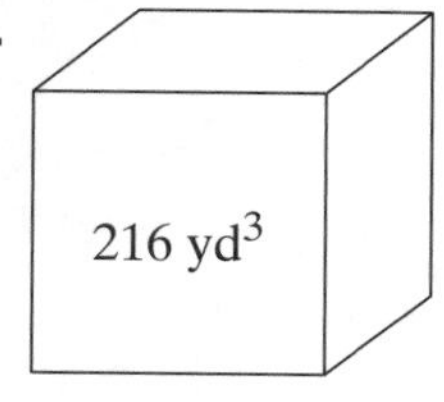

____

14. 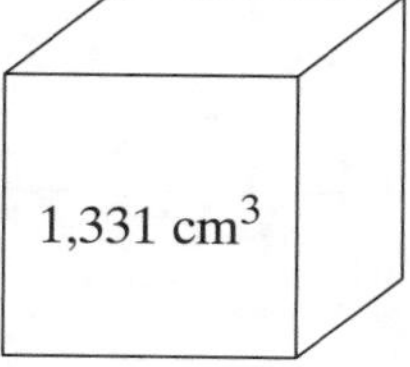

____

15. A bottle of cologne comes in a cube-shaped box that has a volume of 64 cubic inches. What is the length of one side of the box?

____

16. A cube-shaped shipping crate has a volume of 27 cubic feet. What are the dimensions of the crate?

____

17. What is a reasonable estimate for the volume of a number cube: 8 cm^3, 27 in^3, or 1 ft^3?

____

18. A cube-shaped terrarium has a volume of $\frac{27}{64}$ cubic feet. What is the length of its sides?

____

Name ______________________ Class ______________ Date ______________

1-3 • Guided Problem Solving

GPS Student Page 16, Exercise 21:

Find the cube root of 0.216.

Understand

1. When you cube a number, how many times is the number used as a factor?

2. What is a cube root?

Plan and Carry Out

3. Write 0.216 as a fraction.

4. What is the cube root of the numerator?

5. What is the cube root of the denominator?

6. What is the cube root of the fraction?

7. Write the fraction as a decimal.

Check

8. Find the cube of your answer. Is it equal to 0.216?

Solve Another Problem

9. Find the cube root of 0.125.

Name ______________________ Class ______________ Date ______________

Practice 1-4

The Pythagorean Theorem

Find the length of the hypotenuse of each triangle. If necessary, round to the nearest tenth.

1. 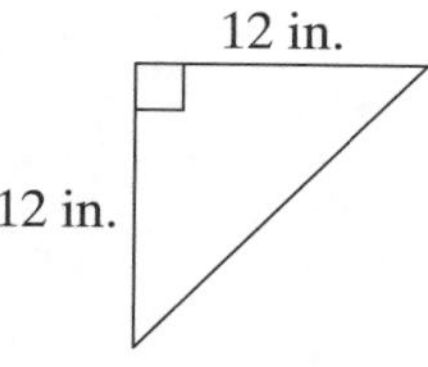

____

2. 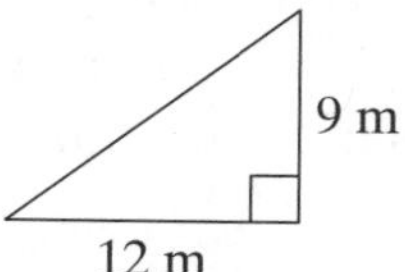

____

3. 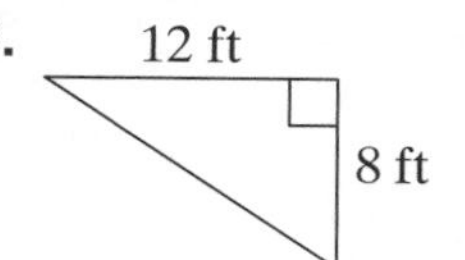

____

4. 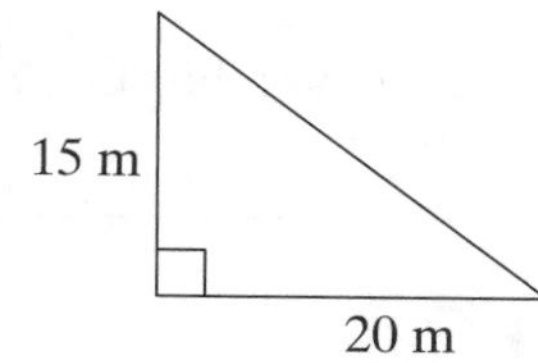

____

Let *a* and *b* represent the lengths of the legs of a right triangle. Find the length of the hypotenuse. If necessary, round to the nearest tenth.

5. $a = 14, b = 18$ ______________

6. $a = 7, b = 23$ ______________

7. $a = 15, b = 8$ ______________

Solve.

8. A circus performer walks on a tightrope 25 feet above the ground. The tightrope is supported by two beams and two support cables. If the distance between each beam and the base of its support cable is 15 feet, what is the length of the support cable? Round to the nearest foot.

____

You are given three circles, as shown. Points *A, B, C, D, E, F,* and *G* lie on the same line. Find each length to the nearest tenth.

9. *HD* ______________

10. *IE* ______________

11. *JD* ______________

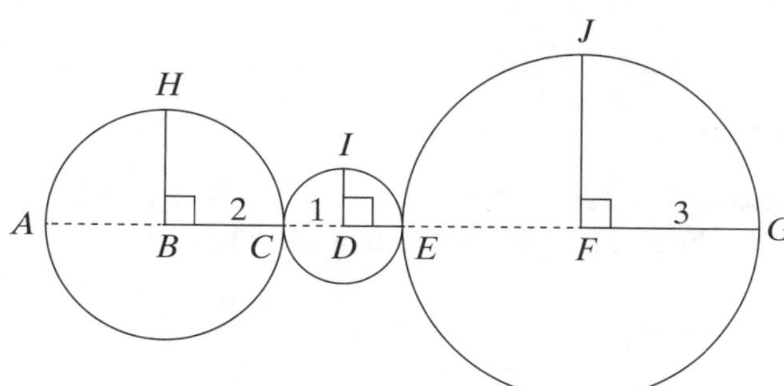

Name ______________________ Class ______________ Date ______________

1-4 • Guided Problem Solving

GPS Student Page 23, Exercise 20:

Two hikers start a trip from a camp walking 1.5 km due east. They turn due north and walk 1.7 km to a waterfall. To the nearest tenth of a kilometer, how far is the waterfall from the camp?

Understand

1. Distances are given for walking in which two directions?

____

2. What are you being asked to find?

____

Plan and Carry Out

3. Draw a picture.
4. Write the formula for the Pythagorean Theorem. ______________
5. What part of the triangle has a missing length? ______________
6. Substitute known values into the Pythagorean Theorem.

____

7. Simplify. ______________________________
8. Add. ______________________________
9. Find the positive square root of the hypotenuse, the missing length.

____

10. Estimate, or simplify, using a calculator. ______________
11. How far is the waterfall from the camp? ______________

Check

12. Is your answer reasonable? Use mental math to check.

____

Solve Another Problem

13. Leah starts at her house and walks 8 blocks east to the library and then 12 blocks south to school. How far is she from her house?

____

Name ______________________ Class ______________ Date ______________

Practice 1-5

Using The Pythagorean Theorem

Find the missing leg length. If necessary, round the answer to the nearest tenth.

1. 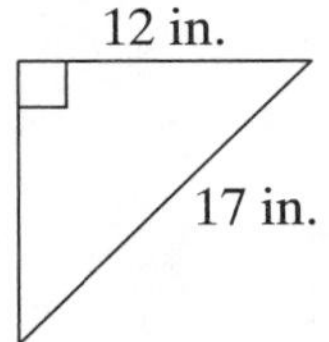

2. 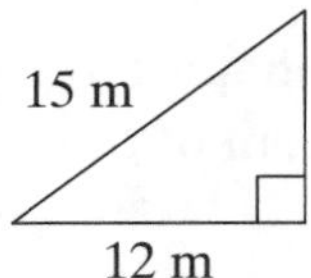

3. 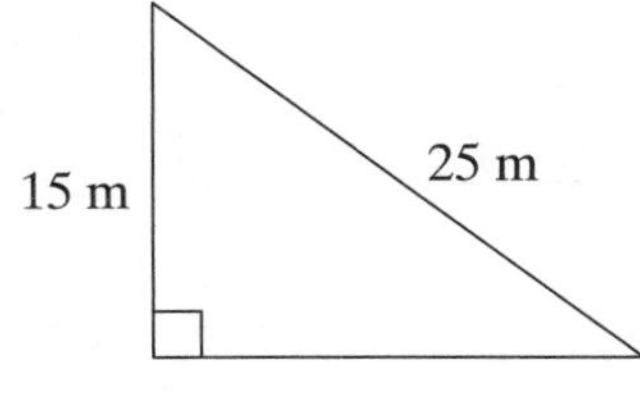

4. 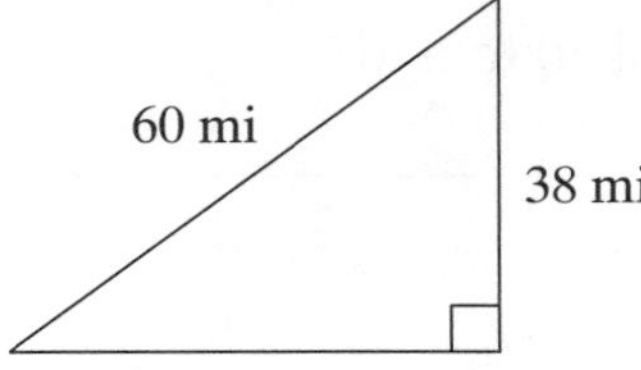

For Exercises 5–14, *a* and *b* represent leg lengths and *c* represents the length of the hypotenuse. Find the missing leg length. If necessary, round to the nearest tenth.

5. $a = 8$ cm, $c = 12$ cm

6. $b = 9$ in., $c = 15$ in.

7. $b = 5$ m, $c = 25$ m

8. $a = 36$ in., $c = 39$ in.

9. $a = 10$ m, $c = 20$ m

10. $b = 24$ mm, $c = 25$ mm

11. $a = 9$ yd, $c = 41$ yd

12. $b = 10$ cm, $c = 26$ cm

13. $b = 27$ yd, $c = 130$ yd

14. $a = 11$ mi, $c = 61$ mi

15. One leg of a right triangle is 4 ft long and the hypotenuse is 5 ft long. Ritchie uses $\sqrt{4^2 + 5^2}$ to find the length of the other leg. Is Ritchie correct in his approach? Why or why not?

Name ____________________ Class ____________ Date ____________

1-5 • Guided Problem Solving

GPS Student Page 29, Exercise 13:

A 10-ft-long slide is attached to a deck that is 5 ft high. Find the distance from the bottom of the deck to the bottom of the slide to the nearest tenth.

Understand

1. What two lengths are given in the problem?

____

2. What are you being asked to find?

____

Plan and Carry Out

3. Draw a picture of the slide, deck, and ground.
4. What kind of a triangle is formed by the picture? ____________
5. Is the unknown length a leg or hypotenuse of the triangle? ____________
6. Write down the formula for the Pythagorean Theorem. ____________
7. Substitute values from your picture into the Pythagorean Theorem. ____________
8. Simplify. ____________
9. Use a calculator to find the square root. Round to the nearest tenth. ____________
10. What is the distance from the bottom of the deck to the bottom of the slide?

____

Check

11. Use the Pythagorean Theorem to check the length of the slide based on your answer, and the height of the deck. Is your answer the same as the given slide length? Why or why not?

____

____

Solve Another Problem

12. Mason is on the southwest corner of a 90° intersection. One street in the intersection is 23 ft wide. If Mason crosses diagonally to the northeast corner, he will walk 34 ft. Find the width of the other street. If necessary, round your answer to the nearest tenth.

____

Name ______________________ Class ______________ Date ______________

Practice 1-6

Converse of the Pythagorean Theorem

Is it possible to construct a triangle with the given side lengths? Explain.

1. 2 yd, 3 yd, 7 yd
2. 4 cm, 4 cm, 8 cm
3. 12 ft, 14 ft, 15 ft
4. 5.4 m, 8.6 m, 13 m
5. $\frac{4}{5}$ in., $3\frac{2}{5}$ in., 4 in.
6. 18 mm, 25 mm, 52 mm

Determine whether the given lengths can be side lengths of a right triangle. Explain.

7. 6 ft, 10 ft, 12 ft
8. 10 in., 24 in., 26 in.
9. 20 m, 21 m, 29 m
10. 15 cm, 17 cm, 21 cm
11. 14 ft, 22.5 ft, 26.5 ft
12. 12 yd, 35 yd, 38 yd

Determine whether the triangles are right triangles. Explain.

13.

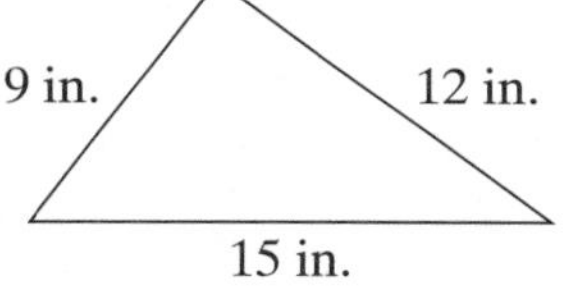

14.

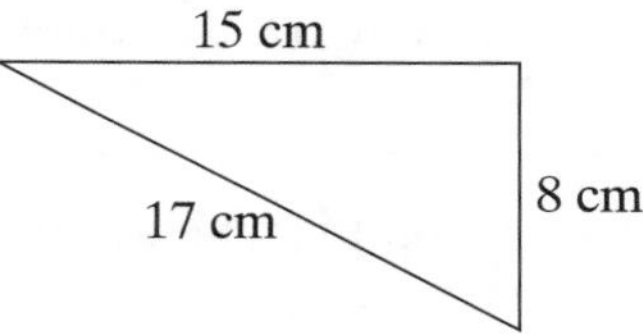

15. A company is designing a new logo in the shape of a triangle. Two of the sides each measure 2 cm. Which of the following is a possible measure for the third side: 3 cm, 4 cm, 5 cm?

16. Three nature trails intersect to form a triangle around a park. The lengths of the trails are 2.8 mi, 3.2 mi, and 4.1 mi. Do the trails form a right triangle? Explain.

17. The sides of a triangular game board are 1 ft, 1 ft, and $\sqrt{2}$ ft in length. Is the game board in the shape of a right triangle? Explain.

18. How do you know that the lengths 6 in., 8 in., and 25 in. cannot form a right triangle without using the Converse of the Pythagorean Theorem?

Name ______________________ Class ______________ Date ______________

1-6 • Converse of the Pythagorean Theorem

GPS Student Page 34, Exercise 27:

You can use the squares of the lengths of the sides of a triangle to find whether the triangle is acute or obtuse.

If $a^2 + b^2 < c^2$, then the triangle is obtuse.
If $a^2 + b^2 > c^2$, then the triangle is acute.

In both cases, c represents the length of the longest side of the triangle. The lengths of the sides of a triangle are 5 m, 6 m, and 7 m. Is the triangle *acute*, *right*, or *obtuse*?

Understand

1. What are you being asked to do?

____

____

2. If $a^2 + b^2 < c^2$, what is true about the triangle?

____

3. If $a^2 + b^2 > c^2$, what is true about the triangle?

____

4. If $a^2 + b^2 = c^2$, what is true about the triangle?

____

Plan and Carry Out

5. Write the values for a, b, and c. ______________
6. What is the value for $a^2 + b^2$? ______________
7. What is the value for c^2? ______________
8. Compare the values for $a^2 + b^2$ and c^2. $a^2 + b^2$ ____ c^2
9. Is the triangle *acute*, *right*, or *obtuse*? ______________

Check

10. How can you check your answer? ______________

____

Solve Another Problem

11. The lengths of the sides of a triangle are 6 cm, 24 cm, and 25 cm. Is the triangle *acute*, *right*, or *obtuse*? ______________

Name ______________________ Class ______________ Date ______________

Practice 1-7

Distance in the Coordinate Plane

Find the distance between each pair of points. If necessary, round to the nearest tenth.

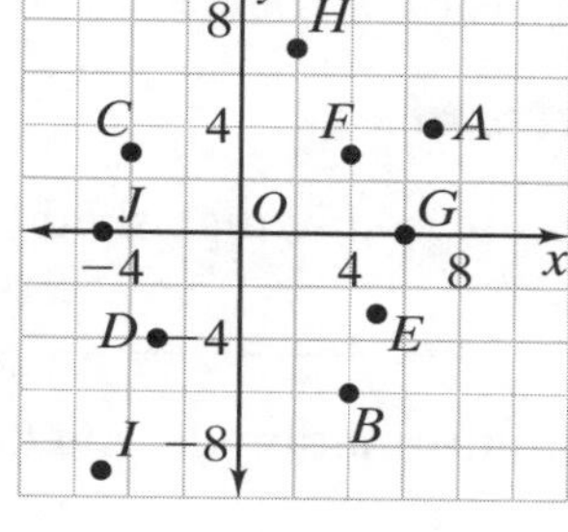

1. $A(7, 4)$ and $H(2, 7)$

____

2. $C(-4, 3)$ and $G(6, 0)$

____

3. $B(4, -6)$ and $D(-3, -4)$

____

4. $E(5, -3)$ and $C(-4, 3)$

____

5. $F(4, 3)$ and $G(6, 0)$

____

6. $A(7, 4)$ and $D(-3, -4)$

____

7. $B(4, -6)$ and $I(-5, -9)$

____

8. $E(5, -3)$ and $F(4, 3)$

____

9. Arnie plotted points on the graph on the right. He placed his pencil point at A. He can move either right or down any whole number of units until he reaches point B. In how many ways can he do this?

____

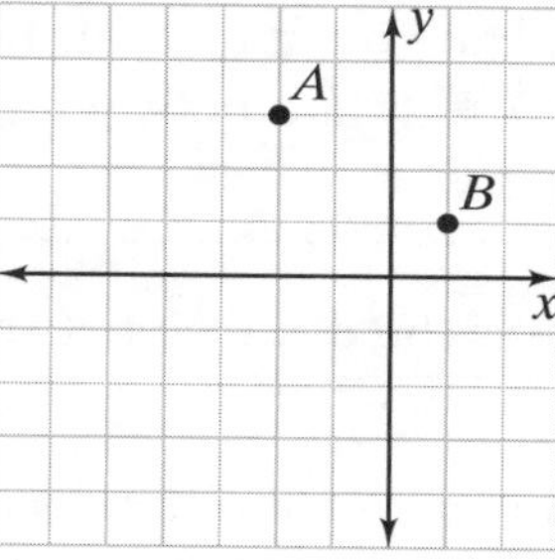

10. Marika had to draw ΔABC that fit several requirements.
    a. It must fit in the box shown.
    b. The endpoints of $\overline{AB}$ have coordinates $A(-2, 0)$ and $B(2, 0)$.
    c. Point C must be on the y-axis and its y-coordinate is an integer.

    Name all the points that could be point C.

____

____

____

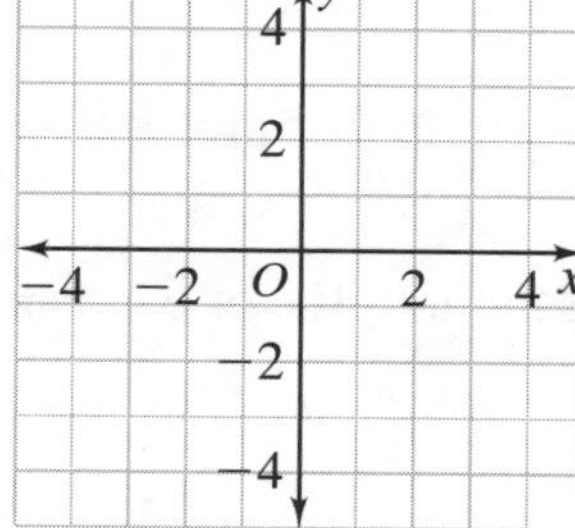

Name ______________________ Class ______________ Date ______________

1-7 • Guided Problem Solving

GPS Student Page 40, Exercise 15:

On a graph, the points (4, −2), (7, −2), (9, −5), and (2, −5) are connected in order to form a trapezoid. To the nearest tenth, what is its perimeter?

Understand

1. What are you being asked to do?

____

2. What information do you know?

____

Plan and Carry Out

3. Plot the points on the graph.

4. How can you find the distance between points (4, −2) and (7, −2) and between the points (2, −5) and (9, −5)?

____

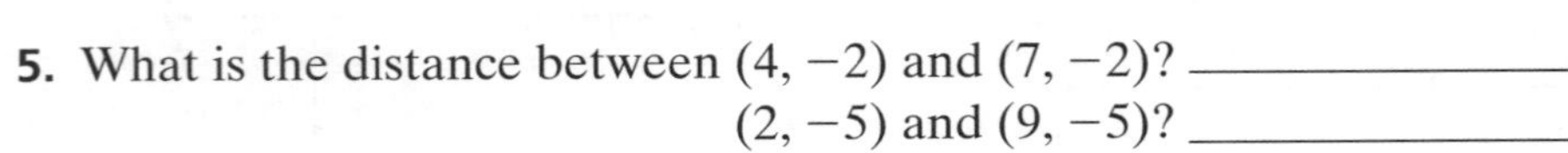

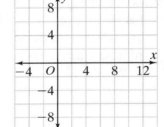

5. What is the distance between (4, −2) and (7, −2)? ____________
(2, −5) and (9, −5)? ____________

6. How can you find the distance between points (4, −2) and (2, −5) and between the points (7, −2) and (9, −5)?

____

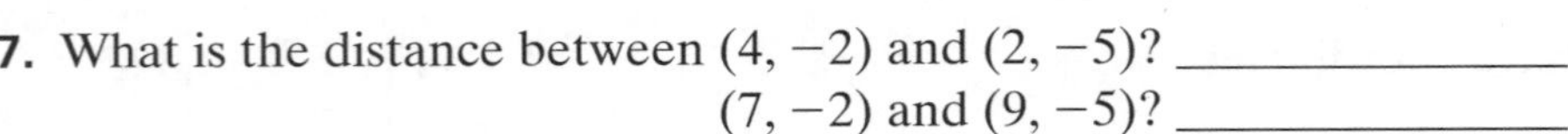

7. What is the distance between (4, −2) and (2, −5)? ____________
(7, −2) and (9, −5)? ____________

8. Add the lengths of each side. What is the perimeter? ____________

Check

9. Is every point plotted correctly to create the figure?

____

Solve Another Problem

10. Plot the following points on the grid at the right. Connect the points in order, connecting the last point to the first. What is the perimeter of the shape formed? (−3, −3), (3, −3), (4, 2), (−4, 2)

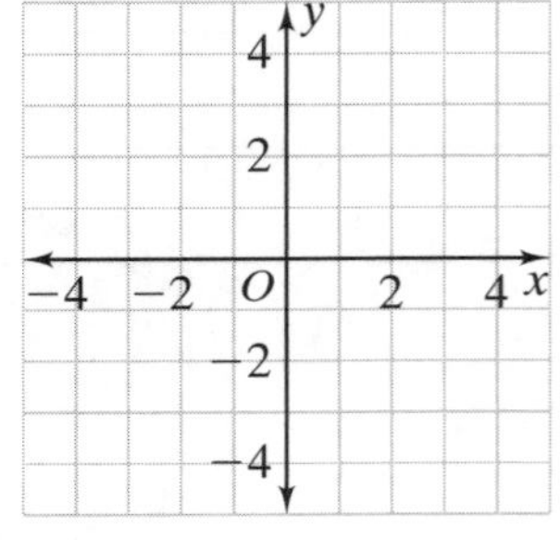

____

Name ______________________ Class ______________ Date ______________

1A: Graphic Organizer

For use before Lesson 1-1

Study Skill When you begin a new chapter in any textbook, take a few minutes to look through the lessons. Get an idea of how the lessons in the chapter are related. When you have completed the chapter, use the notes you have taken to review the material.

Write your answers.

1. What is the chapter title? ______________________
2. How many lessons are there in this chapter? ______________________
3. What is the topic of the Test-Taking Strategies page? ______________________
4. Complete the graphic organizer below as you work through the chapter.
   - In the center, write the title of the chapter.
   - When you begin a lesson, write the lesson name in a rectangle.
   - When you complete a lesson, write a skill or key concept in a circle linked to that lesson block.
   - When you complete the chapter, use this graphic organizer to help you review.

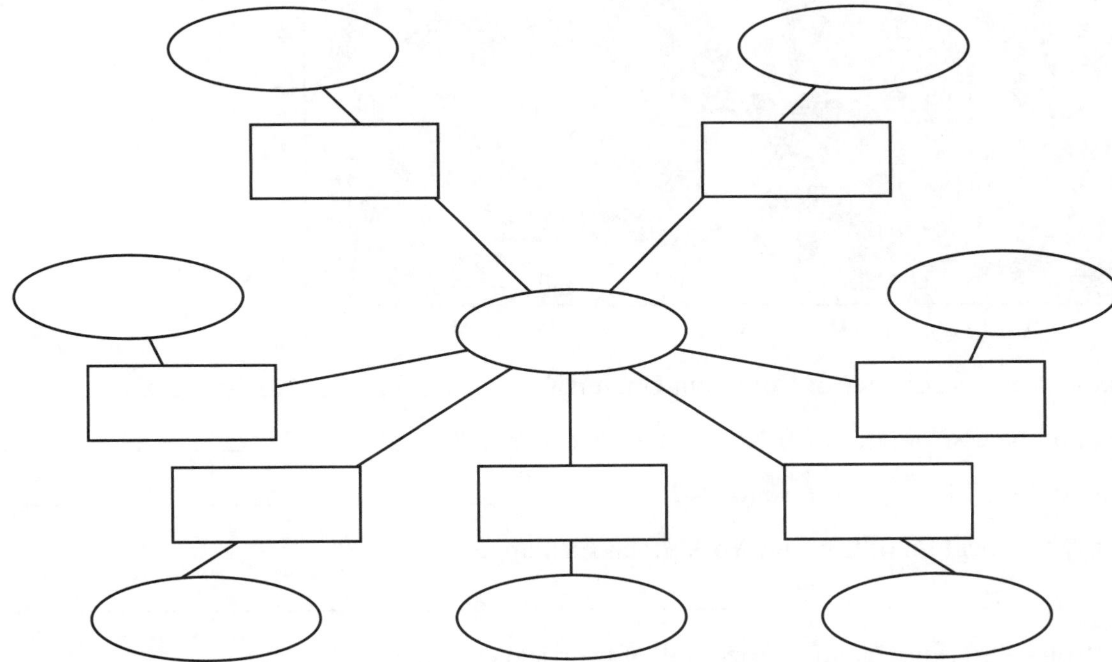

Name ______________________ Class ______________ Date ______________

1B: Reading Comprehension

For use after Lesson 1-7

Study Skill Finish one assignment before starting another. It may help if you begin with the most difficult assignment first.

The map below is a coordinate map of New York City. The horizontal scale uses letters and the vertical scale uses numbers to identify various locations. Use the map to answer the questions below. The letters are typically written first, followed by the numbers.

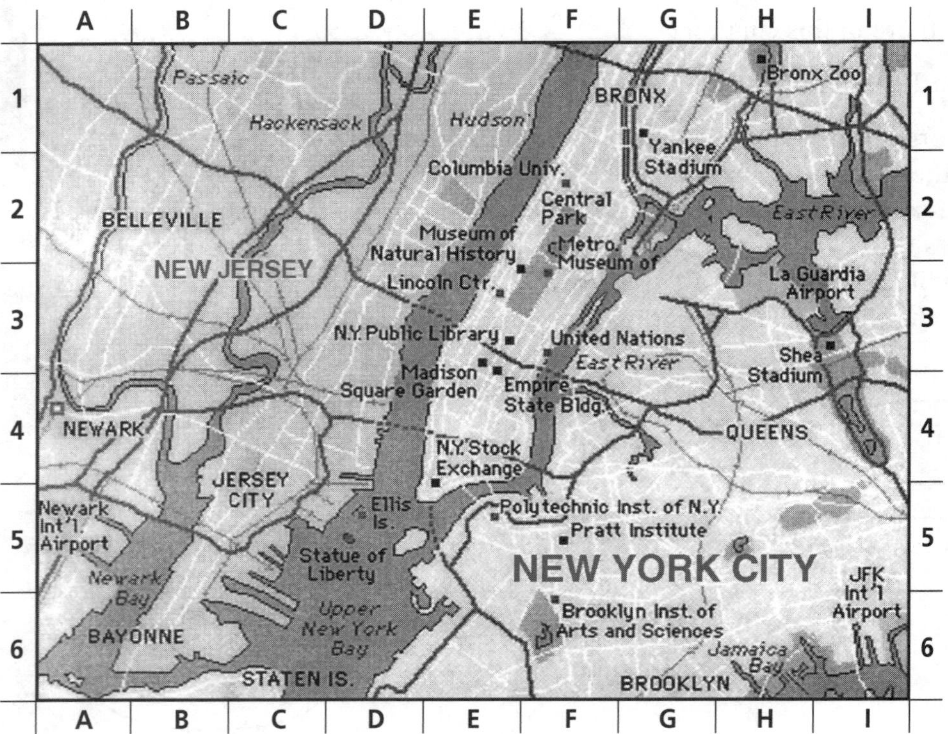

1. What are the coordinates of Columbia University? ______________

2. What are the coordinates of JFK International Airport? ______________

3. What landmark is located close to H4? ______________

4. Identify the location of the New York Stock Exchange.

____

5. The Bronx Zoo is how many horizontal and vertical coordinates from the Statue of Liberty?

____

6. **High-Use Academic Words** In Exercise 4, what does the word *identify* mean?

   a. to show that you recognize something **b.** to have power over

Name ______________________ Class ______________ Date ______________

1C: Reading/Writing Math Symbols

For use after Lesson 1-7

Study Skill Learning is when you figure out how to get past an obstacle.

Vocabulary and Study Skills

Match each number in Column A with its word form in Column B.

	Column A		Column B
1.	8^3	A.	three raised to the seventh power
2.	0.307	B.	three and seven tenths
3.	$\sqrt[3]{8}$	C.	three hundred seven thousandths
4.	3.7	D.	eight cubed
5.	3^7	E.	the cube root of eight

Match each term in Column A with an appropriate example from Column B.

	Column A		Column B
6.	repeating decimal	F.	39.125
7.	ordered pair	G.	$\sqrt[3]{8}$
8.	perfect cube	H.	1.4142135...
9.	terminating decimal	I.	0.0333333...
10.	cube root	J.	64
11.	irrational number	K.	(0, −3)

Write out the following mathematical statements in word form.

12. $4^3 = 64$

____

13. $\sqrt[3]{125} = 5$

____

14. $6^2 > 3^3$

____

Name ______________________ Class ______________ Date ______________

1D: Visual Vocabulary Practice

For use after Lesson 1-4

High-Use Academic Words

Study Skill If a word is not in the glossary, use a dictionary to find its meaning.

Concept List

sum	table	estimate
evaluate	solve	classify
substitute	justify	compare

Write the concept that best describes each exercise. Choose from the concept list above.

1.

$$\frac{z}{8} = 7 - 2$$
$$\frac{z}{8} \times 8 = (7 - 2) \times 8$$
$$z = 5 \times 8$$
$$z = 40$$

____

2.

The World's Longest Rivers

Name	Country	Length
Nile	Egypt	4,160 mi
Amazon	Brazil	4,000 mi
Yangtze	China	3,964 mi

____

3.

You can write $\frac{2}{10}$ as $\frac{1}{5}$ because the two fractions are equivalent.

____

4.

$|-28| > 27$

____

5.

$$3a + 6 + (-4.25) + (-a) + 7 = 2a + 8.75$$

____

6.

$4n - (9 \div m)$ for $n = -3$ and $m = 7$

____

7.

$$x + 29\frac{5}{8} = 42\frac{1}{9}$$
$$x + 30 \approx 42$$
$$x \approx 12$$

____

8.

$6n + 12 = m$, for $n = 3$

$6(3) + 12 = m$

____

9.

$\sqrt{5}$ is an irrational number.
$\sqrt{9}$ is a rational number.

____

Name ______________________ Class ______________ Date ______________

1E: Vocabulary Check

For use after Lesson 1-7

Study Skill Strengthen your vocabulary. Use these pages and add cues and summaries by applying the Cornell Notetaking style.

Write the definition for each word or term at the right. To check your work, fold the paper back along the dotted line to see the correct answers.

perfect square

real numbers

Triangle Inequality Theorem

legs

irrational number

Vocabulary and Study Skills

Name ______________________ Class ______________ Date ______________

1E: Vocabulary Check (continued)

For use after Lesson 1-7

Write the vocabulary word or term for each definition. To check your work, fold the paper back along the dotted line to see the correct answers.

a number that is the square of an integer ______________________

the set of rational and irrational numbers ______________________

The sum of the lengths of any two sides of a triangle is greater than the length of the third side. ______________________

the two shorter sides of a right triangle ______________________

a number that cannot be written as the ratio of two integers ______________________

Name ______________________ Class ______________ Date ______________

1F: Vocabulary Review

For use with the Chapter Review

Study Skill Taking short breaks can help you stay focused. Every 30 minutes, take a 5-minute break, then return to studying.

I. Match the term in Column A with its definition in Column B.

Column A	Column B
1. quadrant	**A.** a decimal that repeats the same digit or group of digits forever
2. origin	**B.** the longest side in a right triangle, which is opposite the right angle
3. hypotenuse	**C.** any one of the four sections into which the coordinate plane is divided
4. real numbers	**D.** the point where the x-axis and the y-axis intersect, indicated by the ordered pair $(0, 0)$
5. Pythagorean Theorem	**E.** The sum of the lengths of any two sides of a triangle is greater than the length of the third side.
6. repeating decimal	**F.** a formula that describes the relationship of length between the legs and the hypotenuse, in a right triangle
7. Triangle Inequality Theorem	**G.** the set of numbers that includes rational and irrational numbers

II. Match the term in Column A with its definition in Column B.

Column A	Column B
1. perfect square	**A.** numbers that cannot be written in the form $\frac{a}{b}$, where a is any integer and b is any nonzero integer
2. coordinate plane	**B.** a decimal that stops
3. ordered pair	**C.** a number that is the cube of a whole number
4. rational numbers	**D.** a number that is the square of a whole number
5. terminating decimal	**E.** a number that can be written in the form $\frac{a}{b}$, where a is any integer and b is any nonzero integer
6. perfect cube	**F.** gives the coordinates of the location of a point
7. irrational numbers	**G.** a grid formed by the intersection of two number lines

Name ____________ Class ____________ Date ____________

Practice 2-1

Solving Two-Step Equations

Solve each equation.

1. $4r + 6 = 14$
2. $9y - 11 = 7$
3. $\frac{m}{4} + 6 = 3$
4. $-\frac{k}{9} + 6 = -4$
5. $-\frac{4}{5}b - 6 = -14$
6. $-\frac{v}{7} + 8 = 19$
7. $3.4t + 19.36 = -10.22$
8. $-\frac{n}{1.6} + 7.9 = 8.4$
9. $4.6b + 26.8 = 50.72$
10. $-\frac{a}{8.06} + 7.02 = 18.4$
11. $-2.06d + 18 = -10.84$
12. $-\frac{e}{95} + 6 = 4$

Write and solve an equation to answer each question.

13. Hugo received $100 for his birthday. He then saved $20 per week until he had a total of $460 to buy a printer. Use an equation to show how many weeks it took him to save the money.

14. A health club charges a $50 initial fee plus $2 for each visit. Moselle has spent a total of $144 at the health club this year. Use an equation to find how many visits she has made.

Solve each equation to find the value of the variable. Write the answer in the puzzle. Do not include any negative signs or any decimal points.

ACROSS

1. $6n - 12 = 2.4$
2. $\frac{n}{3} + 4.6 = 21.6$
4. $x - 3 = 51.29$
6. $2z + 2 = 7.6$

DOWN

1. $\frac{j}{5} - 14 = -9$
2. $3x - 2 = 169$
3. $\frac{x}{4} + 1 = 19$
4. $\frac{x}{3} + 4 = 22$
5. $2x - 2 = 182$

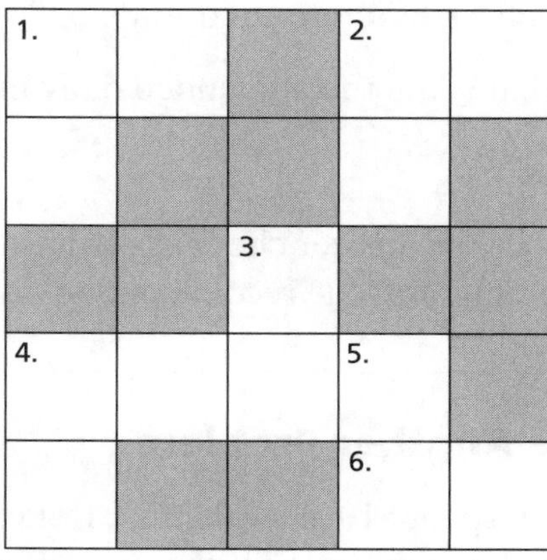

Name ______________________ Class ______________ Date ______________

2-1 • Guided Problem Solving

GPS Student Page 51, Exercise 21:

Nutrition According to the Food and Drug Administration, the recommended daily intake of iron is 18 mg. This is 4 less than twice the recommended daily intake of zinc. What is the recommended daily intake of zinc?

Understand

1. What is the recommended daily intake of iron? ______________________

2. What are you being asked to find? ______________________

   ____

3. Will the recommended daily intake of zinc be more or less than that of iron? ______________

Plan and Carry Out

4. Fill in the names of the minerals to help set up an equation.

   2 times ______________ − 4 = ______________

5. Write an equation, letting z represent the amount of zinc. ______________

6. To solve the equation, what do you do first?

   ____

7. To solve for the recommended amount of zinc, what do you need to do to the equation next? ______________________

8. What is the recommended daily intake of zinc? ______________

Check

9. Does the answer check? Is twice the answer minus 4 milligrams the recommended daily intake of zinc?

   ____

Solve Another Problem

10. You spent \$10.50 at the fair. If it costs \$4.50 for admission and you rode 8 rides which all cost the same, how much does one ride ticket cost?

    ____

Name ______________________ Class ______________ Date ______________

Practice 2-2

Simplifying Algebraic Expressions

Combine like terms. Write your answer in simplest form.

1. $9j + 34j$
2. $2.3s - 1.2s$
3. $5t - 12t + 17t$
4. $6q + 14q - 8q$
5. $7t - 12t + 4t$
6. $-16w + 7w - 5w$
7. $y + \frac{5}{6}y - \frac{1}{6}y$
8. $5z - 2z - 13z$
9. $4x + 2.1x - 0.6x$

Simplify each expression. Write your answer in simplest form.

10. $4a + 7 + 2a$
11. $8(k - 9)$
12. $\frac{2}{3}(w + 3)$
13. $5(b - 6) + 9$
14. $-4 + 3(6 + k)$
15. $\frac{7}{8}j - (\frac{3}{8}j + 7)$
16. $-9 + 8(x + 6)$
17. $4(m + 6) - 3$
18. $28k + 36(7 + k)$
19. $3.09(j + 4.6)$
20. $7.9y + 8.4 - 2.04y$
21. $4.3(5.6 + c)$
22. $9.8d + 8d - 4.6d + 2.9d$
23. $18 + 27m - 29 + 36m$
24. $8(j + 12) + 4(k - 19)$
25. $4.2r + 8.1s + 1.09r + 6.32s$

Solve.

26. Tyrone bought 15.3 gal of gasoline priced at g dollars per gallon, 2 qt of oil priced at q dollars per quart, and a wiper blade priced at $3.79. Write an expression that represents the total cost of these items.

27. Choose a number. Multiply by 2. Add 6 to the product. Divide by 2. Then subtract 3. What is the answer? Repeat this process using two different numbers. Explain.

Name ______________________ Class ______________ Date ______________

2-2 • Guided Problem Solving

GPS Student Page 57, Exercise 31:

On a shopping trip, Kelly buys 3 barrettes and a headband. Her sister buys 2 barrettes and 2 headbands. Define and use variables to represent the total cost.

Understand

1. Place a circle around the number of barrettes purchased and a square around the number of headbands purchased.
2. How many headbands did Kelly buy? ______________
3. Underline what you are being asked to do.

Plan and Carry Out

4. Write an expression for the cost of the items Kelly bought on the shopping trip. Let b = cost of a barrette and h = cost of a headband.

   ____

5. Write an expression for the cost of the items Kelly's sister bought on the shopping trip.

   ____

6. Combine the like terms to represent the total cost of the items bought.

   ____

Check

7. Add the numbers in each shape (circle and square) in the original problem to check your answer.

   ____

Solve Another Problem

8. For a birthday party, you purchase 10 balloons, 8 party hats, and 5 game prizes. At the last minute you find that you will have a few extra guests. You pick up 3 more hats, 2 more balloons, and another game prize. Use variables where b = cost of a balloon, h = cost of a hat, and p = cost of a game prize to represent the total cost.

   ____

Name ______________________ Class ______________ Date ______________

Practice 2-3

Solving Multi-Step Equations

Solve each equation. Check the solution.

1. $2x - 3 + 4x = 39$

2. $0.7w + 16 + 4w = 27.28$

3. $-6(m + 1) = 24$

4. $\frac{2}{3}(k - 8) = 52$

5. $4(1.5c + 6) - 2c = -9$

6. $0.5n + 17 + n = 20$

7. $2(2.5b - 9) + 6b = -7$

8. $3(\frac{3}{4}a + 3) + 6 = 87$

9. $20 = -4(f + 6) + 14$

10. $9a - 4 + 3(a - 11) = 23$

11. You want to join the tennis team. You go to the sporting goods store with $100. If the tennis racket you want costs $80 and the tennis balls cost $4 per can, how many cans of tennis balls can you buy?

12. Johnny wants to ship a package to his friend. A shipping company charges $2.49 for the first pound and $1.24 for each additional pound. If it cost Johnny $11.17 to ship the package, how much did his package weigh?

Name ______________________ Class ______________ Date ______________

2-3 • Guided Problem Solving

GPS Student Page 62, Exercise 22:

Jobs An employee earns \$7.00 an hour for the first 35 hours worked in a week and \$10.50 for any hours over 35. One week's paycheck (before deductions) was for \$308.00. How many hours did the employee work?

Understand

1. How much per hour does the employee make for the first 35 hours? ______________
2. How much per hour does the employee make after 35 hours of work? ______________
3. How much was the week's paycheck? ______________
4. What is it you are asked to find?

   ____

Plan and Carry Out

5. Write an equation for this situation. Multiply the hourly rate by 35 hours. Add the overtime rate multiplied by an unknown, x. Set this sum equal to the total amount of the check.

   ____

6. Solve for x, the number of overtime hours the employee worked.

   ____

7. What do you have to do to find the total hours worked?

   ____

8. How many total hours did the employee work? ______________

Check

9. Does the answer check? Is 35 times \$7 plus the overtime hours times \$10.50 equal to the total check?

   ____

Solve Another Problem

10. A college student has a long-distance phone card. The phone-card rate for the first 100 minutes is 12 cents per minute and then goes to 15 cents per minute after that. If the student had a long distance charge of \$21, how many total minutes did the student talk?

    ____

Name ______________________ Class ______________ Date ______________

Practice 2-4

Solving Equations with Variables on Both Sides

Solve each equation. Check the solution.

1. $10 + 12y = 2y + 40$

2. $6(c + 4) = 4c - 18$

3. $0.5m + 6.4 = 4.9 - 0.1m$

4. $14b = 16(b + 12)$

5. $7 + \frac{2}{5}y = \frac{3}{5}y - 4$

6. $9(d - 4) - 8 = 5d$

7. $12j = 16(j - 8)$

8. $0.7p + 4.6 = 7.3 - 0.2p$

9. $6(f + 5) + 8 = 2f$

10. $4 = -2(4.5p + 25)$

11. Jace owns twice as many DVDs as Louis. Bo has sixty fewer DVDs than five times Louis's collection. If Jace and Bo have the same amount of DVDs, how many DVDs are in Louis's collection?

12. Deborah has two paintings in her portfolio and paints three more each week. Kai has twelve paintings in her portfolio and paints two more each week. After how many weeks will Deborah and Kai have the same number of paintings?

Name ______________________ Class ______________ Date ______________

2-4 • Guided Problem Solving

GPS Student Page 67, Exercise 17:

Efren leaves home at 9 A.M. and walks 4 miles per hour. His brother, Gregory, leaves half an hour later and runs 8.5 miles per hour in the same direction as Efren. Predict the time at which Gregory will catch up to Efren.

Understand

1. What is the distance formula? ______________________

2. What can you say about the distance each boy will have traveled when Gregory catches up to Efren? ______________________

Plan and Carry Out

3. Write an expression for the distance Gregory travels per hour. Let h stand for time in hours. ______________________

4. Write an expression for the distance Efren travels per hour plus the distance he will have traveled when Gregory leaves the house.

   ____

5. Write an equation setting the distance expressions in Steps 3 and 4 equal. ______________________

6. Solve for h. Use your answer to estimate the time at which Gregory will catch up to Efren. ______________________

Check

7. Solve the expressions in Steps 3 and 4 for your value of h. Are the distances equal? ______________________

Solve Another Problem

8. Roshonda begins riding her bike home from school at 3:00 P.M., traveling 12 miles per hour. James leaves school in a bus a quarter of an hour later and travels 35 miles per hour in the same direction. At about what time will James catch up to Roshonda?

   ____

Name ________________ Class ________________ Date ________________

Practice 2-5

Types of Solutions of Linear Equations

Show whether each equation has one solution, infinitely many solutions, or no solution. Justify your answer.

1. $8c = 6 + 5c$

2. $2x + 7 = -8x - 9 + 10x$

3. $-2(b - 4) = -2b + 8$

4. $0.6(2h - 4) = 2.4 + 1.2h$

5. $-6a - 15 = -3(a - 7)$

6. $\frac{1}{2}(4z + \frac{1}{4}) = 2(z + \frac{1}{16})$

7. $3 - 7t = -5t + 3 - 2t$

8. $-3x + 6 = -3(x + 3)$

9. $4(0.8g + 1.5) = 2(3 + 1.6g)$

10. $1 + \frac{2}{3}w + \frac{1}{2} = 2w$

11. One restaurant offers two large pizzas for the same price as two medium pizzas and a $6 pitcher of drinks. The medium pizza costs $3 less than the large pizza. How much could a large pizza cost? Justify your answer.

12. Four less than a number equals four times the sum of a number and 2. Is this statement true for only one number, for all numbers, or for no numbers? Explain your reasoning.

Name ______________________ Class ______________ Date ____________

2-5 • Guided Problem Solving

GPS Student Page 74, Exercise 20a:

Geometry Greg is buying fabric from a store. He has the choice of buying fabric that is 2 feet wide or 3 feet wide. The diagrams show how much fabric of each type he can buy for d dollars. For what value(s) of d is the perimeter of both choices the same?

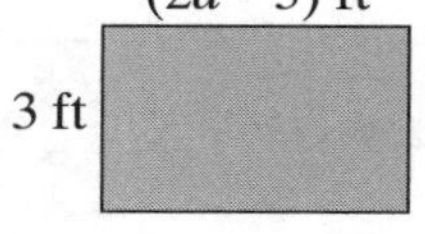

(2d – 4) ft
2 ft

Understand

1. What is the formula for the perimeter of a rectangle?

   ____

2. What is it you are asked to find?

   ____

   ____

Plan and Carry Out

3. Write an expression for the perimeter of the 3-ft wide fabric.

   ____

4. Write an expression for the perimeter of the 2-ft wide fabric.

   ____

5. Write an equation setting the perimeter expressions in Steps 3 and 4 equal. ____

6. Transform the equation into its simplest form. ______________________

7. The lengths of the fabrics must be positive numbers of units. How does this affect the possible values of d? ______________________

   ____

Check

8. Evaluate the expressions in Steps 3 and 4 for several different values of d. Are the perimeters equal? ______________________

Solve Another Problem

9. For what value(s) of s is the perimeter of both isosceles triangles the same? ______________________

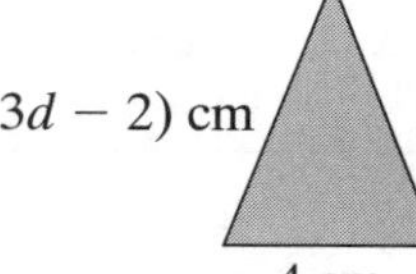

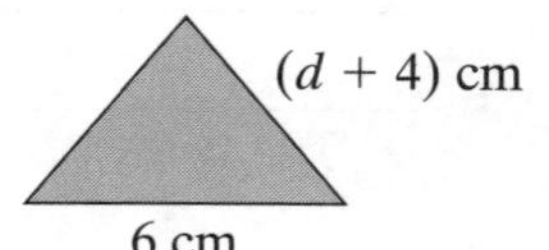

Name ______________________ Class ______________ Date ______________

2A: Graphic Organizer

For use before Lesson 2-1

Study Skill It is important that you fully understand the basic concepts in each chapter before moving on to more complex material. Be sure to ask questions when you are not comfortable with the material you have learned.

Vocabulary and Study Skills

Write your answers.

1. What is the chapter title? ______________________
2. How many lessons are there in this chapter? ______________________
3. What is the topic of the Test-Taking Strategies page?

____

4. Complete the graphic organizer below as you work through the chapter.
   - In the center, write the title of the chapter.
   - When you begin a lesson, write the lesson name in a rectangle.
   - When you complete a lesson, write a skill or key concept in a circle linked to that lesson block.
   - When you complete the chapter, use this graphic organizer to help you review.

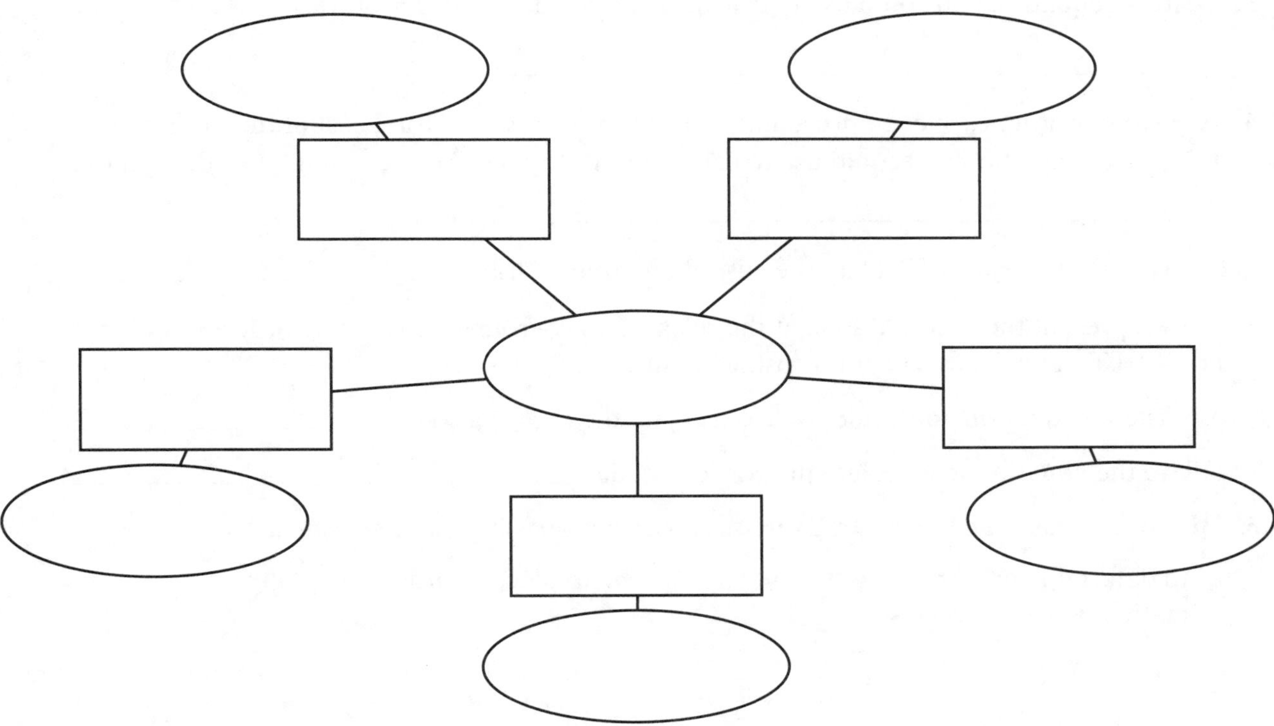

Name ______________________ Class ______________ Date ______________

2B: Reading Comprehension

For use after Lesson 2-2

Study Skill Make a realistic study schedule. Try to balance your study time with before- or after-school free time, meals, and other activities.

Use the paragraph and menu below to answer the questions.

Ian and two of his friends went to a restaurant for lunch. Each of them ordered juice, but they shared an order of fries. The total cost of their order, without tax, was $6.30.

Menu

BLT Sandwich	$2.50
Pizza, slice	$3.50
Hamburger	$3.50
Ice cream	$1.75
Juice	$1.60

1. Let f represent the cost of the fries. What expression describes the cost of the fries for each of the three friends? ______________

2. How much did they spend altogether on juice? ______________________

3. Write an equation you could use to calculate the cost for an order of fries.

   ____

4. A customer orders a slice of pizza and two orders of fries. The total cost of the order is $6.50
   a. Write an equation you could use to calculate the cost for the fries using this information.

   ____

   b. Use the equation to calculate the cost of an order of fries. ______________________

5. Let s represent the cost of a soda at the restaurant. A group of customers orders 4 sodas and 4 BLT sandwiches. The total cost, without tax, is $19.00.

   a. Write an equation you could use to calculate the cost of a soda. ______________________

   b. Use the equation to calculate the cost of a soda. ______________________

6. **High-Use Academic Words** In Exercises 3–5, what does it mean to *calculate*?

   a. to determine using mathematical processes

   b. to place in order

Name ______________________ Class ______________ Date ______________

2C: Reading/Writing Math Symbols

For use after Lesson 2-4

Study Skill Create a list of mathematical symbols and their meanings. Keep the list in your math notebook for reference.

Explain the meaning of the bar (—) in the following examples.

1. $4 - 7$ ______________________
2. $\frac{3}{5}$ ______________________
3. $3 + (-5)$ ______________________
4. $3.\overline{6}$ ______________________

Explain the meaning of the dot (·) in the following examples.

5. 2.7 ______________________
6. $3 \cdot 9$ ______________________
7. 1, 3, 5, 7, . . . ______________________

Write the following expressions using the appropriate math symbols.

8. the sum of four and negative three ______________________
9. the difference between two and five tenths and three point three repeating ______________________
10. six is not equal to the product of three and *n* ______________________
11. the product of eight and *k* is greater than twenty-four ______________________

Vocabulary and Study Skills

Name ________________________ Class ________________ Date ________________

2D: Visual Vocabulary Practice

For use after Lesson 2-4

High-Use Academic Words

Study Skill When making a sketch, make it simple but make it complete.

Concept List

represent	verify	convert
model	explain	pattern
property	solve	graph

Write the concept that best describes each exercise. Choose from the concept list above.

1. c is the total cost ________________	**2.** 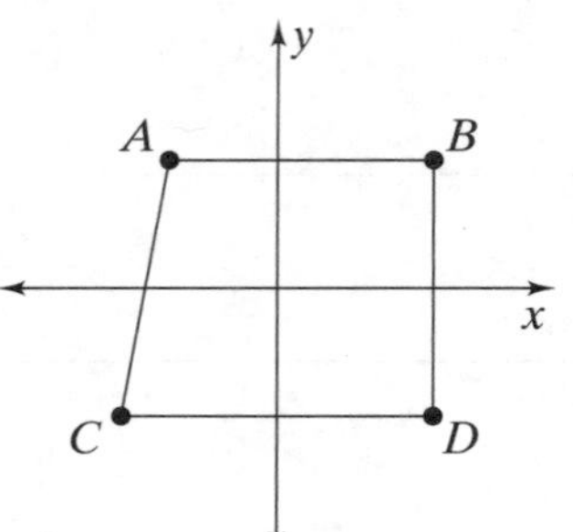 ________________	**3.** $8s + 12 = 52$ $s = 5$ Check: $8(5) + 12 = 52$ $40 + 12 = 52$ $52 = 52$ ________________
4. 1 in. = 2.54 cm ________________	**5.** $2.5 + 4d = 12.8$ Kim jogged 2.5 km on Monday. Then she jogged d km each day for four days. She jogged a total of 12.8 km for the five days. ________________	**6.** $2x - 3 = 4$ 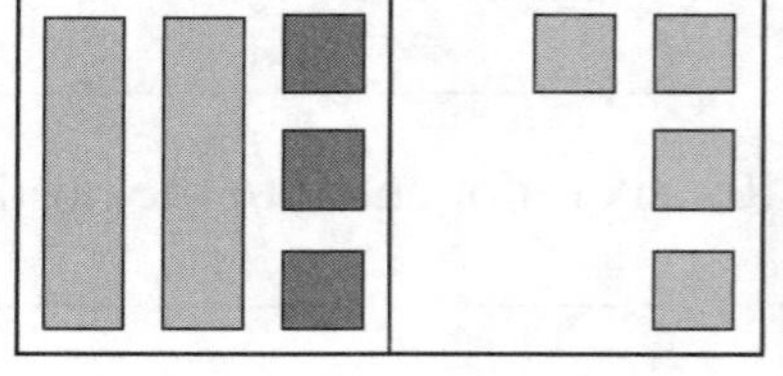 ________________
7. $1 \cdot 11 = 121$ $11 \cdot 111 = 1{,}221$ $11 \cdot 1111 = 12{,}221$ ________________	**8.** $5 + 6m = 35$ $6m = 35 - 5$ $6m = 30$ $m = 30 \div 6$ $m = 5$ ________________	**9.** $a(b + c) = ab + ac$ ________________

Name ______________________ Class ______________ Date ______________

2E: Vocabulary Check

For use after Lesson 2-3

Study Skill Strengthen your vocabulary. Use these pages and add cues and summaries by applying the Cornell Notetaking style.

Write the definition for each word or term at the right. To check your work, fold the paper back along the dotted line to see the correct answers.

Definition	Term
______________________	term
______________________	like terms
______________________	linear equation
______________________	Distributive Property
______________________	Commutative Property

Vocabulary and Study Skills

Name ______________________ Class ______________ Date ______________

2E: Vocabulary Check (continued)

For use after Lesson 2-3

Write the vocabulary word or term for each definition. To check your work, fold the paper back along the dotted line to see the correct answers.

a number, a variable, or the product of a number and a variable ______________________

terms with exactly the same variable factors ______________________

an equation whose graph is a line ______________________

For any numbers a, b, and c, $a(b + c) = ab + ac$ and $a(b - c) = ab - ac$. ______________________

For any numbers a and b, $a + b = b + a$ and $ab = ba$. ______________________

Name ______________________ Class ______________ Date ______________

2F: Vocabulary Review Puzzle

For use with the Chapter Review

Study Skill Turn off the television and radio when studying.

Find each of the words below in the Word Search. Circle the word and cross it off the Word List. Words can be displayed forwards, backwards, up, down, or diagonally.

variable	distributive	integer	exponent
linear	equation	additive inverse	inverse
isolate	like terms	solution	

```
L F E E T P U O M O I I H H H R D K W V
I B T F C C S P R R J N H E I E O B C M
K M A G T J L B X P X T X A E L S T F I
E A V V E Z Y S C I O E B O B O J Z J N
T D L L P A D L S E J G M L L O T D N L
E I Q W C K K C T U O E H U K G N V F I
R S F C Y N R L Z S L R T N S L Z M X N
M T W A D D I T I V E I N V E R S E G E
S R G N R E U I V E O U C M V B A I H A
W I T R R C M O Q N D U V S T M E S L R
R B M Q N N S Y V N L V S I I G X U I T
P U E O M G W A B N Z Y P M I O P S E Y
D T A V Z Y R K A W S D I N K U O A D C
O I B G Q I B I L I C U V Y Q L N U O Z
H V J A A K D I Q U W E I M A L E F N T
K E J B R E N L W T R I F T L D N V W P
T R L R M Q H N S S L D E H E R T K F W
S E E D E W A R E J I R O N G E E W V Y
W T K H T R F F C A R H F U W J K Y F V
E Q U A T I O N T Q N H G H M U N C W C
```

Name ____________________ Class ____________ Date ____________

Practice 3-1

Relating Graphs to Events

Each graph represents a situation. Match a graph with the appropriate situation.

a.
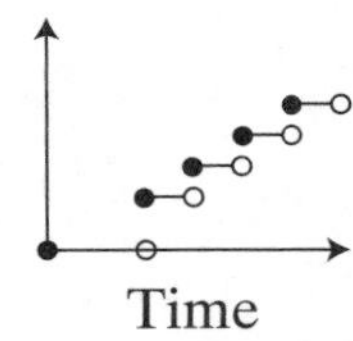

b.
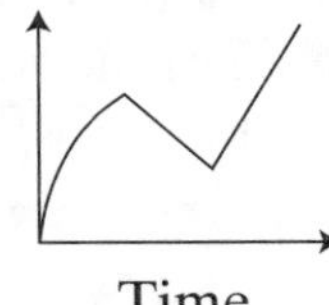

c.
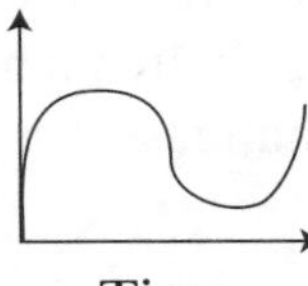

d.
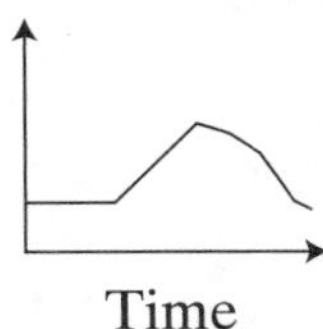

e.
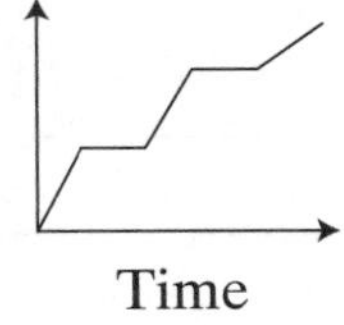

f.
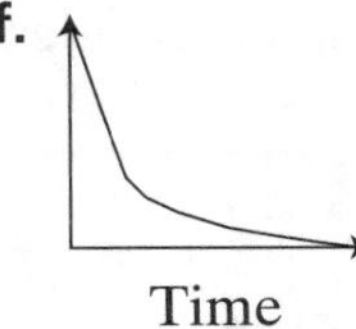

1. the amount of an unpaid library fine ____________
2. the height above ground of a skydiver during a dive ____________
3. one's adrenaline flow when receiving a fright ____________
4. the temperature of the air during a 24-h period beginning at 9:00 A.M. ____________
5. a jogger gradually increases speed, steadily decreases speed, then steadily increases speed ____________
6. elevator ride up with stops ____________
7. Look at graph b above. Suppose the total time shown is 6 min. Estimate the times when the graph is increasing, decreasing, linear, and nonlinear. ____________

____

Sketch and label a graph of each relationship.

8. the height of a football after it has been kicked

9. the distance traveled by a car that was traveling at 50 mph, but is now stopped by road construction

10. The function table at the right shows the distance in feet that an object falls over time.

Time (s)	Distance (ft)
1	16
2	64
3	144
4	256

Name ______________________ Class ______________ Date ______________

3-1 • Guided Problem Solving

GPS Student Page 85, Exercise 19:

Geometry As the length of the side of a square increases, the area of the square increases. Sketch a graph that shows the area of the square as the side length changes.

Understand

1. As the length of one side of a square increases, what happens to the lengths of the other sides?

____

____

Plan and Carry Out

2. What is the formula for the area of a square in terms of one side length? ______________

3. Complete the chart.

Side Length	1	2	3	4	5
Area					

4. Draw a graph with the x-axis labeled "side length" and the y-axis labeled "area." Plot each of the values from Step 3, and draw a line connecting the points.

Check

5. Another way to find the area of a square is to multiply the length times the width. Are your calculations correct? ______________

Solve Another Problem

6. As the length of one side of a square increases, the perimeter of the square increases. Sketch a graph that shows the perimeter of a square as its side length increases in increments of one.

Name ____________ Class ____________ Date ____________

Practice 3-2

Use the function rule $y = 5x + 1$. Find each output.

1. $x = 3$ ____________
2. $x = -6$ ____________
3. $x = 8$ ____________
4. $x = 1.5$ ____________
5. $x = 0$ ____________
6. $x = 30$ ____________

7. **Measurement** The function rule $c = 2.54k$ gives the number of centimeters c that are equivalent to k inches. How many centimeters are equivalent to 4 inches? ____________

8. **Cycling** The function rule $h = \frac{m}{5}$ gives the number of hours h that are needed to travel m miles at a speed of 5 miles per hour. How many hours are needed to travel 32 mi? ____________

Complete the input-output table for each function.

9. $r = 2t - 1$

Input t	Output r
−2	
0	
2	
4	

10. $p = 2v + 12$

Input v	Output p
−0.4	
−0.2	
0	
0.1	

11. $k = 0.3n - 2$

Input n	Output k
−10	
−5	
0	
5	

12. **Unit Pricing** Complete the table of input-output pairs for the function $c = \frac{p}{8}$. The variable c represents the unit cost in dollars of a box of 8 granola bars. The variable p represents the price in dollars of a box of 8 granola bars.

Input p (dollars in price)	Output c (dollars in unit price)
4	
3.60	
3.48	

13. **Merchandising** The function $d = 3r + 5.25$ represents the cost in dollars d for a vase of r roses from a flower shop. Make a table of input-output pairs to show the cost for arrangements with 6, 9, and 12 rows.

Input r (number of roses)	Output d (cost of arrangement in dollars)
6	
9	
12	

Name ______________________ Class ______________ Date ______________

3-2 • Guided Problem Solving

GPS Student Page 90, Exercise 19:

Fruit smoothies cost \$1.50 each plus \$.50 for each fruit mixed into the smoothie. The function $c = 1.5 + 0.5f$ gives the cost c of a smoothie with f fruits. Find the cost of a smoothie with 4 different fruits mixed in.

Understand

1. What do the variables represent?

   ____

   ____

2. Which variable is the input variable? ______________________

3. Circle what you are asked to find.

Plan and Carry Out

4. How can you use a function to find the output when you are given an input?

   ____

   ____

5. Use the function to find the cost of a smoothie with 4 fruits mixed in.

   ____

Check

6. How could you find the answer another way?

   ____

   ____

Solve Another Problem

7. You spent \$4.50 for admission to the fair. Each ride ticket costs \$.75. The function $c = 4.5 + 0.75t$ gives the cost of admission with t ride tickets. Find the cost of 6 ride tickets.

   ____

Name ____________________ Class ____________ Date ____________

Practice 3-3

Proportional Relationships

Determine if the relationship is proportional.

1.

x	*y*
−6	−30
−3	−15
6	30
9	60

______

2.

a	*b*
20	10
40	20
60	30
80	40

______

3.

g	*h*
−8	−6
−4	−2
0	0
4	2

______

4.

r	*s*
8	12
16	20
24	28
32	36

______

5.

c	*d*
25	−10
35	−14
45	−18
55	−22

______

6.

v	*w*
120	24
150	0
180	36
210	40

______

7. **Bagels**
2 for $3
4 for $6
12 for $18

______

8. **Canoe Rentals**
1 hr for $6
2 hr for $10
3 hr for $12

______

9. **Berries**
3 lb for $9
5 lb for $15
10 lb for $30

______

10. **Bottles of Water**
6 for $4
12 for $8
24 for $16

______

11. **Ears of Corn**
4 for $3
6 for $4
12 for $7

______

12. **Bridge Tolls**
5 for $10
10 for $20
25 for $40

______

13. **Swimming** Evan pays $12 per month to belong to a gym so that he can swim in the gym's pool. Each time he swims he pays an additional $2. He uses the function $e = 2t + 12$ to track his monthly swimming expenses, where e represents total expenses and t represents number of times Evan swims. Make an input-output table, graph your results, and determine if the function has a proportional relationship. Explain.

____

____

Name ______________ Class ______________ Date ______________

3-3 • Guided Problem Solving

GPS Student Page 95, Exercise 15:

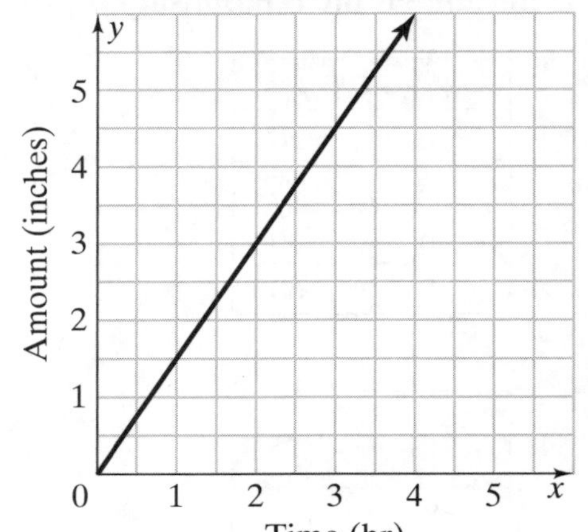

Data Analysis The graph shows the relationship between time and total snowfall for a December blizzard. Based on the graph, estimate how long it will take for the amount of snow to total 18 inches.

Understand

1. Is the relationship shown in the graph proportional or not proportional? ______________
2. What are the input and output values for this relationship?

   ____

   ____
3. What is the scale used on each axis of the graph?

   ____
4. Underline what you are being asked to do.

Plan and Carry Out

5. Find a point on the graph that corresponds to an amount of snowfall that is a factor of 18. Write the ordered pair for that point. ______________
6. What is the ratio in simplest form of input to output for the ordered pair you wrote in Step 5? ______________
7. What input value can you pair with 18 to make the same ratio? ______________
8. About how many hours did it take for 18 inches of snow to fall? ______________

Check

9. Divide 18 inches of snowfall by the number of hours. Compare the rate of inches per hour to the ordered pair for the input 1.

   ____

   ____

Solve Another Problem

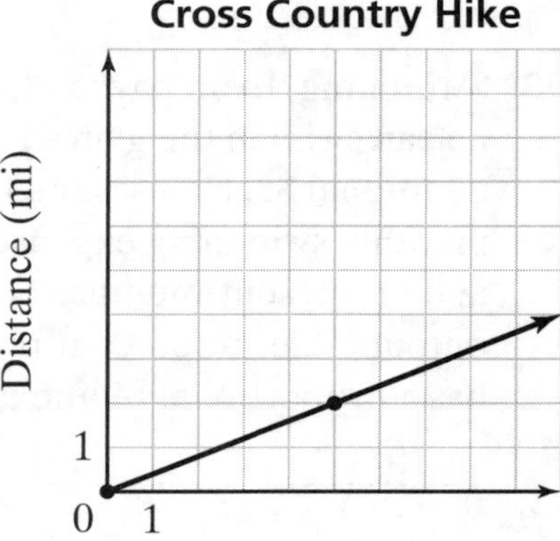

10. The graph shows the relationship between time and total distance covered by a hiker. Based on the graph, estimate how long it will take for the hiker to cover 20 miles.

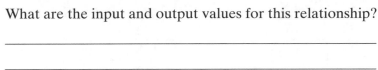

    ____

Name ______________________ Class ______________ Date ______________

Practice 3-4

Linear Functions

Determine if the function represented by the table is linear. Explain.

1.

x	3	5	7	11
y	6	9	12	18

____

2.

x	−4	−1	5	12
y	3	7	15	23

____

3.

x	6	0	−9	−12
y	−2	8	23	28

____

4.

x	−1	5	12	18
y	72	12	2	0

____

5.

x	84	5	−1	−4
y	1	−1	−5	−9

____

6.

x	25	15	0	−10
y	16	8	−4	−12

____

Determine whether the data for each function are *discrete* or *continuous*. Then make a table and graph for the function.

7. The function $I = 1.5h + 6$ represents the height (in inches) of water in a pool that contained 6 inches of water before the refilling began.

____

8. The function $c = 2.25b - 0.5$ represents the cost (in dollars) of b beverages at a snack bar after using a coupon.

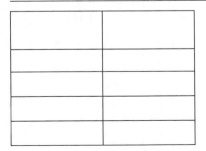

____

Name ______________________ Class ______________ Date ______________

3-4 • Guided Problem Solving

GPS Student Page 101, Exercise 11:

Science The height of a burning candle depends on how long the candle has been burning. For one type of candle, the function $h = 8 - \frac{1}{2}t$ gives the candle's height h (in centimeters) as a function of the time t the candle has burned (in hours). **a.** Graph the function. **b.** What was the original height of the candle? **c.** What is the greatest amount of time the candle can burn?

Understand

1. What are the input and output values for this relationship?

   ____

2. When the candle is at its original height, how many hours will it have burned? __________
3. When the candle has burned the greatest amount of time, what will its height be? __________

Plan and Carry Out

4. Make a table for input values of 0, 1, 2, and 3.

5. Use the table to graph the function. (Hint: Number the x-axis by 2s.)
6. Use the graph to answer these questions.

   a. What was the original height of the candle? __________

   b. What is the greatest amount of time the candle can burn?

   ____

Check

7. Substitute your answers from Step 6 in the function equation. Solve for the corresponding values. Check that the pairs of values represent points on the graph you made in Step 5.

   ____

Solve Another Problem

8. While driving home from a water park, your distance from home depends upon how long you have been driving. The function $d = 9 - 0.6t$ gives the distance d (in miles) as a function of the time t (in minutes) that you have been driving.

   a. Graph the function.

   b. How far is the water park from your home? __________

   c. How long will it take you to reach home? __________

Name ______________________ Class ______________ Date ____________

Practice 3-5

Nonlinear Functions

Identify each function as linear or nonlinear.

1. 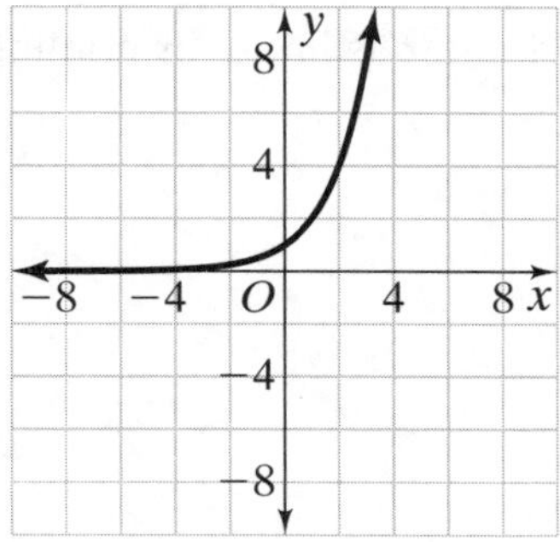

____

2. 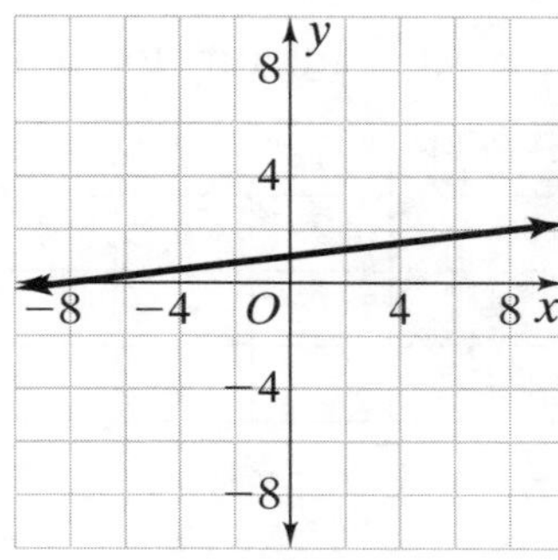

____

Circle the function in each pair that is nonlinear.

3. $y = 2x$
   $y = x^2 - 4x + 6$

4. $y = 2x^3 + 7x - 1$
   $y = 5x + 3$

5. $y = 2(x - 3.5)$
   $y = 0.6x^4 + 2$

6. $y = \frac{2}{5}x^5 - 4x^3 + 5$
   $y = \frac{3}{5}x - 5 + \frac{2}{5}x$

7. $y = 4^x$
   $y = 4x - 1 + 2x$

8. $y = 2.4(5 - x)$
   $y = 3 + 5x - 2x^2$

9.

x	1	6	11	17
y	21	−2	−6−	−10

x	−3	−1	1	3
y	6	5	4	3

10.

x	−2	−3	−4	−5
y	20	23	26	29

x	4	8	12	16
y	5	10	20	40

Determine if the function described is linear or nonlinear. Explain.

11. **Physics** Gravity causes an object to fall from a tall building. A function relates the object's speed while falling and time. ______________________

____

12. **Transportation** A train is traveling at a rate of 80 mi/hr. A function relates the distance the train has traveled to its rate of speed.

____

Name ______________________ Class ______________ Date ______________

3-5 • Guided Problem Solving

GPS Student Page 107, Exercise 17:

Geometry Complete the table. Identify the function relating area and perimeter as linear or nonlinear.

Length of Rectangle (cm)	1	2	3	4	5
Width of Rectangle (cm)	2	3	4	5	6
Perimeter (cm)					
Area (cm^2)					

Understand

1. What are the dimensions of the first rectangle shown in the table?

____

2. What two things are you being asked to do?

____

____

Plan and Carry Out

3. Find the perimeter of each rectangle in the table. Use the formula $P = 2(l + w)$.
4. Find the area of each rectangle in the table. Use the formula $A = lw$.
5. Find the ratios of change in perimeter to the change in area.

____

6. Are the ratios of change the same? ____________
7. Is the function relating area and perimeter linear or nonlinear? ____________

Check

8. On a separate sheet of paper, graph the points representing corresponding areas and perimeters shown in the table. Connect the points and identify whether the graph is a straight line or not.

Solve Another Problem

9. **Geometry** Complete the table. Use the formulas $C = 2\pi r$ and $A = \pi r^2$. Leave the measurements in π notation. Identify the function relating circumference and area as linear or nonlinear.

Length of Radius of Circle (cm)	1	2	3	4	5
Circumference (cm)					
Area (cm^2)					

____

Name ______________________ Class ______________ Date ____________

3A: Graphic Organizer

For use before Lesson 3-1

Study Skill Your textbook includes a Skills Handbook with extra problems and questions. Working these exercises is a good way to review material and prepare for the next chapter.

Write your answers.

1. What is the chapter title? ______________________
2. How many lessons are there in this chapter? ______________________
3. What is the topic of the Test-Taking Strategies page?

____

4. Complete the graphic organizer below as you work through the chapter.
   - In the center, write the title of the chapter.
   - When you begin a lesson, write the lesson name in a rectangle.
   - When you complete a lesson, write a skill or key concept in a circle linked to that lesson block.
   - When you complete the chapter, use this graphic organizer to help you review.

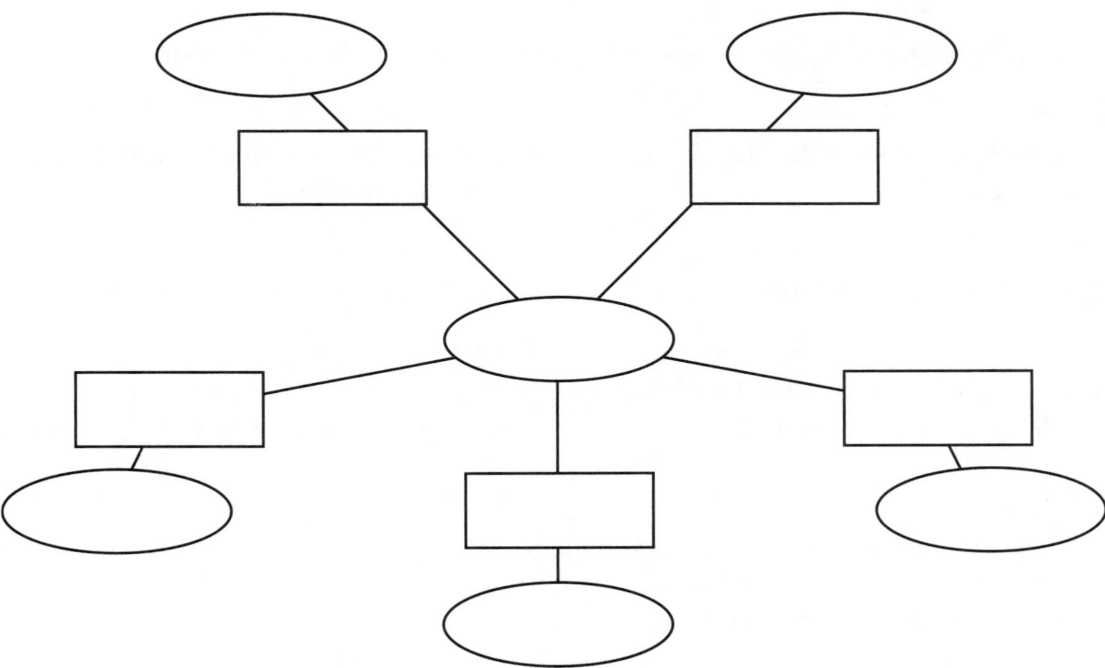

Vocabulary and Study Skills

Name ______________________ Class ______________ Date ______________

3B: Reading Comprehension

For use after Lesson 3-2

Study Skill Pay attention to detail when you read. Try to pick out the important points as you go along.

Read the paragraph below and answer the questions.

The Iditarod is an annual dog sledding competition that begins the first Saturday in March. This event, which covers about 1,850 km, begins in Anchorage and ends in Nome, Alaska. There are two possible routes: a northern route that is used in even-numbered years and a southern route that is used in odd-numbered ones. The weather is often unpredictable, with wind chill temperatures as low as −73°C. The drivers ("mushers") average approximately two hours of sleep each day. In 2005, there were 79 participants who started the race, but only 63 finished. Mushers are required to carry everything they need for the journey in their sleds. A fully loaded sled weighs approximately 150 lb. The first Iditarod was held in 1973 and it took the winner 20 days to complete. In 2005, the winner completed the course in 9 days, 18 hours, and 39 minutes.

1. If there are 1.609 km in a mile, approximately how many miles long is the race?

   ____

2. How many hours of sleep per day do the mushers average?

   ____

3. In 2005, what percentage of participants finished the race?

   ____

4. Which route was used in 2005?

   ____

5. In which month does the race begin?

   ____

6. How many minutes did it take the winner of the 2005 Iditarod to complete the race?

   ____

7. How much longer did it take the 1973 winner to complete the race than the 2005 winner?

   ____

8. The formula for converting Celsius to Fahrenheit is $F = \frac{9}{5}C + 32$. What is the coldest temperature, to the nearest whole degree Fahrenheit, that the racers must endure?

   ____

9. **High-Use Academic Words** What is a *detail*, as mentioned in the study skill?

   a. small part or feature

   b. a short statement of the main part

Name ______________________ Class ______________ Date ______________

3C: Reading/Writing Math Symbols

For use after Lesson 3-4

Study Skill Work in a well-lit, quiet spot with the proper materials.

Vocabulary and Study Skills

Write the meaning of the following mathematical expressions or equations.

1. $f(3) = 2x$ ______________________
2. -12 ______________________
3. $\angle S \cong \angle R$ ______________________
4. $\frac{8}{\$5}$ ______________________
5. $(3, 9)$ ______________________
6. $y < 15$ ______________________
7. $(-16 + 4^2) = 0$ ______________________
8. $12 - x$ ______________________
9. $\sqrt{64} = 8$ ______________________
10. $|-41| = 41$ ______________________
11. $\frac{3}{4} = 75\%$ ______________________
12. $f(x) = x + 3$ ______________________
13. $\triangle ABC \cong \triangle DEF$ ______________________
14. $\pi \approx 3.14$ ______________________
15. $x^2 + 4$ ______________________
16. $\sqrt{48} \approx 7$ ______________________
17. $A = bh$ ______________________

Name ______________________ Class ______________ Date ______________

3D: Visual Vocabulary Practice

For use after Lesson 3-5

Study Skill Mathematics builds on itself, so build a strong foundation.

Concept List

functions	function rule	linear
linear function	nonlinear	nonlinear functions
parabola	proportional relationship	quadratic function

Write the concept that best describes each exercise. Choose from the concept list above.

1.

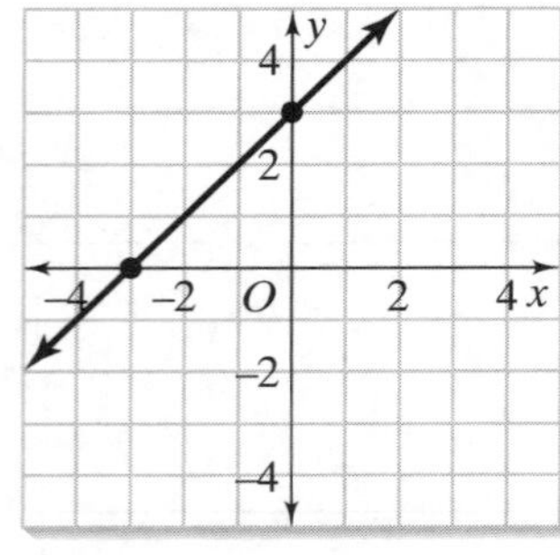

The type of change represented by the graph.

____

2.

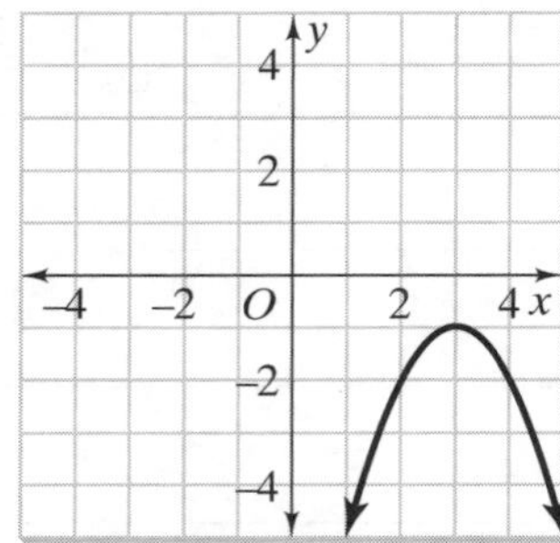

The type of change represented by the graph.

____

3.

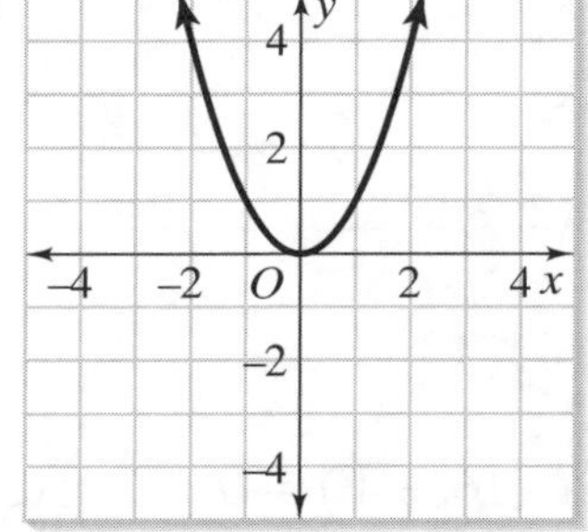

____

4.

$h(x) = \frac{1}{4}x^2 - 8$

____

5.

$y = 3x^2 + 7$

$s = 8k^3 + 4$

____

6.

Cost	Pounds of Tomatoes
\$1.50	1
\$3.00	2
\$4.50	3
\$6.00	4

____

7.

g is six added to the product of three and t

____

8.

$g = 6 + 3t$

____

9.

$h = x^2 + 3$

$k = 4x + 2$

____

Name ______________________ Class ______________ Date ______________

3E: Vocabulary Check

For use after Lesson 3-5

Study Skill Strengthen your vocabulary. Use these pages and add cues and summaries by applying the Cornell Notetaking style.

Write the definition for each word or term at the right. To check your work, fold the paper back along the dotted line to see the correct answers.

Vocabulary and Study Skills

linear

quadratic function

function rule

proportional relationship

function

Name ____________________ Class ______________ Date ______________

3E: Vocabulary Check (continued)

For use after Lesson 3-5

Write the vocabulary word or term for each definition. To check your work, fold the paper back along the dotted line to see the correct answers.

change in data that forms a straight line when graphed ____________________

a nonlinear function in which the greatest exponent of a variable is 2 ____________________

an equation that describes a function ____________________

a relationship between inputs and outputs in which the ratio of inputs and outputs is always the same ____________________

a relationship that assigns exactly one output value for each input value ____________________

Name ______________________ Class ______________ Date ______________

3F: Vocabulary Review

For use with the Chapter Review

Study Skill Take notes while you study. Use a highlighter to emphasize important material in your notes.

Circle the word that best completes the sentence.

1. A rule that assigns to each input value exactly one output value is a (*parabola, function*).
2. A count of items, such as number of people or cars, is (*discrete, continuous*).
3. A function whose points lie on a straight line when the function is graphed is (*linear, nonlinear*).
4. A function whose points do not line on a straight line when the function is graphed is (*linear, nonlinear*).
5. Data where numbers between any two data values have meaning is (*discrete, continuous*).
6. Change in data is (*linear, nonlinear*) if it forms a straight line when graphed.
7. A (*coordinate, function rule*) is an equation that describes a function.
8. A (*proportional, quadratic*) function is one in which the greatest exponent of a variable is 2.
9. Data that produces a curve when graphed is an example of (*linear, nonlinear*) change.
10. A parabola is a (*U-shaped, V-shaped*) curve.
11. A (*quadratic, proportional*) relationship is one in which the ratio of inputs and outputs is always the same.

Name ______________________ Class ______________ Date ______________

Practice 4-1

Understanding Slope

Find the slope of each line.

1. 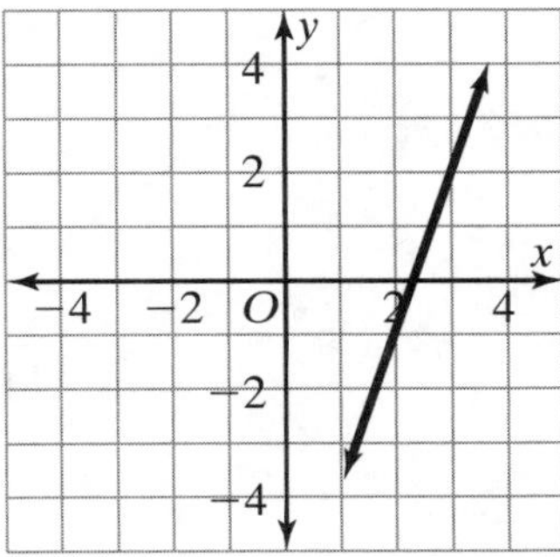

____

2. 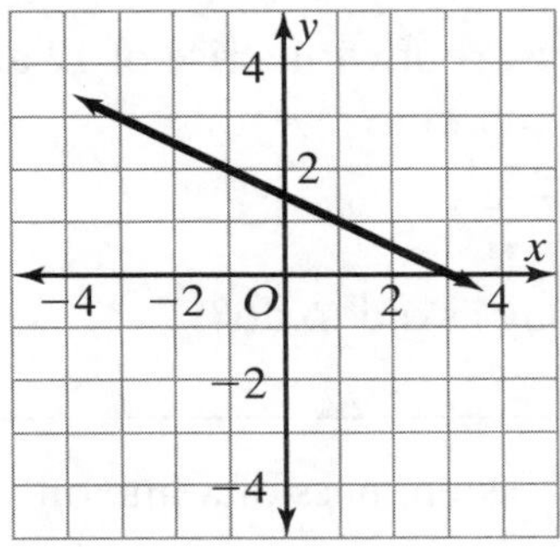

____

3. 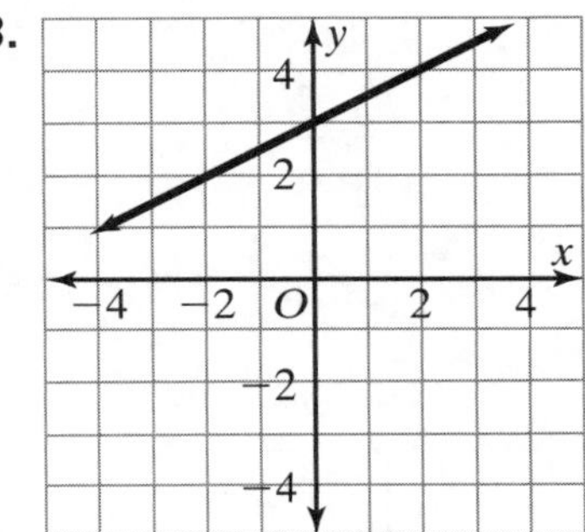

____

4. 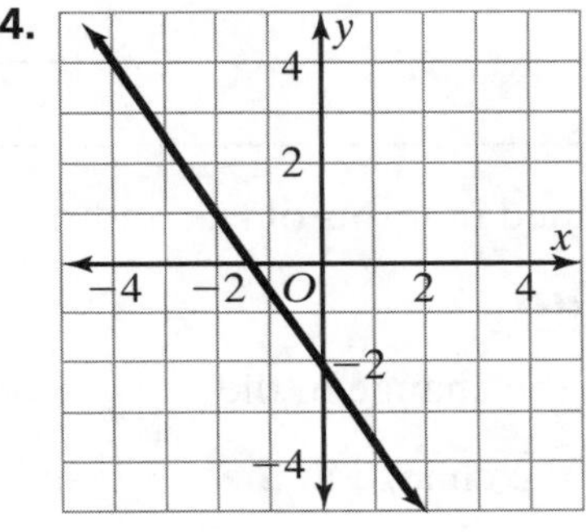

____

The points from each table lie on a line. Use the table to find the slope of each line. Then graph the line.

5.

x	0	1	2	3	4
y	−3	−1	1	3	5

slope = _______________

6.

x	0	1	2	3	4
y	5	3	1	−1	−3

slope = _______________

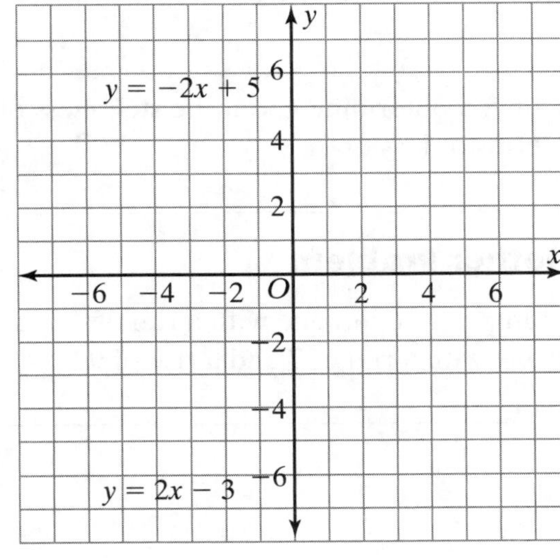

Name ______________________ Class ______________ Date ______________

4-1 • Guided Problem Solving

GPS Student Page 120, Exercise 12:

Which roof is steeper: a roof with a rise of 12 and a run of 7 or a roof with a rise of 8 and a run of 4?

Understand

1. What are you being asked to do?

____

2. What describes the steepness of a line on a coordinate plane?

____

3. What is a good way to visualize this problem?

____

____

4. How is slope defined in terms of run and rise? ____________

Plan and Carry Out

5. The rise involves the change in the ☐ -coordinates.
6. The run involves the change in the ☐ -coordinates.
7. Graph each slope on the coordinate plane.
8. Which roof is steeper?

____

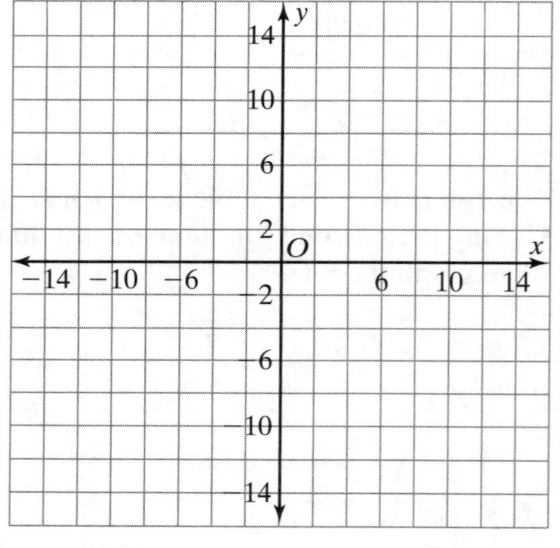

Check

9. What can you determine about the steepness of a line in terms of its slope?

____

Solve Another Problem

10. Which ramp is steeper: one with a run of 4 and a rise of 6, or one with a run of 7 and a rise of 9?

____

Name ______________________ Class ______________ Date ______________

Practice 4-2

Graphing Linear Functions

Find the slope and y-intercept of the graph of each function.

1. $y = x - 2$ ______________

2. $y = -3x + 4$ ______________

3. $y = \frac{4}{5}x + \frac{1}{5}$ ______________

4. $y = -2x$ ______________

5. $y = -\frac{2}{9}x - 8$ ______________

6. $y = 6x + 1$ ______________

Graph each linear function.

7. $f(x) = -x + 4$

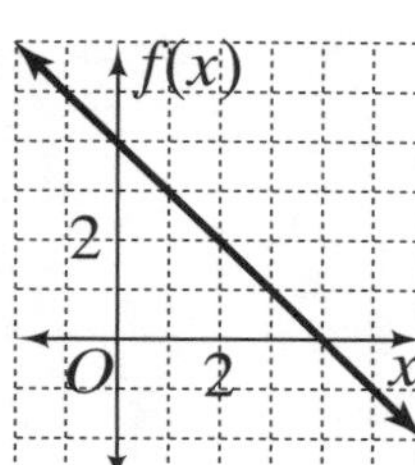

8. $f(x) = \frac{2}{3}x + 1$

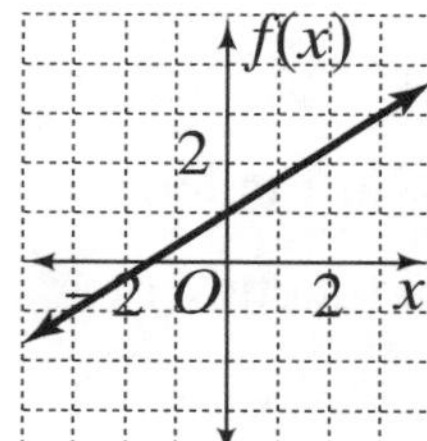

9. $f(x) = -2x + 1$

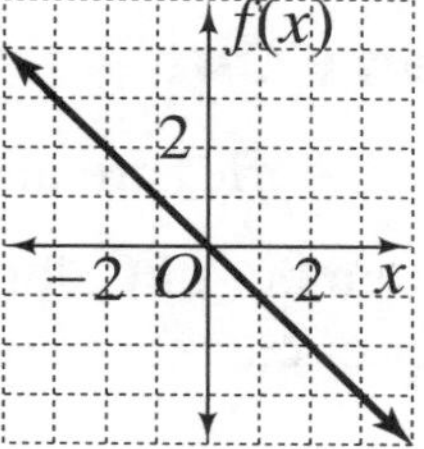

10. $y = \frac{1}{2}x + 3$

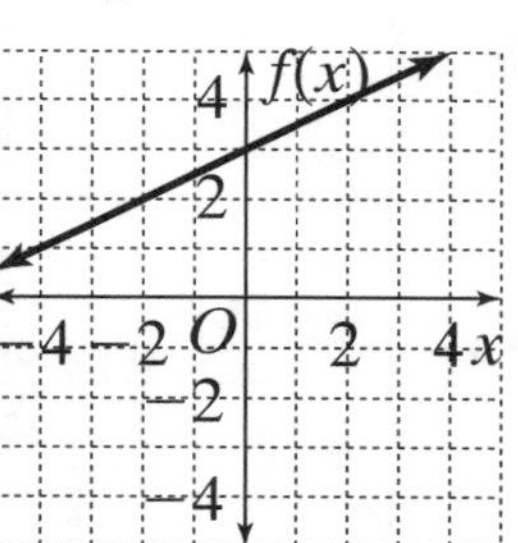

11. $y = -2 - 3x$

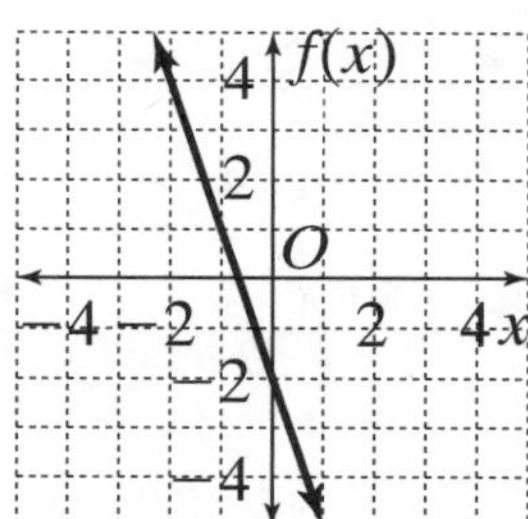

12. $y = 5 - 0.2x$

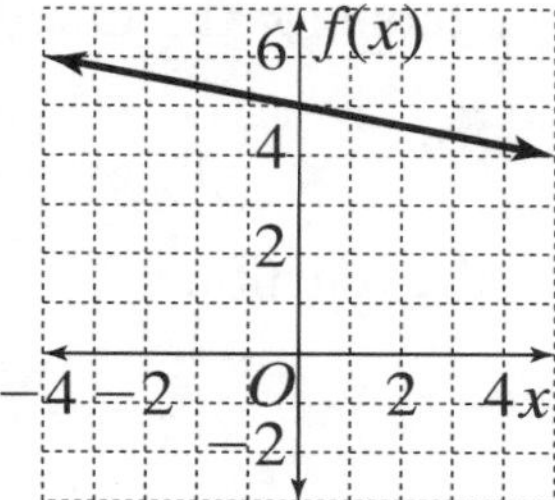

13. On a trip Alex averages 300 mi/day. The distance he covers (y) is a function of the number of days (x). Complete the table and graph the function.

Days	1	2	3	4
Miles				

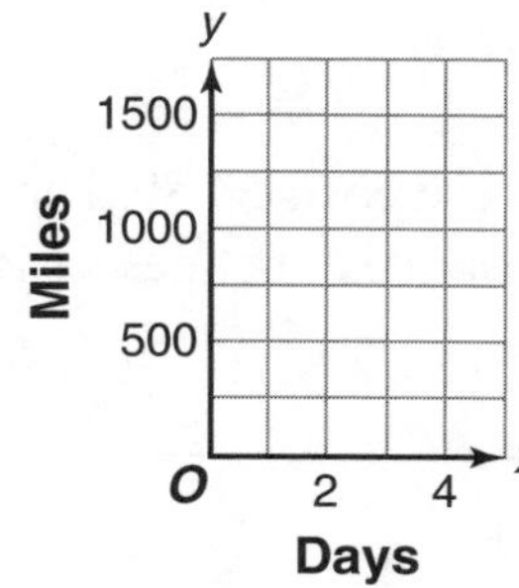

Name ______________________ Class ______________ Date ______________

4-2 • Guided Problem Solving

GPS Student Page 126, Exercise 23:

Nutrition Facts
Serving Size: 8 crackers (31g)
Serving Per Container: about 15
Amount Per Serving
Calories 140 Calories from Fat 35
% Daily Value
Total Fat 4g 6%
Saturated Fat 1g 5%
Monounsaturated Fat 1.5g

Nutrition The label at the right shows the nutrition facts for a package of crackers. Find how many Calories are in one cracker. The number of Calories consumed is a function of the number of crackers eaten. Make a table and a graph for the function.

Understand

1. What are you being asked to do? ______________________

____

____

Plan and Carry Out

2. How many Calories are in 8 crackers? ______ in 1 cracker? ______
3. Write the number of Calories consumed as a function of the number of crackers eaten.

____

____

4. Make a table for the function.

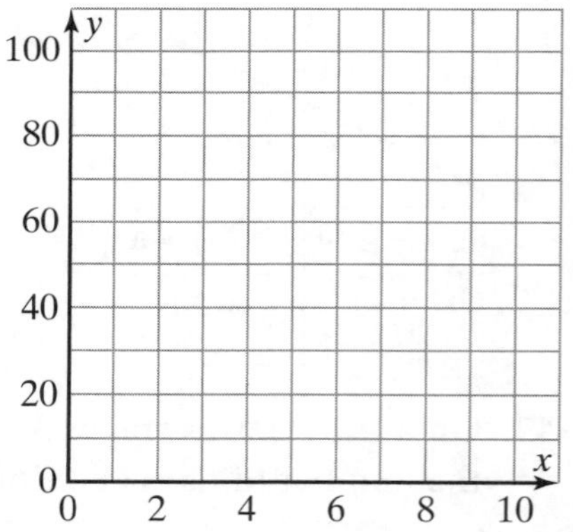

5. Graph the function.

Check

6. How can you check your answer?

____

Solve Another Problem

7. A 16-ounce package of cheese costs $4.80. The cost is a function of the number of ounces of cheese. Make a table and graph for the function.

____

____

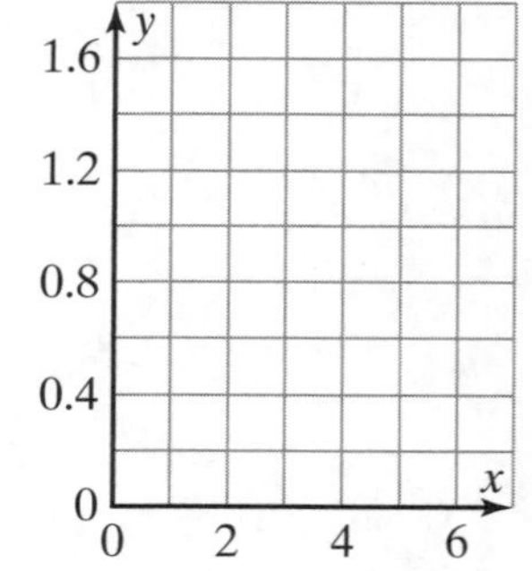

Name ______________________ Class ______________ Date ______________

Practice 4-3

Writing Rules for Linear Functions

Write a linear function rule for each situation. Identify the initial value and rate of change.

1. Amy sells tote bags at a craft fair for a day. She pays $50 to rent a booth. The materials and labor cost on each tote bag is $3.50. Her expenses for the day depend on how many tote bags she sells.

____

2. Ms.Watson receives a base pay of $150 plus a commission of $45 on each appliance that she sells. Her total pay depends on how many appliances she sells.

____

Write a function rule for the data in the table. Find the initial amount and rate of change.

3.

Number of Sessions, x	3	6	9	12
Cost for Music Lessons, y	115	205	295	385

____

4.

Number of People, x	2	4	6	8
Admission Price, y	28	56	84	112

____

5.

Pounds, x	1	2	5	10
Shipping Cost, y	7	11.5	25	47.5

____

6.

Hours, x	2	3	5	8
Cost for Repairs, y	165	225	345	525

____

Write a function rule for the data in the graph. Find the initial amount and rate of change.

7.

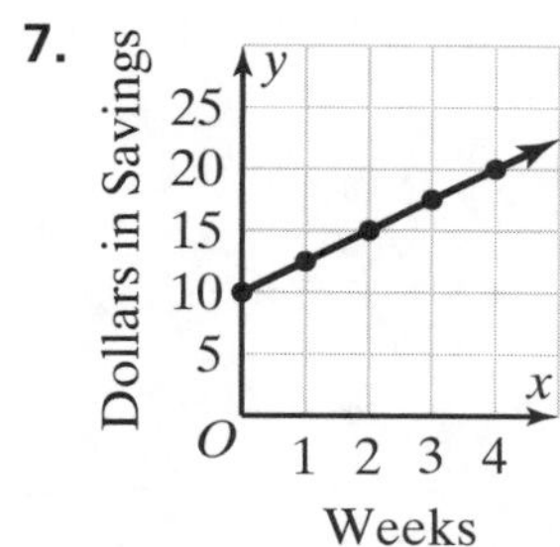

____

8.

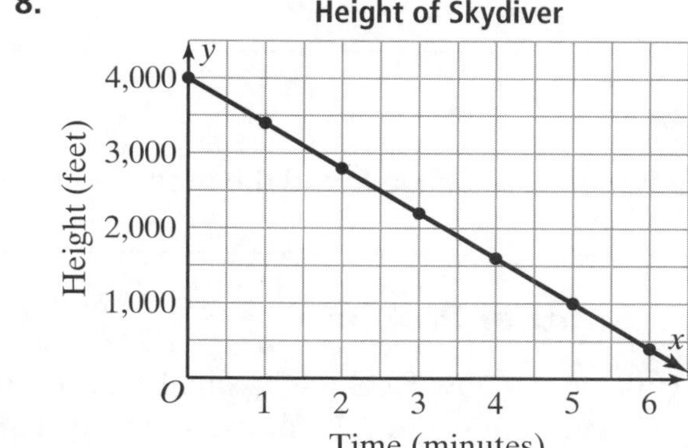

____

Name ______________________ Class ______________ Date ______________

4-3 • Guided Problem Solving

GPS Student Page 131, Exercise 10:

Art At a fair, an artist draws caricatures. He pays the fair $30 for space to set up his table and $2 for each drawing that he sells.

a. Write a function rule to represent the artist's total payment to the fair as a function of the number of drawings he sells. What is the initial payment and rate of change?

b. Reasoning What input is paired with the output $54? What does this input represent?

Understand

1. What is a caricature?

____

____

Plan and Carry Out

2. How much does the artist pay the fair for space rental and each drawing he sells?

____

3. Which function shows the amount of money the artist will pay the fair if *c* represents the number of caricatures he sells?

____

4. Complete the table below.

Number of Caricatures	1	2	3	4	5	6	7	8	9	10	11	12
Total Payment to Fair												

5. What input is paired with an output of $54? ______________________

____

Check

6. How could you have found the input value another way?

____

Solve Another Problem

7. At the craft show, Becky sells small ceramic, painted balls. She pays $25 for booth rental and $.50 for each ceramic ball that she sells. Write a function rule to represent her total payment to the craft show organizers as a function of the number of ceramic balls she sells.

____

Name ______________________ Class ______________ Date ______________

Practice 4-4

Comparing Functions

1. Determine which function has the greater rate of change. ____________

Function 1

x	2	3	5	6
y	6	10	18	22

Function 2

$y = 3x + 8$

2. Determine which function has the greater initial value? ____________

Function 1

When the value of x is 0, the value of y is 3. Each time the value of x increases by 1, the value of y increases by 5.

Function 2

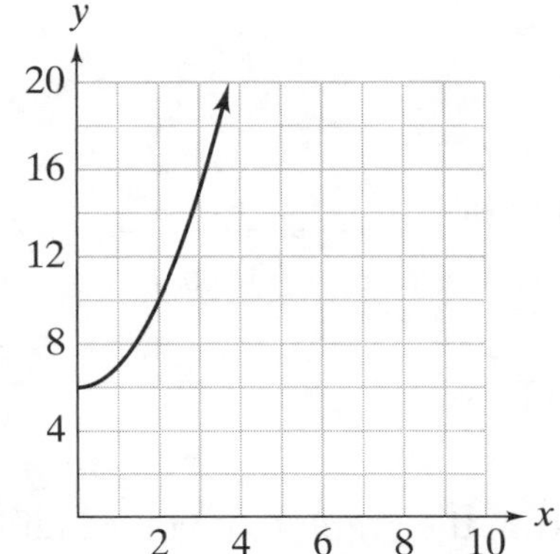

3. The repair costs for two mechanic shops are shown below. Which shop has the greater initial cost?

____

GT Auto Shop	Capital City Auto Service
• $75 to run a diagnostic test • $60 per hour for labor	The ordered pairs (2, 210) and (5, 435) are in the form (number of hours, total cost in dollars).

4. Which car gets better gas mileage (more miles per gallon)?

____

Mrs. Jackson's Car

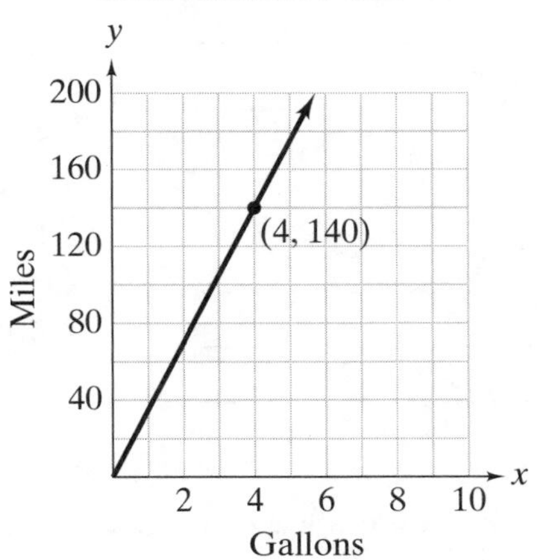

Mr. Padilla's Car

$m = 42g$ where m represents the number of miles and g represents the number of gallons

Name ______________________ Class ______________ Date ______________

4-4 • Guided Problem Solving

GPS Student Page 138, Exercise 13:

Order linear functions G, T, E, and W from least to greatest slope.

G:

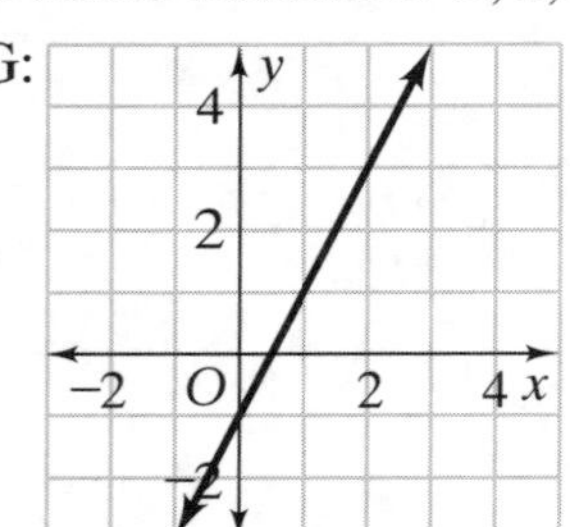

T:

x	−4	0	4	8
y	2	3	4	5

E: $y = \frac{5}{3}x + 2$

W: As x increases by 3 units, y increases by 1 unit.

Understand

1. What are you being asked to do? ______________________

2. Define slope in terms of x-values and y-values.

____

Plan and Carry Out

3. Name two ordered pairs from the graph that you can use to find the slope.

____

4. Name two ordered pairs from the table that you can use to find the slope.

____

5. Find the slope for functions G, T, E, and W. ______________________

6. Order the functions from least to greatest slope. ____________

Check

7. How can you check your answer?

____

____

Solve Another Problem

8. Order the functions A, B, C, and D from least to greatest slope.

A:

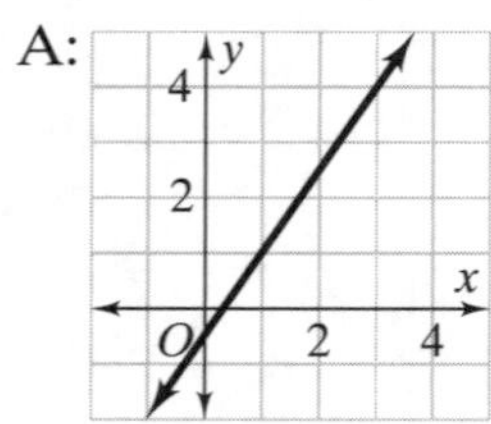

B:

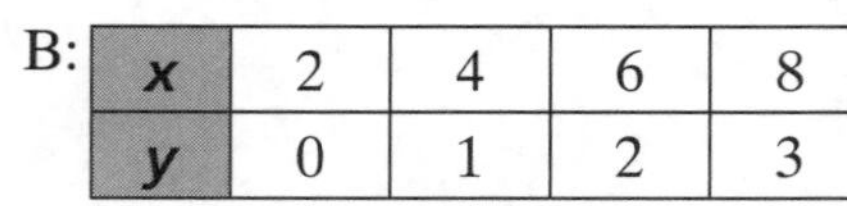

x	2	4	6	8
y	0	1	2	3

C: $y = \frac{1}{4}x + 2$

D: As x increases by 4 units, y increases by 3 units.

Name ______________________ Class ______________ Date ______________

4A: Graphic Organizer

For use before Lesson 4-1

Study Skill Your textbook includes a Skills Handbook with extra problems and questions. Working these exercises is a good way to review material and prepare for the next chapter.

Vocabulary and Study Skills

Write your answers.

1. What is the chapter title? ______________________
2. How many lessons are there in this chapter? ______________________
3. What is the topic of the Test-Taking Strategies page?

____

4. Complete the graphic organizer below as you work through the chapter.
   - In the center, write the title of the chapter.
   - When you begin a lesson, write the lesson name in a rectangle.
   - When you complete a lesson, write a skill or key concept in a circle linked to that lesson block.
   - When you complete the chapter, use this graphic organizer to help you review.

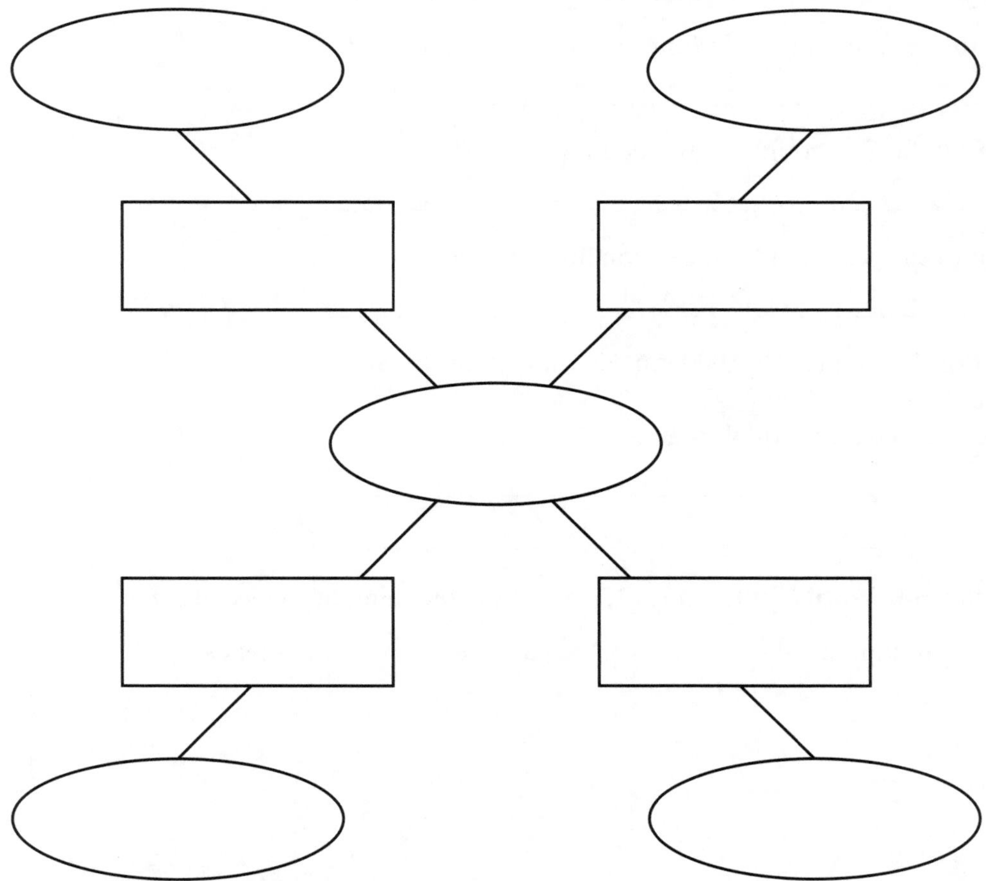

Name ______________________ Class ______________ Date ______________

4B: Reading Comprehension

For use after Lesson 4-2

Study Skill Highlight important information in your notes and on handouts from class.

Read the paragraph below and answer the questions.

A solar eclipse occurs when the moon passes between Earth and the Sun, partially blocking the view of the Sun. On June 11, 2002, a solar eclipse began at sunrise in Indonesia. The coastal town of Toli was the first to see the eclipse. Views of the eclipse lasted about $\frac{1}{4}$ of an hour with approximately $\frac{1}{5}$ of the Sun covered by the moon. In Mexico, residents witnessed about 97 percent of the Sun disappearing behind the moon, while in California about one-quarter of the Sun could be seen.

1. What event is described in the paragraph?

____

2. In Indonesia, how many minutes did the eclipse last?

____

3. How much more of the Sun did Indonesia see than California?

____

4. What percent of the Sun could not be seen in Mexico?

____

5. What percent of the Sun could not be seen in Indonesia?

____

6. The diameter of the Sun is 1,390,000 km. How much of the Sun's area could not be seen in Indonesia?
Hint: The area of a circle is equal to πr^2.

____

____

7. **High-Use Academic Words** In Exercise 1, what is the meaning of the word *event*?

   a. something that happens　　**b.** a result or consequence

Name ____________ Class ____________ Date ____________

4C: Reading/Writing Math Symbols

For use after Lesson 4-3

Study Skill To be successful in mathematics, you need to be able to read and understand mathematical symbols. These symbols will help you to determine relationships between figures and diagrams.

Vocabulary and Study Skills

Write each of the following expressions or statements in words.

1. $|5|$ ____________
2. -6 ____________
3. $-|8|$ ____________
4. $-2 < -1$ ____________
5. $3 \neq 5$ ____________
6. $|-2| = |2|$ ____________
7. $803 \text{ cm} \approx 8 \text{ m}$ ____________
8. $\frac{9}{2} = 4.5$ ____________

Write each of the following expressions using appropriate symbols.

9. the absolute value of negative four ____________
10. four times a number increased by five ____________
11. the quotient of a number and twelve ____________
12. the opposite of negative seven ____________
13. The opposite of three is less than zero. ____________
14. Four less than a number is six. ____________
15. One degree Celsius is approximately 32 degrees Fahrenheit. ____________

Name ______________________ Class ______________ Date ______________

4D: Visual Vocabulary Practice

For use after Lesson 4-4

Study Skill Mathematics builds on itself, so build a strong foundation.

Concept List

rate of change	initial value	line
3	slope of a line	slope-intercept form
−3	steepness	y-intercept

Write the concept that best describes each exercise. Choose from the concept list above.

1. 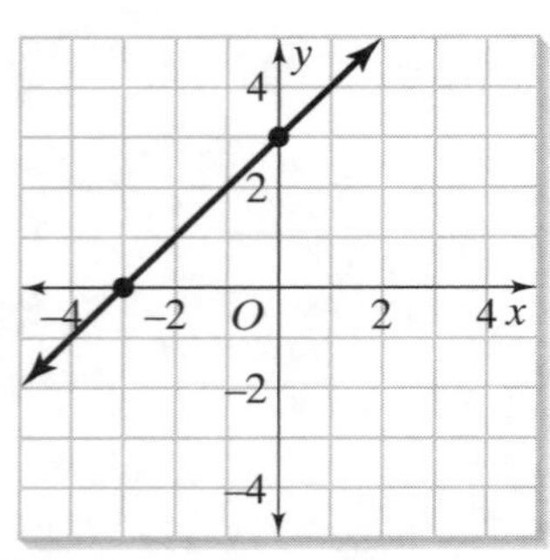 3 for the line in the graph ______________	**2.** The slope of a line describes the line's ______________. ______________	**3.** 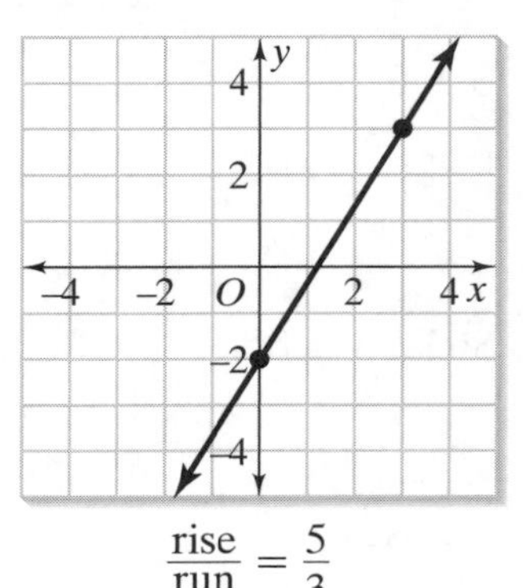 $\frac{\text{rise}}{\text{run}} = \frac{5}{3}$ ______________
4. In a function rule, what the slope represents. ______________	**5.** In a function rule, what the y-intercept represents. ______________	**6.** The graph of a linear function is this. ______________
7. For the line $y = 3x - 2$, the slope ______________	**8.** $y = mx + b$ ______________	**9.** The slope of the line passing through the points $(1, 4)$ and $(0, 7)$ ______________

Name ____________ Class ____________ Date ____________

4E: Vocabulary Check

For use after Lesson 4-4

Study Skill Strengthen your vocabulary. Use these pages and add cues and summaries by applying the Cornell Notetaking style.

Write the definition for each word or term at the right. To check your work, fold the paper back along the dotted line to see the correct answers.

Vocabulary and Study Skills

Definition	Term
____________	*y*- intercept
____________	slope-intercept form
____________	linear function
____________	slope
____________	function

Name ________________ Class ________________ Date ________________

4E: Vocabulary Check (continued)

For use after Lesson 4-4

Write the vocabulary word or term for each definition. To check your work, fold the paper forward along the dotted line to see the correct answers.

the point where the graph of a line crosses the y-axis ________________

an equation written in the form, $y = mx + b$ ________________

its graph has points that lie on a line ________________

a ratio that describes the steepness of lines in the coordinate plane ________________

a relationship that assigns exactly one output value for each input value ________________

Name ______________________ Class ______________ Date ______________

4F: Vocabulary Review Puzzle

For use with the Chapter Review

Study Skill Read problems carefully. Pay special attention to units when working with measurements.

Complete the crossword puzzle below. For help, use the Glossary in your textbook.

Here are the words you will use to complete this crossword puzzle:

geometric	circumference	equilateral	right	scalene
combination	permutation	arithmetic	coefficient	mean
parabola	perpendicular	function	linear	solution

ACROSS

2. sequence in which each term is found by multiplying the previous term by a fixed number
3. relationship that assigns exactly one output value to each input value
5. triangle with three congruent sides
6. distance around a circle
9. value that makes an equation true
12. sum of the values in a data set divided by the number of items in the data set
13. sequence in which each term is found by adding a fixed number to the previous term
14. angle measuring exactly 90°
15. arrangement of items in which the order of the items is not considered

DOWN

1. two lines that intersect and form a right angle
4. type of function whose points lie in a line
7. number that is multiplied by a variable
8. arrangement of objects in a particular order
10. shape of the graph of a quadratic function
11. triangle with no congruent sides

Name ______________________ Class ______________ Date ______________

Practice 5-1

Proportional Relationships

Solve each system of equations by graphing. Check your solution.

1. $y = x + 3$
$y = 4x - 3$

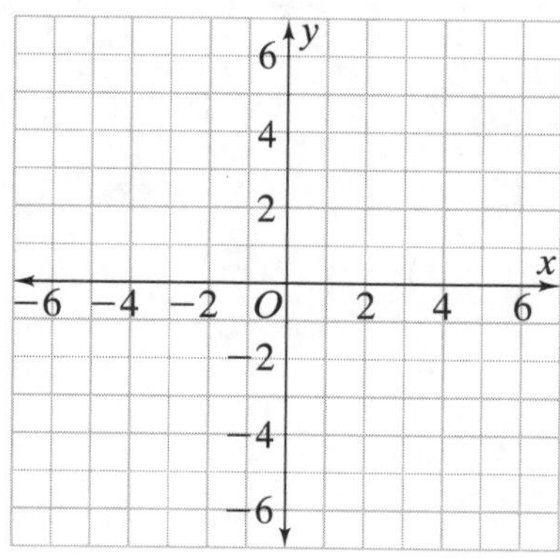

____

2. $y = \frac{1}{3}x + \frac{4}{3}$
$y = -\frac{1}{2}x + \frac{11}{2}$

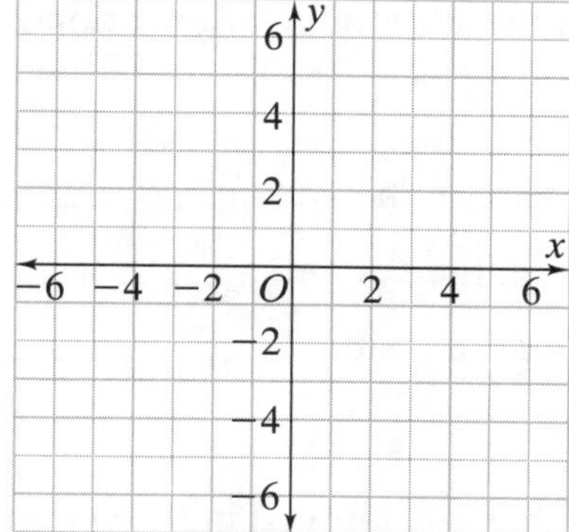

____

3. $x + y = -1$
$-2x + y = 5$

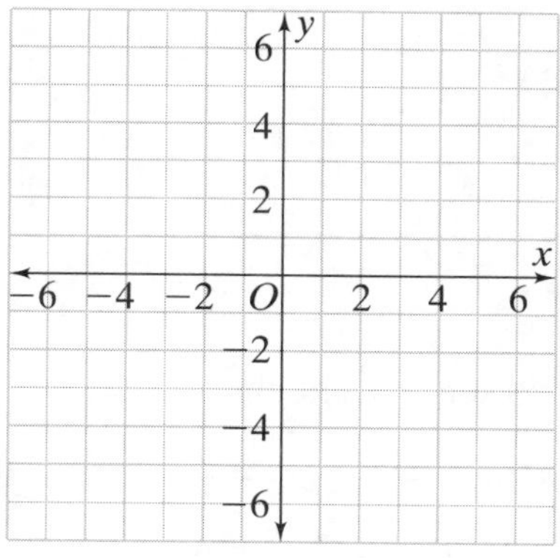

____

4. $\frac{1}{2}x - y = 4$
$x + 2y = -4$

____

5. During a football game, a concession stand sold a family 3 hamburgers and 2 hotdogs for a total of \$13. It sold another family 2 hamburgers and 5 hotdogs for a total of \$16. What are the prices of a hamburger and a hotdog?

____

Name ______________________ Class ______________ Date ______________

5-1 • Guided Problem Solving

GPS Student Page 151, Exercise 20:

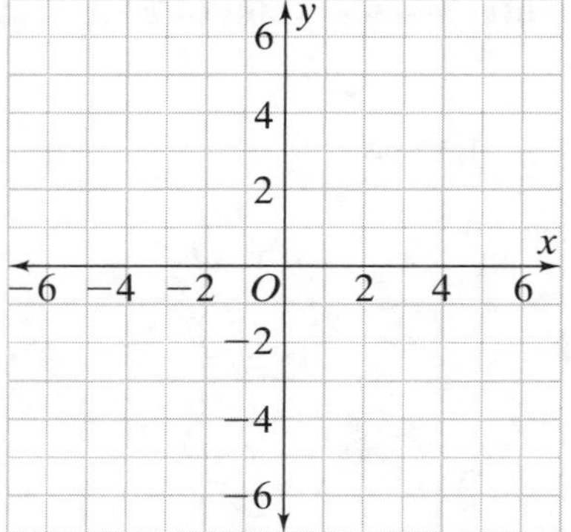

Open Ended One equation in a linear system is $y = x - 4$.

a. Graph $y = x - 4$ and a second linear equation so that the solution of the system is $(4, 0)$.

b. Write an equation of the second linear equation in the system.

Understand

1. How many equations are in the system? ______________
2. What is one equation in the system? ______________
3. What is the solution of the system? ______________

Plan and Carry Out

4. Graph the equation that you know is in the system. ______________
5. Draw a point on the graph to represent the solution of the system.

____

6. What point do you know that the second equation passes through? ______________
7. How many different lines can be drawn through this point? ______________
8. Draw one possible line to represent the second equation in the system.

____

9. Write the equation for the line you drew. ______________

Check

10. Substitute the solution of the system in the equation you wrote to see if it checks.

____

Solve Another Problem

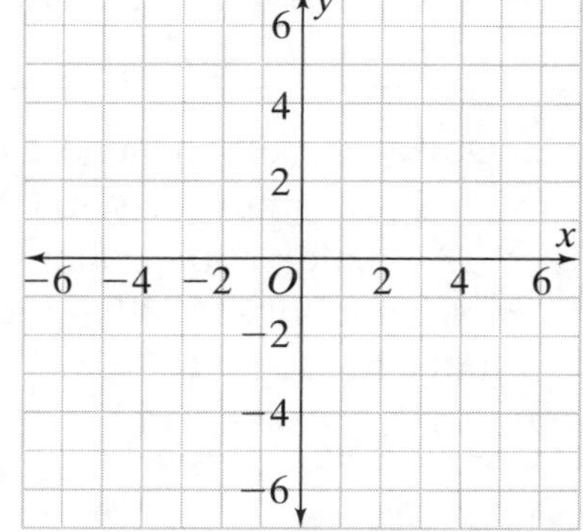

11. **Open Ended** One equation in a linear system is $y = 2x - 3$.

a. Graph $y = 2x - 3$ and a second linear equation so that the system has a solution of $(1, -1)$.

b. Write the equation of the second linear equation in the system.

____

Name ______________________ Class ______________ Date ______________

Practice 5-2

Solving Systems by Substitution

Solve each system of equations using substitution. Check your answer.

1. $y = x - 2$
   $-2x + 3y = -1$

   ____

2. $3y - 2x = 0$
   $y = 4x - 1$

   ____

3. $x - 3y = -13$
   $4x + 2y = 4$

   ____

4. $2y - \frac{3}{4}x = -10$
   $y + \frac{1}{4}x = 0$

   ____

5. A gym charges a one-time registration fee as well as a monthly fee. The cost of joining the gym for 4 months is \$370, and the cost of joining for 6 months is \$530. Write and solve a system of equations to find the registration fee and monthly fee.

   ____

   ____

   ____

Name ______________________ Class ______________ Date ______________

5-2 • Guided Problem Solving

GPS Student Page 157, Exercise 16:

A grocery store makes a 20 pound mixture of almonds and cashew nuts. The store charges $4.00 per pound for almonds and $5.50 per pound for cashews. The total value of the mixture is $92. How many pounds of each type of nut are in the mixture?

Understand

1. What is in the mixture? ______________________
2. How much does the mixture weigh? ______________________
3. How much does 1 pound of almonds cost? ______________________
4. How much does 1 pound of cashews cost? ______________________
5. How much does the mixture cost? ______________________

Plan and Carry Out

6. Write an equation that represents the total weight of the mixture. Let x = pounds of almonds and y = pounds of cashews.

   ____

7. Write an equation that represents the total cost of the mixture.

   ____

8. The equations in Steps 6 and 7 form a system. Use substitution to solve the system.

   ____

9. How many pounds of almonds and cashews are in the mixture?

   ____

Check

10. Substitute the solution in each of the original equations.

    ____

Solve Another Problem

11. A deli makes up a cheese tray with colby and jack cheese. There is a total of 6 pounds of cheese. The colby cheese costs $5.00 per pound, and the jack cheese costs $4.50 per pound. The total value of the cheese tray is $28. How many pounds of each type of cheese are on the tray?

    ____

Name ________________ Class ________________ Date ________________

Practice 5-3

Solving Systems by Elimination

Solve each system of equations by elimination. Check your solution.

1. $x - y = 5$
   $x + y = 11$

   ____

2. $9x + 4y = 7$
   $6x - 4y = 2$

   ____

3. $-3x + 6y = 15$
   $-3x - 2y = -1$

   ____

4. $-\frac{9}{4}x + 3y = 12$
   $\frac{1}{4}x - 6y = 10$

   ____

5. At the craft store, Lisa bought 3 clay blocks and 2 molds for \$15.50. Tony bought 6 clay blocks and 1 mold for \$19.00. Write and solve a system of equations to find the cost of each clay block and each mold.

   ____

   ____

   ____

Name ______________________ Class ______________ Date ______________

5-3 • Guided Problem Solving

GPS Student Page 184, Exercise 11:

Writing in Math Explain how to solve the system below using the elimination method.

$$5x - 6y = 8$$
$$-3x + 11y = 10$$

Understand

1. What are you being asked to do?

____

2. How will you find the answer?

____

Plan and Carry Out

3. Multiply the first equation by 3.

4. Multiply the second equation by 5.

5. Add the equations to eliminate x.

6. Substitute the value for y. Solve for x.

7. What is the solution of the system? ______________________

Check

8. How can you check your answer?

____

Solve Another Problem

9. Explain how to solve the system below using the elimination method.

$$4x + 2y = 28$$
$$3x - 3y = 3$$

____

Name ______________________ Class ______________ Date ______________

Practice 5-4

Systems in the Real World

Solve each linear system. Explain why you chose the method that you used.

1. $x + 4y = 18$
   $x + 8y = 38$

   ____

2. $0.6x + 5y = 11$
   $3x + 2y = 28$

   ____

3. $x + y = -7$
   $2x + 2y = -14$

   ____

4. $5x - 2y = 22$
   $y = \frac{1}{3}x - \frac{7}{3}$

   ____

5. Marco is selling comic books and other paperback books at a yard sale. The comic books cost \$3 each, and the other paperbacks cost \$0.75 each. Marco has 60 books to sell in all. If he sells all of them, he will make \$135. Write a system of equations and find how many comic books and how many other paperback books Marco has to sell. Explain why you chose the method you used.

   ____

   ____

   ____

Name ______________________ Class ______________ Date ______________

5-4 • Guided Problem Solving

GPS Student Page 170, Exercise 16:

The Ahmed family wants to get satellite television service. Satellite Focus charges a monthly rate of \$50 plus a one-time installation fee of \$150. Dish Dynamics charges a monthly rate of \$55 plus a one-time installation fee of \$100. How should the Ahmeds choose which satellite television company to use? Justify your response.

Understand

1. Draw an oval around the cost for Satellite Focus. Draw a box around the cost for Dish Dynamics.

Plan and Carry Out

2. Write an equation that represents the cost of Satellite Focus's service. Then write an equation that represents the cost of Dish Dynamics' service. Let x = number of months and y = total cost.

   ____

3. When does the service from both companies cost the same?

   ____

4. What decision should the Ahmeds make?

   ____

   ____

   ____

Check

5. Substitute the solution in each of the original equations.

   ____

Solve Another Problem

6. The Miller family is planning to order a pizza. Papa's Pizza charges \$14 for a large cheese pizza and \$1.50 for each additional topping. Zeke's Pizzeria charges \$12 for a large cheese pizza and \$2 for each additional topping. How should the Millers choose which pizza company to order from? Justify your response.

   ____

   ____

   ____

Name ______________________ Class ______________ Date ______________

5A: Graphic Organizer

For use before Lesson 5-1

Study Skill Take notes when your teacher presents new material in class and when you read the lesson yourself. Organize your notes, reviewing them as you go.

Write your answers.

1. What is the chapter title? ______________________
2. How many lessons are there in this chapter? ______________________
3. What is the topic of the Test-Taking Strategies page? ______________________
4. Complete the graphic organizer below as you work through the chapter.
   - In the center, write the title of the chapter.
   - When you begin a lesson, write the lesson name in a rectangle.
   - When you complete a lesson, write a skill or key concept in a circle linked to that lesson block.
   - When you complete the chapter, use this graphic organizer to help you review.

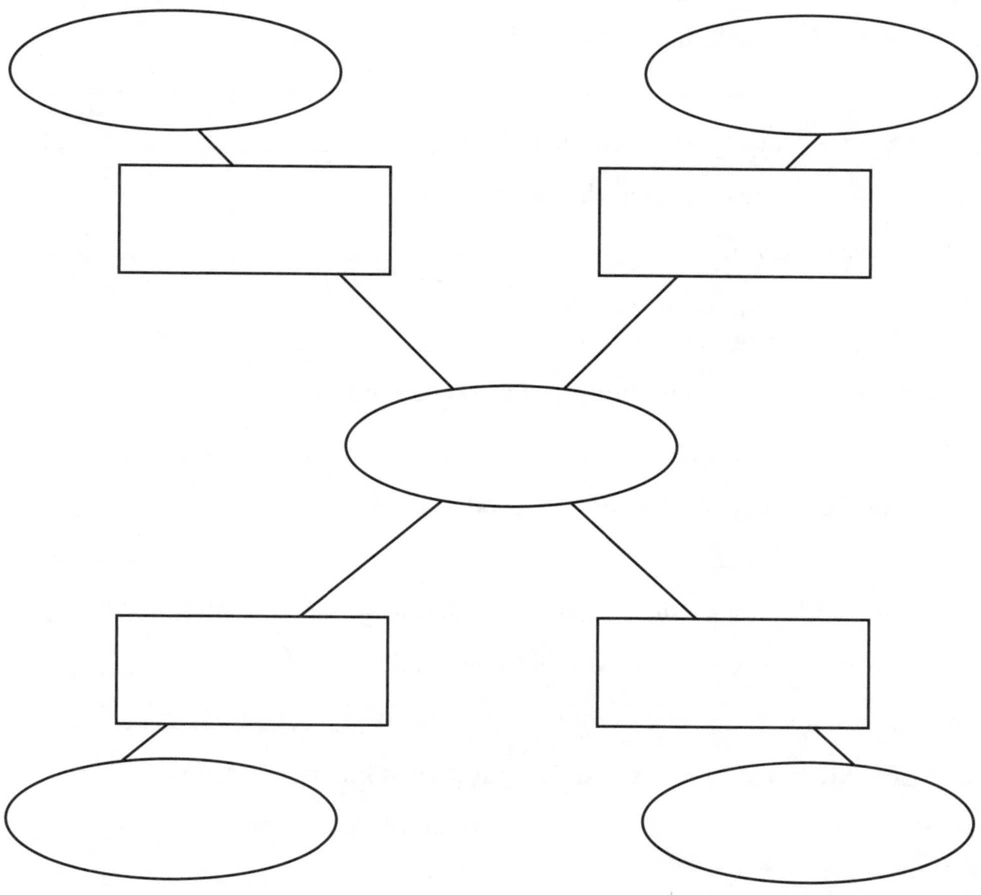

Vocabulary and Study Skills

Name ______________________ Class ______________ Date ______________

5B: Reading Comprehension

For use after Lesson 5-4

Study Skill Make a realistic study schedule. Try to balance your study time with before- or after-school free time, meals, and other activities.

Use the recipe below to answer the questions.

Saffron Rice Salad

2 tablespoons white wine vinegar
1 teaspoon olive oil
2 to 3 drops hot pepper sauce, optional
1 clove garlic, minced
$\frac{1}{4}$ teaspoon ground white pepper
$2\frac{1}{2}$ cups cooked rice (cooked in chicken broth and $\frac{1}{8}$ teaspoon saffron or ground turmeric), cooled to room temperature
$\frac{1}{2}$ cup diced red bell pepper
$\frac{1}{2}$ cup diced green bell pepper
$\frac{1}{2}$ cup sliced green onions
$\frac{1}{4}$ cup sliced black olives

Combine vinegar, oil, pepper sauce (if desired), garlic, and white pepper in large bowl; mix well. Add rice, peppers, onions, and olives; toss lightly. Serve on lettuce leaves. Serves four.

1. What can you make by combining the ingredients above?

   ____

2. How many ingredients are used in the recipe? ______________
3. What is the smallest quantity used in the recipe? ______________
4. How many servings can you make using this recipe? ______________
5. How many ingredients require an amount that is a rational number but not an integer? ______________
6. Which ingredient(s) require an amount that is a mixed number?

   ____

7. Calculate the total quantity of bell peppers used in the recipe.

   ____

8. For a picnic, you need to make the saffron rice salad to serve 6 people.
   a. How many cups of sliced black olives will you need? ______________
   b. How many cups of sliced green onions will you need? ______________
9. **High-Use Academic Words** In Exercise 7, what does it mean to *calculate*?
   a. to determine using mathematical processes
   b. to place in order

Name ______ Class ______ Date ______

5C: Reading/Writing Math Symbols

For use after Lesson 5-2

Study Skill Create a list of mathematical symbols and their meanings. Keep the list in your math notebook for reference.

Explain the meaning of the bar (–) in the following examples.

1. $4 - 7$ ______
2. $\frac{3}{5}$ ______
3. $3 + (-5)$ ______
4. $3.\overline{6}$ ______

Explain the meaning of the dot (·) in the following examples.

5. 14.2222 . . .
6. 2.7
7. $3 \cdot 9$
8. Sarah is 6 years old.
9. 1, 3, 5, 7, . . .

Write the following expressions using the appropriate math symbols. Use a bar or a dot.

10. the sum of four and negative three ______
11. the difference between two and five tenths and three point three repeating ______

Name ______________________ Class ______________ Date ______________

5D: Visual Vocabulary Practice

For use after Lesson 5-4

Study Skill When a math exercise is difficult, try to determine what makes it difficult. Is it a word that you don't understand? Are the numbers difficult to use?

Concept List

substitution method	factors	system of equations
prime numbers	graphing	infinite
least common multiple	elimination method	none

Write the concept that best describes each exercise. Choose from the concept list above.

1. Set of two or more equations that have the same variables ________________	**2.** The number 336 represents this for the numbers 28 and 48. ________________	**3.** 30 → 6, (5); 6 → (2), (3) ________________
4. By replacing one variable with an equivalent expression containing the other variable, you create a one-variable equation to solve. ________________	**5.** 2, 13, 23, and 37 are examples of these. ________________	**6.** Can be used to solve systems of two linear equations in two variables. ________________
7. In this method, use the Addition or Subtraction Properties of Equality to add or subtract equations in order to eliminate one variable. ________________	**8.** The number of solutions for this system of equations: $3x + 4y = 5$ $3x + 4y = 7$ ________________	**9.** The number of solutions for this system of equations: $x + y = 3$ $3x + 3y = 9$ ________________

Name ________________ Class ________________ Date ________________

5E: Vocabulary Check

For use after Lesson 5-4

Study Skill Strengthen your vocabulary. Use these pages and add cues and summaries by applying the Cornell Notetaking style.

Write the definition for each word or term at the right. To check your work, fold the paper back along the dotted line to see the correct answers.

substitution method

system of equations

solution of a system

elimination method

graphing method

Name ______________________ Class ______________ Date ______________

5E: Vocabulary Check (continued)

For use after Lesson 5-4

Write the vocabulary word or term for each definition. To check your work, fold the paper forward along the dotted line to see the correct answers.

solve one equation for one variable, then substitute the value of the variable into the other equation to solve for the other variable	______________
set of two or more equations that have the same variables	______________
ordered pair that satisfies all equations in the system	______________
with this method the Addition and Subtraction properties of Equality are used to add and subtract equations to eliminate one variable	______________
graph each equation and determine any points of intersection	______________

Name ______________________ Class ______________ Date ______________

5F: Vocabulary Review

For use with the Chapter Review

Study Skill Take notes while you study. Go back and review your notes before quizzes and tests.

Circle the word that best completes the sentence.

1. A (*percent, sentence*) is a ratio that compares a number to 100.
2. Percent increase is equal to the change in price divided by the (*new, original*) price, times 100.
3. A (*solution, letter*) is a value for a variable that makes an equation true.
4. A(n) (*outlier, range*) is a data value that is much greater than or less than the other values in a set of data.
5. An (*expression, equation*) is a mathematical sentence with an equal sign.
6. The original deposit into a bank account is called the (*rate, principal*).
7. The (*mean, median*) is the number that is the middle value of a data set that is ordered from least to greatest values.
8. The amount a store increases the price of an item is called the (*selling price, markup*).
9. The (*absolute value, opposite*) of a number is its distance from 0 on a number line.
10. A collection of all possible outcomes in an experiment is called the (*event, sample space*).
11. A(n) (*equation, proportion*) states that two ratios are equal.
12. A(n) (*variable, expression*) is a letter that stands for an unknown quantity.

Name ______________________ Class ______________ Date ______________

Practice 6-1

Scientific Notation

Write each number in scientific notation.

1. 45 ______
2. 250 ______
3. 90 ______
4. 670 ______
5. 4,100 ______
6. 500 ______
7. 43,200 ______
8. 97,100 ______
9. 38,050 ______
10. 480,000 ______
11. 900,000 ______
12. 8,750,000 ______

Write each number in standard form.

13. 3.1×10^1 ______
14. 8×10^2 ______
15. 4.501×10^4 ______
16. 9.7×10^6 ______
17. 2.86×10^5 ______
18. 3.58×10^6 ______
19. 8.1×10^1 ______
20. 9.071×10^2 ______
21. 4.83×10^9 ______
22. 2.73×10^8 ______
23. 2×10^5 ______
24. 8.09×10^4 ______

Order each set of numbers from least to greatest.

25. $8.9 \times 10^2, 6.3 \times 10^3, 2.1 \times 10^4, 7.8 \times 10^5$

______

26. $2.1 \times 10^4, 2.12 \times 10^3, 3.46 \times 10^5, 2.112 \times 10^2$

______

27. A mulberry silkworm can spin a single thread that measures up to 3,900 ft in length. Write the number in scientific notation.

______

Write each number in scientific notation.

28. 0.025 ______
29. 0.00003 ______
30. 0.00197 ______
31. 0.000407 ______

Write each number in standard form.

32. 8.1×10^{-3} ______
33. 3.42×10^{-5} ______
34. 9.071×10^{-6} ______
35. 2×10^{-4} ______

Name ______________________ Class ______________ Date ______________

6-1 • Guided Problem Solving

GPS Student Page 181, Exercise 33:

Astronomy When the sun emits a solar flare, the blast wave can travel through space at 3×10^6 km/h. Use the formula $d = rt$ to find how far the wave will travel in 30 min.

Understand

1. What does each of the variables stand for in the formula?

____

2. What are being asked to find?

____

Plan and Carry Out

3. Which variable are you solving for in the formula? ____________

4. To write the rate in standard form, which way and how many places will you move the decimal point? What is the rate in standard form?

____

5. Convert 30 minutes to hours. ____________

6. Substitute what you know into the formula and solve.

____

7. Write the distance back into scientific notation. Which way will you move the decimal point and how many places?

____

Check

8. How can you check to see if your answer is reasonable?

____

____

Solve Another Problem

9. A state animal shelter had 4.2×10^4 unwanted animals dropped off last year. If the goal of the shelter is to decrease the number by one-sixth this year, how many fewer animals will enter the shelter? Write your answer in scientific notation.

____

Name ____________ Class ____________ Date ____________

Practice 6-2

Exponents and Multiplication

Write each expression using a single exponent.

1. $3^2 \cdot 3^5$
2. $1^3 \cdot 1^4$
3. $(-3)^{12} \cdot (-3)^5$
4. $0.8^3 \cdot 0.8$
5. $(-1.3)^2 \cdot (-1.3)^4$
6. $4.5^8 \cdot 4.5^2$
7. $3^3 \cdot 3 \cdot 3^4$
8. $2^2 \cdot 2^2 \cdot 2^2$
9. $5 \cdot 5^4 \cdot 5^3$

Simplify each expression.

10. $a^1 \cdot a^2$
11. $m^5 \cdot m$
12. $(-y)^3 \cdot (-y)^2$
13. $(3x) \cdot (3x)$
14. $4d \cdot 9d^8$
15. $x^2y \cdot xy^2$
16. $10jk^5 \cdot 3j^3k^2$
17. $2p^3q^2 \cdot 3p^2q^3$
18. $5x^2 \cdot x^6 \cdot x^3$

Replace each ? with =, <, or >.

19. 3^8 ? $3 \cdot 3^7$
20. 49 ? $7^2 \cdot 7^2$
21. $5^3 \cdot 5^4$? 25^2

22. A square has a side length of $7x^4$ in. Find the area of the square.

23. The formula for the volume of a rectangular prism is $V = \ell \cdot w \cdot h$. What is the volume of a prism with length $2x^2$ mm, width $4x$ mm, and height x^3 mm?

24. One meter is equal to 10^2 centimeters. One kilometer is equal to 10^3 meters. How many centimeters are in one kilometer?

Name ____________________ Class ____________ Date ____________

6-2 • Guided Problem Solving

GPS Student Page 187, Exercise 34:

Geometry The formula for the area of a square is $A = s^2$. What is the area of a square whose sides are $3x^2$ cm?

Understand

1. What are you being asked to do? ____________________
2. What do you know? ____________________

Plan and Carry Out

3. Write the formula for the area of the square as a multiplication sentence.
4. Substitute the side length of the square for s in the formula you wrote in Problem 3.
5. Rewrite the formula by using the Commutative Property of Multiplication to group numbers and to group variables that have the same base.
6. How do you multiply numbers or variables that have the same base?
7. What is the area of the square in simplest form?

Check

8. How can you check your answer? ____________________

Solve Another Problem

9. What is the area of a rectangle whose length is $5x$ ft and whose width is $8x^2$ ft?

Name ______________________ Class ______________ Date ______________

Practice 6-3

Multiplying with Scientific Notation

Find each product. Write the answers in scientific notation.

1. $(3 \times 10^4)(5 \times 10^6)$ ______________
2. $(7 \times 10^2)(6 \times 10^4)$ ______________
3. $(4 \times 10^5)(7 \times 10^8)$ ______________
4. $(9.1 \times 10^6)(3 \times 10^9)$ ______________
5. $(8.4 \times 10^9)(5 \times 10^7)$ ______________
6. $(5 \times 10^3)(4 \times 10^6)$ ______________
7. $(7.2 \times 10^8)(2 \times 10^3)$ ______________
8. $(1.4 \times 10^5)(4 \times 10^{11})$ ______________

Choose the most reasonable unit to describe the quantity.
Then use scientific notation to describe the quantity using the other unit.

9. The mass of a bicycle is about 6 _____. (g, kg) ______________
10. The length of a school bus is 12 _____. (m, km) ______________
11. Double the number 4.6×10^{15}. Write the answer in scientific notation.

    ____

12. Triple the number 2.3×10^3. Write the answer in scientific notation.

    ____

13. A company manufactures 3.2×10^4 cell phones per month. How many cell phones does it manufacture per year?

    ____

14. Yosemite National Park covers about 7.6×10^5 acres. There are about 4.36×10^4 square feet in one acre. How many square feet does the national park cover?

    ____

Name ____________________ Class ____________ Date ____________

6-3 • Guided Problem Solving

GPS Student Page 191, Exercise 20:

Geography The Sahara is a desert of about 3.5 million square miles. There are about 2.79×10^7 square feet in a square mile. About how many square feet does the Sahara cover? Write your answer in scientific notation.

Understand

1. What are you being asked to do?

____

____

2. What form will your answer be in? ____________________

Plan and Carry Out

3. Write 3.5 million in standard form. ____________________
4. Write 3.5 million in scientific notation. ____________________
5. To convert from square miles to square feet, what operation will you use?

____

6. Write the conversion for square feet to square miles.

____

7. Convert the square miles of the Sahara to square feet.

____

Check

8. Use another method to solve the problem. Does your answer check?

____

____

____

Solve Another Problem

9. The human body contains about 3.2×10^4 microliters of blood per pound of body weight. How many microliters of blood would a 185-pound man have circulating in his body? Write your answer in scientific notation.

____

Name ____________________ Class ____________ Date ____________

Practice 6-4

Exponents and Division

Simplify each expression.

1. 8^{-2}
2. $(-3)^0$
3. 5^{-1}
4. 18^0
5. 2^{-5}
6. 3^{-3}
7. 2^{-3}
8. 5^{-2}
9. $\frac{4^4}{4}$
10. $8^6 \div 8^8$
11. $-\frac{(3)^6}{(3)^8}$
12. $\frac{8^4}{8^0}$
13. $1^{15} \div 1^{18}$
14. $7 \div 7^4$
15. $-\frac{(4)^8}{(4)^4}$
16. $\frac{10^9}{10^{12}}$
17. $\frac{b^{12}}{b^4}$
18. $\frac{g^9}{g^{15}}$
19. $x^{16} \div x^7$
20. $v^{20} \div v^{25}$

Complete each equation.

21. $\frac{1}{3^5} = 3^{?}$
22. $-\frac{1}{(2)^7} = -2^{?}$
23. $\frac{1}{x^2} = x^{?}$
24. $-\frac{1}{125} = (-5)^{?}$
25. $\frac{1}{1,000} = 10^{?}$
26. $\frac{5^{10}}{?} = 5^5$
27. $\frac{z^{?}}{z^8} = z^{-3}$
28. $\frac{q^5}{?} = q^7$

Is each statement true or false? Explain your reasoning.

29. $(-1)^3 = 1^{-3}$
30. $3^{-1} \cdot 3^{-1} = 3^1$
31. $2^2 \cdot 2^{-2} = 1$
32. $7^2 \cdot (-7)^3 = (-7)^{-6}$

Name ______________________ Class ______________ Date ______________

6-4 • Guided Problem Solving

GPS Student Page 197, Exercise 24:

Earth Science Earth's crust is divided into large pieces called tectonic plates. The Pacific tectonic plate is moving northwest at a rate of about 4^{-2} m each year. At this rate, how long will it take the plate to move 4^6 m (about 2.5 miles)?

Understand

1. The equation $d = rt$ represents the relationship between distance d, rate r, and time t. What measurements are given in the problem?

____

2. What measurement are you asked to find?

____

Plan and Carry Out

3. Solve the equation $d = rt$ for t.

____

4. Substitute the values that are known into the equation for t.

____

5. What is the common base?

____

6. When dividing powers with the same base, what do you do to the exponents?

____

7. Solve the equation for t.

____

Check

8. Solve the problem by writing the numbers in standard form. Does your answer check?

____

Solve Another Problem

9. A rectangular plot of land covers an area of 2^{13} square feet. You measure the length of the plot to be 2^7 feet. What is the width?

____

Name ______________________ Class ______________ Date ______________

Practice 6-5

Dividing with Scientific Notation

Divide. Write each quotient in scientific notation.

1. $\dfrac{6.8 \times 10^7}{3.4 \times 10^5}$ ______________

2. $\dfrac{7.3 \times 10^3}{4.5 \times 10^6}$ ______________

3. $\dfrac{2.6 \times 10^5}{5.1 \times 10^3}$ ______________

4. $\dfrac{1.9 \times 10^{-4}}{3.3 \times 10^1}$ ______________

5. $\dfrac{7.9 \times 10^5}{2.3 \times 10^3}$ ______________

6. $\dfrac{6.2 \times 10^7}{5.6 \times 10^{-8}}$ ______________

7. $\dfrac{8.2 \times 10^5}{6}$ ______________

8. $\dfrac{12}{4.3 \times 10^2}$ ______________

9. $\dfrac{3.4 \times 10^7}{9}$ ______________

Which of the following numbers is greater?

10. 5.2×10^4 or 5.8×10^3 ______________

11. 6×10^3 or 8×10^{-3} ______________

12. 3.42×10^6 or 3.24×10^6 ______________

13. 8.1×10^{-7} or 8.1×10^{-8} ______________

Estimate how many times the first number is than the second number.

14. 6×10^{12} and 2×10^{10} ______________

15. 4×10^9 and 8×10^5 ______________

16. The height of the thermosphere is about 2.95×10^5 feet above Earth. There are 5,280 feet in 1 mile. About how many miles above earth is the thermosphere?

____

17. The speed of light is about 3.0×10^8 m/s. The speed of sound is about 3.4×10^2 m/s. How much faster does light travel than sound?

____

18. The distance between Los Angeles, California, and Washington, D.C., is 4.3×10^6 m. The distance between New York City, New York, and Washington, D.C., is 3.6×10^5 m. How much farther is Los Angeles from Washington, D.C., than New York City?

____

Name ______________________ Class ______________ Date ______________

6-5 • Guided Problem Solving

GPS Student Page 205, Exercise 19:

The sun's diameter is 1.39×10^6 kilometers. Earth's diameter is 1.28×10^4 kilometers. How many times greater is the sun's diameter than Earth's diameter?

Understand

1. Which diameter is larger? ______________________
2. What are you being asked to find?

____

____

Plan and Carry Out

3. The diameters are in scientific notation, and the numbers 1.28 and 1.39 are close in value, so what do you need to compare?

____

4. When dividing powers with the same base, what do you do to the exponents?

____

5. Subtract the exponents and write the power in standard form.

____

6. How many times greater is the sun's diameter than Earth's?

____

Check

7. What strategy could you use to check your answer?

____

____

Solve Another Problem

8. When you donate a pint of blood, you lose about 2.3×10^{12} red blood cells. If your body can produce about 2×10^6 red blood cells per second, about how many seconds would it take for your body to replenish the red blood cells lost through donation? Write your answer in standard form.

____

Name ____________________ Class ____________ Date ____________

6A: Graphic Organizer

For use before Lesson 6-1

Study Skill Your textbook includes a Skills Handbook with extra problems and questions. Working these exercises is a good way to review material and prepare for the next chapter.

Write your answers.

1. What is the chapter title? ____________________
2. How many lessons are there in this chapter? ____________________
3. What is the topic of the Test-Taking Strategies page?

   ____
4. Complete the graphic organizer below as you work through the chapter.
   - In the center, write the title of the chapter.
   - When you begin a lesson, write the lesson name in a rectangle.
   - When you complete a lesson, write a skill or key concept in a circle linked to that lesson block.
   - When you complete the chapter, use this graphic organizer to help you review.

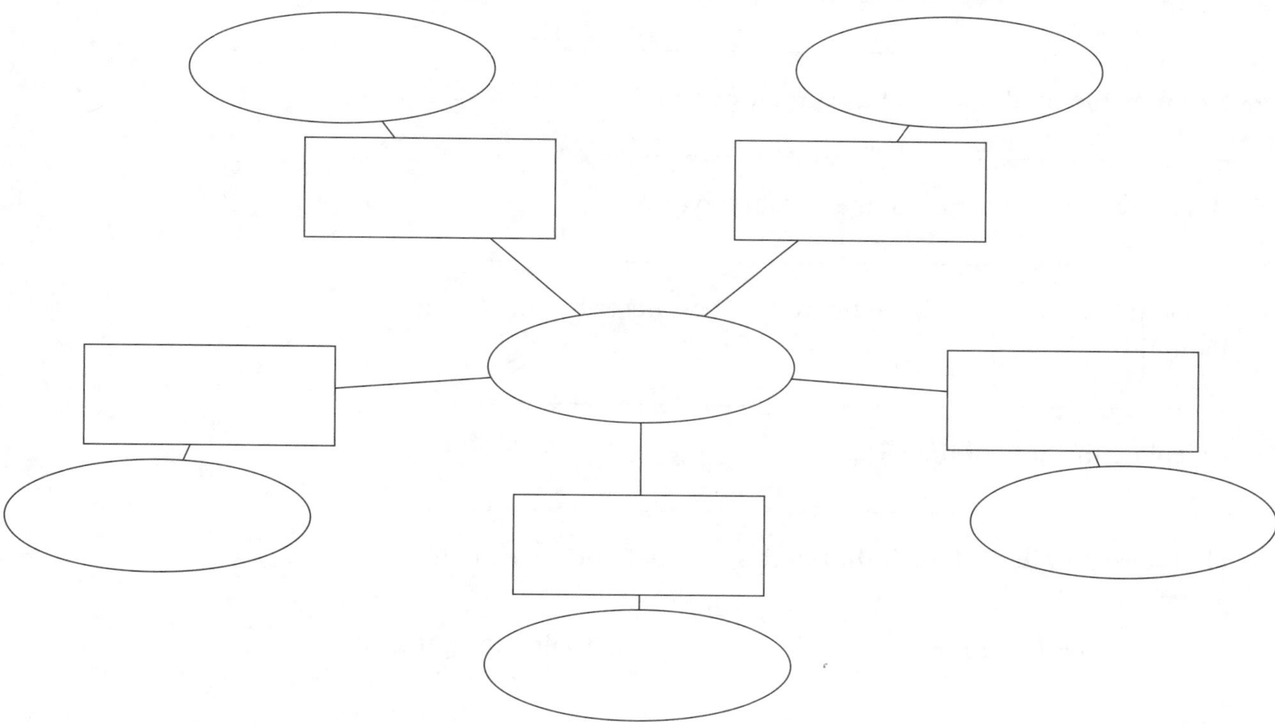

Name ______________________ Class ______________ Date ______________

6B: Reading Comprehension

For use after Lesson 6-3

Study Skill Attitude is everything.

Read the paragraph below and answer the questions that follow.

The Great Pyramid of Giza, one of the Seven Wonders of the World, is located just outside the city of Cairo, Egypt. It was built between 2589 and 2566 B.C. by the pharaoh Khufu. The walls are set at an incline of approximately 52 degrees. The square base is 745 feet on each side and the height is 449 feet. The pyramid is oriented to face the four cardinal directions: north, south, east, and west. It is composed of more than 2.3 million stone blocks that weigh about 2.5 tons each on average. The heaviest stones weigh almost 9 tons.

1. How long did it take to build the Great Pyramid?

   ____

2. About how many stone blocks were used? Give your answer in scientific notation.

   ____

3. On average, how much does each block weigh?

   ____

4. Estimate the total weight of the Great Pyramid.

   ____

5. What are the dimensions of the pyramid base?

   ____

6. Name the three-dimensional figure that best describes the Great Pyramid.

   ____

7. Calculate the area of the base.

   ____

8. **High-Use Academic Words** In Exercise 6, what does it mean to *name*?

   a. to identify something

   b. to find the value of

Name ______________________ Class ______________ Date ______________

6C: Reading/Writing Math Symbols

For use after Lesson 6-5

Study Skill Appreciate your efforts even when you have yet to see them pay off.

Vocabulary and Study Skills

Match each expression in Column A to its meaning in Column B.

Column A	Column B
1. $6^{(4-2)}$	**A.** $1 - P(6)$
2. $6!$	**B.** 1
3. 6^{-2}	**C.** a^4
4. 0.06×10^4	**D.** 600
5. $P(\text{not } 6)$	**E.** $\frac{1}{6^2}$
6. $(-6a)^0$	**F.** $6 \times 5 \times 4 \times 3 \times 2 \times 1$
7. $\frac{a^6}{a^2}$	**G.** 6^2

Write each statement using appropriate mathematical symbols.

8. five raised to the *n* plus three power

____

9. The square root of 168 is approximately thirteen.

____

10. *y* is equal to three times *x* plus eleven.

____

11. eight and sixty-five hundredths, multiplied by ten raised to the ninth power

____

12. the quantity seven plus *z*, squared

____

13. the number of ways 3 objects can be chosen from 25 where order does matter

____

14. Line segment *XY* is congruent to line segment *AB*.

____

Name ______________________ Class ______________ Date ______________

6D: Visual Vocabulary Practice

For use after Lesson 6-5

Study Skill Making sense of mathematical symbols is like reading a foreign language that uses different letters.

Concept List

9,000,000	constant	c^4
coefficient	6^3	a^{-n}
400	like terms	linear function

Write the concept that best describes each exercise. Choose from the concept list above.

1. $\frac{6^9}{6^6}$ ______________	**2.** The factor in scientific notation that multiplies a power of 10. ______________	**3.** $f(x) = -2x + 11$ ______________
4. $\frac{1}{a^n}$ ______________	**5.** $2y$ and $-8y$ in the expression $2y + 3y^2 - 8y - 5$ ______________	**6.** -4 in the expression $-\frac{4}{5}x^5 - 6x^4 + 4x - 4$ ______________
7. 9×10^6 in standard form. ______________	**8.** $c \times c \times c \times c$ ______________	**9.** $\frac{8 \times 10^5}{2 \times 10^3}$ ______________

Name ______________________ Class ______________ Date ______________

6E: Vocabulary Check

For use after Lesson 6-5

Study Skill Strengthen your vocabulary. Use these pages and add cues and summaries by applying the Cornell Notetaking style.

Write the definition for each word or term at the right. To check your work, fold the paper back along the dotted line to see the correct answers.

Definition	Term
______________________	scientific notation
______________________	standard form
______________________	base
______________________	squared
______________________	power

Vocabulary and Study Skills

Name ______________________ Class ______________ Date ______________

6E: Vocabulary Check (continued)

For use after Lesson 6-5

Write the vocabulary word or term for each definition. To check your work, fold the paper forward along the dotted line to see the correct answers.

a number where the first factor is greater than or equal to one and the second factor is a power of 10 ______________________

a number not written as a product of factors ______________________

in the expression, 5^2, what 5 represents ______________________

a number taken to the second power ______________________

in the expression of a^n, what n represents ______________________

Name ________________ Class ________ Date ________

6F: Vocabulary Review Puzzle

For use with the Chapter Review

Study Skill Read problems carefully. Pay special attention to exponents when working with polynomials.

Complete the crossword puzzle below. For help, use the Glossary in your textbook.

Here are the words you will use to complete this crossword puzzle:

distributive	constant
binomial	polynomial
variable	exponent
coefficient	scientific notation
like terms	monomial

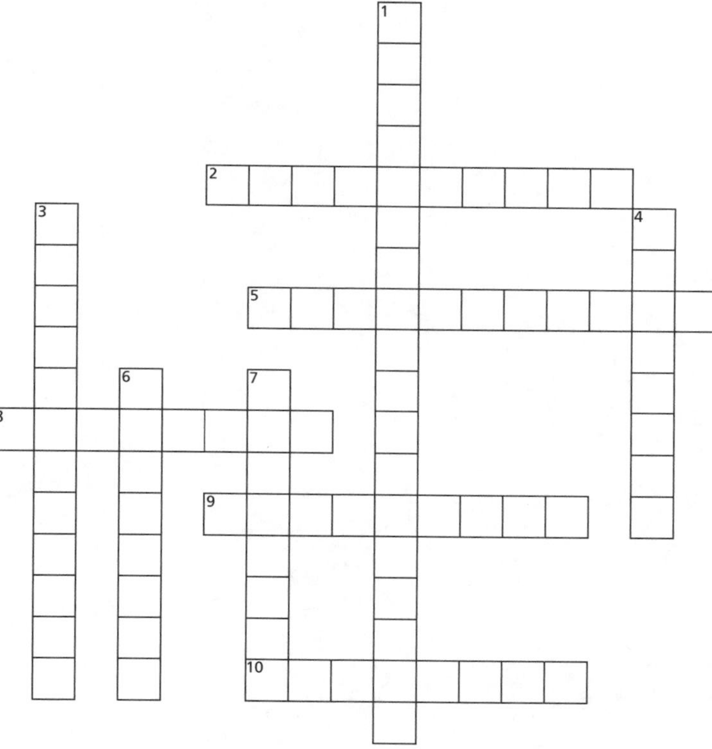

ACROSS

2. may be one term or the sum or difference of two or more terms
5. the numerical factor in any term of a polynomial
8. a polynomial with two terms
9. terms with exactly the same variable factors
10. tells how many times a number, or base, is used as a factor

DOWN

1. a way to write a number as two factors, the second of which is always a power of ten
3. $a(b + c) = ab + ac$ is an example of the ______ Property.
4. $4m$, for example
6. a term in a polynomial that does not contain a variable
7. a letter that stands for a number

Name ______________________ Class ______________ Date ______________

Practice 7-1

Pairs of Angles

Name a pair of vertical angles and a pair of adjacent angles in each figure. Find $m\angle 1$.

1.

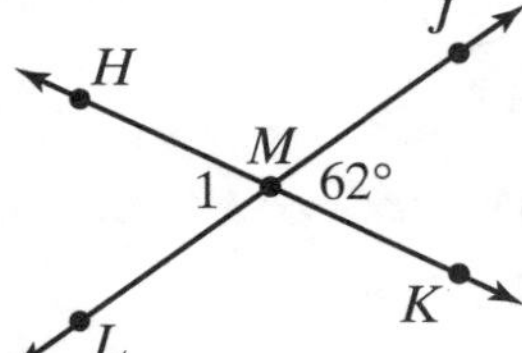

2.

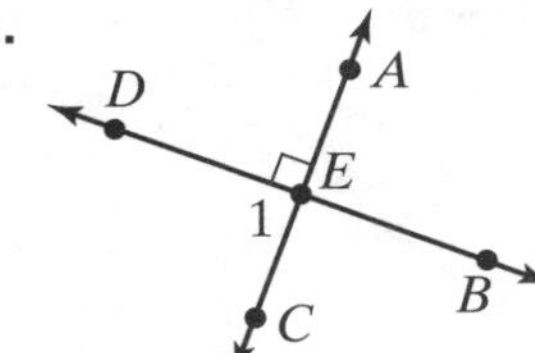

3.

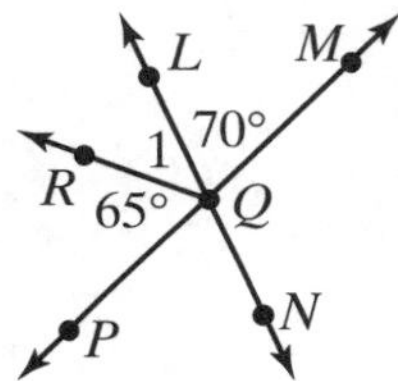

4.

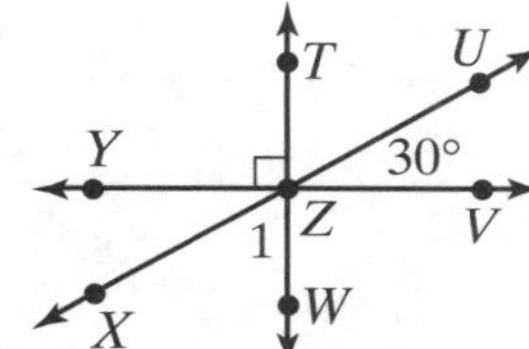

Find the measure of the supplement and the complement of each angle.

5. 10°

6. 42.5°

7. 80°

Use the diagram at the right for Exercises 8–14. Decide whether each statement below is true or false.

8. $\angle GAF$ and $\angle BAC$ are vertical angles. ______

9. $\angle EAF$ and $\angle EAD$ are adjacent angles. ______

10. $\angle CAD$ is a supplement of $\angle DAF$. ______

11. $\angle CAD$ is a complement of $\angle EAF$. ______

12. $\angle DAF = 109°$ ______

13. $\angle BAC \cong \angle EAF$ ______

14. $\angle CAE \cong \angle DAF$ ______

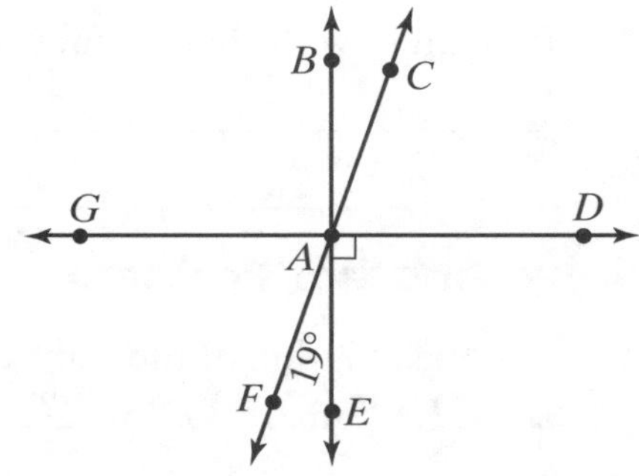

Name ______________________ Class ______________ Date ______________

7-1 • Guided Problem Solving

GPS Student Page 217, Exercises 28–31:

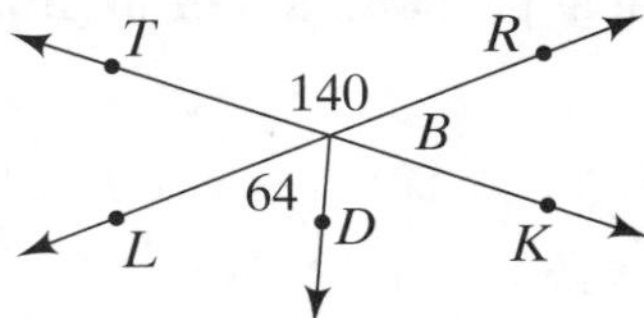

Use the diagram for Exercises 28–31.

28. $\angle LBD$ and $\angle TBL$ are __?__ angles.

29. $\angle RBT$ and $\angle$ __?__ are vertical angles.

30. $m\angle KBL =$ __?__

31. $m\angle DBK =$ __?__

Understand

1. What are you asked to do?

____

2. What is true about the measures of two vertical angles?

____

3. What are adjacent angles?

____

____

Plan and Carry Out

4. Do angles $\angle LBD$ and $\angle TBL$ share a side? If so, what is it?

____

5. What type of angles are $\angle LBD$ and $\angle TBL$? ______________

6. What pairs of vertical angles are formed by the intersection of $\overleftrightarrow{TK}$ and $\overleftrightarrow{RL}$?

____

7. What is the measure of angle KBL? ______

8. $m\angle LBD + m\angle DBK =$ ______

9. Which angle is adjacent to $\angle LBD$?

____

10. Substitute what you know into the equation in step 8 and solve.

____

Check

11. Explain how to check your answer in Step 10.

____

____

Solve Another Problem

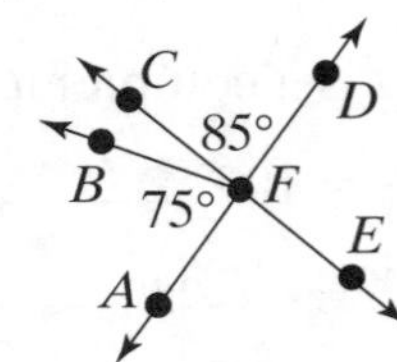

12. Use the diagram at the right to solve.

a. $\angle CFA$ and $\angle DFE$ are __?__ angles.

b. $m\angle BFC =$ __?__ °

______________ ______________

Name ______________________ Class ______________ Date ______________

Practice 7-2

Angles and Parallel Lines

Identify each pair of angles as *vertical, adjacent, corresponding, alternate interior,* or *none of these.*

1. ∠7, ∠5 ______________
2. ∠1, ∠2 ______________
3. ∠1, ∠7 ______________
4. ∠4, ∠7 ______________

Use the diagrams at the right for Exercises 5 and 6.

5. Name four pairs of corresponding angles.

____

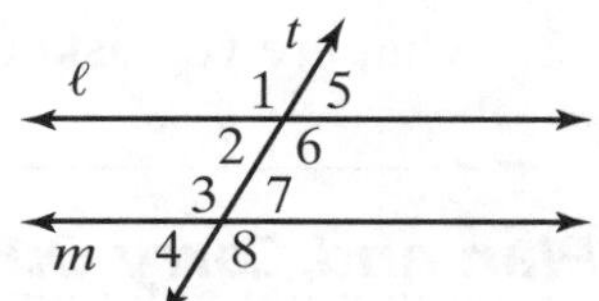

6. Name two pairs of alternate interior angles

____

In each diagram below, ℓ ∥ *m*. Find the measure of each numbered angle.

7.

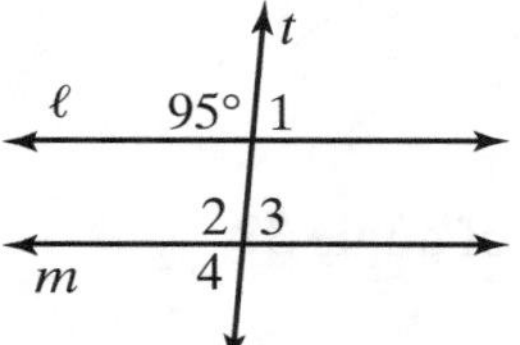

$m\angle 1 =$ __________

$m\angle 2 =$ __________

$m\angle 3 =$ __________

$m\angle 4 =$ __________

8.

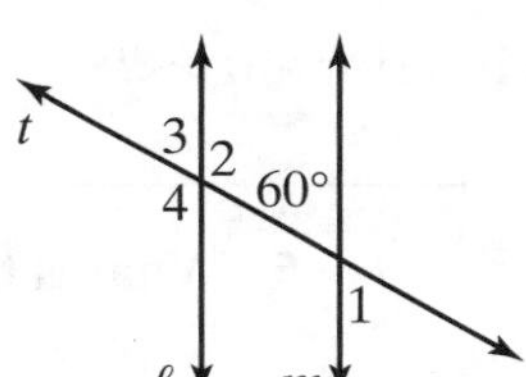

$m\angle 1 =$ __________

$m\angle 2 =$ __________

$m\angle 3 =$ __________

$m\angle 4 =$ __________

9.

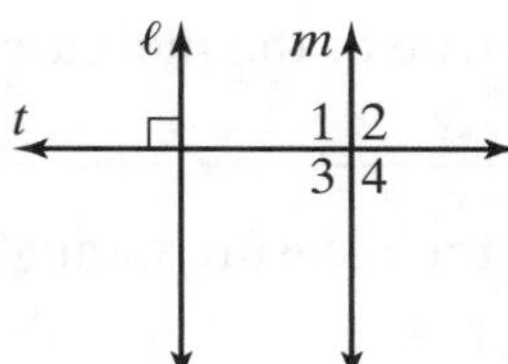

$m\angle 1 =$ __________

$m\angle 2 =$ __________

$m\angle 3 =$ __________

$m\angle 4 =$ __________

10. Use the figure at the right. Is line ℓ parallel to line *m*? Explain how you could use a protractor to support your conjecture.

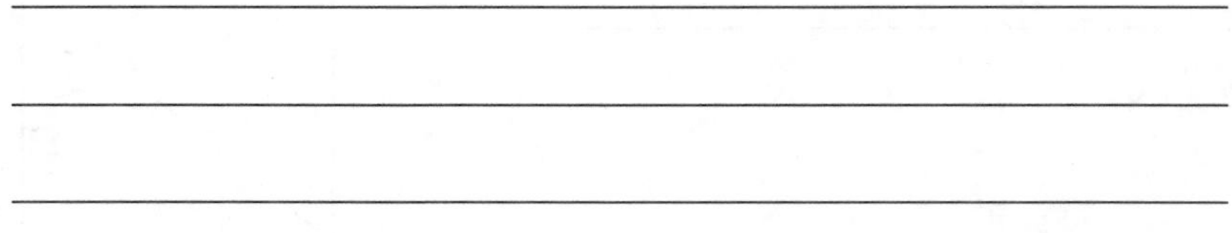

____

____

____

____

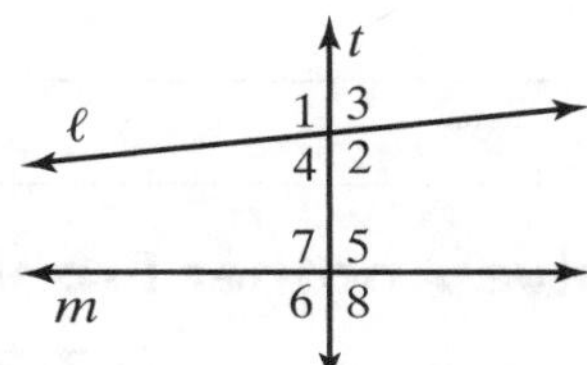

Name ______________________ Class ______________ Date ______________

7-2 • Guided Problem Solving

GPS Student Page 221, Exercise 31:

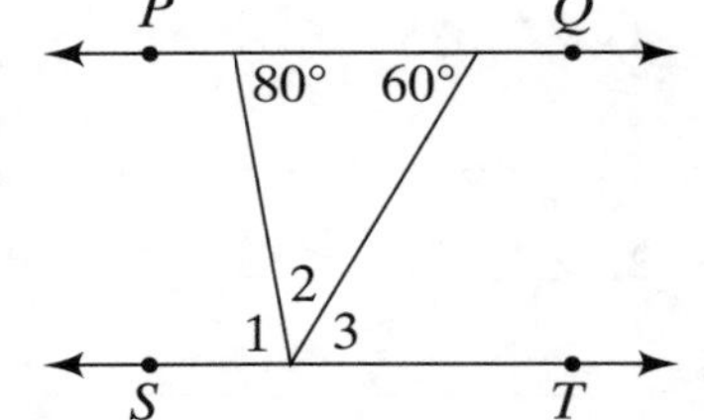

a. In the diagram at the right, $\overleftrightarrow{PQ} \parallel \overleftrightarrow{ST}$. Find the measure of each numbered angle.

b. What is the sum of the angle measures of the triangle?

Understand

1. What are alternate interior angles?

____

____

2. What are you asked to do?

____

Plan and Carry Out

3. Use angle 1 and angle 3 to name two pairs of alternate interior angles.

____

4. What is true of the measure of alternate interior angles?

____

5. What is the measure of angle 1?

____

6. What is the measure of angle 3?

____

7. What type of angle do angles 1, 2 and 3 form?

____

8. How many degrees are in a straight angle?

____

9. Use the information from Steps 5 and 6 to help find the measure of angle 2.

____

10. What is the sum of the angle measures in the triangle?

____

Check

11. Explain your answer from Step 10.

____

____

Solve Another Problem

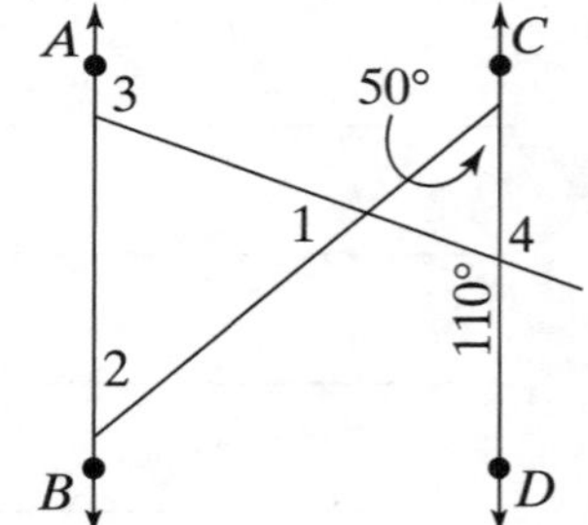

12. In the diagram, $\overleftrightarrow{AB} \parallel \overleftrightarrow{CD}$. Find the measure of each numbered angle.

____

Name ______________________ Class ______________ Date ______________

Practice 7-3

Congruent Figures

Determine whether each pair of triangles is congruent. Explain.

1. 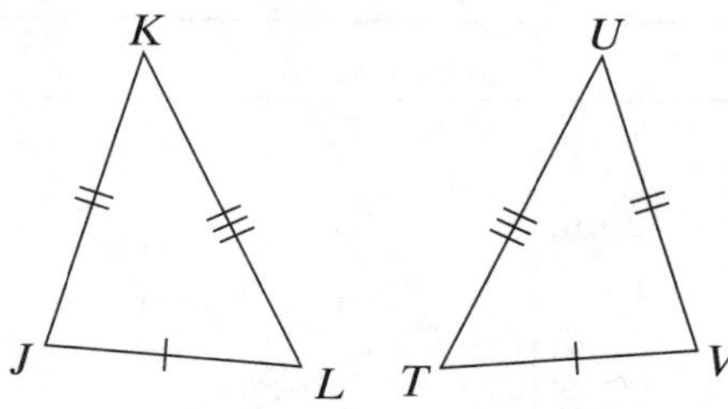

____

2. 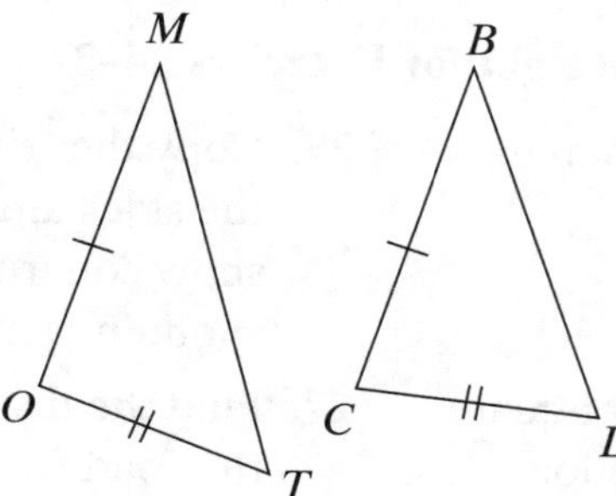

____

3. 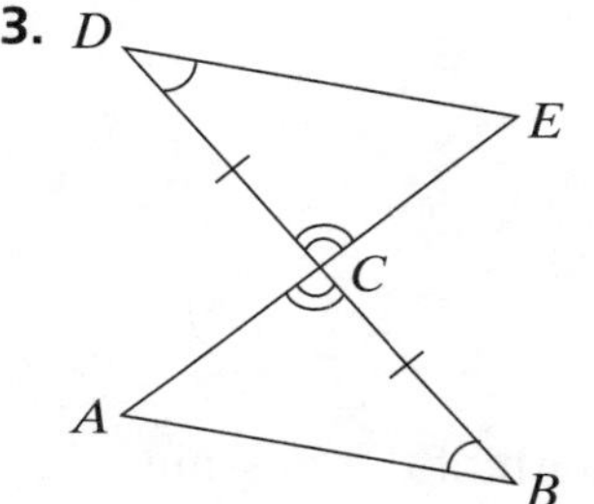

____

4. 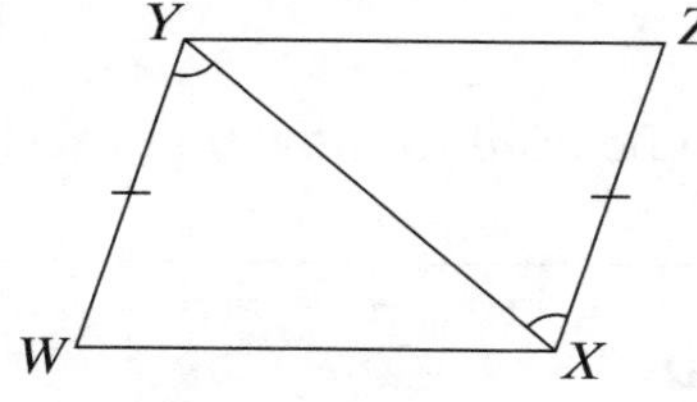

____

Determine if each triangle in Exercises 5–7 must be congruent to $\triangle XYZ$ at the right.

5. 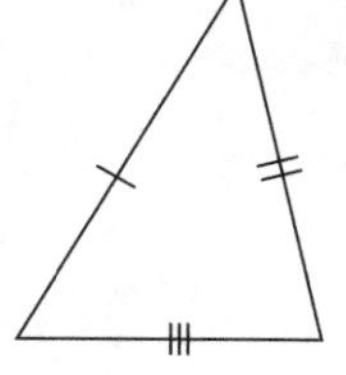

____

6. 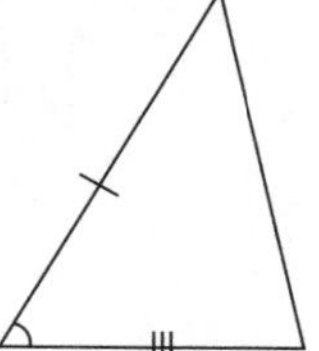

____

7. 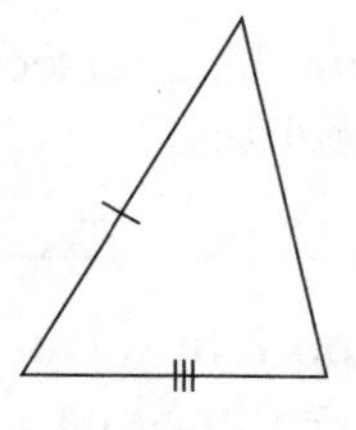

____

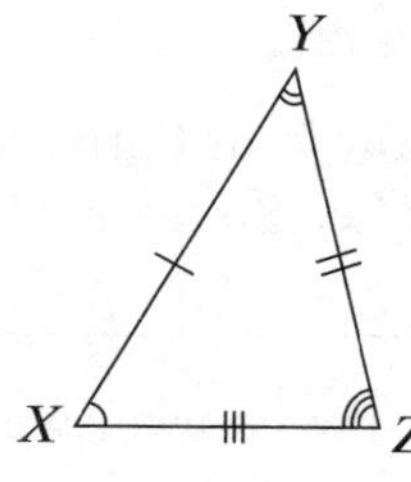

For Exercises 8–9, use the triangles at the right.

8. $\triangle XYZ \cong$ ______________ by ______________

9. Find the missing measures for $\triangle XYZ$.

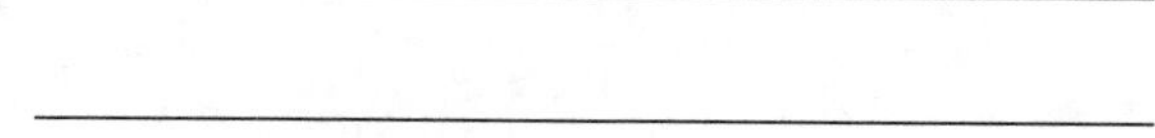

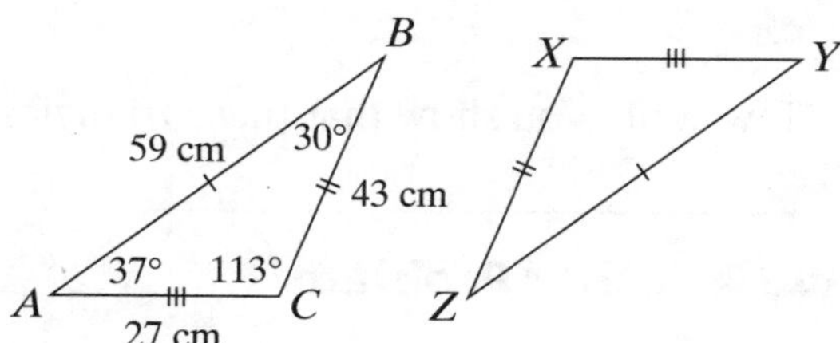

Name ____________________ Class ____________ Date ____________

7-3 • Guided Problem Solving

GPS Student Page 226, Exercises 24–27:

Maps Use the map at right for Exercises 24–27.

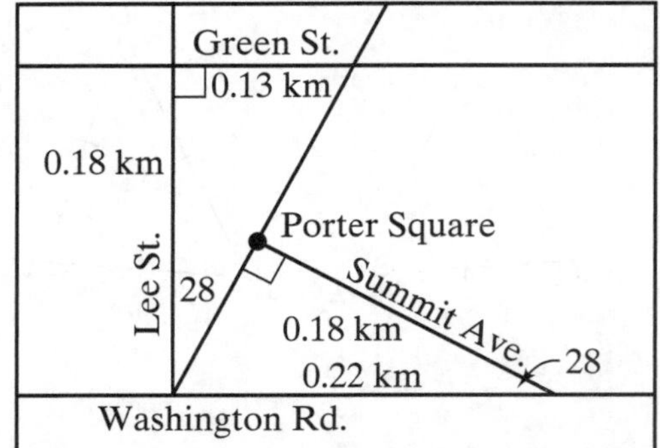

24. Show that the triangles in the map are congruent.

25. Copy the triangles. Mark the sides and angles to show congruent corresponding parts.

26. How far is Porter Square from the intersection of Lee Street and Washington Road?

27. Find the distance along the road from Porter Square to Green Street.

Understand

1. What methods can be used to show that two triangles are congruent?

____

Plan and Carry Out

2. How can you find the length of a missing side?

____

3. What is the total length of the missing hypotenuse?

____

4. Are the two triangles congruent? Why?

____

5. Sketch the two triangles. Mark their corresponding parts.

6. How far is Porter Square from the intersection of Lee Street and Washington Road?

____

____

7. What is the total length of the street from Washington to Green by the way of Porter Square? ______________

8. Using your answer from Step 7, how can you find the distance from Porter Square to Green Street?

____

Check

9. How could you show that these triangles are congruent by another method?

____

Solve Another Problem

10. Explain why the pair of triangles shown are congruent. Find the missing measures in the diagram.

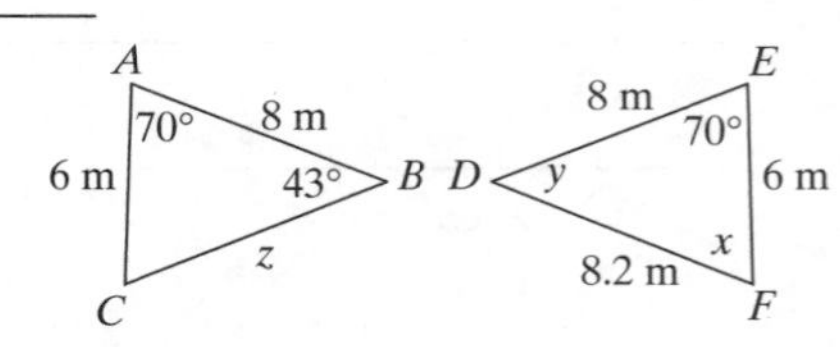

____

Name ____________ Class ____________ Date ____________

Practice 7-4

Similar Figures

Tell whether each pair of polygons is similar. Explain why or why not.

1. 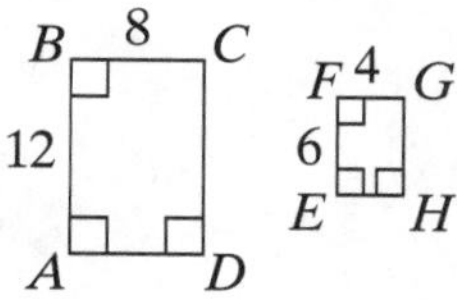

2. 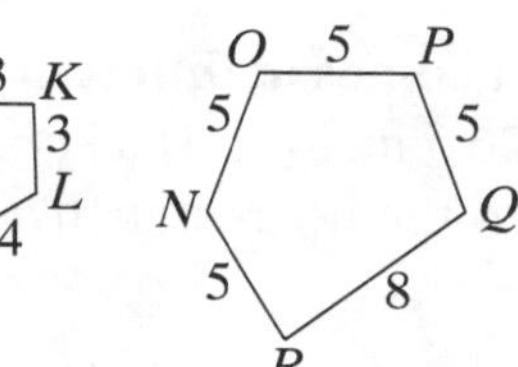

3. 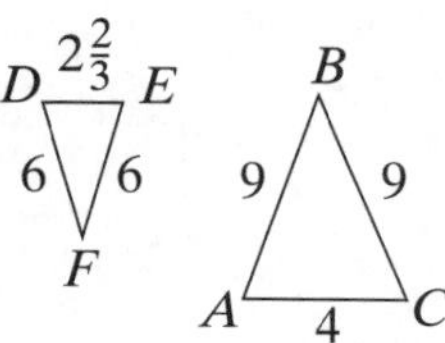

4. 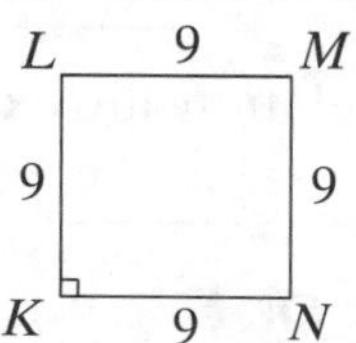

Exercises 5–12 show pairs of similar polygons. Find the unknown lengths.

5. 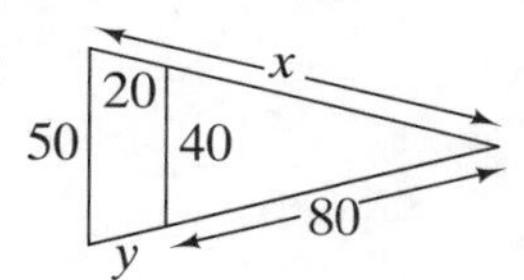

6. 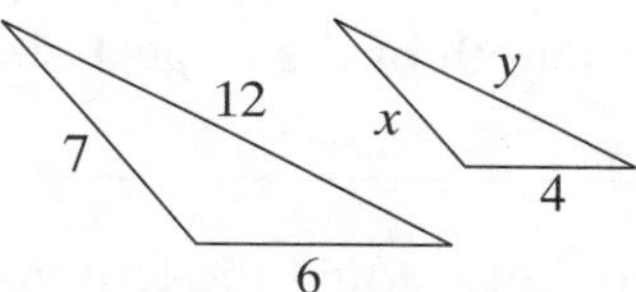

7. 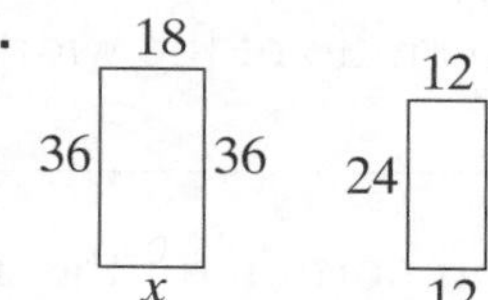

8. 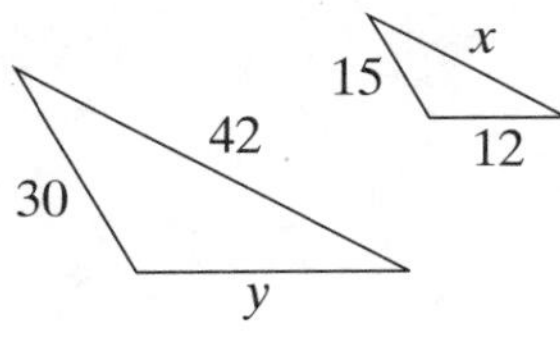

9. 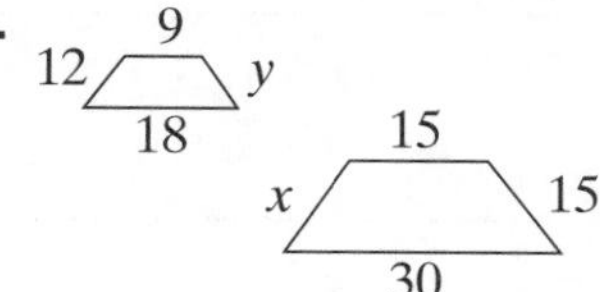

10. 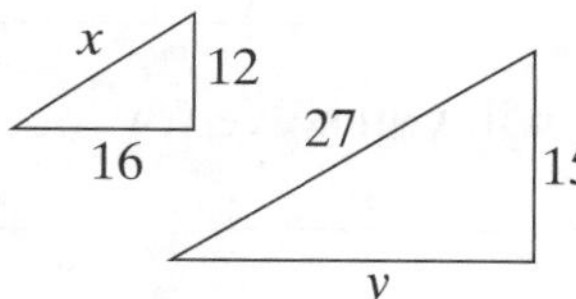

11. 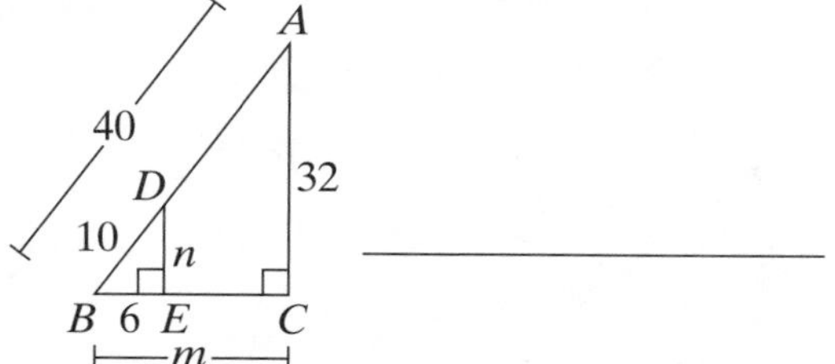

12. 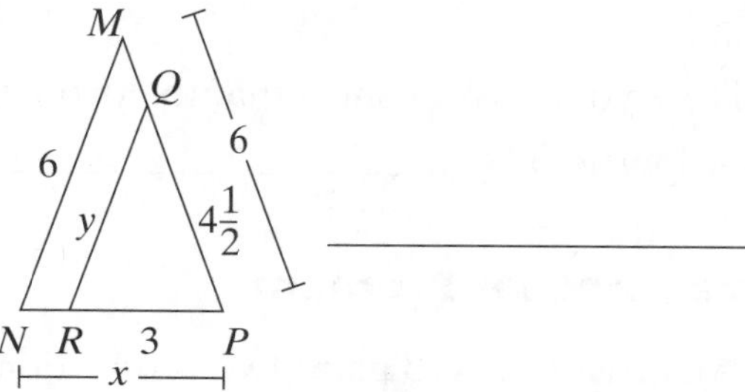

Solve.

13. A rock show is being televised. The lead singer, who is 75 inches tall, is 15 inches tall on a TV monitor. The image of the bass player is 13 inches tall on the monitor. How tall is the bass player?

14. A 42-inch-long guitar is 10.5 feet long on a stadium screen. A drum is 21 inches wide. How wide is the image on the stadium screen?

Name ______________________ Class ______________ Date ______________

7-4 • Guided Problem Solving

GPS Student Page 231, Exercise 15:

Clothing A T-shirt comes in different sizes. A large T-shirt is 21.5 in. wide and 26.5 in. long. If a small T-shirt is 15.5 in. wide, what is its length to the nearest inch?

Understand

1. What are you being asked to find? ______________________

____

2. What type of relationship exists between the two shirts?

____

Plan and Carry Out

3. What are the dimensions of the large T-shirt? ______________

____

4. What is the ratio of the width to the length of the large T-shirt?

____

5. Set up a proportion for the situation. Let y equal the length of the small T-shirt.

____

6. How will you solve for the variable y?

____

7. What is the value of y? ______________________

Check

8. Does your answer show that the two T-shirt sizes are proportional? ______________________

Solve Another Problem

9. An artist wants to paint two proportional rectangular paintings on canvas. One painting is larger than the other. The large painting is 20 in. wide and 8 in. long. The smaller painting is 16 in. wide and 6 in. long. Are the two paintings proportional in size?

____

____

Name ______________________ Class ______________ Date ______________

Practice 7-5

Proving Triangles Similar

Determine the unknown angle measure in each triangle.

1.

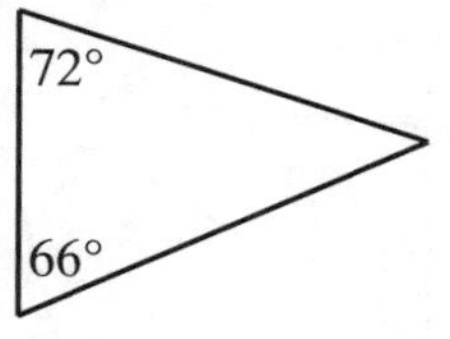

____

2.

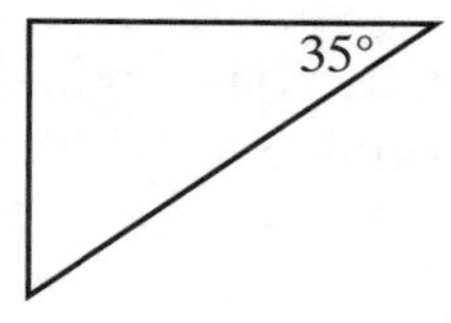

____

3.

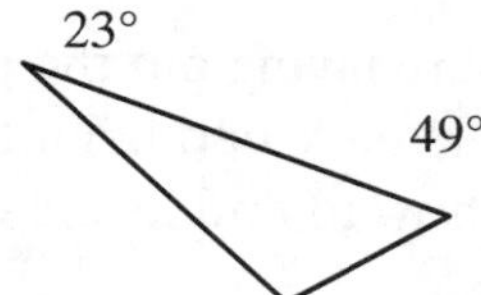

____

4.

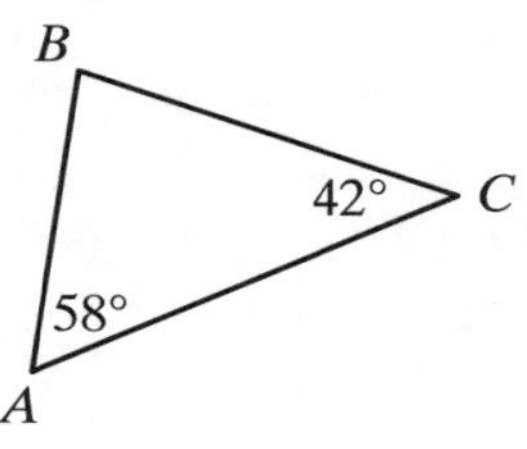

____

5.

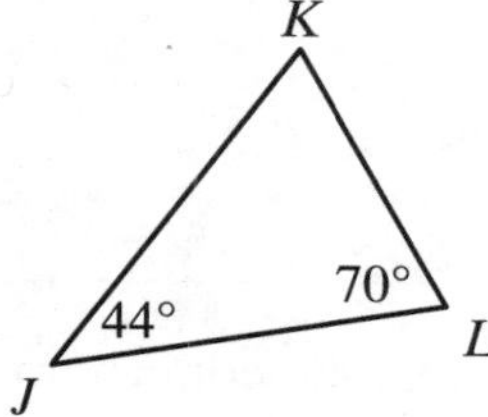

____

6.

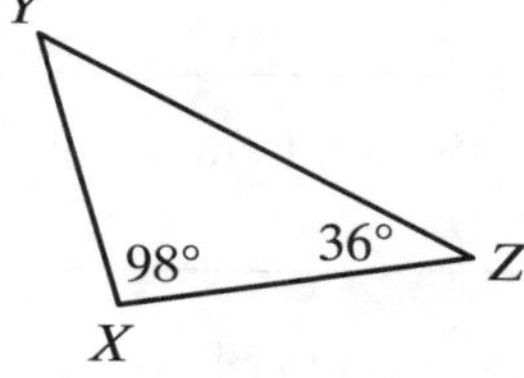

____

Show that each pair of triangles is similar.

7.

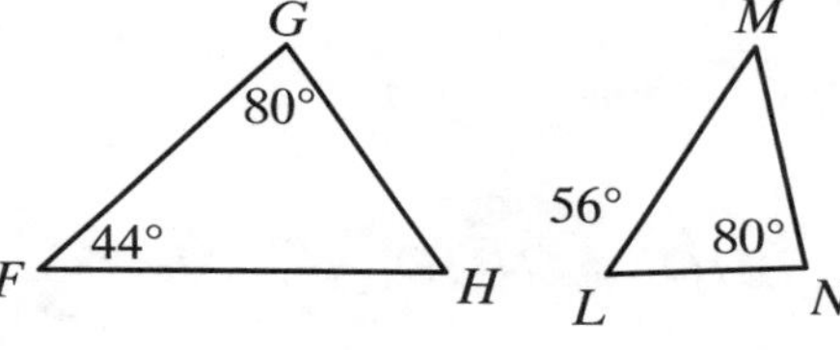

____

8.

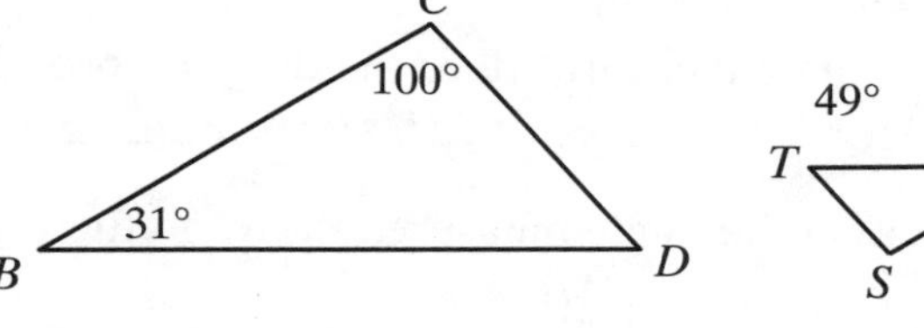

____

9.

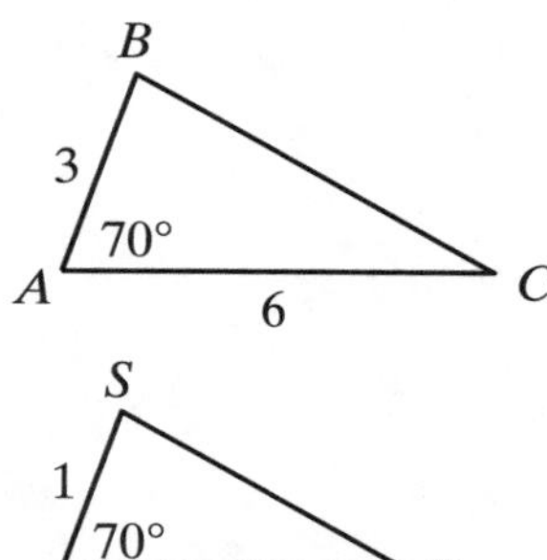

____

Solve.

10. A stained glass window has a triangular piece of purple glass with a right angle and another angle that measures 45°. What is the measure of the third angle of the purple glass? __________

Name ______________________ Class ______________ Date ____________

7-5 • Guided Problem Solving

Proving Triangles Similar

GPS Student Page 235, Exercise 13:

City workers are laying out the paths in a new park, as shown in the diagram. Do the workers have enough information to determine $m\angle Q$? If so, explain how to find its measure. If not, explain why not.

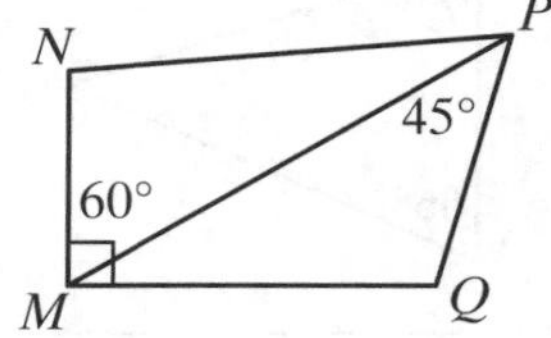

Understand

1. What are you being asked to find?

____

2. What is the angle measure of a right angle?

____

3. How many pairs of corresponding angles must be congruent in order for two triangles to be similar?

____

Plan and Carry Out

4. What angle measures does the diagram provide?
$\angle NMQ =$ ________ $\angle NMP =$ ________ $\angle MPQ =$ ________

5. Based on the angle measures shown in the diagram, you can find $m\angle PMQ$. $\angle PMQ = \angle NMQ - \angle NMP =$ ______

6. Now that you know the measure of two angles in $\triangle MQP$, use angle sum of a triangle to find $\angle Q$. $180° - (\angle PMQ + \angle MPQ) = \angle Q =$ ______

7. Is $\triangle MQP \sim \triangle PNM$? How do you know?

____

____

Check

8. Given the angle measure you found for $\angle Q$, what is the angle sum of $\triangle MQP$? Show each angle measure ____________________

Solve Another Problem

9. For part of a theater set, students are supposed to build two similar triangular wood frames. The first frame has the following side/angle/side measure: 20 cm/80°/24 cm. The second frame has a different side-angle-side measures: 15 cm/80°/18 cm. Are the frames similar triangles? Explain.

____

____

Name ______________________ Class ______________ Date ______________

Practice 7-6

Angles and Polygons

Classify each polygon by its number of sides.

1. 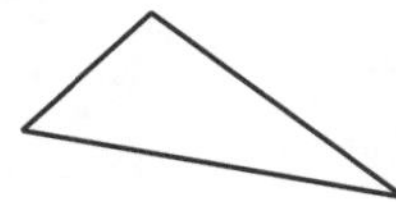

____

2. 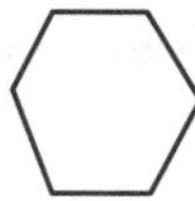

____

3. 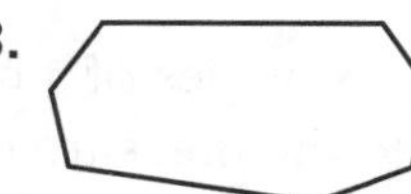

____

4. a polygon with 8 sides

____

5. a polygon with 10 sides

____

6. Find the measure of each angle of a regular hexagon.

____

7. The measures of four angles of a pentagon are 143°, 118°, 56°, and 97°. Find the measure of the missing angle.

____

8. Four of the angles of a hexagon measure 53°, 126°, 89°, and 117°. What is the sum of the measures of the other two angles?

____

9. Four of the angles of a heptagon measure 109°, 158°, 117°, and 89°. What is the sum of the measures of the other three angles?

____

10. Complete the chart for the total of the angle measures in each polygon. The first three have been done for you.

Polygon	Number of Sides	Sum of Angle Measures
triangle	3	180°
rectangle	4	360°
pentagon	5	540°
hexagon		
heptagon		
octagon		
nonagon		
decagon		

11. From the table you completed in Exercise 10, what pattern do you see? Explain.

____

____

Name ______________________ Class ______________ Date ______________

7-6 • Guided Problem Solving

GPS Student Page 243, Exercise 28:

The measures of six angles of a heptagon are 145°, 115°, 152°, 87°, 90°, and 150°. Find the measure of the seventh angle.

Understand

1. How many sides does a heptagon have? ______________
2. How many interior angles does a heptagon have?

   ____

3. What are you asked to find?

   ____

Plan and Carry Out

4. For a polygon with n sides, the sum of the measures of the interior angles is $(n - 2)180°$. Substitute what you know into the formula to find the sum of the interior angles. Show your work.

   ____

5. Find the total of the measures of the six interior angles given in the problem.

   ____

6. Subtract the total you found in Step 5 from the total number of degrees in a heptagon that you found in Step 4.

   ____

Check

7. Add all seven angles to verify that they total 900°.

   ____

Solve Another Problem

8. A decagon has interior angle measures of 156°, 178°, 124°, 132°, 138°, 142°, 116°, 178°, and 159°. Find the measure of the missing angle.

   ____

Name ______________________ Class ______________ Date ______________

7A: Graphic Organizer

For use before Lesson 7-1

Study Skill As your teacher presents new material in the chapter, keep a paper and pencil handy to write down notes and questions. If you miss class, borrow a classmate's notes so you don't fall behind.

Vocabulary and Study Skills

Write your answers.

1. What is the chapter title? ______________________
2. How many lessons are there in this chapter? ______________________
3. What is the topic of the Test-Taking Strategies page? ______________________
4. Complete the graphic organizer below as you work through the chapter.
   - In the center, write the title of the chapter.
   - When you begin a lesson, write the lesson name in a rectangle.
   - When you complete a lesson, write a skill or key concept in a circle linked to that lesson block.
   - When you complete the chapter, use this graphic organizer to help you review.

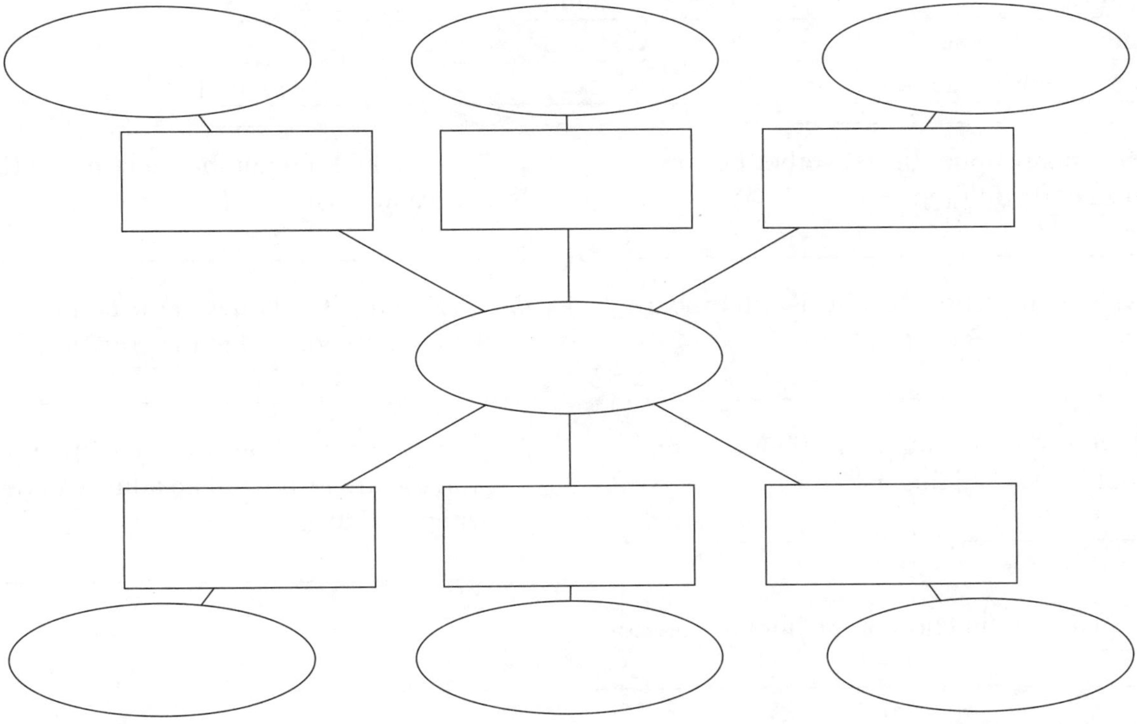

Name ____________________ Class ____________ Date ____________

7B: Reading Comprehension

For use after Lesson 7-2

Study Skill Use tables when you need to organize complex information. The columns and rows allow you to display different types of information in a way that is easy to read. Make sure you use appropriate headings.

Read the paragraph and chart below to answer the questions.

The human skeletal system helps support the body and protects its organs from being damaged. At birth, a human skeleton is made up of 275 different bones. As the body ages, some of the bones fuse together leaving the adult skeleton with 206 bones. There are two major systems of bones in the human body; the axial skeleton which is made up of 80 bones, and the appendicular skeleton which has 126 bones. The following chart lists the types and number of bones located in various parts of the adult body.

Human Bones

Fingers (per hand)	14	Toes (per foot)	14
Each Palm	5	Instep of Each Foot	5
Each Wrist	8	Each Ankle	7
Facial Bones	14	Cranium	8
Lumbar Vertebrae	5	Cervical Vertebrae	7
Thoracic Vertebrae	12	Ribs	12 pairs

1. How many bones fuse together between birth and adulthood?

____

2. What is the total number of bones in the hand and wrist?

____

3. What is the ratio of cervical vertebrae to thoracic vertebrae?

____

4. What percent of bones in the adult skeleton are located in the cranium?

____

5. What is the total number of bones in an adult's toes and fingers?

____

6. What percent of bones in the human skeleton are located in an adult's ankle, instep, and toes?

____

7. Explain the function of the human skeleton.

____

8. **High-Use Academic Words** In question 7, what does the word *explain* mean?

   a. to display using illustrations, tables, or graphs

   b. to give facts and details that make an idea easier to understand

Name ______________________ Class ______________ Date ______________

7C: Reading/Writing Math Symbols

For use after Lesson 7-6

Vocabulary and Study Skills

Study Skill Take notes while you study. Use a highlighter to emphasize important material in your notes.

Write the following mathematical expressions or equations in words.

1. $m\angle 1 = 50^\circ$

____

2. $\angle JKL$ ______________________________

3. $a \parallel b$ ______________________________

4. $\overline{GH} \cong \overline{LK}$

____

5. $\angle R \cong \angle T$

____

6. $\overleftrightarrow{AB} \parallel \overleftrightarrow{CD}$

____

7. $\overrightarrow{AB}$ ______________________________

8. t^5 ______________________________

9. $\overleftrightarrow{AB} \perp \overleftrightarrow{JK}$

____

Write each of the following statements using mathematical symbols.

10. Segment AB and segment SR are equal in length. ______________

11. angle STU ______________________________

12. Segment BA is parallel to segment RK. ______________

13. The measure of angle JKL is 43 degrees. ______________

14. Angle R is congruent to angle Y. ______________

15. x raised to the sixth power ______________

16. arc TY ______________________________

17. The sum of the measures of angles ABC and XYZ is 90 degrees.

____

Name ____________________ Class ____________ Date ____________

7D: Visual Vocabulary Practice

For use after Lesson 7-6

Study Skill Use Venn Diagrams to understand the relationship between words whose meanings overlap such as squares, rectangles, and quadrilaterals or real numbers, integers, and counting numbers.

Concept List

obtuse triangle	transversal	rhombus
supplementary	complementary	120 degrees
corresponding angles	isosceles triangle	alternate interior angles

Write the concept that best describes each exercise. Choose from the concept list above.

1.

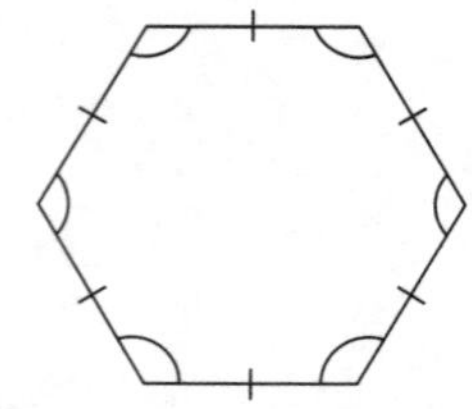

the measure of each interior angle

____

2.

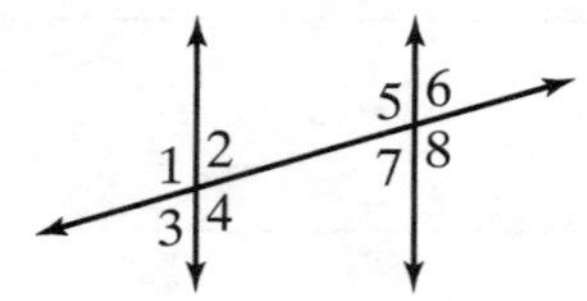

$\angle 2$ and $\angle 7$

____

3.

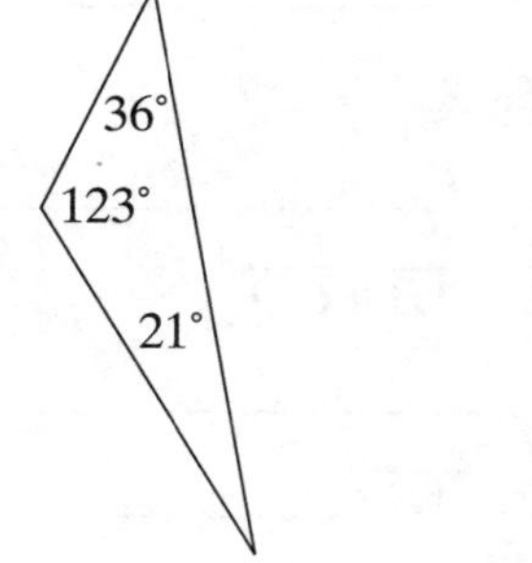

____

4.

$m\angle 1 = 30°$ and $m\angle 2 = 60°$

____

5.

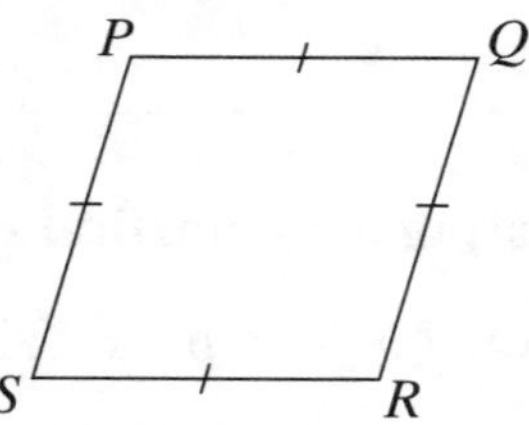

____

6.

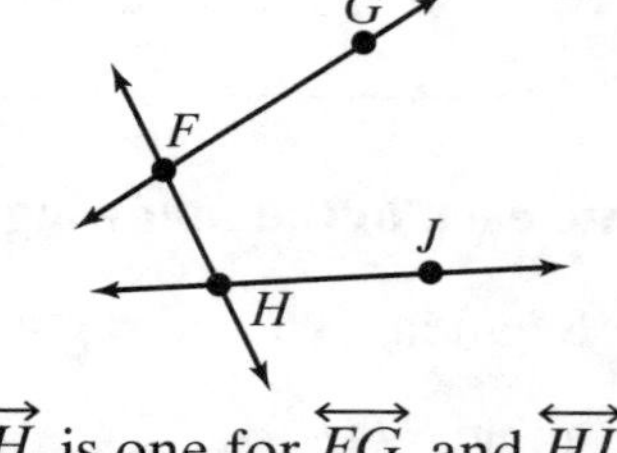

$\overleftrightarrow{FH}$ is one for $\overleftrightarrow{FG}$ and $\overleftrightarrow{HJ}$

____

7.

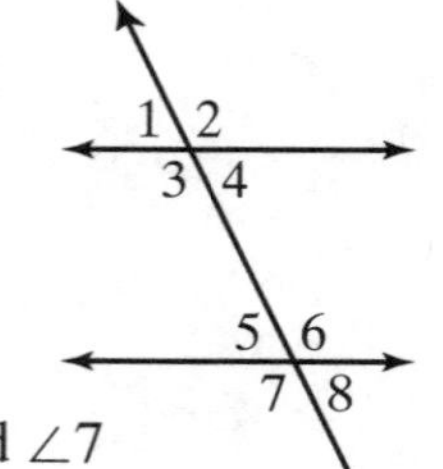

$\angle 2$ and $\angle 7$

____

8.

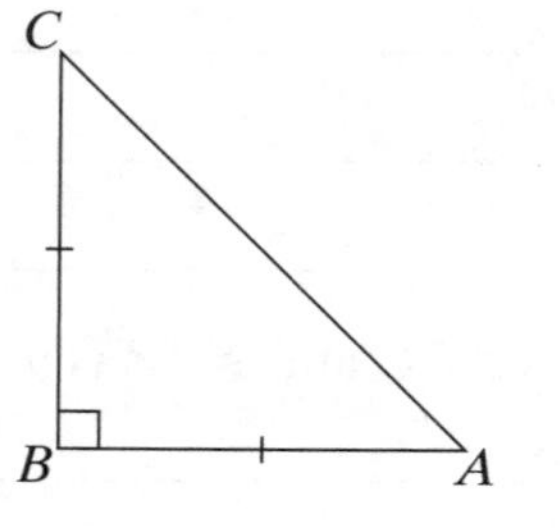

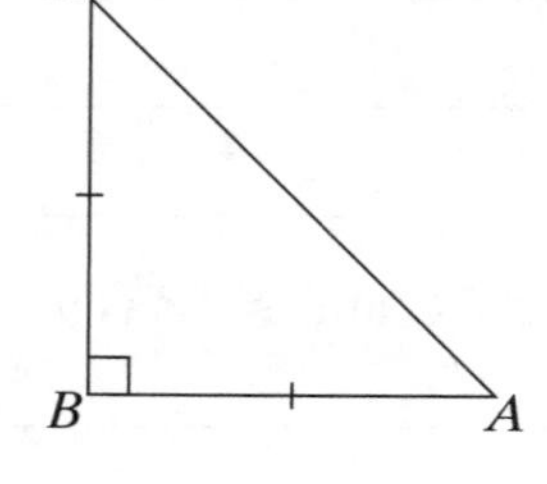

____

9.

$m\angle ABC = 24°$ and
$m\angle XYZ = 156°$

____

Name ______________________ Class ______________ Date ______________

7E: Vocabulary Check

For use after Lesson 7-6

Study Skill Strengthen your vocabulary. Use these pages and add cues and summaries by applying the Cornell Notetaking style.

Write the definition for each word or term at the right. To check your work, fold the paper back along the dotted line to see the correct answers.

vertical angles

adjacent angles

similar polygons

congruent polygons

perpendicular lines

Name ______________________ Class ______________ Date ______________

7E: Vocabulary Check (continued)

For use after Lesson 7-6

Write the vocabulary word or term for each definition. To check your work, fold the paper forward along the dotted line to see the correct answers.

angles that are formed by intersecting lines and are opposite of each other ______________________

angles that share a common vertex and a common side ______________________

polygons that have congruent corresponding angles and corresponding sides in proportion ______________________

polygons that have the same size and shape ______________________

lines that intersect to form right angles ______________________

Name ______________________ Class ______________ Date ______________

7F: Vocabulary Review Puzzle

For use with the Chapter Review

Study Skill As you read through a new lesson, write new vocabulary words and the definitions on index cards.

Complete the crossword puzzle below. For help, use the glossary in your textbook.

Here are the words you will use to complete this crossword puzzle.

right	square	trapezoid	vertical	supplementary
scalene	acute	isosceles	circumference	complementary
obtuse	adjacent	rectangle	transversal	parallelogram

ACROSS

1. two angles whose sum is 180 degrees
5. a triangle with one angle measuring 90 degrees
6. a triangle with angles each measuring less than 90 degrees
8. a triangle with at least two sides congruent
9. two angles whose sum is 90 degrees
12. a type of angle formed by intersecting lines
13. a parallelogram with four right angles and four congruent sides
14. a quadrilateral with exactly one pair of parallel sides

DOWN

1. a triangle with no congruent sides
2. a quadrilateral with two pairs of opposite sides that are parallel
3. a line that intersects two other lines in different points
4. a parallelogram with four right angles
7. the distance around a circle
10. a triangle with one angle larger than 90 degrees
11. two angles that share a vertex and a side but have no common interior points

Name ______________________ Class ______________ Date ______________

Practice 8-1

Translations

Use arrow notation to write a rule that describes the translation shown on each graph.

1\. 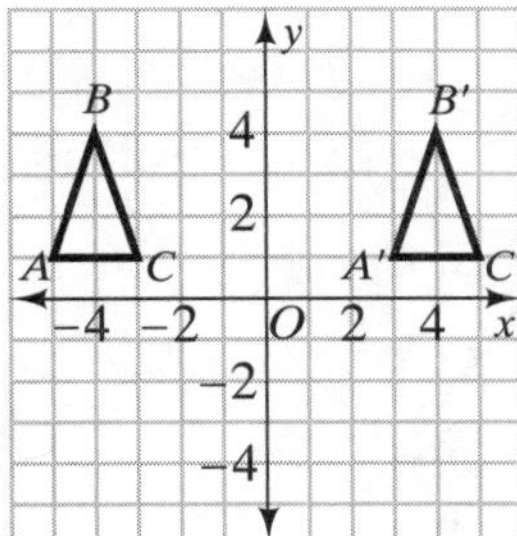

2\. 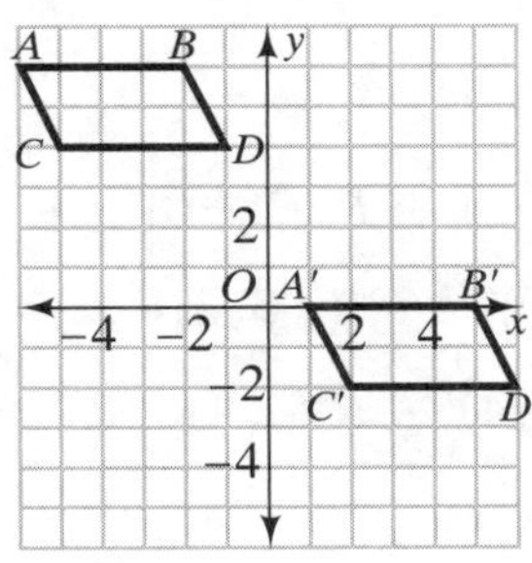

3\. 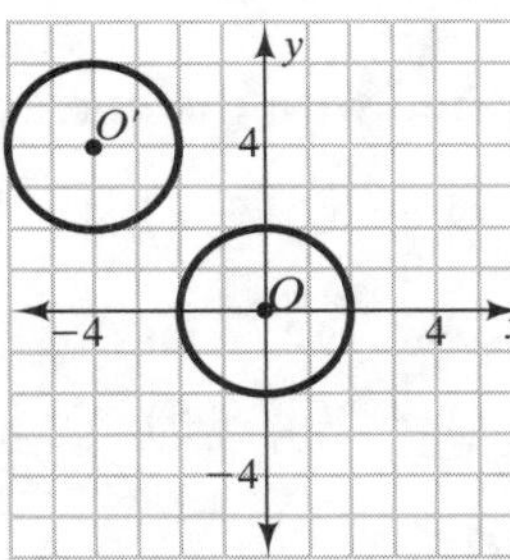

_______________ _______________ _______________

Copy $\triangle MNP$. Then graph the image after each translation. List the coordinates of each image's vertices.

4\. left 2 units, down 2 units

____

5\. right 2 units, down 1 unit

____

6\. left 2 units, up 3 units

____

Copy $\square RSTU$. Then graph the image after each translation. List the coordinates of each image's vertices.

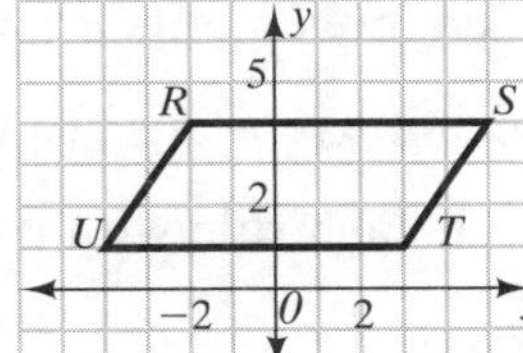

7\. right 1 unit, down 2 units

____

8\. left 3 units, up 0 units

____

9\. right 2 units, up 4 units

____

Use the graph at the right for Exercises 10 and 11.

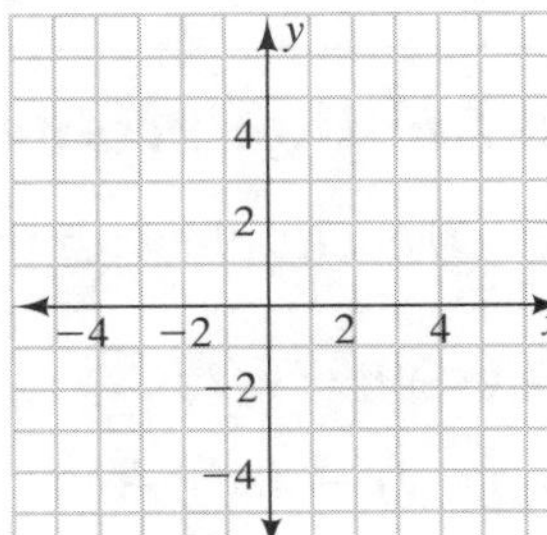

10\. A rectangle has its vertices at $M(1, 1)$, $N(6, 1)$, $O(6, 5)$, and $P(1, 5)$. The rectangle is translated to the left 4 units and down 3 units. What are the coordinates of M', N', O', and P'? Graph the rectangles $MNOP$ and $M'N'O'P'$.

____

11\. Use arrow notation to write a rule that describes the translation of $M'N'O'P'$ to $MNOP$.

____

Name ______________________ Class ______________ Date ______________

8-1 • Guided Problem Solving

GPS Student Page 257, Exercises 16–18:

Match each rule with the correct translation.

A. $(x, y) \rightarrow (x - 6, y + 2)$ **I.** $P(4, -1) \rightarrow P'(3, -6)$

B. $(x, y) \rightarrow (x + 3, y)$ **II.** $Q(3, 0) \rightarrow Q'(-3, 2)$

C. $(x, y) \rightarrow (x - 1, y - 5)$ **III.** $R(-2, 4) \rightarrow R'(1, 4)$

Understand

1. What are you asked to do?

____

Plan and Carry Out

2. Use the words *left* or *right* and *up* or *down* to describe the movement between each point and its image. Be sure to give the number of units each coordinate is translated.

Point $P(4, -1)$ to $P'(3, -6)$ ______________________

Point $Q(3, 0)$ to $Q'(-3, 2)$ ______________________

Point $R(-2, 4)$ to $R'(1, 4)$ ______________________

3. Which movements are written as addition? ______________

4. Which movements are written as subtraction? ______________

5. Match each rule with its translation.

A = __________ B = __________ C = __________

Check

6. How could you check your answers?

____

____

Solve Another Problem

7. Match each rule with the correct translation.

A. $(x, y) \rightarrow (x - 3, y - 4)$ **I.** $P(5, -2) \rightarrow P'(5, -5)$

B. $(x, y) \rightarrow (x + 4, y + 2)$ **II.** $Q(1, 6) \rightarrow Q'(5, 8)$

C. $(x, y) \rightarrow (x, y - 3)$ **III.** $R(-4, 2) \rightarrow R'(-7, -2)$

____

Name ______________________ Class ______________ Date ______________

Practice 8-2

Reflections and Symmetry

How many lines of symmetry can you find for each letter?

1. W __________ 2. X __________ 3. H __________ 4. T __________

Graph the given point and its image after each reflection. Name the coordinates of the reflected point.

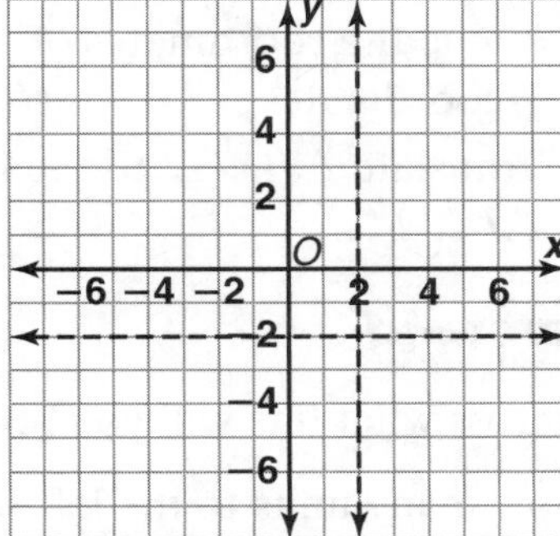

5. $A(5, -4)$ over the vertical dashed line

____

6. $B(-3, 2)$ over the horizontal dashed line

____

7. $C(-5, 0)$ over the y-axis

____

8. $D(3, 4)$ over the x-axis

____

$\triangle ABC$ has vertices $A(2, 1)$, $B(3, -5)$, and $C(-2, 4)$. Graph $\triangle ABC$ and its image, $\triangle A'B'C'$, after a reflection over each line. Name the coordinates of A', B', and C'.

9. the x-axis

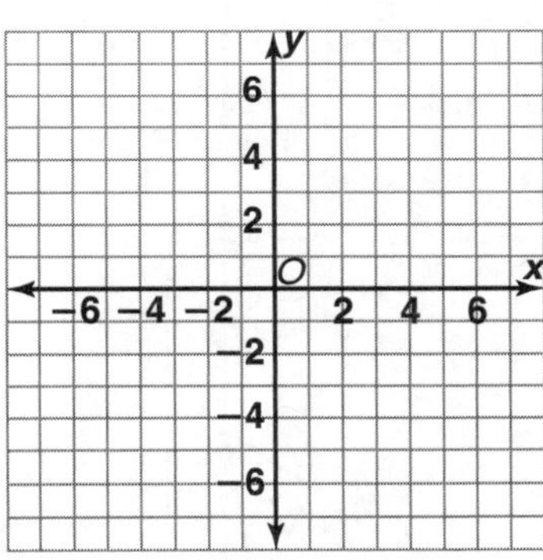

____

____

10. the line through $(-1, 2)$ and $(1, 2)$

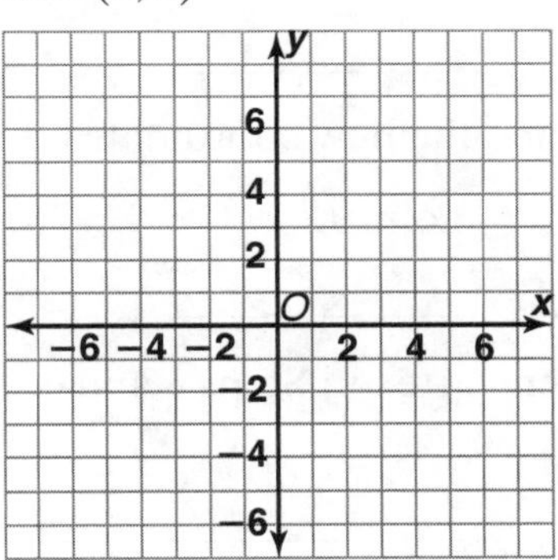

____

____

11. the y-axis

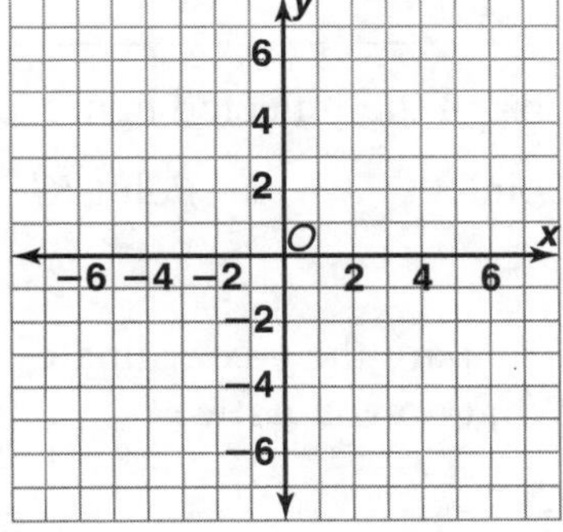

____

____

Fold your paper over each dashed line. Are the figures reflections of each other over the given line?

12.

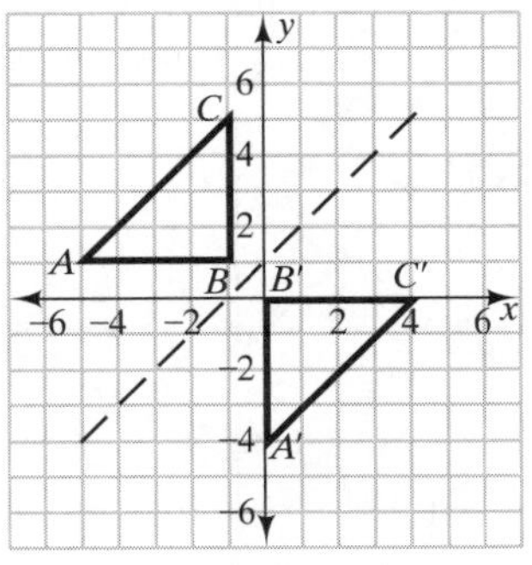

____

13.

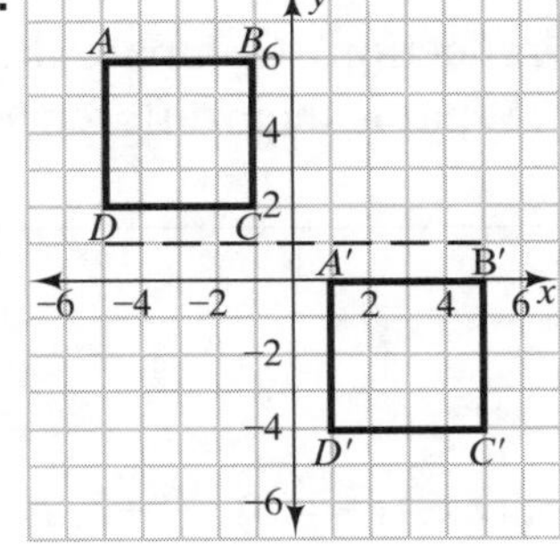

____

14.

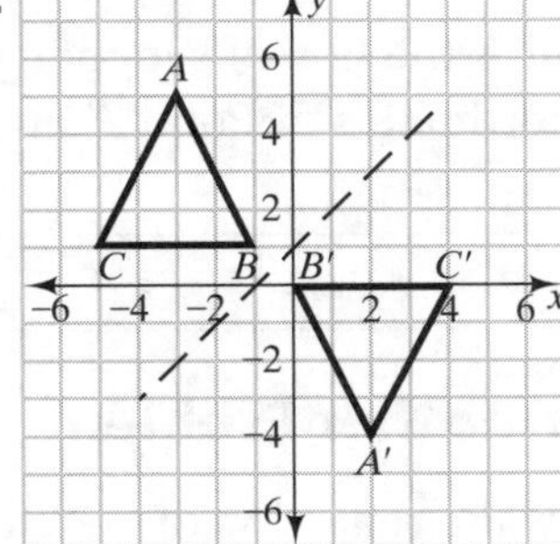

____

Name ______________________ Class ______________ Date ______________

8-2 • Guided Problem Solving

GPS Student Page 262, Exercise 22:

a. Graph the image of $\triangle JKL$ after it is reflected over the line m. Name the coordinates of $\triangle J'K'L'$. What do you notice about the y-coordinates?

b. Translate $\triangle J'K'L'$ to the left 3 units. Name the coordinates of $\triangle J''K''L''$.

Understand

1. Across what line will you reflect $\triangle JKL$? ______________

2. How many units to the left will you translate $\triangle JKL$? ________

Plan and Carry Out

3. Write the coordinates for each vertex of $\triangle JKL$.

Point J ________ Point K ________ Point L ________

4. Graph the reflected figure and name the new coordinates.

Point J' ________ Point K' ________ Point L' ________

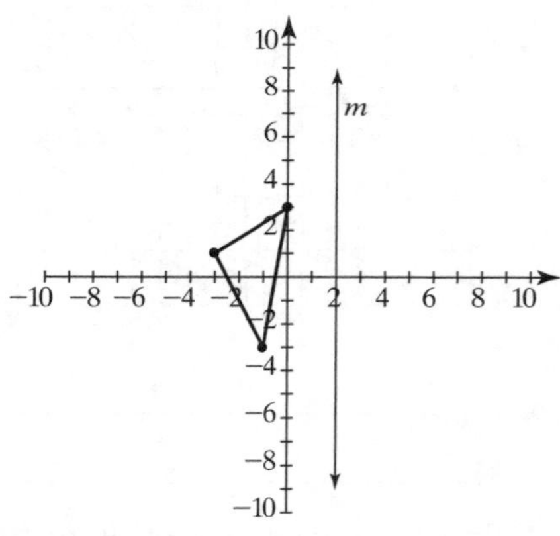

5. Compare the y-coordinates of each vertex in Steps 3 and 4. What do you notice? ______________________________

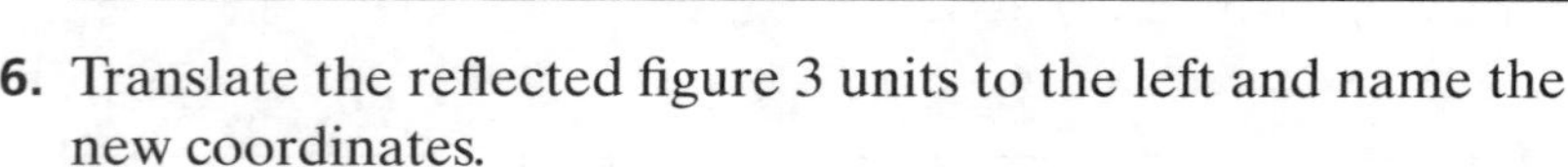

6. Translate the reflected figure 3 units to the left and name the new coordinates.

Point J'' ________ Point K'' ________ Point L'' ________

Check

7. What is the line of symmetry in your reflection? Compare the x-coordinates of Point J' and Point J''. What is their difference?

Solve Another Problem

8. Draw the reflection of $\triangle ABC$ with vertices $A(-1, 0)$, $B(-3, 2)$, and $C(-2, 3)$ across the y-axis. Give the coordinates of the reflection's vertices. ______________________

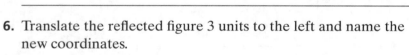

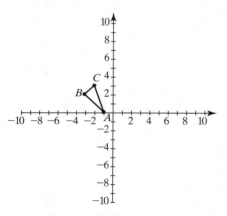

Name ______________________ Class ______________ Date ______________

Practice 8-3

Rotations

Graph each point. Then rotate it the given number of degrees about the origin. Give the coordinates of the image.

1. $V(2, -3)$; 90° ______________
2. $M(-4, 5)$; 270° ______________
3. $V(0, 5)$; 180° ______________
4. $V(3, 4)$; 360° ______________
5. Graph $\triangle RST$ with vertices $R(-1, 3)$, $S(4, -2)$, and $T(2, -5)$. Graph the image formed by rotating the triangle about the origin by each angle.

a 90°

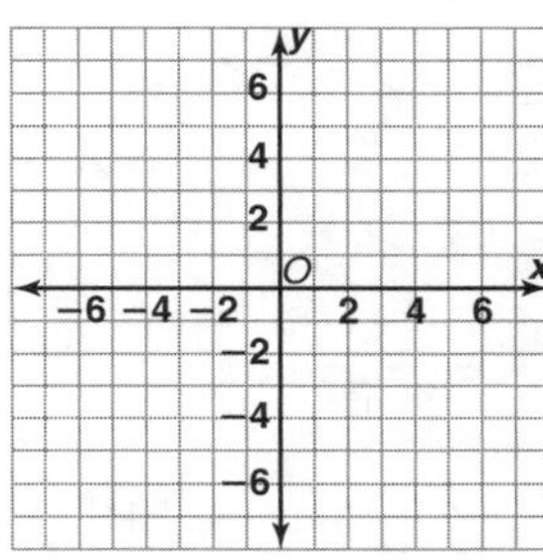

b 180°

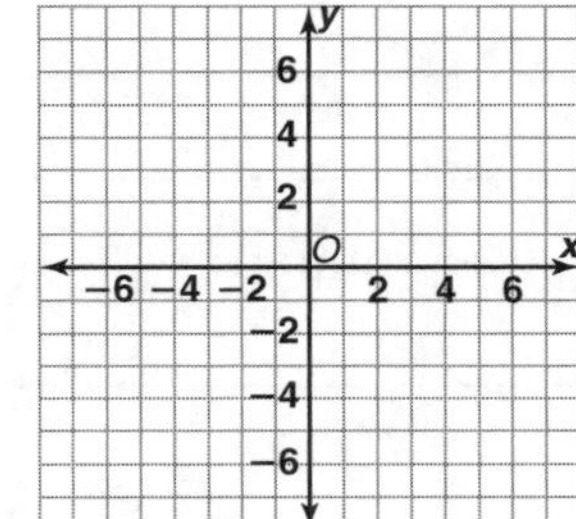

c 270°

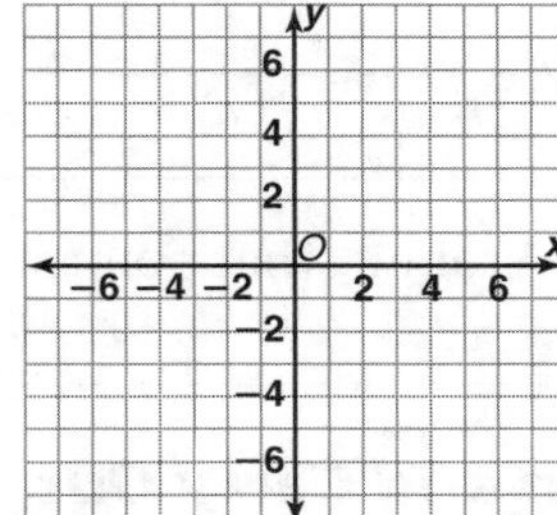

Determine if each figure could be a rotation of the figure at the right. For each figure that could be a rotation, tell what the angle of rotation appears to be.

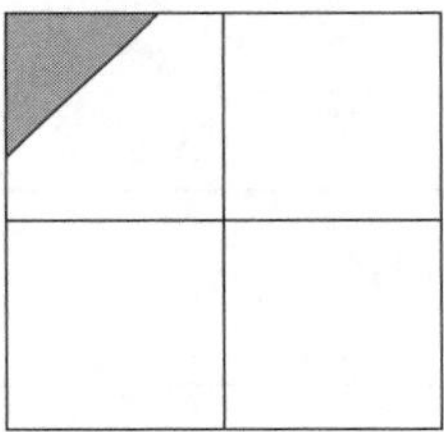

6.

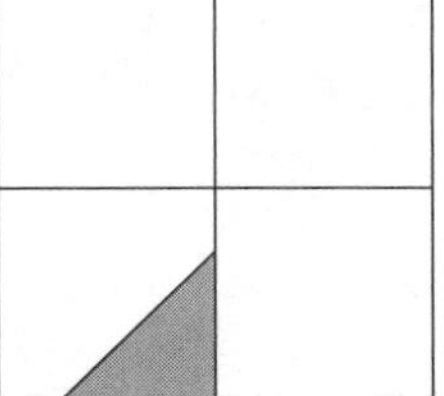

____

7.

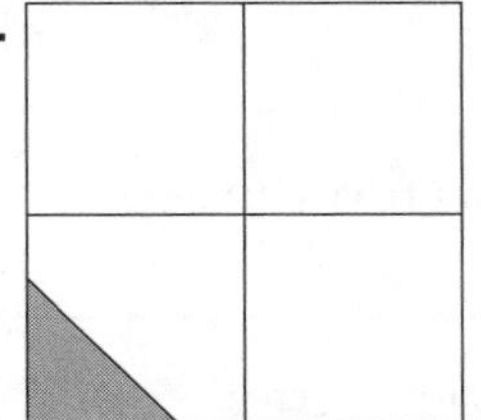

____

8.

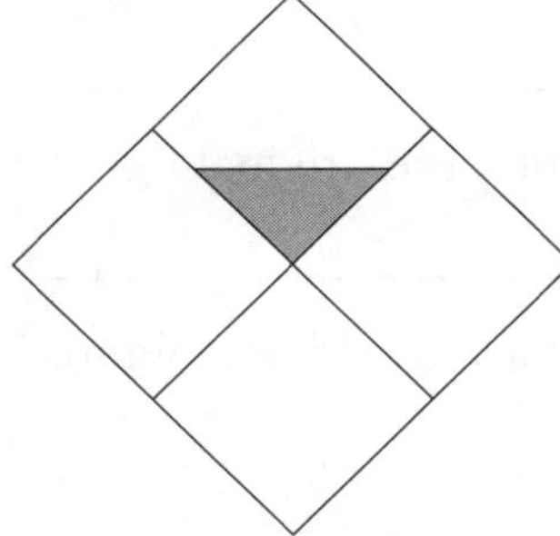

____

9.

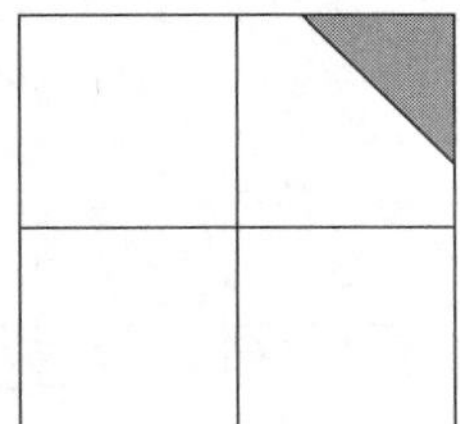

____

10.

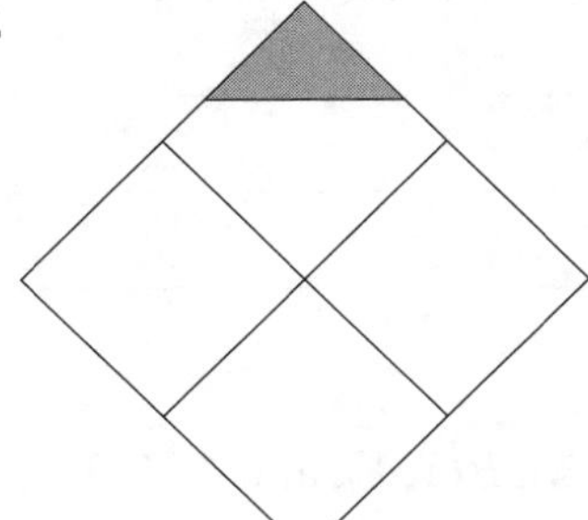

____

11.

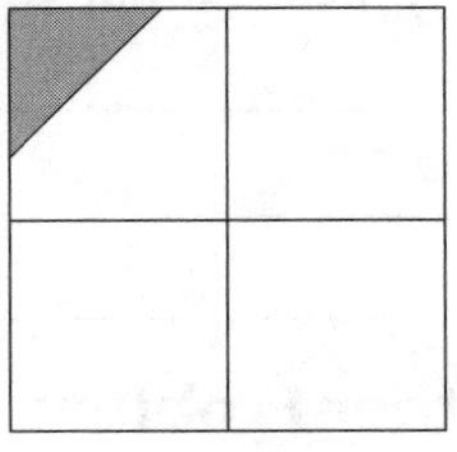

____

Name ______________________ Class ______________ Date ______________

8-3 • Guided Problem Solving

GPS Student Page 267, Exercise 12:

Graph $\triangle JKL$ with vertices $J(1, -3)$, $K(6, -2)$, and $L(6, -4)$. Graph the three images formed by rotating the triangle 90°, 180°, and 270° about the origin. Give the coordinates of the vertices of each image.

Understand

1. What are you asked to do?

____

____

2. Around what point will the triangle be rotated?

____

Plan and Carry Out

3. Graph the triangle. ______________________________

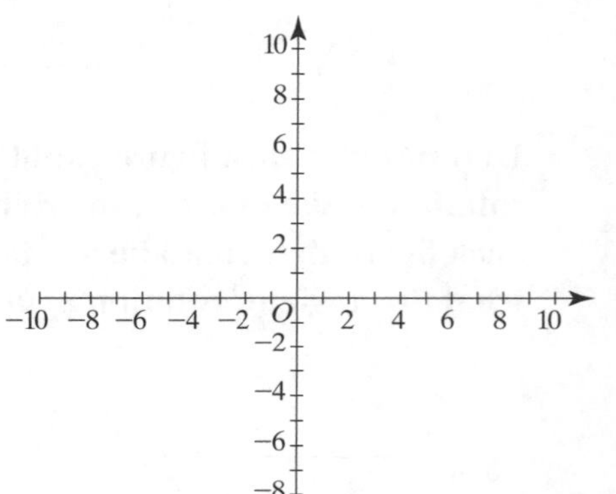

4. What is a rotation?

____

5. What direction does the figure rotate?

____

6. Rotate the figure 90° and mark each vertex.

____

7. Rotate the original figure 180° and mark each vertex.

____

8. Rotate the original figure 270° and mark each vertex.

____

Check

9. How can you check that your figures are rotated correctly?

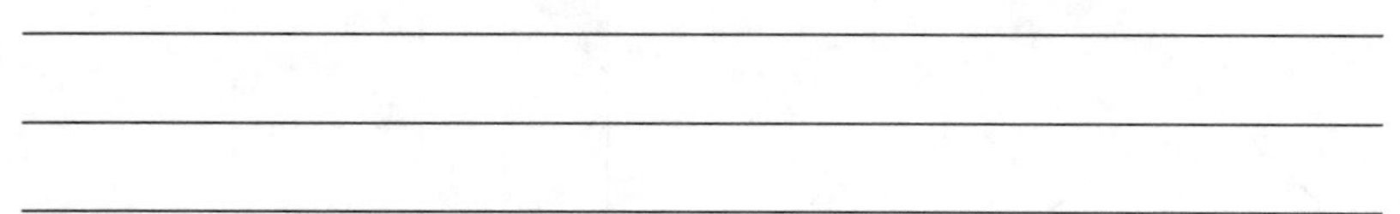

____

____

____

Solve Another Problem

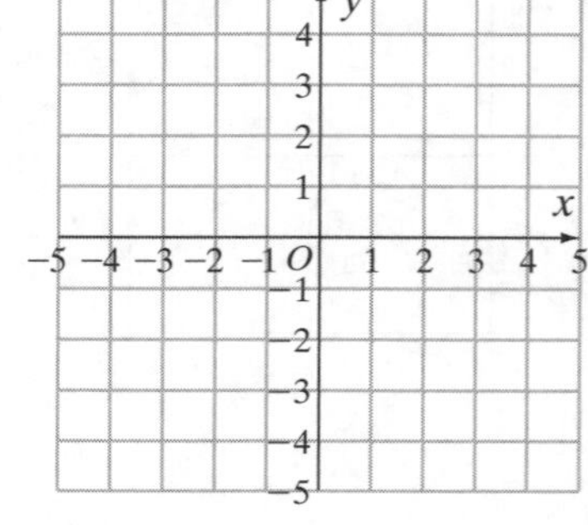

10. a. Graph $\triangle ABC$ with vertices $A(2, 2)$, $B(1, 1)$, and $C(1, 3)$.

b. Draw the three images formed by rotating the triangle 90°, 180°, and 270° about the origin.

Name ______________________ Class ______________ Date ______________

Practice 8-4

Transformations and Congruence

The three figures in each diagram are congruent. Describe the sequence of transformations that maps the original figure onto the final image.

1.

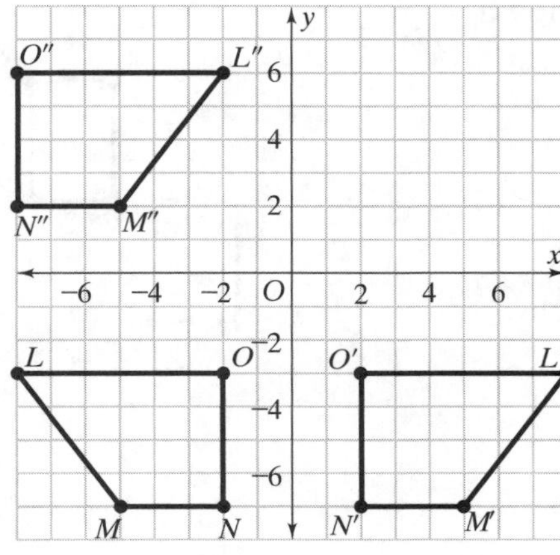

2.

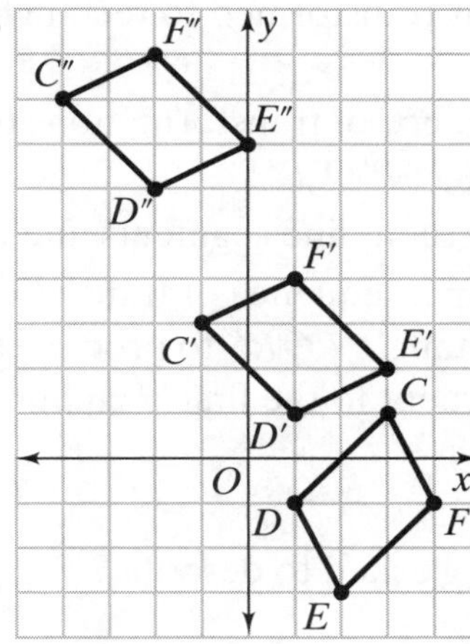

Determine whether the two figures in each diagram are congruent. If the figures are congruent, tell what sequence of transformations will map one figure onto the other. Then write a congruence statement. If they are not congruent, explain why.

3.

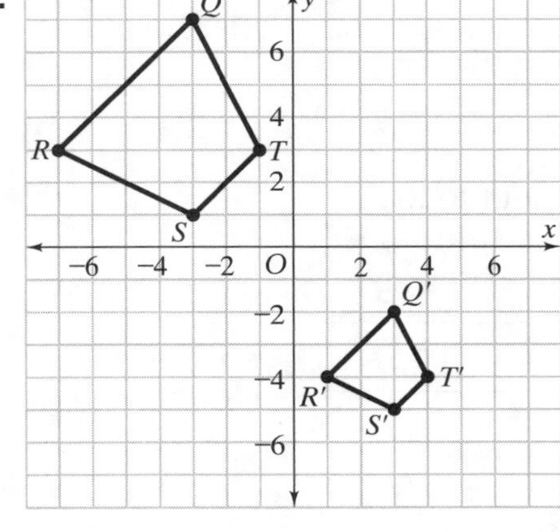

4.

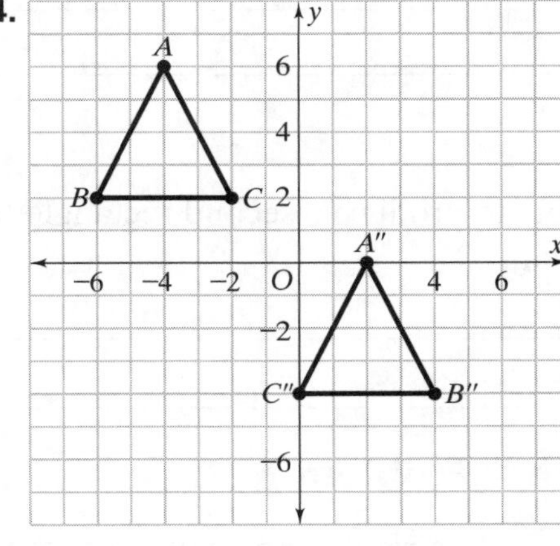

Name ______________________ Class ______________ Date ______________

8-4 • Guided Problem Solving

Transformations and Congruence

GPS Student Page 272, Exercise 10:

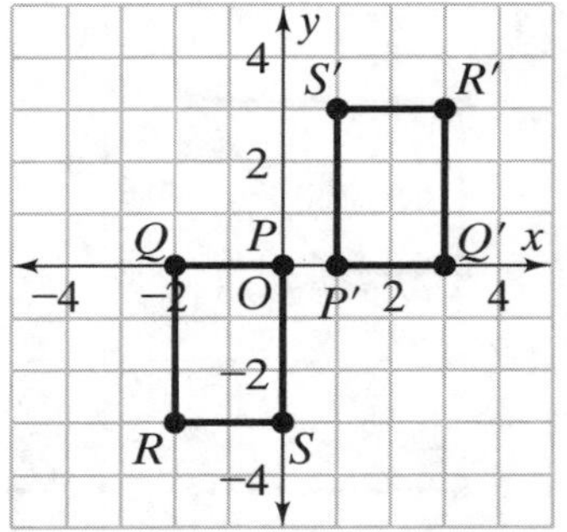

10. Rectangle *PQRS* is transformed to rectangle *P'Q'R'S'* as shown on the graph.

a. Describe a sequence of transformations to map rectangle *PQRS* to rectangle *P'Q'R'S'*.

b. Identify all congruent line segments and angles.

c. Can you perform a sequence of translations, reflections, or rotations on rectangle *PQRS* to produce a second rectangle that is *not* congruent to the first? Explain.

Understand

1. What are you being asked to describe?

____

2. What are you being asked to identify?

____

Plan and Carry Out

3. List the corresponding line segments. ______________________________

4. To map rectangle *PQRS* onto rectangle *P'Q'R'S'* should you start by translating, reflecting, or rotating rectangle *PQRS*? What transformation should you perform second?

____

____

Check

5. Is it possible to produce a second rectangle that is not congruent to the first? Explain.

____

____

Solve Another Problem

6. Graph and label a right triangle in the coordinate plane. Describe a sequence of transformations. Then draw and label the final transformation image. Give the coordinates of the vertices of both the original triangle and its final transformation image.

Name ______________________ Class ______________ Date ______________

Practice 8-5

Transformations and Congruence

Graph quadrilateral $ABCD$ with the given vertices. Find the coordinates of the vertices of its image $A'B'C'D'$ after a dilation with the given scale factor.

1. $A(2, -2), B(3, 2), C(-3, 2), D(-2, -2)$; scale factor 2

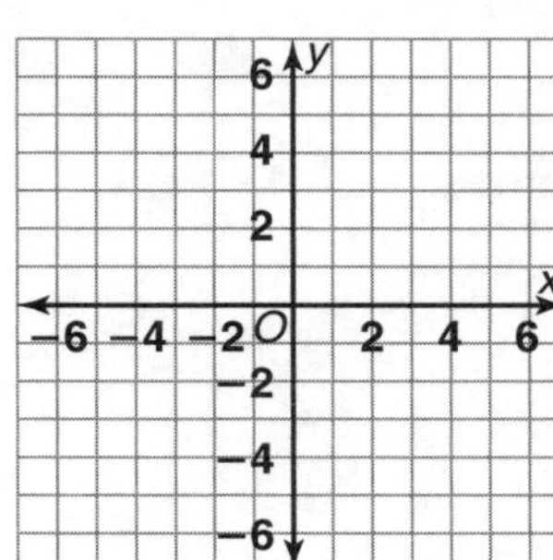

2. $A(6, 3), B(0, 6), C(-6, 2), D(-6, -5)$; scale factor $\frac{1}{2}$

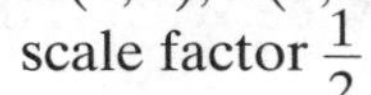

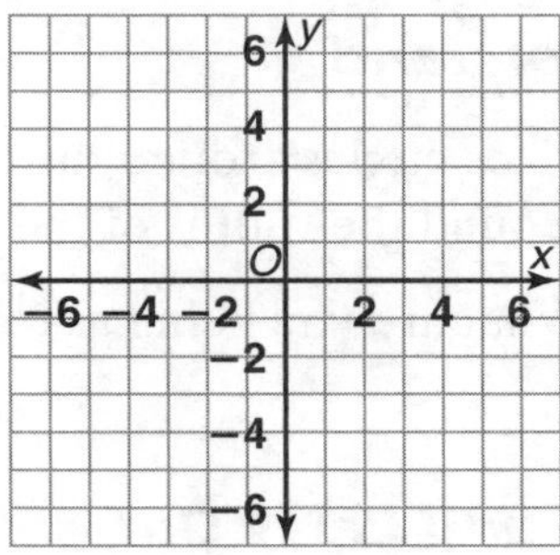

Quadrilateral $A'B'C'D'$ is a dilation image of quadrilateral $ABCD$. Find the scale factor. Classify each dilation as an *enlargement* or a *reduction*.

3.

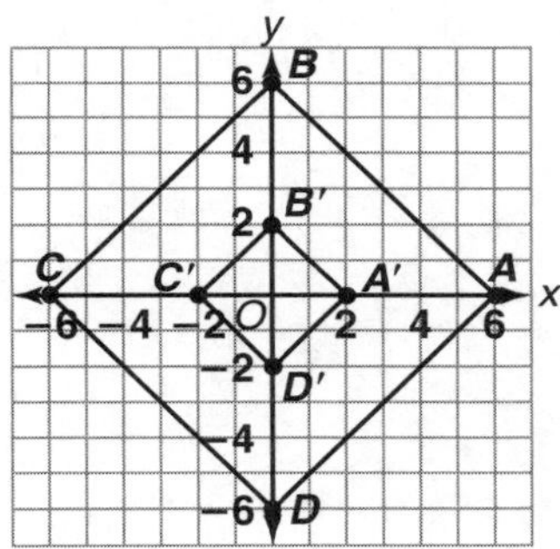

4.

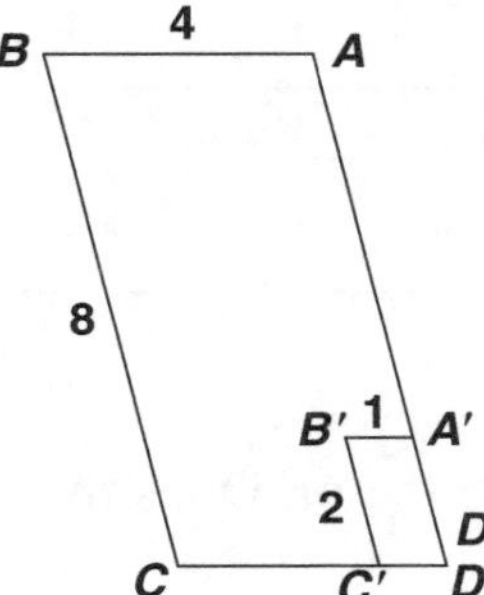

5.

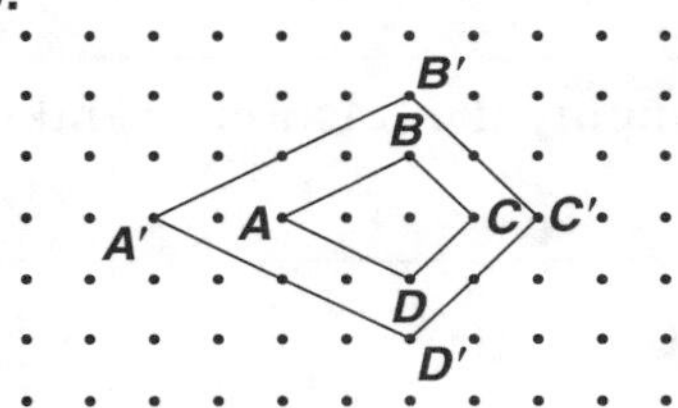

______________ ______________ ______________

6. A triangle has coordinates $A(-2, -2)$, $B(4, -2)$, and $C(1, 1)$. Graph its image $A'B'C'$ after a dilation with scale factor $\frac{3}{2}$. Give the coordinates of $A'B'C'$, and the ratio of the areas of the figures $A'B'C'$ and ABC.

____

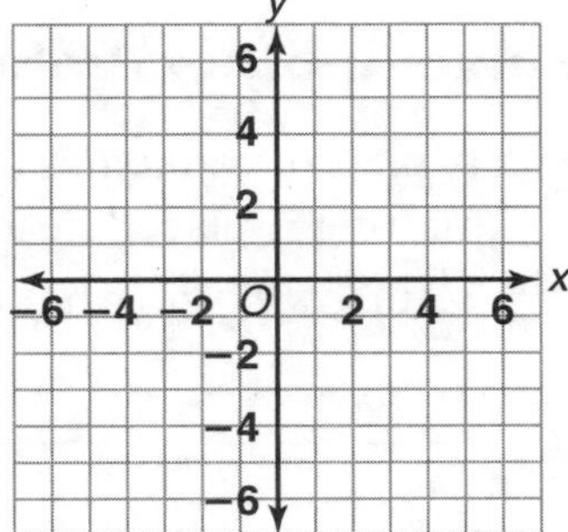

Name ______________________ Class ______________ Date ______________

8-5 • Guided Problem Solving

GPS Student Page 280, Exercise 14:

Computers A window on a computer screen is $1\frac{1}{2}$ in. high and 2 in. wide. After you click the "size reduction" button, the window is reduced to $1\frac{1}{8}$ in. high and $1\frac{1}{2}$ in. wide. What is the scale factor?

Understand

1. Place circles around the heights of the window and squares around the widths of the window.

2. What are you being asked to find?

____

Plan and Carry Out

3. Use the width dimension to find the scale factor by placing the values in the formula $\frac{\text{image}}{\text{original}}$.

____

4. Simplify the fraction to find the scale factor.

____

Check

5. Use the height dimension to find the scale factor. Does the value match your answer to Step 4?

____

Solve Another Problem

6. A picture frame has an opening that is 12 in. by 15 in. If a matting is placed inside the frame to create an opening that is $7\frac{1}{2}$ in. by $9\frac{3}{8}$ in., what is the scale factor of the reduction?

____

Name ______________________ Class ______________ Date ______________

Practice 8-6

1. You and a friend decide to start a lawn cutting business. You use a graphics program to make a flyer advertising your business. You choose a picture for your flyer and place it on the top, left of the computer screen. The size of the picture on your screen is 12 cm wide. It looks much too large, so you reduce it to 4 cm wide. You then center the picture both horizontally and vertically on the page. Describe the sequence of transformations that maps the original picture on the flyer to the final version.

____

____

The two figures in each diagram are similar. Describe the sequence of two transformations that maps the original figure onto the final image.

2.

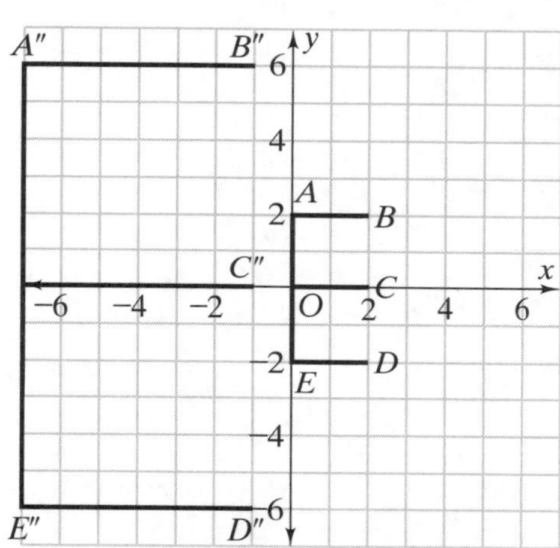

____

____

3.

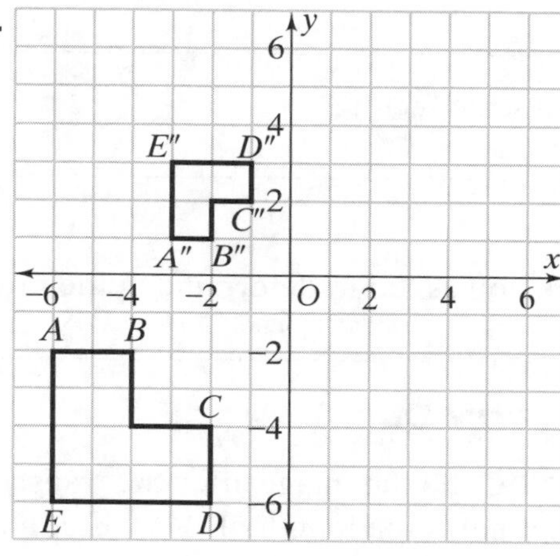

____

____

4.

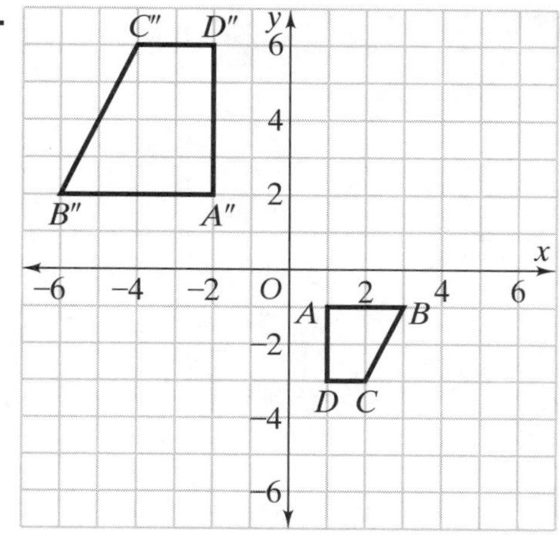

____

____

5.

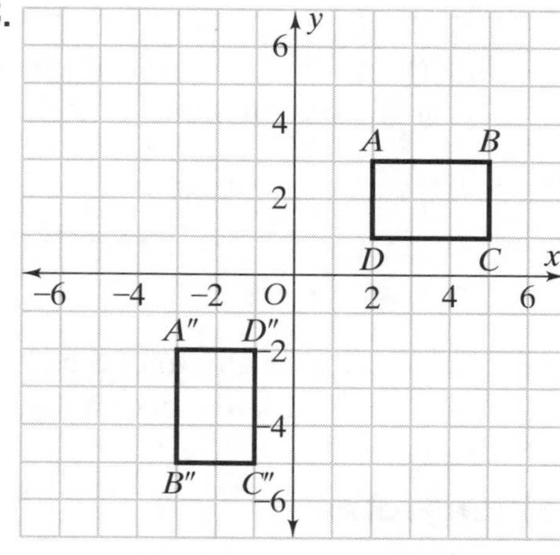

____

____

Name ______________________ Class ______________ Date ______________

8-6 • Guided Problem Solving

GPS Student Page 285, Exercise 13:

A translation 6 units down followed by a dilation with scale factor $\frac{1}{2}$ maps $\triangle ABC$ onto $\triangle A''B''C''$. If $\overline{AB} = 8$ units, what is the length of $\overline{A''B''}$?

Understand

1. What is a translation?

____

____

2. What is a dilation?

____

____

3. What is a scale factor?

____

____

4. What are you asked to determine in the problem?

____

Plan and Carry Out

5. Let $\triangle A'B'C'$ be the image after the translation but before the dilation. What is the length of $\overline{A'B'}$ after a translation of $\triangle ABC$ 6 units down? Explain your answer.

____

____

6. What is the length of $\overline{A''B''}$ after a dilation of $\triangle A'B'$ with a scale factor of $\frac{1}{2}$? Explain your answer.

____

____

Check

7. Draw a triangle with a side length of 8 units on a coordinate grid. Then translate and dilate it according to the directions to check your answer.

Solve Another Problem

8. A reflection across the y-axis is followed by a dilation with scale factor $\frac{1}{3}$ maps $\triangle ABC$ onto $\triangle A''B''C''$. If $AB = 15$ units, what is the length of $\overline{A''B''}$? ______________________

Name ______________________ Class ______________ Date ______________

8A: Graphic Organizer

For use before Lesson 8-1

Study Skill Many skills build on each other. Before you begin a new lesson, do a quick review of the material covered in earlier lessons. Ask for help if there are any concepts you did not understand.

Write your answers.

1. What is the chapter title? ______________________
2. How many lessons are there in this chapter? ______________________
3. What is the topic of the Test-Taking Strategies page? ______________________
4. Complete the graphic organizer below as you work through the chapter.
   - In the center, write the title of the chapter.
   - When you begin a lesson, write the lesson name in a rectangle.
   - When you complete a lesson, write a skill or key concept in a circle linked to that lesson block.
   - When you complete the chapter, use this graphic organizer to help you review.

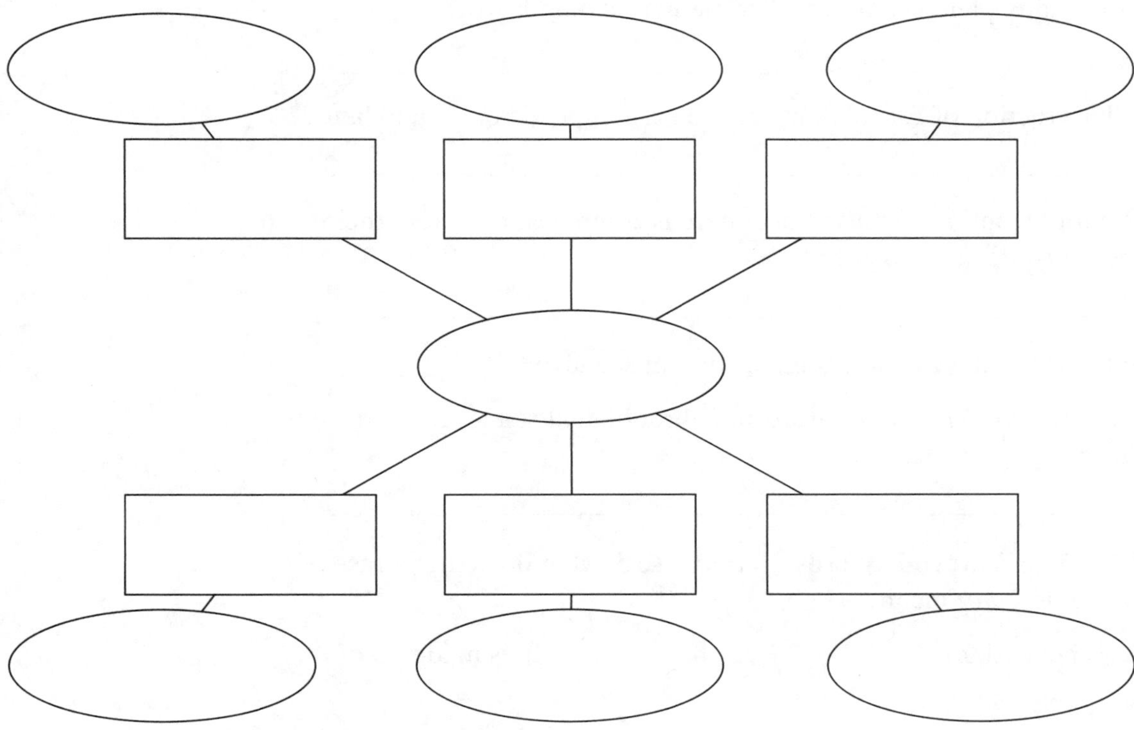

Name ______________________ Class ______________ Date ______________

8B: Reading Comprehension

For use after Lesson 8-3

Study Skill Read problems carefully. Pay special attention to units when working with measurements.

Read the paragraph below and answer the questions.

Earth has an average diameter of 7,926.2 miles. It is not a sphere, since it bulges slightly at the equator. Of the nine major planets in our solar system, Earth is the middle planet in average diameter. The composition of the Earth's surface area is 70% water and 30% air and land. The atmosphere is composed of 78% nitrogen, 21% oxygen, and a mixture of several other gases. The average temperature at sea level is 15°C. The Earth is about 93 million miles from the sun.

1. What is the paragraph about?

   ____

2. What is Earth's radius?

   ____

3. How many planets have smaller diameters than Earth? ________

4. Why is Earth not a sphere? ______________________________

5. What fraction of Earth's surface area is composed of air and land?

   ____

6. What percent of Earth's atmosphere is composed of gases other than nitrogen and oxygen?

   ____

7. What is Earth's average temperature at sea level? ____________

8. Find the average temperature, in Fahrenheit, at sea level. *Hint:* $F = \frac{9}{5}C + 32$.

   ____

9. **High-Use Academic Words** In Exercise 5, what does the phrase *is composed of* mean?

   a. is needed for

   b. is made up of

Name ______________________ Class ______________ Date ______________

8C: Reading/Writing Math Symbols

For use after Lesson 8-5

Study Skill Use a notebook or a section of a loose-leaf binder for homework assignments.

Write a mathematical statement of expression for each word description.

1. Six and six hundredths percent

____

2. Triangle XYZ is similar to triangle ABC.

____

3. Thirty-nine percent is approximately equal to four tenths.

____

4. Angle G is congruent to angle K.

____

5. One fourth equals twenty-five percent.

____

6. Five elevenths is greater than 45 percent.

____

In the diagram below, $\triangle ABC \cong \triangle A'B'C'$. Use the diagram to write the meaning of each mathematical statement.

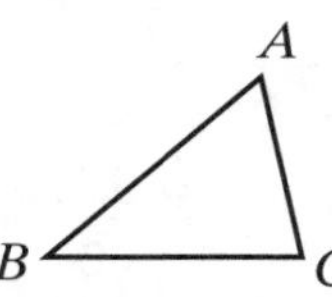

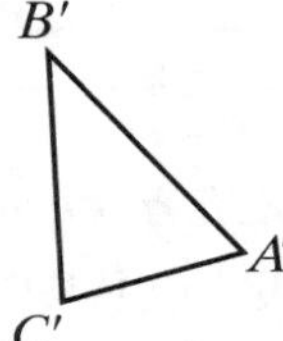

7. $\overline{AC}$ _______________________________
8. $\overrightarrow{CB}$ _______________________________
9. A' _______________________________
10. $\angle B'$ _______________________________
11. $\overline{AC} \cong \overline{A'C'}$ _______________________________

Name ____________________ Class ____________ Date ____________

8D: Visual Vocabulary Practice

For use after Lesson 8-6

High-Use Academic Words

Study Skill If a word is not in the glossary, use a dictionary to find its meaning.

Concept List

sum	table	estimate
evaluate	solve	define
order	equivalent	compare

Write the concept that best describes each exercise. Choose from the concept list above.

1.

$$\frac{z}{8} = 7 - 2$$
$$\frac{z}{8} \times 8 = (7 - 2) \times 8$$
$$z = 5 \times 8$$
$$z = 40$$

____

2.

The World's Longest Rivers

Name	Country	Length
Nile	Egypt	4,160 mi
Amazon	Brazil	4,000 mi
Yangtze	China	3,964 mi

____

3.

$7\frac{1}{6}$ and $7.1\overline{6}$

____

4.

$|-28| > 27$

____

5.

$3a + 6 + (-4.25) + (-a) + 7$
$= 2a + 8.75$

____

6.

$4n - (9 \div m)$ for $n = -3$ and $m = 7$

____

7.

$$x + 29\frac{5}{8} = 42\frac{1}{9}$$
$$x + 30 \approx 42$$
$$x \approx 12$$

____

8.

A *transformation* is a change in the position, shape, or size of a figure.

____

9.

$-10.1, 6.7, -10\frac{2}{3}, -4, 7.8$
$-10\frac{2}{3}, -10.1, -4, 6.7, 7.8$

____

Name ____________________ Class ____________ Date ____________

8E: Vocabulary Check

For use after Lesson 8-6

Study Skill Strengthen your vocabulary. Use these pages and add cues and summaries by applying the Cornell Notetaking style.

Write the definition for each word or term at the right. To check your work, fold the paper back along the dotted line to see the correct answers.

____________________	reflectional symmetry
____________________	rotation
____________________	transformation
____________________	translation
____________________	dilation

Vocabulary and Study Skills

Name ______________________ Class ______________ Date ______________

8E: Vocabulary Check (continued)

For use after Lesson 8-6

Write the vocabulary word or term for each definition. To check your work, fold the paper back along the dotted line to see the correct answers.

when a figure can be reflected over a line so that its image matches the original ______________________

a transformation that turns a figure about a fixed point ______________________

a change in position, shape, or size of a figure ______________________

a transformation that moves each point of a figure the same distance and in the same direction ______________________

a transformation in which the figure and its image are similar ______________________

Name ______________________ Class ______________ Date ______________

8F: Vocabulary Review

For use with the Chapter Review

Study Skill Some concepts are very difficult to grasp on your own. If you pay attention in class, you can ask questions about concepts you do not understand.

Vocabulary and Study Skills

I. Match the term in Column A with its definition in Column B.

Column A	Column B
1. angle of rotation	A. a figure is flipped over this
2. center of rotation	B. when a figure can be flipped over a line and match its original figure
3. line of reflection	C. when a figure can be rotated 180° or less and exactly match its original figure
4. scale factor	D. the number of degrees a figure rotates
5. reflectional symmetry	E. the ratio of a length in an image to the corresponding length in the original figure
6. rotational symmetry	F. a fixed point from which a figure is rotated

II. Match the term in Column A with its definition in Column B.

Column A	Column B
1. enlargement	A. a transformation that moves each point of a figure the same distance and in the same direction
2. transformation	B. a dilation with a scale factor less than 1
3. dilation	C. a transformation that flips a figure over a line
4. image	D. a dilation with a scale factor greater than 1
5. translation	E. the figure after a transformation
6. reduction	F. a transformation that turns a figure
7. rotation	G. a transformation in which a figure and its image are similar
8. reflection	H. a change in the position, shape, or size of a figure

Name ____________________ Class ____________ Date ____________

Practice 9-1

Solids

For each figure, describe the base(s) of the figure, and name the figure.

1. 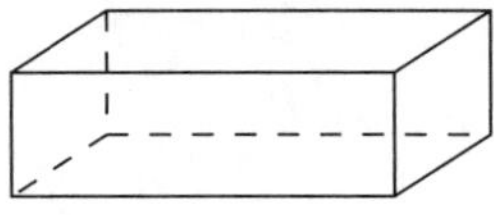

____

____

2. 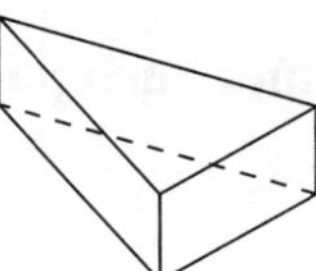

____

____

3. 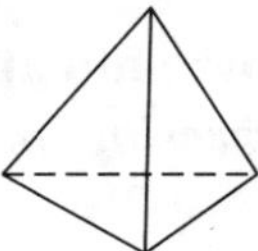

____

____

4. 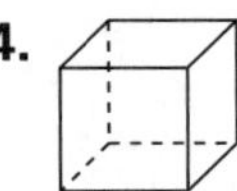

____

____

5. 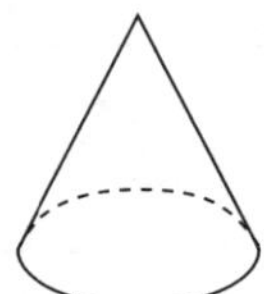

____

____

6. 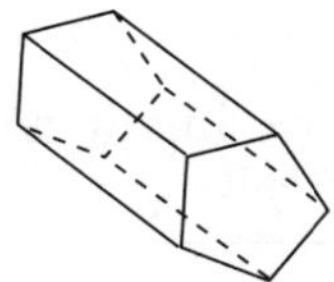

____

____

Name the solid that describes each item.

7. bowling ball ______________

8. DVD player ______________

9. soup can ______________

Complete.

10. A ______________ has exactly two circular bases.
11. A hexagonal prism has ______________ faces.
12. A cube has ______________ edges.
13. A pentagonal pyramid has ______________ faces.
14. A pentagonal pyramid has ______________ edges.

Name the figure described.

15. a space figure with six congruent square faces

____

16. a space figure with parallel bases that are congruent, parallel circles

____

Name ______________________ Class ______________ Date ______________

9-1 • Guided Problem Solving

GPS Student Page 299, Exercise 14–16:

Use the rectangular pyramid at the right. State whether each pair of line segments is *intersecting, parallel,* or *skew*.

14. $\overline{CO}, \overline{CE}$ **15.** $\overline{OR}, \overline{CE}$ **16.** $\overline{CT}, \overline{ER}$

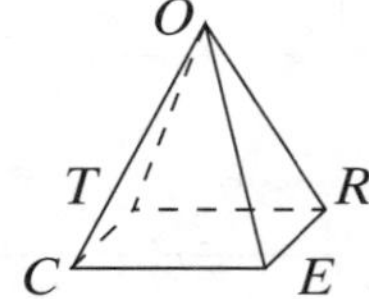

Understand

1. What figure is formed by the line segments?

____

2. What are intersecting lines?

____

3. What are parallel lines?

____

____

4. What are skew lines?

____

____

Plan and Carry Out

5. Trace $\overline{CO}$ and $\overline{CE}$ on the rectangular pyramid.
6. If you extended these two line segments what would happen to them? ______________________________
7. Therefore, these line segments are ______________________________
8. Repeat Steps 5–7 for segments $\overline{OR}$ and $\overline{CE}$ and for segments $\overline{CT}$ and $\overline{ER}$. ______________________________

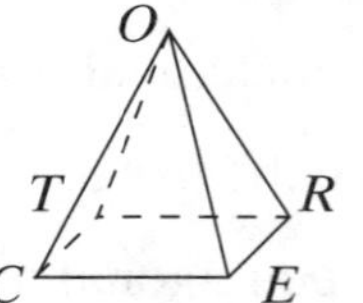

Check

9. If $\overline{CE}$ and $\overline{TR}$ are parallel, what must then be true about the relationship between $\overline{OT}$ and $\overline{TR}$?

____

Solve Another Problem

10. In the rectangular pyramid at the right, state whether line segments $\overline{MN}$ and $\overline{PQ}$ are intersecting, parallel, or skew.

____

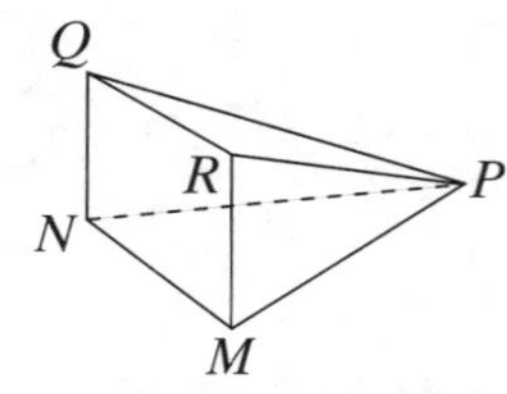

Name ______________________ Class ______________ Date ____________

Practice 9-2

Volumes of Prisms and Cylinders

Find the volume of each solid to the nearest whole number.

1. 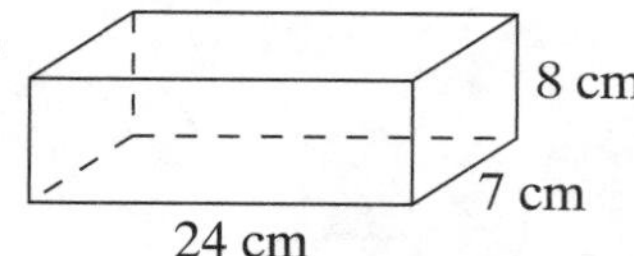

2. 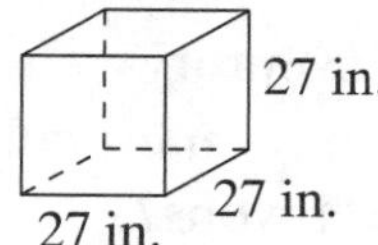

3. 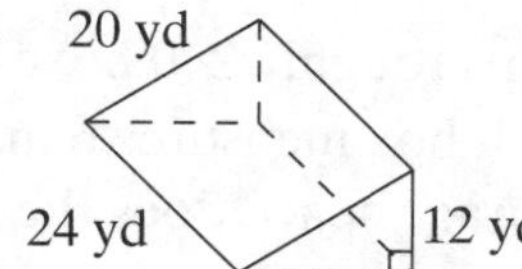

4. 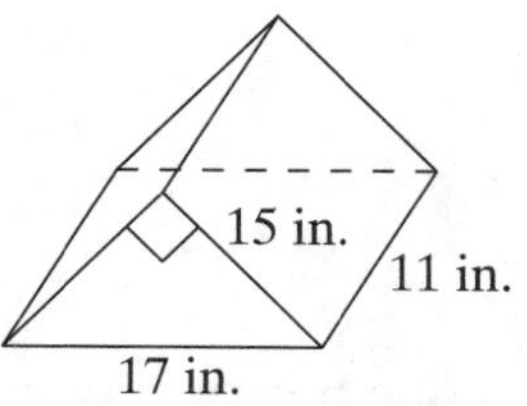

5. 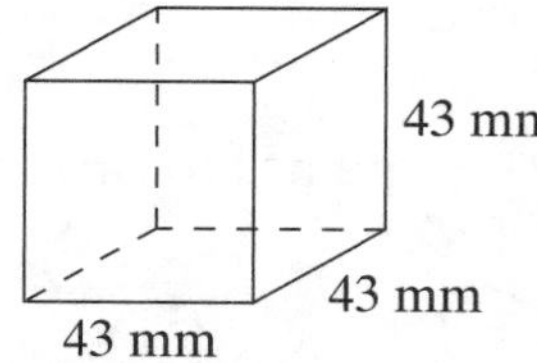

6. 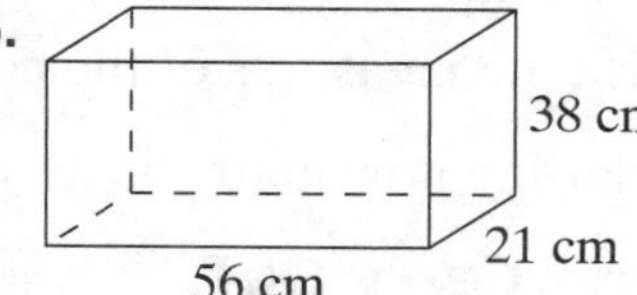

7. 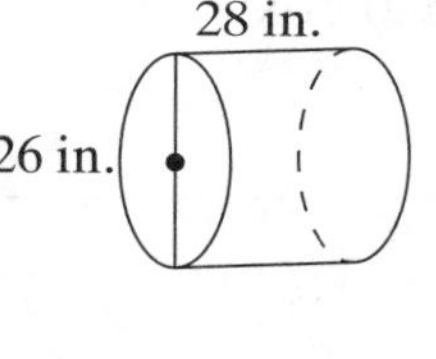

8. 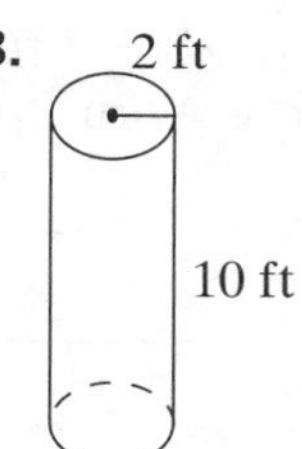

9. 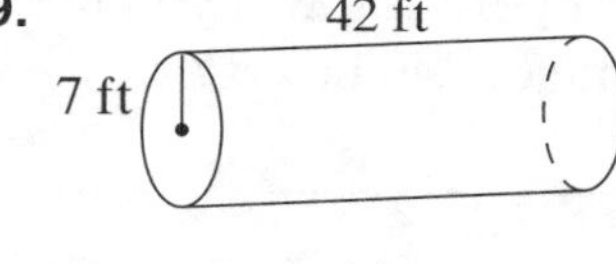

10. Suppose you want to buy concrete for a 36 ft by 24 ft by 9 in. patio. If concrete costs $55/yd^3, how much will the concrete for the patio cost?

11. A cylinder has a volume of about 500 cm^3 and a height of 10 cm. What is the length of the radius to the nearest tenth of a cm?

Name ______________________ Class ______________ Date ______________

9-2 • Guided Problem Solving

GPS Student Page 305, Exercise 20:

A store keeps roughly 240 boxes of crayons in its inventory.

a. If each box measures 6 in. by 2.5 in. by 4 in., how many cubic inches of storage space does the store need for the crayons?

b. One cubic foot is equal to $(12 \text{ in.})^3$, or 1,728 in.^3. Find the number of cubic feet necessary for storing 240 boxes of crayons.

Understand

1. Circle the measures of the crayon boxes.
2. Underline how many boxes the art supply store has for inventory.

Plan and Carry Out

3. What formula will you use to find the volume of one box of crayons?

____

4. What is the volume of one box of crayons?

____

5. What operation will you use to find the volume of 240 boxes?

____

6. What is the volume of 240 boxes of crayons?

____

7. How many cubic inches are in one cubic foot? ______________________

8. How can you change cubic inches to cubic feet?

____

9. How many cubic feet are necessary for storing 240 boxes of crayons?

____

Check

10. What is a way to check the problem?______________________

____

____

Solve Another Problem

11. A video store keeps approximately 350 boxes of storage cases in its inventory.

a. If each storage case measures 1 in. by 5.5 in. by 8.75 in., how many cubic inches of storage space does the store need for the boxes of storage cases?

____

b. Find the number of cubic feet necessary for storing 350 boxes of cases. ______________________

Name ______________________ Class ______________ Date ______________

Practice 9-3

Volumes of Pyramids and Cones

Find the volume of each figure to the nearest cubic unit.

1. 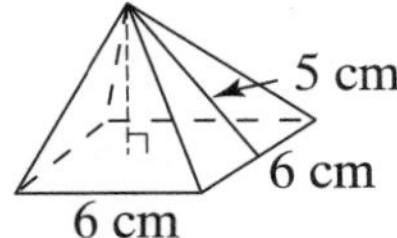

____

2. 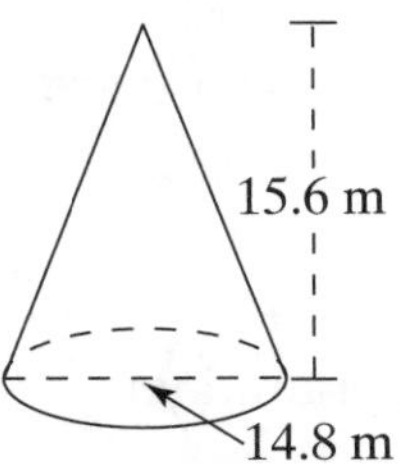

____

3. 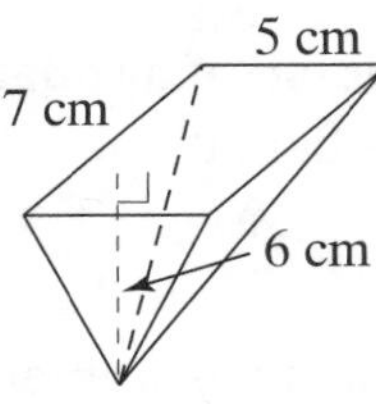

____

4. 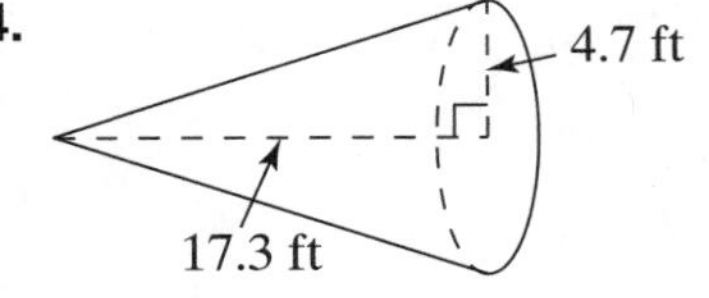

____

5. 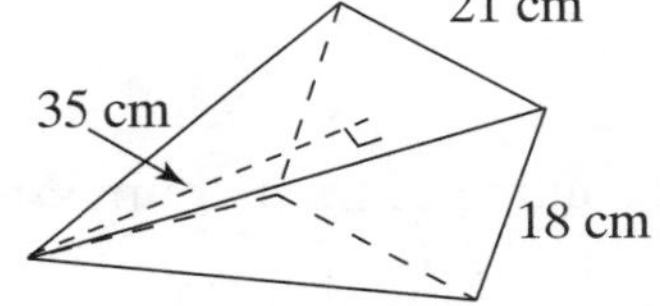

____

6. 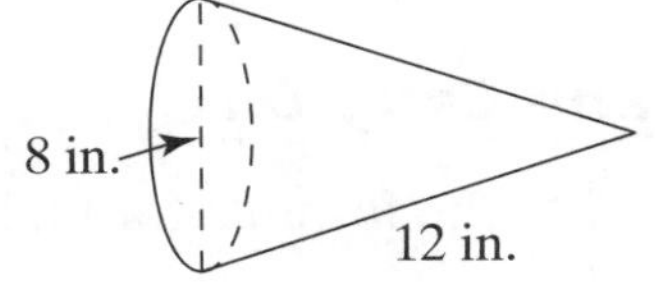

____

Find the missing dimension for each three-dimensional figure to the nearest tenth, given the volume and other dimensions.

7. rectangular pyramid, $l = 8$ m, $w = 4.6$ m, $V = 88$ m^3

____

8. cone, $r = 5$ in., $V = 487$ in.^{3}

____

9. square pyramid, $s = 14$ yd, $V = 489$ yd^3

____

10. square pyramid, $h = 8.9$ cm, $V = 56$ cm^3

____

11. Find the volume of a 4 ft by 2 ft by 3 ft rectangular prism with a cylindrical hole, radius 6 in., through the center.

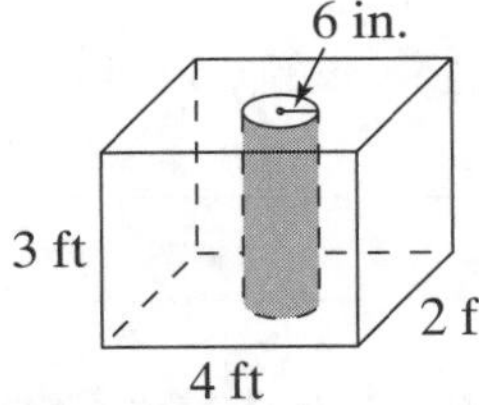

____

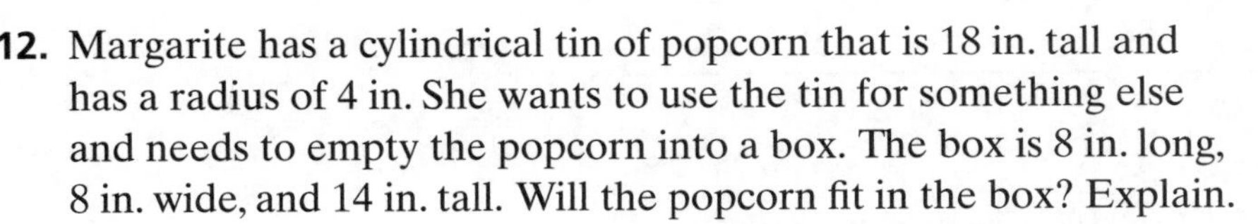

12. Margarite has a cylindrical tin of popcorn that is 18 in. tall and has a radius of 4 in. She wants to use the tin for something else and needs to empty the popcorn into a box. The box is 8 in. long, 8 in. wide, and 14 in. tall. Will the popcorn fit in the box? Explain.

____

____

Name ______________________ Class ______________ Date ______________

9-3 • Guided Problem Solving

GPS Student Page 312, Exercise 17:

Algebra The volume of a square pyramid is 15 ft^3. Its base area is 27 ft^2. What is its height?

Understand

1. Underline the measurements of the square pyramid you are given.
2. What are you asked to find?

   ____

Plan and Carry Out

3. What is the formula for finding the volume of a square pyramid?

   ____

4. What measurements are you given?

   ____

5. Substitute what you know into the formula.

   ____

6. What variable are you solving for? ______________
7. Solve.

   ____

Check

8. How can you check your answer?

   ____

   ____

Solve Another Problem

9. The volume of a cone is 113.04 ft^3. Its base area is 28.26 ft^2. What is its height?

   ____

   ____

Name ______________________ Class ______________ Date ______________

Practice 9-4

Spheres

Find each sphere's surface area and volume to the nearest whole number.

1.

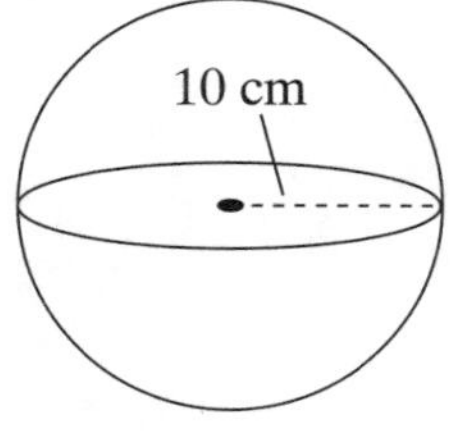

____

____

2.

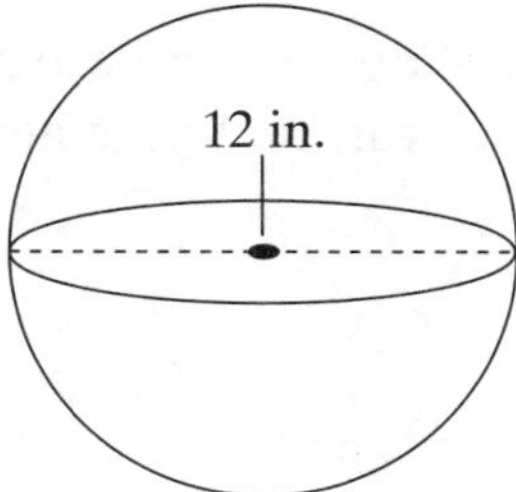

____

____

3.

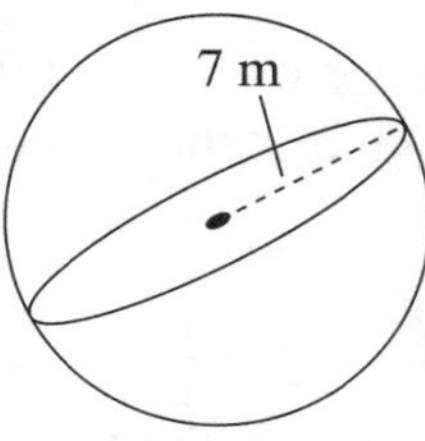

____

____

4.

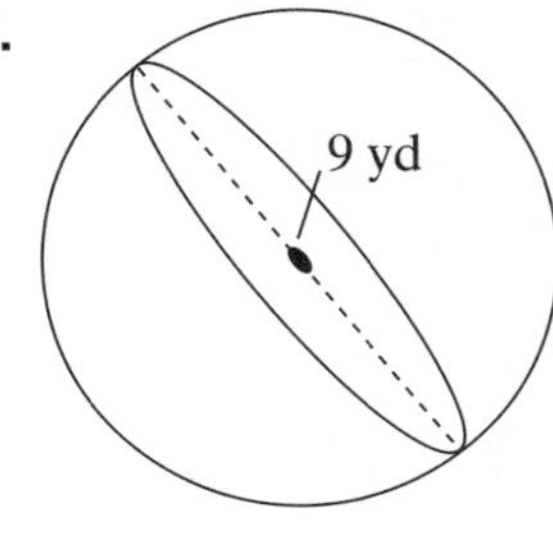

____

____

5.

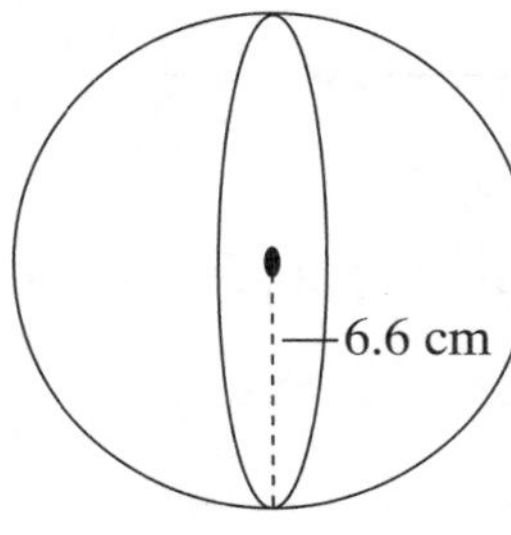

____

____

6.

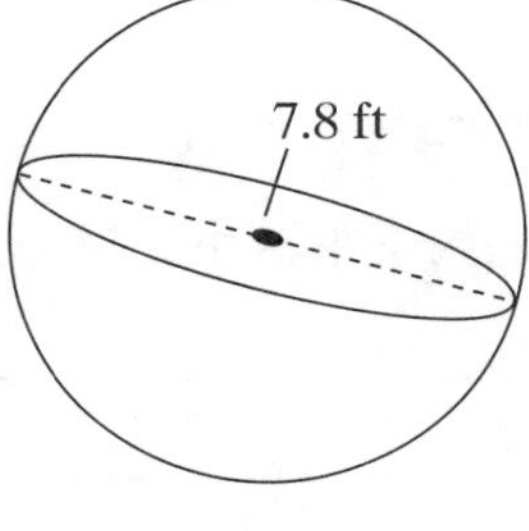

____

____

7. A sphere has a radius of 9 ft. Find its surface area to the nearest whole square unit.

____

8. A geography professor has a spherical globe with a diameter of 14 in. What is the volume of the globe?

____

9. Jenny has four marbles that are all of different sizes and colors. They have diameters of 18 mm, 19 mm, 21 mm, and 24 mm. What is the average surface area of the four marbles?

____

Name ______________________ Class ______________ Date ______________

9-4 • Guided Problem Solving

GPS Student Page 316, Exercise 16:

The circumference of a glass terrarium in the shape of a sphere is about 12.5 in. What is the surface area of the terrarium to the nearest square inch?

Understand

1. What is the given measurement? ______________________
2. What formula do you use to find circumference?

    ____

3. What are you being asked to find?

    ____

Plan and Carry Out

4. How can you use the circumference to find the surface area?

    ____

    ____

5. What is the radius of the terrarium?

    ____

6. How will you find the surface area of the terrarium?

    ____

7. What is the surface area of the terrarium to the nearest square inch?

    ____

Check

8. Does your answer check? Is your answer consistent with the circumference given in the question?

    ____

Solve Another Problem

9. The volume of a weather balloon is about 33.5 ft^3. What is the surface area of the weather balloon? Round your answer to the nearest whole square unit.

    ____

    ____

Name ____________________ Class ____________ Date ____________

Practice 9-5

Complete the table for each prism.

	Original Size		Doubled Dimensions		
	Dimensions (m)	**S.A. (m^2)**	**Dimensions (m)**	**S.A. (m^2)**	**New S.A. 4 Old S.A.**
1.	$2 \times 3 \times 4$				
2.	$5 \times 5 \times 9$				
3.	$7 \times 7 \times 7$				
4.	$8 \times 12 \times 15$				
5.	$15 \times 15 \times 20$				
6.	$32 \times 32 \times 32$				

7. What conclusion can you draw?

____

____

8. A rectangular prism is 8 cm by 10 cm by 15 cm. What are the volume and surface area of the prism?

____

9. In Exercise 8, if each dimension of the prism is halved, what are the new volume and surface area?

____

Use the triangular prism shown at the right for Exercises 10 and 11.

10. Find the volume and surface area.

____

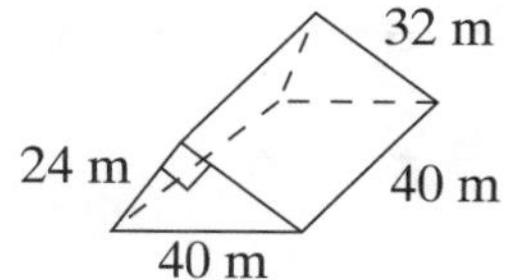

11. If each dimension of the prism is doubled, what are the new volume and surface area?

____

12. A rectangular prism is 8 cm long, 24 cm wide, and 43 cm high. The length is doubled, and the width is tripled. What happens to the volume?

____

Name ______________________ Class ______________ Date ______________

9-5 • Guided Problem Solving

GPS Student Page 322, Exercise 14:

Carpentry Gina used 78 square feet of plywood to build a storage bin to hold her gardening supplies. How much plywood will she need to build a similar box for her hand tools if the dimensions of the box are half the dimensions of the bin?

Understand

1. What are you asked to do?

____

____

2. How many square feet of plywood did Gina use? ____________

Plan and Carry Out

3. What is the ratio for the surface area of similar solids? ________
4. What are the dimensions of the similar box?

____

____

5. What is the ratio of the surface areas? ____________
6. Write a proportion. ____________
7. Solve. ____________

Check

8. How can you tell if your answer is reasonable?

____

____

____

Solve Another Problem

9. In pottery class, Mark made a small cylindrical bowl with a volume of 75 in.^{3} and a radius of 2 inches. He also made a larger bowl with a similar shape. It has a diameter of 8 inches. Find the volume of the larger bowl.

____

Name ______________________ Class ______________ Date ______________

9A: Graphic Organizer

For use before Lesson 9-1

Study Skill Try to read new lessons the night before your teacher presents them in class. Important information is sometimes printed in bold face type or highlighted inside a box with color. Pay special attention to this information.

Write your answers.

1. What is the chapter title? ______________________
2. How many lessons are there in this chapter? ______________________
3. What is the topic of the Test-Taking Strategies page? ______________________
4. Complete the graphic organizer below as you work through the chapter.
   - In the center, write the title of the chapter.
   - When you begin a lesson, write the lesson name in a rectangle.
   - When you complete a lesson, write a skill or key concept in a circle linked to that lesson block.
   - When you complete the chapter, use this graphic organizer to help you review.

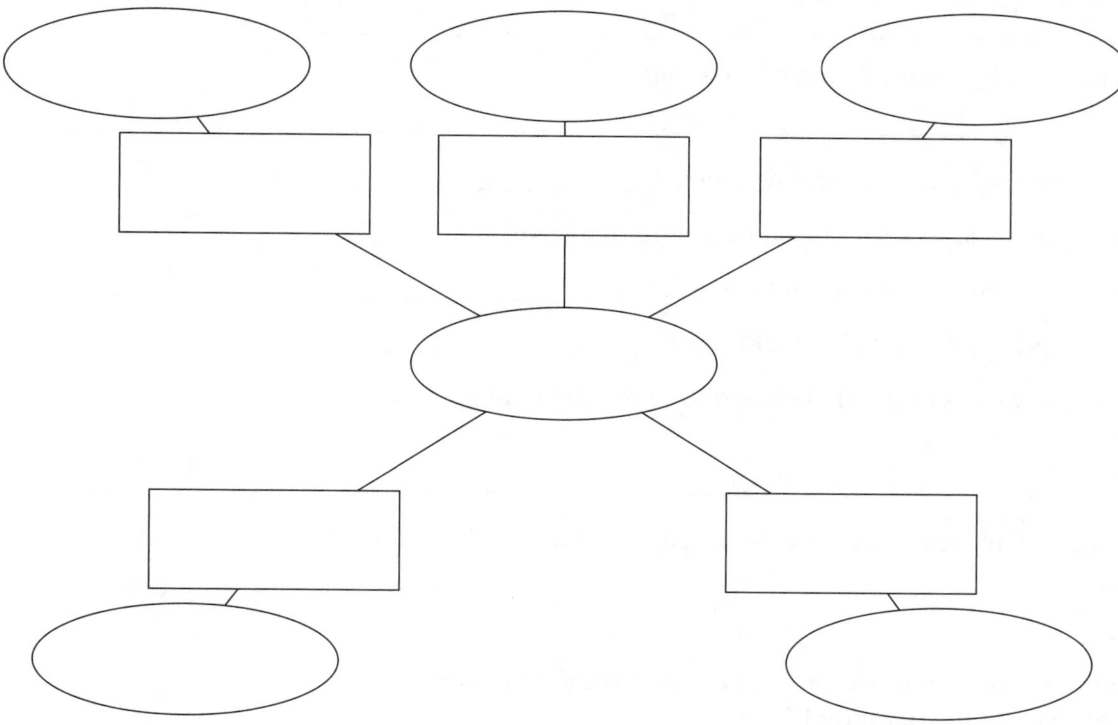

Vocabulary and Study Skills

Name ______________________ Class ______________ Date ______________

9B: Reading Comprehension

For use after Lesson 9-3

Study Skill Try to visualize math concepts when possible. Having a mental picture of something might help you remember it better.

Read the paragraph below and answer the questions.

Traffic signs are devices placed beside, above, or at the intersection of roadways.They control the flow of traffic which includes cars, trucks, bicycles, and pedestrians. Signs are necessary for safety and proper control of traffic.

Shape	Use	Notes
octagon	stop signs only	most expensive to produce
equilateral triangle	yield signs	points downward
circle	railroad warning signs	
trapezoid	recreational guide signs	
rectangle	guide signs	horizontal
rectangle	regulatory signs	vertical
pentagon	school zone signs	

1. What are the paragraph and chart about?

   ____

2. How many sides does a stop sign have? ______________

3. How many sides does a railroad warning sign have? __________

4. How many sides does a school zone sign have? ____________

5. What kind of a triangle is a yield sign? ______________

6. How many pairs of parallel sides does a recreational guide sign have?

   ____

7. How many more sides does a stop sign have than a school zone sign?

   ____

8. **High-Use Academic Words** What does it mean to *control*, as mentioned in the paragraph?

   a. to direct the action of **b.** to make a choice

Name ______________________ Class ______________ Date ______________

9C: Reading/Writing Math Symbols

For use after Lesson 9-5

Vocabulary and Study Skills

Study Skill In mathematics, abbreviations or certain letter combinations take on special meanings. It is important that you recognize these abbreviations and know what they mean.

Below are some common mathematical abbreviations and letter combinations. Write the meaning of each.

1. SAS ______________________ **2.** ASA ______________________

3. S.A. ______________________ **4.** L.A. ______________________

5. SSS ______________________

Write each of the following formulas in words and give a brief description of what the formula is used to find.

6. $V = \frac{4}{3}\pi r^3$

____

____

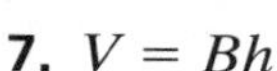

7. $V = Bh$

____

____

8. $C - \pi d$

____

____

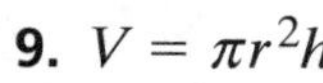

9. $V = \pi r^2 h$

____

____

10. $V = \frac{1}{3}Bh$

____

____

____

11. $\text{S.A.} = 4\pi r^2$

____

____

____

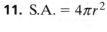

Name ______________________ Class ______________ Date ______________

9D: Visual Vocabulary Practice

For use after Lesson 9-5

Study Skill When learning a new concept, try to draw a picture to illustrate it.

Concept List

prism	cone	cylinder
base plan	lateral area	volume
skew lines	surface area	pyramid

Write the concept that best describes each exercise. Choose from the concept list above.

1.

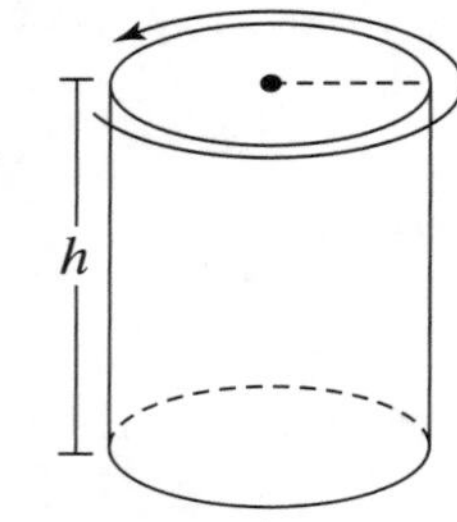

$C \times h$

____

2.

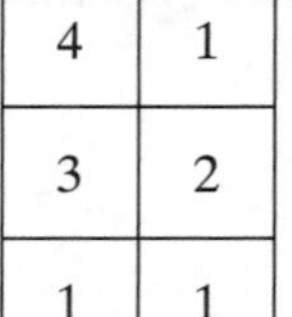

Right

Front

____

3.

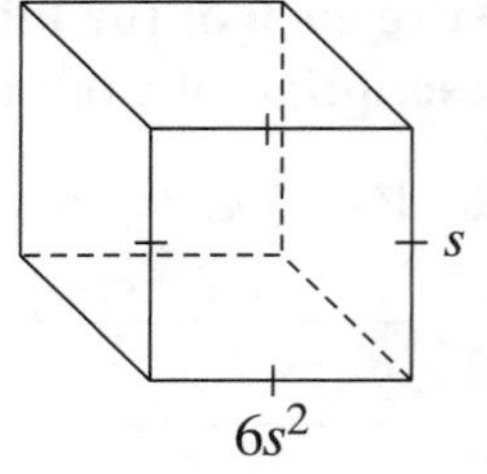

____

4.

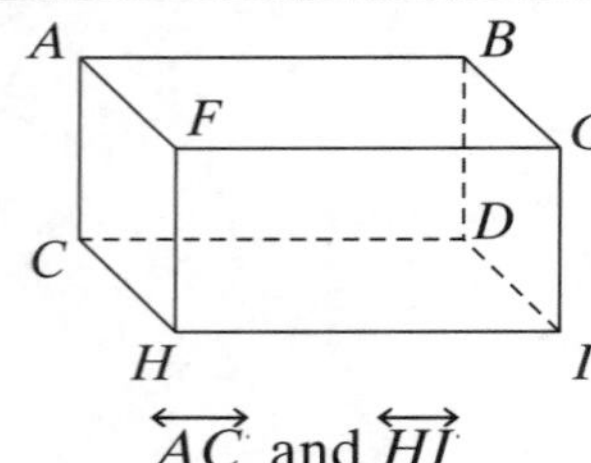

$\overleftrightarrow{AC}$ and $\overleftrightarrow{HI}$

____

5.

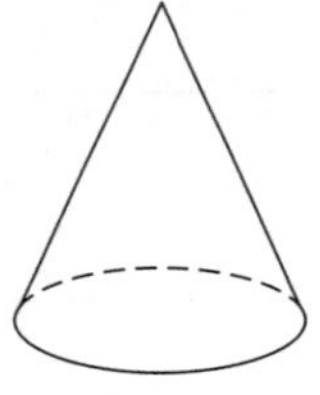

____

6.

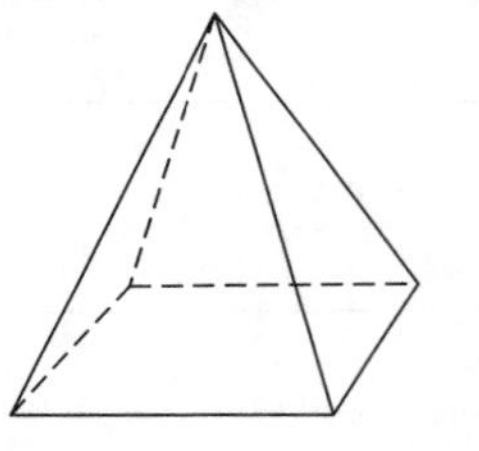

____

7.

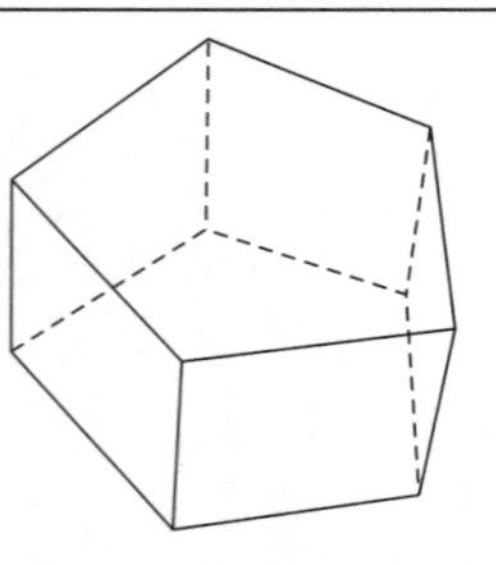

____

8.

$\frac{1}{3}(\pi r^2) \times h$

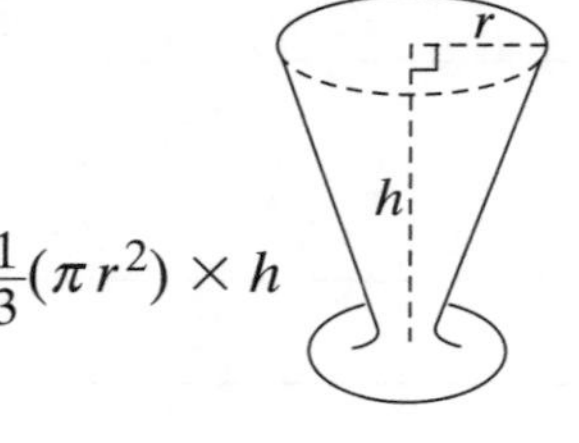

____

9.

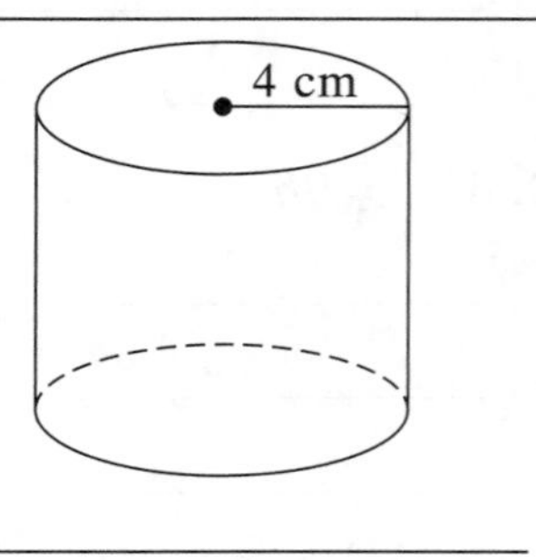

____

Name ______________________ Class ______________ Date ______________

9E: Vocabulary Check

For use after Lesson 9-5

Study Skill Strengthen your vocabulary. Use these pages and add cues and summaries by applying the Cornell Notetaking style.

Write the definition for each word or term at the right. To check your work, fold the paper back along the dotted line to see the correct answers.

polyhedron

skew lines

volume

sphere

similar solids

Vocabulary and Study Skills

Name ____________________ Class ____________ Date ____________

9E: Vocabulary Check (continued)

For use after Lesson 9-5

Write the vocabulary word or term for each definition. To check your work, fold the paper forward along the dotted line to see the correct answers.

a solid with a polygon for each face ____________________

lines that lie in different planes that are neither parallel nor intersecting ____________________

the number of unit cubes, or cubic units, needed to fill a solid ____________________

the set of all points in space that are the same distance from a center point ____________________

two solids that have the same shape and have corresponding dimensions that are proportional ____________________

Name ______________________ Class ______________ Date ______________

9F: Vocabulary Review Puzzle

For use with the Chapter Review

Study Skill Take a few minutes to relax before and after studying. Your mind will absorb and retain more information if you alternate studying with brief rest intervals.

Find and circle each of the words below in the puzzle. Words can be displayed forwards, backwards, up, down, or diagonally.

prism	pyramid	cylinder	cone
skew	polyhedron	space figures	obtuse
precision	isometric view	base plan	slant height
scale factor	parallelogram	square	rectangle
rhombus	acute	straight	

Q	D	R	S	N	O	U	T	A	L	L	E	S	S	E	T	H	M
O	R	H	V	A	W	I	X	L	R	R	U	P	M	R	E	N	B
N	U	O	Q	Z	E	J	J	E	A	S	Y	A	P	C	W	U	G
O	C	M	O	J	I	I	J	E	N	R	F	P	R	I	S	M	X
R	Y	B	W	R	V	X	N	E	A	O	F	B	H	S	R	Y	M
D	L	U	R	L	C	V	O	M	F	S	C	A	Z	Q	V	A	R
E	I	S	E	E	I	Y	I	B	Z	W	K	S	A	U	S	Z	G
H	N	U	C	S	R	D	E	K	F	F	S	E	K	A	L	N	Y
Y	D	R	T	U	T	J	G	B	B	Z	T	P	W	R	A	O	Y
L	E	P	A	T	E	S	T	O	H	V	R	L	D	E	N	I	B
O	R	B	N	B	M	T	K	F	E	S	A	A	O	D	T	S	O
P	U	R	G	O	O	F	A	Q	R	H	I	N	N	G	H	I	O
I	C	J	L	F	S	Z	H	K	Z	X	G	B	S	U	E	C	P
C	J	X	E	J	I	C	N	P	H	J	H	U	Y	O	I	E	V
N	F	I	S	X	X	N	X	L	V	E	T	U	C	A	G	R	I
P	A	R	A	L	L	E	L	O	G	R	A	M	E	N	H	P	V
X	O	N	F	S	C	A	L	E	F	A	C	T	O	R	T	Y	R
A	X	J	S	E	R	U	G	I	F	E	C	A	P	S	J	I	K

Name ______________________ Class ______________ Date ______________

Practice 10-1

Scatter Plots

Use the given scatter plots to complete Exercises 1 and 2.

1. What does the point (12, 40) represent?

Daily Rates People Paid for Car Rental in a City

Daily Rate ($)

Days Rented

2. What does the point (7, 10) represent?

Total Miles Jogged by Runners During an 8-Day Period

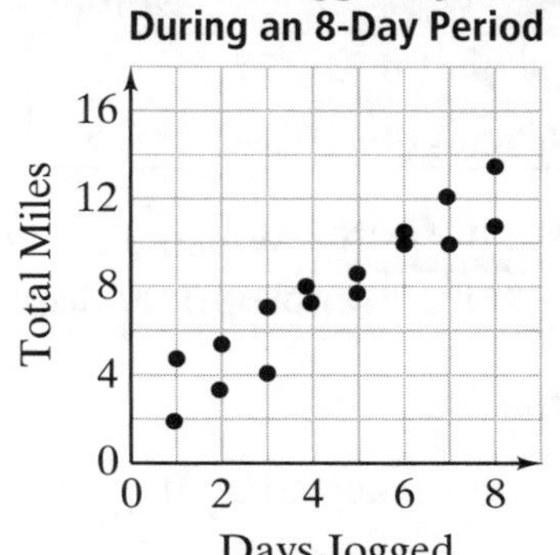

Make a scatter plot for each set of data.

3.

Weeks	7	4	6	8	2	3
Hours	28	20	25	36	10	12

Total Hours Worked

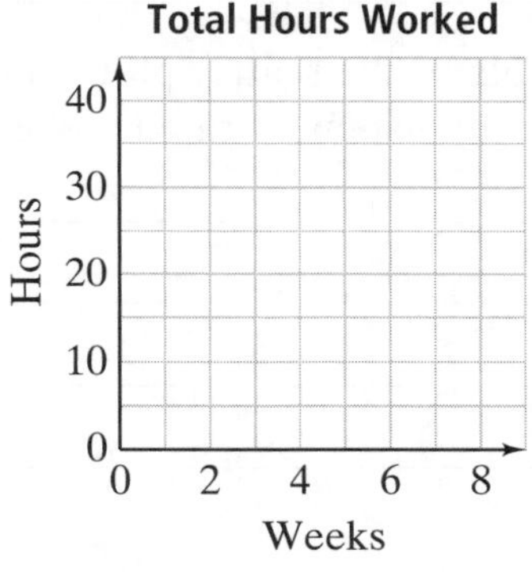

4.

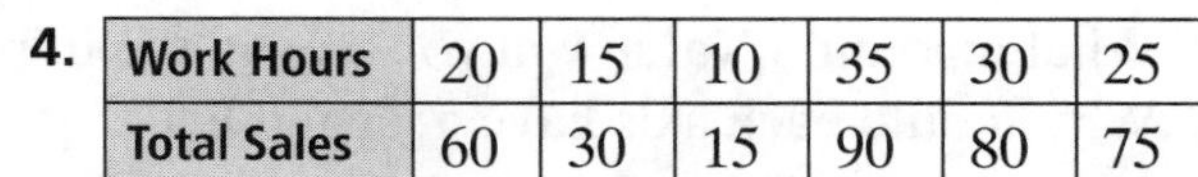

Work Hours	20	15	10	35	30	25
Total Sales	60	30	15	90	80	75

Total Sales for Different Number of Hours Worked

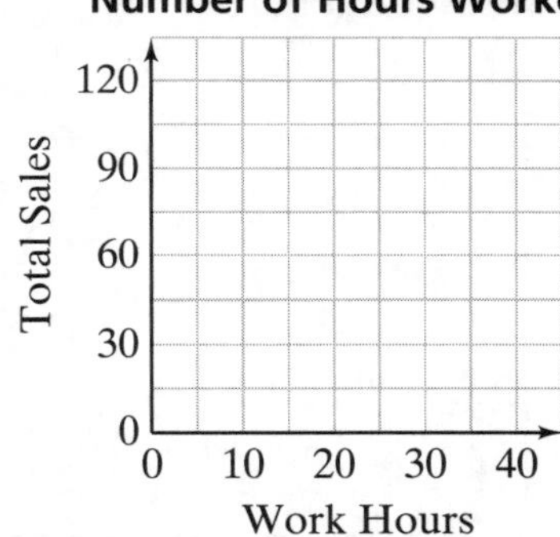

5.

Length (cm)	20	15	40	35	30	5
Height (cm)	15	35	10	40	25	15

Heights and Lengths of Packages

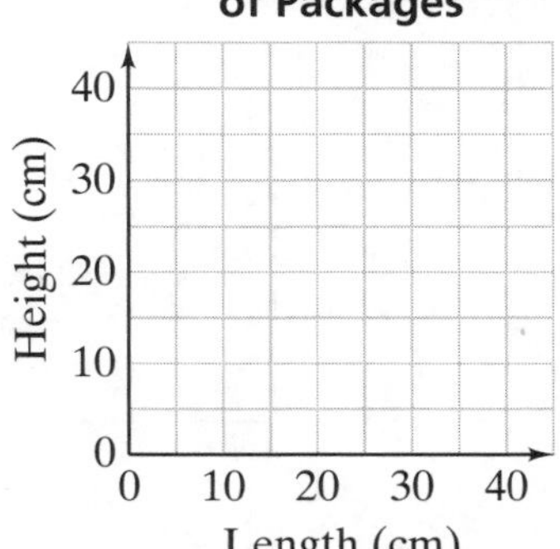

6.

Distance (mi)	6	2	0	5	3	8
Runners	6	15	16	11	12	2

Number of Runners Still in the Race At Different Distances

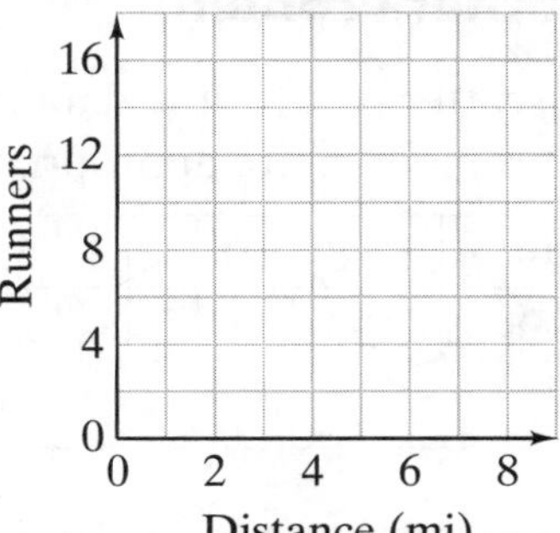

Name ______________________ Class ______________ Date ______________

10-1 • Guided Problem Solving

GPS Student Page 333, Exercise 11:

a. Make a scatter plot for the data in the table below.

Height and Weight of Football Players

Height (in.)	77	75	76	70	70	73	74	74	73
Weight (lb)	230	220	212	190	201	245	218	260	196

b. **Writing in Math** Which display—the table or the scatter plot—do you think is a more appropriate display of the data? Explain your reasoning.

Understand

1. What are you asked to do in part *a* and part *b*?

____

Plan and Carry Out

2. What maximum value will you use on the horizontal and vertical axes? Why should each axis have a jagged line?

____

3. Draw your graph below.

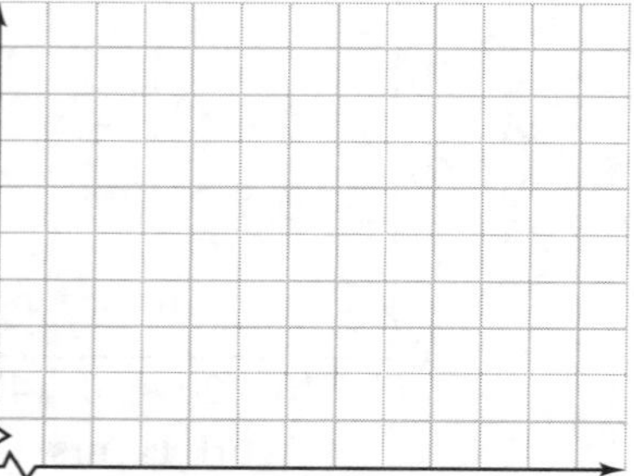

4. Is the table or the scatter plot a more appropriate display of the data? Explain.

____

____

____

____

Check

5. Did you correctly plot all data points? Did you label the axes and include a title?

Solve Another Problem

6. Make a scatter plot for the data in the table. Is the table or the scatter plot a more appropriate display of the data? Explain.

Height (in.)	2	8	10	4	3	6
Weight (lb)	1	3	4	5	4	2

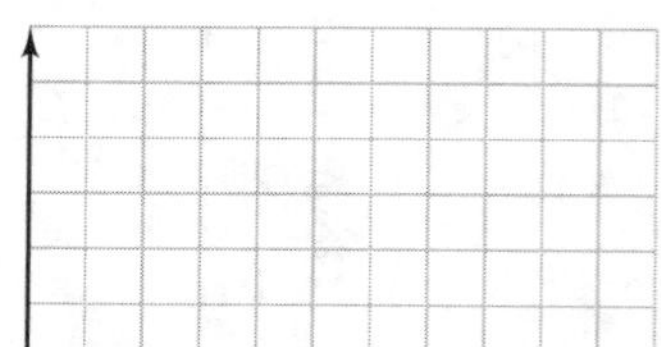

____

____

Name ______________________ Class ______________ Date ______________

Practice 10-2

Analyzing Scatter Plots

Make a scatter plot for the data in the table. Identify any clustering or outliers in the data.

1.

Average Test Grade	82	94	81	95	93	92	84
Number of Students in the Class	19	42	20	18	16	23	22

Clustering between ______ and ______ students

Outlier(s) at (______, ______)

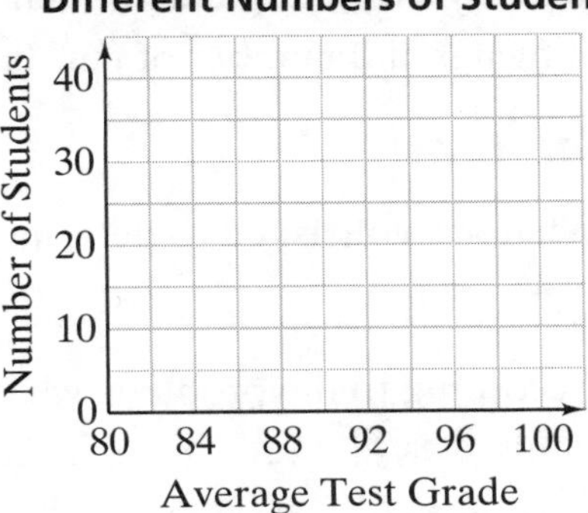

Describe the association of each graph: *positive, negative,* or *no association.*

2.

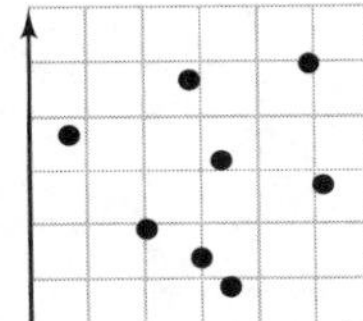

____

3.

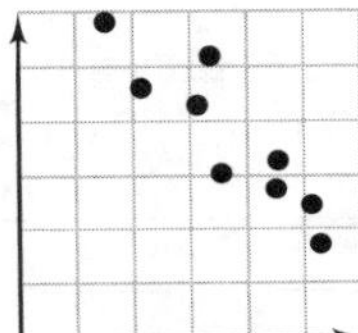

____

4.

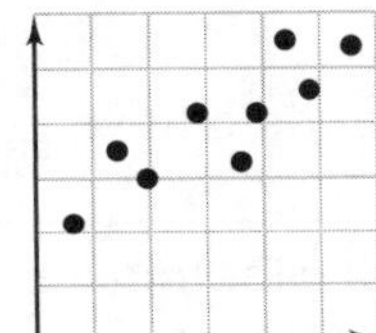

____

Make a scatter plot for each set of data. Tell whether the data show a linear association or a nonlinear association.

5. (7, 0), (3, 9), (1, 12), (6, 4)
(4, 6), (1, 10), (5, 6)

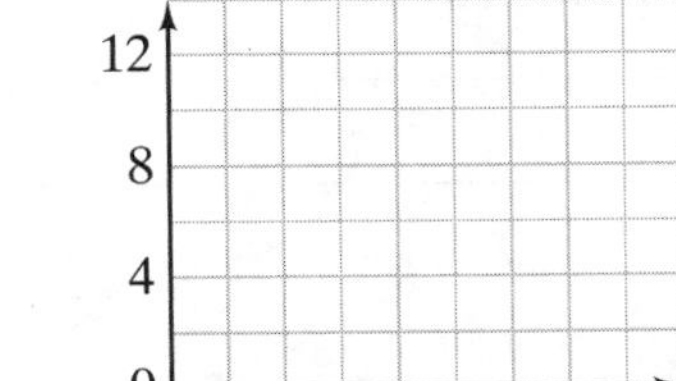

______ association

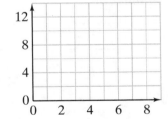

6. (2, 30), (8, 30), (9, 50), (1, 50),
(5, 15), (3, 20), (7, 20)

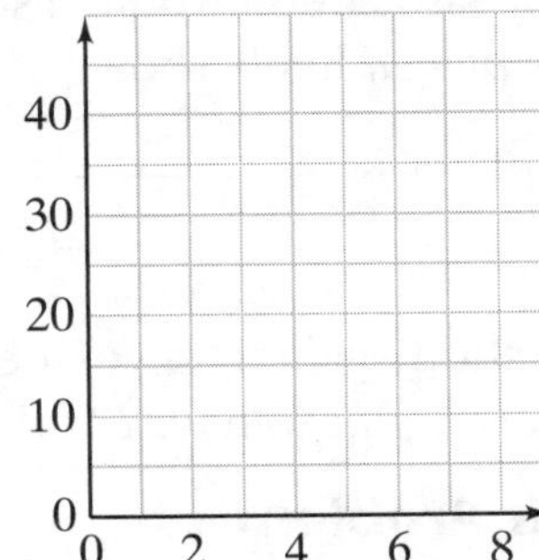

______ association

Name ______________________ Class ______________ Date ______________

10-2 • Guided Problem Solving

GPS Student Page 338, Exercise 12:

For each topic, decide which type of association a scatter plot of the data would likely show. Explain your choice.
age of owner and number of pets currently owned

Understand

1. What are you asked to determine in the problem?

____

2. According to the problem, what are the two sets of data that the scatter plot would describe? ____

Plan and Carry Out

3. Complete the following about the three ways you can describe the association of two data sets:
   (1) Two sets of data have ________ association if
   ____
   The scatter plot looks like ______________________
   (2) Two sets of data have ________ association if
   ____
   The scatter plot looks like ______________________
   (3) Two sets of data have ________ association if
   ____
   The scatter plot looks like ______________________

4. Which type of association would a scatter plot of *age of owner* and *number of pets currently owned* likely show? ______________________

5. Explain your choice. ______________________

Check

6. Read the question again. Did you describe the association you would expect the scatter plot to have? Did you explain your choice?

Solve Another Problem

7. Decide which type of association a scatter plot of the data would likely show. Explain your choice. Highest temperature each day in summer and the number of snow cones a shop sells each day.

____

____

Name ______________________ Class ______________ Date ______________

Practice 10-3

Modeling Data With Lines

Make a scatter plot for each set of data. If possible, draw a trend line and describe the trend.

1.

Grade Average	70	85	78	92	97	88	82	90
Test Scores	720	805	798	860	889	775	810	870

2.

Years	3	7	10	14	16	20	22	25
Quail per Acre	27	114	185	210	170	198	240	356

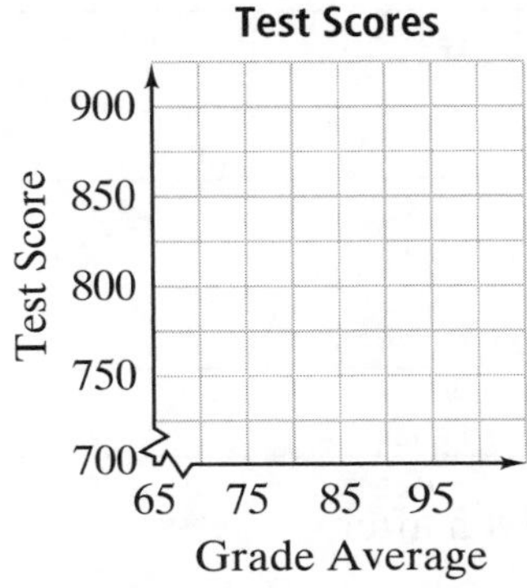

Describe the trend:

____

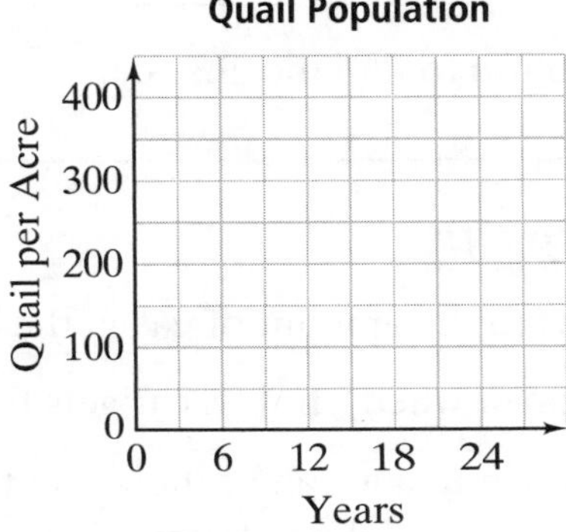

Describe the trend:

____

For each scatter plot, find a better trend line than the one shown.

3.

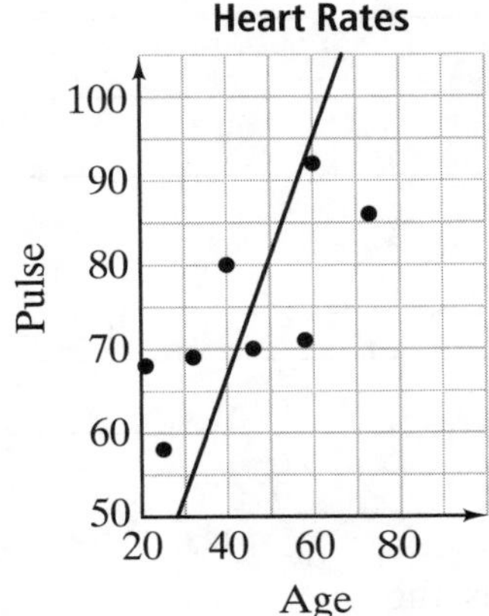

4.

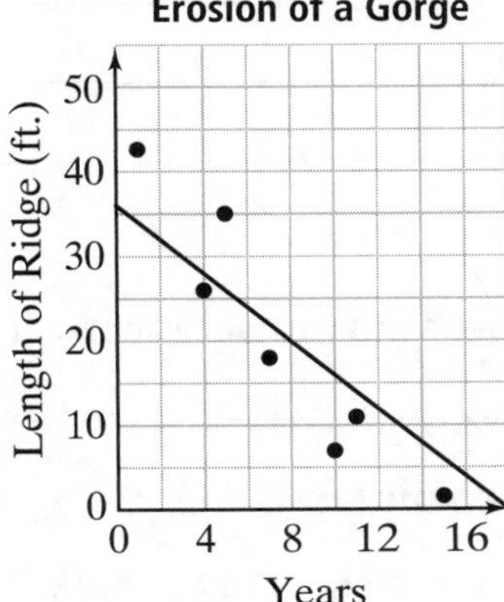

Name ______________________ Class ______________ Date ____________

10-3 • Guided Problem Solving

GPS Student Page 344, Exercise 10:

Mr. Li fills his car with gas. The farther he drives, the less gas his car has. Would it be reasonable to use this negative association to predict the amount of gasoline in Mr. Li's tank after he has driven 500 miles? Explain.

Understand

1. What are you being asked to do?

____

____

2. What will you use to find the answer?

____

Plan and Carry Out

3. What happens to the amount of gas in the car as Mr. Li drives? ______________
4. What will happen when Mr. Li's car gets too low on gas? ______________
5. What will happen to a graph of the gas in the tank vs. miles driven after Mr. Li fills his tank? Make a sketch of this graph.

____

6. Would it be reasonable to use a negative association to predict the amount of gasoline in Mr. Li's tank after he has driven 500 miles?

____

____

____

Check

7. How can you prove your answer is correct? ______________

____

Solve Another Problem

8. Allen runs a lemonade stand in the park. The more lemonade he sells, the fewer lemons he has. Would it be reasonable to use this negative association to predict the number of lemons he has after he sells 1,000 cups of lemonade?

____

____

____

Name ______________________ Class ______________ Date ______________

Practice 10-4

Two-Way Tables

1. Forty people were surveyed at a sporting goods store about their favorite outdoor activities. Below are the results.
   - 10 men and 3 women chose water skiing.
   - 5 men and 7 women chose wakeboarding.
   - 1 man and 2 women chose hiking.
   - 8 men and 4 women chose fishing.

   a. Construct a two-way frequency table for the data.

Favorite Outdoor Activity

   b. According to the survey, what is the least popular activity? ________
   What is the most popular activity? ________________

2. The frequency table shows the uniform preferences of 45 band members.

Favorite Color

Accessories	Black	White	Gray	Total
Ribbons	3	6	1	10
Ruffles	2	8	6	16
Sequins	11	6	2	19
Total	16	20	9	45

   a. Make a two-way table of relative frequencies. Find the relative frequencies for each column.

   b. Is there evidence that those who prefer black also prefer sequins to ruffles? Explain. ______________________________

____

____

Name ______________________ Class ______________ Date ______________

10-4 • Guided Problem Solving

GPS Student Page 350, Exercise 10:

The Venn diagram shows the results of a survey of the types of electronic devices used most often in 124 households. The area within the rectangle but outside the circles represents households that do not use a tablet or smartphone. Construct a two-way frequency table that displays the data.

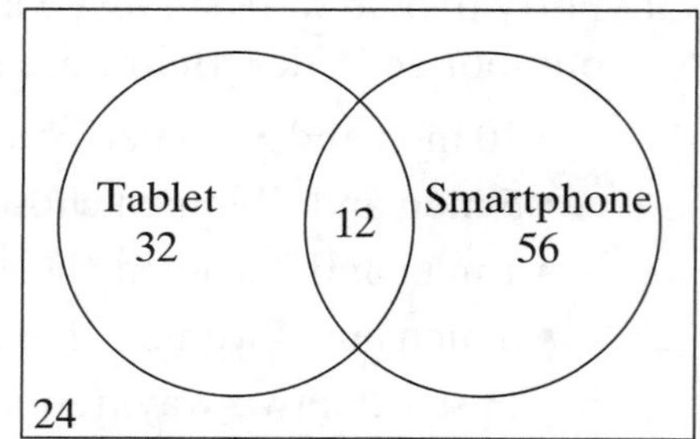

Understand

1. What are you being asked to do?

____

2. What will you use to create the display?

____

Plan and Carry Out

3. What categories should the two-way table include? ______________________________

____

4. Based on the Venn diagram, how many households have each of the following?

Tablet but no smartphone ________ Smartphone but no tablet ________

Tablet and smartphone ________ Neither ________

5. Draw the two-way table.

	Smartphone	No Smartphone	Total
Tablet			
No Tablet			
Total			

Check

6. How can you show that your table is correct?

____

Solve Another Problem

7. The Venn diagram shows the results of a survey of the kinds of vehicles owned by 124 households. The area within the rectangle but outside the circles represents households that do not own a car or pickup truck. Construct a two-way frequency table that displays the data.

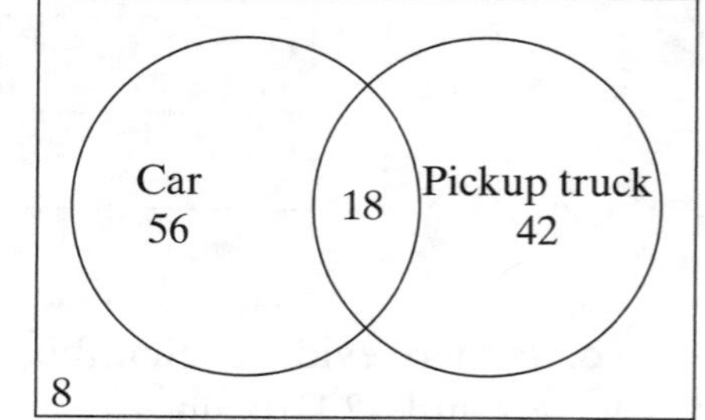

Name ______________________ Class ______________ Date ______________

10A: Graphic Organizer

For use before Lesson 10-1

Study Skill Pay attention in class and concentrate when reading assignments so information does not slip out of your "short-term" memory.

Write your answers.

1. What is the chapter title? ______________________
2. How many lessons are there in this chapter? ______________________
3. What is the topic of the Test-Taking Strategies page? ______________________
4. Complete the graphic organizer below as you work through the chapter.
   - In the center, write the title of the chapter.
   - When you begin a lesson, write the lesson name in a rectangle.
   - When you complete a lesson, write a skill or key concept in a circle linked to that lesson block.
   - When you complete the chapter, use this graphic organizer to help you review.

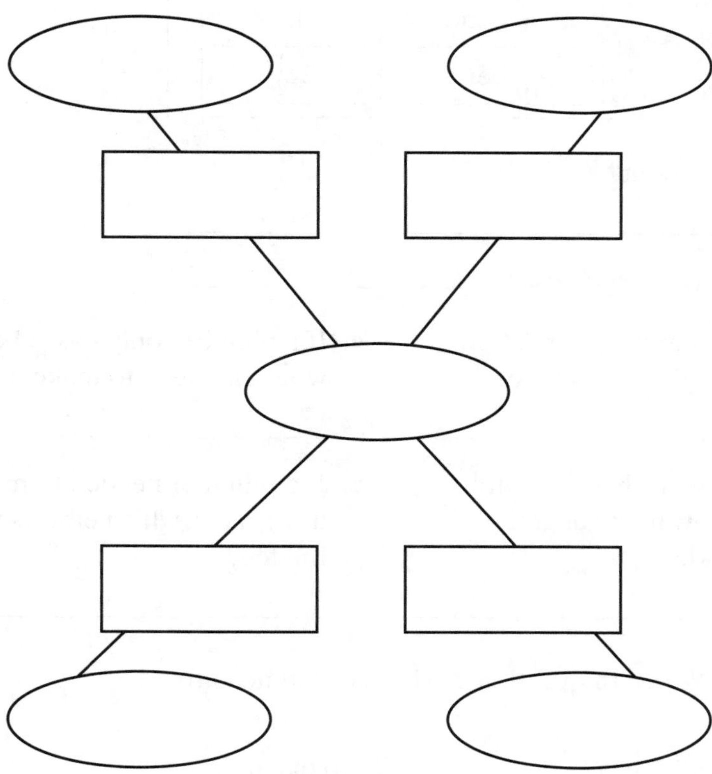

Vocabulary and Study Skills

Name ____________________ Class ____________ Date ____________

10B: Reading Comprehension

For use after Lesson 10-2

Study Skill Participating in class discussions might help you remember new material better. Sometimes, explaining or questioning a new concept can help you understand.

Read the paragraph below and answer the questions.

Plumbers often use a non-metallic pipe called PVC pipe for sink and toilet drain lines. The four most common diameters of PVC pipe are $1\frac{1}{2}$ in., 2 in., 3in., and 4 in. When plumbers need to combine pipes with diameters of difference sizes, they use a bushing or reducer coupling. Elbows or "bends" help make turns when connecting pipes. There are three different sizes of elbows and two common fittings that are used. A "wye" is a straight fitting with a 45° elbow attached to one end, and a "tee" is a straight fitting with a 90° elbow attached to one end. Pipes are connected by cleaning and priming the ends and then fitting them together. Liquid cement is applied to each piece and the pieces are twisted together slightly to ensure an even coating of cement on the pieces.

Elbows	
$\frac{1}{4}$ bend	90°
$\frac{1}{8}$ bend	45°
$\frac{1}{16}$ bend	$22\frac{1}{2}$°

1. What is the paragraph about?

____

2. How are PVC pipe sizes categorized? ______________

3. If a plumber joins a tee and a $\frac{1}{8}$ bend, how many degrees is the angle he has made?

____

4. If a plumber only has $\frac{1}{16}$ bends, how many would he need to make a 90° turn?

____

5. If a plumber joins a wye with a sixteenth and an eighth bend, how many degrees is the angle he has made?

____

6. If a plumber needed to make a $157\frac{1}{2}$° angle using a tee, which elbows would he join to the tee?

____

7. **High-Use Academic Words** In question 2, what does it mean to *categorize?*

   a. to classify

   b. to expand

Name ________________________ Class ________________ Date ______________

10C: Reading/Writing Math Symbols

For use after Lesson 10-3

Vocabulary and Study Skills

Study Skill Read aloud or recite when you are studying at home. Reciting a rule or formula can help you to remember it and recall it for later use.

Write each of the following mathematical symbols or formulas in words.

1. $\cong$ ____________________
2. $>$ ____________________
3. $|x|$ ____________________
4. $\geq$ ____________________
5. $=$ ____________________
6. -4 ____________________
7. $\times$ ____________________
8. $\div$ ____________________
9. % ____________________
10. $\angle$ ____________________
11. $\neq$ ____________________
12. $\sqrt{}$ ____________________
13. $R : L = S : T$ ____________________

____

14. $\triangle ABC \sim \triangle DEF$ ____________________

____

15. $\widehat{BC}$ ____________________
16. $V = Bh$ ____________________

____

17. $A = bh$ ____________________
18. $C = \pi d$ ____________________

____

Name ______________________ Class ______________ Date ______________

10D: Visual Vocabulary Practice

For use after Lesson 10-4

High-Use Academic Words

Study Skill When you feel you're getting frustrated, take a break.

Concept List

acronym	symbolize	predict
classify	abbreviate	equal
analyze	deduce	dimensions

Write the concept that best describes each exercise. Choose from the concept list above.

1. 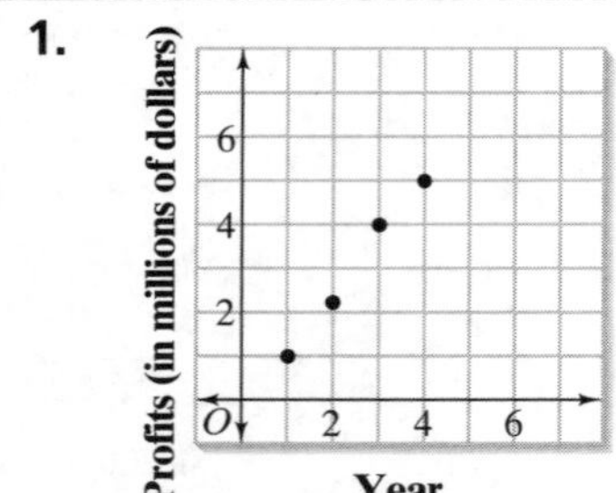 In year five, profits will increase. ______	**2.** $60\% = 0.6 = \frac{3}{5}$ ______	**3.** Find the range and mean on the data set and identify any outliers. ______
4. qt for quarts ______	**5.** A transversal *t* intersects parallel lines *m* and *n* such that *t* is perpendicular to *m*. *t* is perpendicular to *n*. ______	**6.** $l \times w \times h$ ______
7. angle $\angle$ parallel $\parallel$ perpendicular $\perp$ ______	**8.** Write SAS for Side Angle Side. ______	**9.** Prisms and pyramids are polyhedrons; cylinders and cones are not. ______

Name ____________________ Class ____________________ Date ____________________

10E: Vocabulary Check

For use after Lesson 10-4

Study Skill Strengthen your vocabulary. Use these pages and add cues and summaries by applying the Cornell Notetaking style.

Write the definition for each word or term at the right. To check your work, fold the paper back along the dotted line to see the correct answers.

Vocabulary and Study Skills

bivariate data

scatter plot

trend line

clustering

outlier

Name ______________________ Class ______________ Date ______________

10E: Vocabulary Check (continued)

For use after Lesson 10-4

Write the vocabulary word or term for each definition. To check your work, fold the paper forward along the dotted line to see the correct answers.

shows the relationship between two variables ______________________

a graph that displays bivariate data in the form of ordered pairs ______________________

the line drawn on a graph to approximate the relationship between data sets ______________________

data points grouped closely together on a scatter plot ______________________

an item in a data set that is much higher or much lower that the other items in a data set ______________________

Name ______________________ Class ______________ Date ______________

10F: Vocabulary Review

For use with the Chapter Review

Study Skill Taking short breaks can help you stay focused. Every 30 minutes, take a 5-minute break, then return to studying.

I. Match the term in Column A with its definition in Column B.

Column A	Column B
1. negative association	**A.** type of graph used to show changes over time
2. positive association	**B.** as one set of values increases, the other set tends to increase
3. bivariate data	**C.** two angles whose sum is 90 degrees
4. trend line	**D.** line on a scatter plot that approximates the relationship between data sets
5. clustering	**E.** data points grouped closely together
6. complementary	**F.** as one set of values increases, the other set tends to decrease
7. line graph	**G.** two angles whose sum is 180 degrees
8. supplementary	**H.** shows relationship between two variables

II. Match the term in Column A with its definition in Column B.

Column A	Column B
1. slope	**A.** divides the data into four equal parts
2. two-way table	**B.** lines that intersect to form right angles
3. frequency	**C.** number of times an item occurs
4. quartiles	**D.** a type of graph used to show trends
5. bar graph	**E.** used to organize and display data pertaining to two different categories
6. perpendicular	**F.** a ratio that describes the steepness of a line
7. circle graph	**G.** the difference between the greatest and least values in a data set
8. range	**H.** a graph that shows parts of a whole